THE TRANSFORMATIONS OF MAGIC

THE MAGIC IN HISTORY SERIES

FORBIDDEN RITES
A Necromancer's Manual of the Fifteenth Century
Richard Kieckhefer

CONJURING SPIRITS
Texts and Traditions of Medieval Ritual Magic
Edited by Claire Fanger

RITUAL MAGIC
Elizabeth M. Butler

THE FORTUNES OF FAUST
Elizabeth M. Butler

THE BATHHOUSE AT MIDNIGHT
An Historical Survey of Magic and
Divination in Russia
W. F. Ryan

SPIRITUAL AND DEMONIC MAGIC
From Ficino to Campanella
D. P. Walker

ICONS OF POWER
Ritual Practices in Late Antiquity
Naomi Janowitz

BATTLING DEMONS
Witchcraft, Heresy, and Reform in the
Late Middle Ages
Michael D. Bailey

PRAYER, MAGIC, AND THE STARS IN THE
LATE ANCIENT AND ANTIQUE WORLD
Edited by Scott Noegel, Joel Walker,
and Brannon Wheeler

BINDING WORDS
Textual Amulets in the Middle Ages
Don C. Skemer

STRANGE REVELATIONS
Magic, Poison, and Sacrilege in
Louis XIV's France
Lynn Wood Mollenauer

UNLOCKED BOOKS
Manuscripts of Learned Magic in the Medieval
Libraries of Central Europe
Benedek Láng

ALCHEMICAL BELIEF
Occultism in the Religious Culture of Early
Modern England
Bruce Janacek

The Magic in History series explores the role magic and the occult have played in European culture, religion, science, and politics. Titles in the series bring the resources of cultural, literary, and social history to bear on the history of the magic arts, and contribute to an understanding of why the theory and practice of magic have elicited fascination at every level of European society. Volumes will include both editions of important texts and significant new research in the field.

THE TRANSFORMATIONS OF MAGIC

ILLICIT LEARNED MAGIC *in the* LATER MIDDLE AGES *and* RENAISSANCE

FRANK KLAASSEN

THE PENNSYLVANIA STATE UNIVERSITY PRESS
UNIVERSITY PARK, PENNSYLVANIA

Library of Congress Cataloging-in-Publication Data

Klaassen, Frank F.
The transformations of magic : illicit learned magic in the later Middle
Ages and Renaissance / Frank Klaassen.
p.   cm. — (The magic in history series)
Summary: "Explores two principal genres of illicit learned magic in late
Medieval manuscripts: image magic, which could be interpreted and
justified in scholastic terms, and ritual magic, which could
not"—Provided by publisher.
Magic and natural philosophy—Scholastic image magic before
1500—Some apparent exceptions: image magic or necromancy?
The *ars notoria* and the sworn book of Honorius—The magic of demons
and angels—Sixteenth-century collections of magic texts—Medieval
ritual magic and Renaissance magic.
Includes bibliographical references and index.
ISBN 978-0-271-05626-5 (cloth : alk. paper)
1. Magic—Manuscripts—History.
2. Manuscripts, Medieval.
3. Manuscripts, Renaissance.
4. Magic—Religious aspects—Christianity.
5. Magic—England—History.
I. Title.

BF1593.K56 2012
133.4'309—dc23
2012028139

FOR MY PARENTS

Ruth and Walter Klaassen

CONTENTS

PREFACE

Manuscripts of illicit magic present considerable methodological challenges for modern historians. While they may communicate in excruciating detail their constituent operations, they simultaneously give little explicit information about their authors, scribes, and collectors. Because magic texts often claim ancient lineage, they unsurprisingly deemphasize their more modern transmitters; good counsel would also have suggested the value of anonymity when copying an illicit work. As a result, that someone chose to transmit a magic text tells us that he thought it was worth the effort, but little more. Was the transmitter a practitioner, a kind of antiquarian, or just a slavish scribe copying the next text in a volume? Did he copy it so as to develop arguments against magic, as a kind of curiosity, or just to make money? With few exceptions, what we know about the people behind the letters has been revealed unselfconsciously or inferred from the broader historical context. And, in fact, historians of medieval magic are usually delighted just to find a new manuscript, anonymous or not.

In an unusually stimulating seminar with Brian Stock at the University of Toronto, the intellectual spark that gave rise to this study was first struck. I began to wonder what could be learned about medieval magic by focusing on the manuscripts themselves: their mise-en-page, their organization, the works with which they were bound together, and how they were recorded in inventories and catalogues. I was also interested to know whether a broad survey of surviving manuscripts might reveal patterns that could help us understand the intellectual culture surrounding learned magic in the later Middle Ages and Renaissance. This gave rise to my doctoral dissertation and to much of my intellectual production since that time. As in any study of magic, I have had to move well beyond the skeletal evidence this approach provides, but the manuscript of magic and the codex that contains it have remained my intellectual rudders.

In this study I do not seek to provide a comprehensive treatment of the traditions of illicit learned magic in the late Middle Ages and Renaissance. Instead, I follow two principal genres of magic manuscripts, identify some of the defining features of the intellectual cultures they represent, and attempt to draw some general conclusions about the history of magic. Although I believe that this book reflects the spirit of my sources, the rich intellects of my colleagues in the study of this literature continually drive me to recognize the limitations of this project. I also owe each of them a tremendous debt: to Robert Mathiesen for his generosity with his research materials and stability of spirit; to Richard Kieckhefer and Charles Burnett for their sage advice; and to Sophie Page for her incisive critique, for long hours of discussion, and for thinking in ways that I do not. I owe my most significant intellectual debt to my colleague and friend Claire Fanger, who read this manuscript several times, made innumerable suggestions for its improvement, and reviewed my translations and transcriptions. If this project even approaches the high standards she maintains, I will be content. Any remaining errors are my own.

I also owe thanks to many others, and the following is not an exhaustive list. This project was supported and nurtured in its early stages by Bert Hall, Joseph Goering, Kenneth Bartlett, and Andrew Hughes. The subsequent advice and expertise of Tom Cohen, Elizabeth Cohen, James Carley, Mildred Budney, Nicholas Watson, Jan Veenstra, Nicolas Weill-Parot, Julien Véronèse, Benedek Láng, Walter Klaassen, and Sharon Wright have been invaluable. Laura Mitchell, Erin Ayles, Winston Black, and Margaret Dore worked tirelessly as research assistants, and Edwin Bezina assisted with my manuscript database. Suzanne Wolk's editorial skills contributed significantly to the quality of the volume. Finally, members of the Classical, Medieval, and Renaissance Studies Colloquium and the Faculty Research Colloquium of the History Department, both at the University of Saskatchewan, have provided important feedback. The Social Sciences and Humanities Research Council of Canada provided financial support in the form of a Standard Research Grant. The University of Saskatchewan also provided financial assistance in the form of research grants and production costs. The Department of History, out of its own resources, granted me a teaching release that enabled me to devote myself to research.

I thank my intellectual and life partner, Sharon Wright, and my children, Jessica, Isaac, and Ahren, for their indulgence at times when they, and not this book, should have been the focus of my attention. My pleasure in seeing this project reach completion does not overcome my sense of loss for those moments. To have achieved less might have been to attain more.

INTRODUCTION

This book is about illicit learned magic in England and the ways in which it was transformed between 1300 and 1600. It concerns the changes, sometimes subtle and sometimes dramatic, that took place each time a medieval author, scribe, or collector set out to understand and practice learned magic, and then to copy the associated texts or write new ones. It also deals with the transformations that entire genres of this literature underwent in the later Middle Ages and the sixteenth century. It seeks to understand what motivated these changes and what this tells us about the intellectual culture of late medieval magic.

The history of learned magic in the Latin West may be understood in part as a series of attempts to reconcile theologically problematic practices and ideas with Christian orthodoxy. This was a matter that concerned not only the authors of magic books but also the scribes and collectors who transmitted or preserved such texts. The nature of each reconciliation could, in principle, be quite distinctive and depended on a wide variety of factors, including the nature of the text received, any known authoritative reactions to it or the kind of magic it promoted, the context in which it was transmitted, and the copyist's interests. A desire to see magic in terms of natural philosophy would, for example, demand a fundamentally different approach from a desire to regard it as a kind of mystical technology or religious exercise. A text known to have been condemned by an authoritative voice might generate a different response from one that had not. In addition, the intellectual world of late medieval scribes was not only a matter of solving abstract problems; it was circumscribed and informed by a number of broader conditions, such as the kinds of texts available and the professional context of the individual author, scribe, or collector. A monk's interests, abilities, and resources were different from those of a medical doctor, student, or priest. A copyist's profession affected not only what texts were available but also how they were interpreted, copied, and altered.

The processes involved in copying were thus very complex, and even where the original text was not altered in any way, the act of copying was not passive. On the contrary, it involved a wide range of choices, conscious or otherwise, that might fundamentally alter the sense of the received text. Which text would one choose, and which version? How would one find the text one wanted if one did not already have it? How should its legitimacy and value be judged? Should one alter the contents, omit parts, or extract a portion from its original context? If it was corrupt or fragmentary, how would one correct or supplement it so that it made sense? Might it be incorporated into a new text? How would it be presented on the page? Did it deserve its own folios or was it fit only for the margins, some loose parchment, or a pastedown? Would it be copied in a notebook, a schoolbook, or an illuminated manuscript? Once written, would it be annotated, glossed, indexed, or cross-referenced? Would it be strictly for personal use or available in a library? Finally, assuming that the scribe had the luxury of such a choice, in what kind of book would it be placed, that is to say, with what other kinds of texts should it be gathered for easy reference? Evidence of at least some of these decisions remains in each manuscript. To appreciate the broader changes in magic across the two and a half centuries covered by this book, and the interests and assumptions that lay behind them, we must begin by examining such data.

The transformations were far from random, and clear patterns emerge. The literature of illicit magic, and the way in which it was understood and treated, fall into two major streams. To illustrate the intellectual culture that in part determined the course of these streams, the first two sections of this book are introduced by the stories of two men, an unnamed apothecary and John of Morigny. In each case, the protagonist faces an essentially unsolvable problem. The apothecary must decide whether to believe that an astrological image that made him rich derived its power from occult natural properties or from deceptive demons. Brother John, by contrast, struggles to reconcile the fact that ritual magic was transmitted in books—books that one should assume were corrupt—but could only be learned, practiced, and understood through experiences that were not really communicable through the written word. How, then, could one learn to perform this magic, decide whether what one discovered was true or legitimate, and pass it on to others, when any written text might ultimately be corrupted? These problems form the creative core of the traditions of late medieval Scholastic astrological image magic collections and the literature of ritual magic.

The apothecary's dilemma derives from the rationalist context of twelfth- and thirteenth-century Scholasticism and its Arabic forebears. A few key writers in this intellectual tradition offered the hope that the magical effects of astrological images might derive from natural processes rather than demonic deception. An intellectual debate concerning images, inspired by the writings of the ninth-century Arab philosopher al-Kindī, took hold in the twelfth-century Latin West and engaged the energies of many of the major Scholastic philosophers. It sought to evaluate this kind of magic with reference to authoritative discussions of the natural world and through a process of logical analysis. Although astrological image magic texts contained significant elements that could not be accommodated to naturalistic explanation, the associated debates about the natural world remained the intellectual rudder for how they were treated, a fact that transformed the library of image magic. While scribes tended to alter the contents of these works very little, the decisions they made about which ones to copy were powerfully influenced by authoritative discussions, particularly the *Speculum astronomiae*. Consequently, of the scores of texts once available, a relatively small group came to dominate the library. The transformation was also one of perspective: scribes understood these texts to be reconcilable with Scholastic ideas or, at a minimum, to belong to the larger discourse of natural philosophy. Even where we find no evidence of theoretical concerns, scribes still associated the texts with the genre of *naturalia*. In this way, a significant library of texts, many of which were not intended as—and did not claim to be—natural magic, were collected with other works concerning the natural world.

Part I of the book treats this topic. Chapter 1 describes how writers from Augustine, through al-Kindī, to Aquinas understood astrological images. It argues that, despite clear authoritative statements to the contrary, medieval intellectuals persisted in regarding these images as part of the literature of *naturalia*. Chapter 2 examines the manuscripts of astrological image magic and argues that in the later Middle Ages, particularly under the influence of the *Speculum astronomiae*, a pattern of collection developed that was so regular that it should be understood as a genre: the Scholastic image magic collection. Chapter 3 examines the few exceptions to the rule and argues that these manuscripts tend to confirm the rules in other ways. The habits of mind and patterns of collection in this literature stand in stark contrast to the literature of ritual magic, to which the next chapters turn.

Brother John's dilemma arose from ritual magic, a different set of texts that flowed in an almost entirely discrete stream of transmission: demon conjuring, angel magic, and the theurgic arts, such as the *Ars notoria*, that emphasized the mechanisms of religious rites, dreams, and visions. For enthusiasts of this sort of magic, discovering truth was less about logical elaboration than about experience and revelation. The textual tradition they produced lacked the stabilizing effect that Scholastic debates had provided for astrological image magic. In fact, the mythologies written into the texts themselves encouraged the view that truth might very well not be found in *any* magic text, since ritual magic was less a repository of truth than a vehicle for its discovery. Authors, scribes, and collectors of these sorts of texts also acted with similar assumptions. A text had to accord with their ideas about what magical and/ or religious rites should look like, and if its rituals produced any subjectively convincing experiences, these too could affect how the text was understood or treated. It is clear that scribes evaluated magic texts and regularly altered them on the basis of changing religious sensibilities, practical experience, or even what they took to be instruction by numinous powers brought about by their practices. Arguably, scribes were driven to this approach to truth as the only way to counterbalance the lack of clarity generated by the unstable transmission of ritual magic manuscripts: in order to make systematic sense of unsystematic traditions, suprahuman assistance was needed. The need to defend a tradition that was otherwise impossible to justify also pressed practitioners to claim divine guidance and sanction for their texts and practices through visionary experiences. This knot of problems helps us understand not only the far more unstable nature of ritual magic but also the resiliency and longevity of a form of magic that survives in a relatively robust form to the present day.

Accordingly, part II of the book concerns the literature of ritual magic. It examines and compares the mythologies or literary representations of ritual magic practitioners within magic texts, the magical processes those texts ordained, and the way practicing magicians actually operated, including how they interacted with and transformed their texts. It argues that, unlike astrological image magic collections, ritual magic collections evince no interest in the literature of *naturalia* and lack stable textual traditions. Instead, their authors, scribes, and collectors had a strong interest in ritual processes, in highly personal or individualistic forms of magic, and in direct experiences of the numinous. This part of the book also argues that in this tradition, practitioners were encouraged by a variety of factors to transform received texts: ambivalence toward received texts, a mythology that encouraged practitioners to think of themselves as divinely guided editors or authors, and operations that emphasized the fundamental importance of individual experience, including subjectively convincing experiences of the numinous. Chapter 4 addresses the theurgic and largely angelic magic of the *Ars notoria*, John of Morigny's *Liber visionum*, and the *Liber iuratus Honorii*. Chapter 5 examines the literature of necromancy, that is, operations involving both angels and demons.

Once we appreciate the distinguishing features of these two streams of thought, the distinctive blend of new and old in magic after 1480 comes clearly into view. This is the subject of part III. Chapter 6 argues that although the late fifteenth and early sixteenth centuries are often characterized as a period when the superstitious "old dirty" magic of the Middle Ages was shed in favor of a more elegant magic of Hermetic or kabbalist inspiration, often associated with natural and astrological image magic, the magic manuscripts of this period exhibit no such shift.[1] The most commonly copied texts of illicit learned magic at that time were works of late medieval ritual magic. Astrological image magic, on the other hand, and most particularly the Scholastic image magic collection, enjoyed its highest level of copying during the fourteenth and fifteenth centuries. It then almost vanished as an independent genre, and its texts, when they were copied at all, were typically subsumed within the larger literature of ritual magic. This situation cannot be explained by the increased availability of magic texts in print.

Chapter 7 attempts to make sense of all this by comparing the manuscript evidence with the magic of Marsilio Ficino, Cornelius Agrippa, and John Dee. It argues that the major occultists of the sixteenth century, particularly Agrippa and Dee, stood firmly in the tradition of late medieval demonic and angelic magic. Even Ficino's magic, often understood as a limited kind of natural magic, was in fact a distinctively Neoplatonic system with great similarities to medieval ritual magic, highly ritualized and with powerfully religious, interior, experiential, and personal dimensions. Also like their medieval forebears, all three writers took up and transformed the older traditions, and they understood themselves as part of a divinely inspired renovation of magic. In short, Brother John's dilemma lies at the heart of Renaissance magic.

Scholarly Context

This study begins with manuscripts. Unlike most studies of learned magic, however, and particularly works on Renaissance magic, it focuses upon a wide spectrum of scribes, collectors, and authors of magic works. The weakness of this approach is that the most eloquent proponents or elucidators of magic in the period are not treated in detail. The subtleties of their positions and the intellectual power of their writing often fade in a sea of intellectual mediocrity. The strengths of this approach, however, are considerable. First, by examining copyists and collectors rather than just authors, we discover important traditions, such as the *Ars notoria*, that have become invisible in the intervening years. Second, because most people are not exceptional, any understanding of the cultural world of late medieval magic should at least take cognizance of more ordinary intellectuals. Third, the exceptional Renaissance occultists, among them Ficino, Agrippa, Trithemius, Bruno, and Dee, did not write their works in a vacuum: great writers often become so through their ability to engage the concerns of their age. Their popularity, intellectual lineage, and originality are therefore better understood in the context of broader intellectual trends. In order to understand the significance of their books, we must understand their readers, on the one hand, and the magic traditions with which they were familiar, on the other. This approach also provides a kind of aerial view of the literature that transcends the divisions into which scholarship conventionally has fallen.

Until relatively recently, the historiography of illicit learned magic has fallen roughly into two streams that correspond to the two streams of transmission just identified. In one, historians concentrated on the relationship between science and magic, and in the other on the relationship between religion and magic. Lynn Thorndike's eight-volume *History of Magic and Experimental Science* epitomizes the first approach. Although this monumental work includes a great deal of information on magic of a more "religious" kind, Thorndike's treatment of necromancy and the *Ars notoria* is very limited, no doubt owing to the limited connections between these texts and the discourse of natural philosophy. Frances Yates significantly extended this approach to the Renaissance, emphasizing the connections of science with Renaissance magic, which she understood as fundamentally concerned with natural magic.

In the other stream, which emphasizes the relationship between religion and magic, such scholars as Keith Thomas, Norman Cohn, and Edward Peters have examined the relationship of magic to broader cultural issues, and have worked to locate magic in the complex nexus of moral, legal, and religious thought. Thomas's classic *Religion and the Decline of Magic* assumed as its starting point that religion and magic were inextricably interwoven in the medieval period. Norman Cohn sought to understand the part that ritual magic played in late medieval conceptions of witchcraft and evil.[2]

Scholars have also tended tacitly to assume a division between magic before and after the 1480s, when Marsilio Ficino and Pico della Mirandola produced their powerful new syntheses. Some, like Frances Yates, have explicitly contrasted medieval and Renaissance magic; but for the most part this has been an unspoken divide that few scholars have crossed.[3] Like the division in scholarship between the scientific and religious aspects of medieval magic, this divide arises from and to a certain extent is justified by the sources. Renaissance writers incorporated the traditions of Neoplatonism and kabbalism in novel and very sophisticated ways. They also self-consciously rejected earlier traditions, particularly necromantic magic, and constructed their systems not only in opposition to prior magic texts but also in the self-conscious assumption that their age was engaged in a broad-based intellectual renovation that drew on the knowledge of antiquity. At the same time, this rejection belied the debts owed to their medieval forebears, and recent scholarship on the traditions of learned magic in the late Middle Ages and Renaissance demands that this division be reconsidered, or at least that the transition between medieval and Renaissance magic be better and more clearly articulated.

In recent decades scholars have begun to pick up the diverse threads of Lynn Thorndike's remarkable survey of Western magic manuscripts in an attempt to open up this considerable and important literature. David Pingree and Charles Burnett in particular have broken new ground with their close studies of individual figures and texts associated with medieval traditions of Arabic magic.[4] Although he had already published many articles on magic in the West (in addition to his survey *Magic in the Middle Ages*), Richard Kieckhefer's edition and study of a fifteenth-century necromancer's manual, *Forbidden Rites*, initiated a flood of editions and studies of specific texts, many by a new generation of scholars. The dean of magic studies in France, Jean-Patrice Boudet, produced a variety of important examinations of the *Ars notoria* and other texts and has led the way in editing the corpus of Solomonic literature in the Latin West.[5] An edition of the *Liber iuratus Honorii* by Gösta Hedegård, followed by studies by Robert Mathiesen, Kieckhefer, Katelyn Mesler, Boudet, and Jan Veenstra, has expanded our awareness of this important text.[6] Don Skemer has produced a study of textual amulets. Paola Zambelli has produced an edition and analysis of the *Speculum astronomiae*. Julien Véronèse's important study and edition of the *Ars notoria* is perhaps the single most remarkable achievement, given the vast number of manuscripts involved. Sophie Page, Benedek Láng, and I have conducted studies of manuscript collection and transmission and have contributed to a growing body of scholarship on specific texts and manuscripts.[7] Veenstra and Véronèse have provided important studies of other ritual magic texts as well.[8] The profoundly compelling materials left behind by John of Morigny have been partially edited by Claire Fanger and Nicholas Watson, who are currently at work on additional parts of his corpus.[9]

Work on Renaissance magic has also shifted to more focused examinations in recent decades; the literature is so vast that I can mention only a few studies that are directly relevant to this book. Brian Copenhaver, Michael J. B. Allen, Christopher Celenza, and Chaim Wirszubski have examined Ficino's *De vita coelitus comparanda* and Pico della Mirandola's *Oration on the Dignity of Man*, contributing substantially to our understanding of these difficult but central texts.[10] Paola Zambelli, Michael Keefer, Vittoria Perrone Compagni, and Christopher Lehrich have expanded our understanding of Cornelius Agrippa's *De occulta philosophia*.[11] The magic of John Dee has been treated in detail by Nicholas Clulee, Deborah Harkness, Stephen Clucas, and an array of other authors.[12]

In addition to this more focused scholarship, a number of important surveys now provide guidance to the broader traditions of medieval magic. Boudet's study *Entre science et nigromance* is the most important general treatment of magic in the later Middle Ages and in many ways supersedes Kieckhefer's *Magic in the Middle Ages*. Perhaps its greatest virtue is its tremendous breadth, including an examination of divination and astrology as well. Nicolas Weill-Parot's *Les "images astrologiques" au Moyen Âge et à la Renaissance* surveys the literature of astrological image magic and the reactions of medieval scholars from al-Kindī to Ficino. Paolo Lucentini and Vittoria Perrone Compagni's list of manuscripts of Hermetic texts (many of them concerning image magic) has superseded Thorndike's work on this literature, as have comparable lists in the works of Boudet, Weill-Parot, and Véronèse.[13] In addition to these, recent years have seen a wide array of thematic treatments of these and related subjects. William Eamon's study of books of secrets and William Newman's work on alchemy, while not focused precisely on magic, provide a useful backdrop against which other traditions of magic may be measured. At the same time, few studies of magic have attempted to survey illicit magic in general in both the medieval and Renaissance periods, a gap this study attempts to fill.

The relationship to this book of some of the scholarship I have mentioned merits explicit treatment here, particularly its relation to studies that attempt to outline broader historical developments in the history of illicit magic in the later Middle Ages and Renaissance. Keith Thomas's classic *Religion and the Decline of Magic* argues that an inherently magical medieval church tended to preserve or even promote the practice of magic, its support fading with the Reformation. While my study does tend to confirm the argument that religion and the practice of ritual magic cannot be easily disentangled, it suggests, on the one hand, that this integration of magic and religion is one of the factors that allowed ritual magic to survive and to thrive after the Reformation, and, on the other, that magic, particularly medieval astrological image magic, cannot comfortably be collapsed under the broad rubric of religion, at least not in the Latin West. Instead, many of its proponents argued (or evidently assumed) that image magic was natural magic and was thereby as discontinuous with the practice of religion as any other natural tool would be. It was more precisely, as Weill-Parot has argued, the subject of an ongoing Scholastic *debate* surrounding what he has called its "addressativity," that is, the uncomfortable reality that this form of magic appears to, or actually does, address spiritual beings that medieval theology insisted had to be demons. This study also confirms Weill-Parot's contention that the high point of this genre was reached in the fifteenth century.[14] I also follow Boudet's suggestion, in *Entre science et nigromance*, that the medieval period was characterized by a fundamental ambivalence toward magic, but Boudet casts his net further than I cast mine, including the broader literature of astrology and divination. He also delves much more deeply into the connections between the history of magic and medieval institutions and the growth in the sophistication and tenor of condemnations of magic in the later Middle Ages. It is curious that this period of increasing condemnation was accompanied by a growing interest in magic, and Véronèse has suggested that it was also characterized by the development of the "author-magician."[15] I have developed, and articulate more fully here, a similar and parallel argument that the highly individual-centered magician of the later Middle Ages and Renaissance flows naturally from the practices and mythologies of ritual magic, which promoted the importance of the individual practitioner and the idea of the magician as a divinely guided editor. With respect to the transition between the Middle Ages and Renaissance, evidence presented here suggests that the stark division of medieval and Renaissance magic promoted by many scholars, particularly by Frances Yates, cannot be sustained. Despite my reservations about Brian Vickers's evaluation of Renaissance magic, he is quite right to note that most magic in the sixteenth century looked very little like what Yates imagined and rather more like what she called the "old dirty magic" of the Middle Ages.[16] In addition to demonstrating the continuity of Renaissance magic with medieval traditions, then, I hope that this study will help redeem the old magic and prove it worthy of study.

Two other scholars not directly concerned with magic also deserve mention here. William Eamon's *Science and the Secrets of Nature* emphasizes the division between Scholastic natural philosophy and the literature of *naturalia*, particularly books of secrets, on the grounds that the former offered explanations for observed realities, whereas the latter, at best, offered demonstrations of those ideas.[17] While recognizing the *quia–propter quid* division, my study emphasizes the continuity between debates in Scholastic natural philosophy (*propter quid*) and habits of mind in the wider literature of *naturalia*, including experiments, secrets, divination, and astrological image magic (largely *quia*), and argues in particular that Scholastic natural philosophy fundamentally influenced the fortunes of astrological image magic texts. Eamon's work also emphasizes the practical nature of much of the secrets literature. In a similar vein, and like William Newman's *Promethean Ambitions*, which focuses heavily upon the practice of alchemy, my study takes seriously the idea that magic, even when it was a largely theoretical activity, was still a *practice* involving habits of authorship, translation, selection, copying, analysis, and practical application. These habits provide crucial evidence for understanding the intellectual culture of illicit learned magic in the premodern world.

Assumptions and Terminology

I use the terms "magic" and, less often, "religion" and "science" as useful general categories only. The modifiers "religious" and "scientific" are easily understood ways of referring to a very real division in premodern treatments of magic. Naturally, those who copied astrological image magic texts into volumes containing works of Scholastic natural philosophy were no less religious than the scribes of ritual magic, nor were the latter less "scientific" than the former. Yet the manuscripts do reveal different ways of approaching and thinking about the texts. If the Scholastic approach to magic texts was framed by religious questions (and it certainly could be), it was, at the same time, fundamentally concerned with physical processes, natural phenomena, and related theoretical questions. Similarly, if ritual magic texts reveal a more explicit desire to connect with the numinous, to perform powerful liturgical rites, and to engage in magic in an effective way, almost all of their scribes would have had Scholastic training. So there is no reason to assume that these approaches were in any way mutually exclusive. That some medieval scribes participated in both traditions, and that Renaissance writers and scribes merged these two streams, argues very strongly that they are better understood as distinctive modalities of relation or discourse. Similarly, the term "magic" is tremendously vague. I engage in a modern anachronism when I use this term, for many of my scribes did not use it, nor did they necessarily regard their practices as "magic." Nevertheless, use of the term may be justified by the fact that most authorities would have regarded all of the practices considered in this book as illicit, and therefore as magic.

Boudet has pointed out that writers commonly used the term "nigromancy" to refer to magic of which they approved and "necromancy" for magic of which they did not. A practitioner of demon conjuring was thus likely to refer to himself as a nigromancer, and it follows that to use the term "necromancer" to describe him might be anachronistic. However, the term "nigromancy" lacks precision, as it was used to refer both to astrological image magic and also to ritual magic, traditions that this book seeks to distinguish. Further, when a medieval catalogue identifies a book as necromantic or nigromantic, this does not necessarily mean that it was a work of demon conjuring. For example, a German medieval catalogue refers to works of astrological image magic simply as necromantic.[18] This was simply a negative valuation of astrological image magic, but in the absence of the accompanying description it is impossible to know whether the texts were astrological image magic or explicit demon conjuring. The terms are thus inherently ambiguous and depend on the (perhaps unknown) point of view of the author. For this reason, I use the term "necromancy" in the conventional sense, to refer only to those activities that the authors, scribes, and collectors explicitly regarded as involving the conjuring and deploying of demons.

An additional problem with the term "magic" is that it can be taken to imply a practice that is inherently inefficacious. I do not regard medieval assumptions about the world as in any way absolutely true. But the magical processes they described were assumed to be real, and I do accept that, in many cases, *they did work*. Certainly, practitioners could assign results to their magical operations in retrospect, but subjective experience of magic is far more complex than this.[19] Ritual magic employed human mediums, reflecting surfaces (fingernails, mirrors, water, or "show stones"), transparent substances (crystals or vials), and randomly moving things (fire or smoke), which could have evocative power even in the absence of meditative or trance states. Dreams, a fairly regular occurrence in everyday human experience, were also common vehicles for ritually induced visionary experiences. Recent studies, such as those by Tanya Luhrmann, have demonstrated that the techniques of modern magic, which differ in only limited ways from their medieval forebears, can result in subjectively convincing and even life-altering experiences.[20] Certainly, the medieval worldview provided abundant encouragement for the belief that these kinds of experiences could occur: conventional Christianity commonly employed visions and reports of visions as a way to access divine mysteries, and as Richard Kieckhefer has observed, very few people in the medieval period did not believe in demons and angels.[21] Given a state of suggestibility or altered awareness brought about by an ongoing discipline of meditation or visualization and more immediate evocative stimuli, it should be unsurprising that experiences ranging from feelings or impressions to visual or auditory hallucinations might follow. Of course, it is conceivable that some authors and scribes failed in their magical efforts, but we have every reason to assume that they copied magic texts under the assumption that the practices described therein could work. Similar conditions surrounded image magic: although there was some debate about *how* it worked—whether it operated because of astrological influence or demonic intervention—the assumption remained that it did work. Throughout this study I assume that the practices described probably did achieve some subjectively convincing results, and if not, that the practitioners would have better cause to doubt their texts or techniques than to question the principle that magic could work.

Sensitive readers will also be aware that it is problematic to use the term "scribe" to indicate the person whose intents and interests are reflected in the text. It is, of course, unclear whether the texts were copied by professional scribes or were the work of the person directly interested in magic. It may be that both participated in the selection and transmission of the text. In fact, a single manuscript may reveal a startling complexity of "archeological" layers, each represented by a different person. It may have been assembled from several previous books, each assembled by a different person. The complete surviving codex, or any of the parts of which it is made up, may have been owned, that is, collected, by numerous people. It also may contain any number of the various levels of authorship or authorial intervention. This is one of the great riches of the medieval codex, but any attempt to reflect this complexity can make for some very clumsy writing. In order to simplify things, and to avoid the endless repetition of awkward phrases like "the scribe, the person who directed the copying or paid for it, the collector or the group who collaborated on this manuscript, the authors, extractors, or those who in some way made authorial interventions," I often simply refer to this person or group in the singular as "the author, scribe, or collector," or sometimes "the scribes." I trust that my readers will indulge me in this matter.

PART I | THE APOTHECARY'S DILEMMA

The story goes that the thirteenth-century astrologer Guido Bonatti took pity upon a poor apothecary with whom he used to play chess: "Guido gave him a wax image of a ship, telling him that if he kept it hidden in a box in a secret place he would grow rich, but that if he removed it he would grow poor again."[1] In time, the apothecary became very wealthy. But he began to worry about the condition of his soul—was the magic diabolical?—and so he confessed to a priest, who advised him to destroy the image. The hapless apothecary did as he was told and soon was reduced to poverty once again. Evidently, having reconsidered the value of his condition, he returned to Bonatti to ask for a replacement. Bonatti chastised him, saying that the effects of the image were not magical but natural, derived from astrological conditions that would not recur for fifty years. In another story of the use of image magic, this one from late fourteenth-century London, a man by the name of Tresilian was about to be executed. After being forced by a beating to climb the gallows, the condemned man proclaimed loudly, "So long as I do wear anything upon me, I shall not die." At this the executioner had him stripped and "found certain images painted like to the signs of the heavens, and the head of a devil painted, and the names of many of the devils wrote in parchment."[2] These being removed, Tresilian was duly hanged without his clothes, after which his throat was cut, and he was left to hang until morning to be sure he was dead.

Most medieval morality tales about magic involving written signs, and most philosophical discussions of the subject warn that demonic powers lurk just beneath the surface. Yet the fear of demons conflicts with another powerful impulse encouraged by a few influential philosophical texts, the desire to carve out a small circle of entirely natural and legitimate image magic. The apothecary's concern was understandable because—philosophical arguments aside—the trappings of image magic could easily leave one in doubt about what powers might make it work. Had he been familiar with books containing astrological image magic, he might have been less concerned, since most of its scribes and collectors assumed that it belonged to the genre of *naturalia,* and at least some also evidently believed that it could be legitimate and nondemonic. At the same time, most philosophical treatments of the subject rejected astrological images as ineffective or demonic. As the report of Tresilian's execution illustrates, even astrological talismans and ligatures (i.e., objects suspended from the neck) were sometimes regarded as diabolical. While the story recognizes the astrological basis of a number of the images, the talismans were assumed to name and depict demons. In the mind of the author, there was no clear line between astrological and demonic images.

Concern about demonic involvement was also frequently raised in regard to the texts of image magic, and not without justification. While the images they describe rarely if ever explicitly name demons in the Christian sense of the word, it would have been very difficult for the uninitiated (and perhaps for anyone) to be sure. The spirit or angel names employed in such texts might be in transliterated or "pig" Hebrew, Arabic, Greek, or Chaldee (i.e., Syriac), if Latin characters were used at all. The texts might also employ a mathematical figure such as a magic square. The image one was to carve or draw might be strange or disturbing and have no apparent relation to the more familiar signs of the zodiac or planets. Perhaps more to the point, some texts advocate using various ritual procedures in the making of astrological images, a practice that would justifiably raise concerns for a late medieval reader. If the source of the image's power was purely natural, why employ a ritual procedure? To whom might the signs, mysterious words, ritual gestures, incantations, and suffumigations be significant, if not to some other sentient being like a demon? That most collectors of the texts of image magic (even those of the apparently necromantic variety) regarded their texts as belonging to the broad category of *naturalia,* and that some appeared to regard the processes as entirely natural, would have been cold comfort.

The stories of the apothecary and Tresilian also illustrate the importance of examining the manuscript evidence for late medieval interest in magic. Literary sources and court records leave a great deal in question and often communicate information third- or fourthhand. Moreover, these sources exist precisely because of their dramatic content; the use of magic has always added color and danger to a story. In the case of court records, one justifiably doubts the veracity of many of the charges of magic, which appear to have provided a useful, if concocted, addition to standard charges of sedition. They also made for an interesting elaboration upon a story such as Tresilian's. His cowardly behavior before mounting the gallows is compounded by his vain and rather pathetic attempt to regain some dignity through his defiant claims about magical protection. His use of magic not only further demonstrates his lack of manliness but also hints strongly at the sin of despair. One rightly suspects some elaboration by the writer of this account.

On the other hand, if accurate, the account is still problematic, as most such records are. To have been prosecuted for these kinds of crimes usually required an imprudent involvement in political conflicts or rash public displays. These sources may raise interesting questions about legal procedure, dissent, and nonconformity, but they do not accurately represent the much larger number of people who were interested in magic and who read, considered, and transmitted magic literature. While examination of the manuscript sources will not ultimately solve the apothecary's dilemma, it can provide an understanding of the worldview of those interested in magic in the late Middle Ages, the vast majority of whom were never brought to trial or memorialized in legend. To begin with, however, we must establish the broad intellectual context that framed their ideas about magic.

Powerful and influential articulations of the apothecary's dilemma—in his case, either keep the wax image and remain rich but in spiritual peril, or forsake the image and suffer the consequences of penury—may be found in the learned discussions of image magic. These discussions tended to take two forms. A few philosophical treatments labored to mark off small portions of magic literature as legitimate but most condemned it; moral and theological condemnations, *often by the same authors who had treated magic positively elsewhere,* argued that all magic was evil and functioned by the exercise of demonic power. The differences in treatment were occasioned in part by the stylistic requirements of the different contexts in which this topic was discussed. Taken together, they illustrate the fundamental ambivalence that dominates evaluations of magic in the Latin West. Since the principal concern of this study is with those who copied, collected, or wrote magic texts, it is desirable to establish the questions about orthodoxy and sin that might have occupied their minds. I begin with a brief exploration of the standard condemnations of magic and the ways in which the practice of magic, image magic in particular, could be considered unorthodox or sinful. I then turn to a brief discussion of the relationship of image magic to natural philosophy.

1

MAGIC AND NATURAL
PHILOSOPHY

Magic, Orthodoxy, and Sin: Questions in the Mind of the Collector

In his *Dialogue on Miracles,* the late twelfth- and early thirteenth-century Cistercian Caesarius of Heisterbach relates the story of a group of German students studying necromancy in Toledo. After several months of intense study, they had seen no concrete results. By threatening his life, they convinced their master to give them a demonstration of his art. He took them to a deserted place, drew a circle around them, and warned them not to leave the circle for any reason. The master then summoned a group of demons who first appeared as knights, attempting to frighten the students out of their protective circle. When this did not work, the demons took the form of voluptuous women, dancing seductively about them. One of the students was overcome by the display and accepted a ring from one of the demons. He was instantly dragged off to hell, and the whole apparition vanished. After they had recovered from the shock, the remaining students persuaded the master, with further threats to his life, to attempt to retrieve their friend. In turn, he managed to persuade the demonic forces to hold a sort of trial to decide whether the student had been dealt with justly. It was concluded that he did not deserve so radical a punishment, and he was returned in a predictably ruinous state. He subsequently entered a monastery, where he lived out the remainder of his days.[1]

The subject of magic rarely evokes weak reactions, largely because it serves to mediate basic tensions in the human psyche. Our desire for power accompanies a sense of powerlessness. We wish for control in a world where most things are beyond our control. We fear that there are hidden machinations affecting our lives, and we wish to discover them. We are drawn to, and fascinated by, the wondrous but fearful of the strange and unknown. The themes of magic and irrational evil persist in modern suspense and horror films. Not only did accounts of demonic magic evoke the same kind of reactions as the modern horror film evokes in us; they also tended to embrace that genre's radical or simplistic moralizing. When the student of necromancy was whisked away to hell, a moment of weakness had dragged him into what was potentially eternal perdition. His reaction upon being saved from indescribable horrors was similarly radical. He entered a monastery, where he remained to the end of his days. As in modern horror films, there is a playful element to this story, but this does not obviate its horrific features: demons and the torments of hell were very real and immanent. Medieval condemnations of magic drew upon these powerful resources.

Magic was a complex sin. Authors vary widely in how they classify magic, and the great variation in treatment testifies not only to the imagination of the authors but also to the variety of potentially sinful behavior that magic might involve. The diversity of the practices that magic included, and the variety of human impulses that drove it, made magic difficult to categorize. John Gower discussed it as a form of gluttony.[2] Thomas of Chobham included some magical practices under *luxuria*.[3] Bernardino of Siena's classification of certain magical practices under the sin of pride is particularly resonant with the grandiose pretensions of learned magic.[4] Much of the magic literature features the creation of illusions, presumably intended to impress others. It also proposes to make available powers over some very fearsome forces—powers usually attributed only to saints—and knowledge not available to the vast majority of humankind. The potential for the sin of pride is clearly high. The use of magical techniques suggests a certain lack of faith in providence, a pride in one's ability to avoid misfortune through magic as opposed to faith in God, and a despair that God will not ultimately provide for one. As it involved images and sometimes apparently worshipful acts, it was sometimes associated with idolatry and paganism. Finally, most learned magic was not characterized as superstitious in the sense that it made undue use of holy things or involved, as it were, a surplus of religious fervor that flowed into dubious practices. Our purpose here, however, is not to catalogue the complex variations on this theme but rather to illustrate the ambivalence commonly associated with image magic. To this end, let us turn to a single representative case.

Vincent of Beauvais's *Speculum maius,* probably the single most important medieval encyclopedia, bases its discussion of magic and orthodoxy almost entirely upon the fundamental text of canon law, Gratian's *Decretum,* but this does not make it less representative.[5] Vincent probably employed Gratian simply because general treatments of the topic by accepted authorities could easily be found there, gathered together in a rational order. It saved a great deal of time, and he was, no doubt, not the only one to use Gratian as a general reference work. The definitive statements of great authorities such as Augustine or Hugh of St. Victor (represented here by Richard of St. Victor, who reiterates his ideas) retained their power over time. Thus, although Edward Peters is quite correct that there has been a tendency to overemphasize canon law as a source in the history of magic and witchcraft, this does not obviate the importance of legal texts as general reference sources, much less the authorities to which the legal texts themselves referred. Further, although they began to speak directly to a known body of literature, the later moralists did not alter or develop the established themes in any significant way. The subtleties developed in the philosophical discussions of William of Auvergne, Nicole Oresme, Aquinas, and Albertus Magnus were not of great concern to the moralist. Not at all surprisingly, the principal patristic authority, Augustine, is by far the most frequently cited author. Thus the discussion employed in the *Speculum maius* (subdivided into three volumes, the *Speculum historiale, Speculum doctrinale, and Speculum naturale*) had a wide currency due to the popularity of the work, the general influence of Augustine, and, of course, the ubiquitous presence of the *Decretum*. But as Vincent's goal was to present the "standard version" of human knowledge, it may also be regarded as a constituent part of a conservative, orthodox position on magic. In particular, it exemplifies the questions that might occupy the mind of one attempting to make a decision about the orthodoxy of a magic text.

Vincent's *Speculum doctrinale* is divided roughly into six fields of knowledge: literary, moral, mechanical, physical, mathematical, and theological.[6] As one could infer from the sources he used, Vincent treats magic as a crime, and his general position is clear. Magic is a sinful art involving an inappropriate relation to the natural or spiritual world. No explicit allowances are made for natural magic. Although a few of the authorities might be interpreted as sympathetic to the practice of magic, their statements are weak and indirect. One terse passage from Richard of St. Victor that does not appear in the explicit discussion of magic begins with a distinction between astrology and astronomy, and then between legitimate and illegitimate astrology. Legitimate astrology is limited to uses in medicine and weather prediction, but the rest of the art is vanity.[7] Among the sections of the work directly concerned with magic, only chapter 121 gives magic a somewhat more positive treatment. Perhaps showing the influence of late twelfth- and early thirteenth-century thought, Raymond of Pennafort is quoted as saying that there may be a natural and irreproachable rationale for the observance of what appear to be

superstitious or magical practices.[8] Yet this by no means argues for the legitimacy of magical images or incantations, and it certainly lacks the authority
of Augustine, who dominates the discussion with his unequivocal condemnation of any kind of magical practice.

The Augustine passages are all drawn directly from Gratian and ultimately derive from standard works such as the *City of God, On Christian
Doctrine,* and *Confessions.* In addition, some of the passages derive from the
opuscule *De divinatione daemonum* (On the Divination of Demons).[9] Augustine's position on magic is relatively conservative, emphasizing the real or
possible involvement of demons in any magical practices.[10] His ideas about
magic and astrology lack the subtle treatment of physical processes found in
Scholastic authors and, of course, relate clumsily to the image magic texts of
the twelfth and thirteenth centuries. Nonetheless, Augustine remained the
dominant influence in this period's antimagic arguments. Chapter 116 of the
Speculum doctrinale contains a passage from *On Christian Doctrine* rejecting all characters, ligatures, and incantations as patent evidence of demonic
involvement.[11] Implicit in this discussion is the association of magic with
pagan religious practices and idolatry. This leaves no room for any practice
involving incantations, images, or even things hung about the neck or bound
on the body. A lengthy section in chapter 117 is devoted to a passage from
De divinatione daemonum, which explains that demons' ability to perform
seemingly miraculous deeds derives from the clear senses of their aerial bodies and the experience afforded by a long life. Not only do demons perceive
the world in a more precise fashion than humans but they also live much
longer, allowing them time to learn a great deal more. This passage concludes
with the warning that God permits demons to carry out magical operations
partly as a test for Christians.[12] So not only does any form of image or incan-
tatory magic function by means of demonic intervention, but these highly
intelligent, powerful, and malevolent beings make magic "work" in order to
deceive humans.

The arguments found in the legal sources Vincent includes are less
comprehensive but betray similar themes. Like Augustine,[13] the legal writers regard magic, even if innocent of demonic involvement, as bordering
on idolatry and paganism. So, for example, early in this section Vincent
includes a discussion that equates various divinatory practices (*sortes*) with
the observance of lucky and unlucky days (Egyptian days), idolatry, and
pagan rites. Later in the *Speculum,* the text explains that the drawing of
lots is not bad in itself but should be avoided as idolatrous.[14] A similar
position is taken on the question of the efficacy of verbal formulae that
may be legitimate if they are Christian prayers, spoken by the devout.[15]

Several papal prohibitions against various pagan practices are also listed. The threat of demonic involvement also forms the basis for the condemnations of two church councils. A decision from the Council of Toledo and a passage from William of Thorigne seek to extirpate superstitious practices among clerics.[16] The latter passage bans the use of charms in connection with the Mass or on particular days.[17] Other church council decisions seek the eradication of more popular forms of magic. They include the infamous description and condemnation of the witches' sabbath (commonly known by its incipit as "Canon episcopi"),[18] and an exhortation to priests to rid their parishes of the art of magic.[19] Although the groups are treated separately, each having its own peculiar superstitious practices, the message in both cases is essentially the same: magic is a criminal and superstitious practice, a species of idolatry, which more often than not involves the threat of demonic temptation and deception. Finally, chapter 119 records Richard of St. Victor's attempt to present a general taxonomy of magical practices of all varieties. Richard's classifications are similar to, and seem to be drawn from, Isidore of Seville's through Hugh of St. Victor, which explains the presence of such practices as augury, which probably had not been practiced for centuries.

As a discussion of an art, even a criminal one, Vincent's presentation is scattered and somewhat unsatisfying. At the same time, it is more or less characteristic of twelfth- and early thirteenth-century thought. The interpenetration of moral and legal sources was common in the later medieval discussions and depictions of magic.[20] In most contexts, little attention was given to the actual content of the magical arts, except for what one might infer from their names. The discussion is dominated by theological and legal prohibitions, in particular those of Augustine, who had addressed a tradition of magical practices in the Mediterranean region almost a millennium earlier. The resulting lack of accuracy was of little concern and did not diminish the condemnatory power of the passages. The authority of the authors and the general force of their arguments were far more important. There are weak hints of instances where magic-like practices might be legitimate if the symbols were Christian ones, the verbal formulas were prayers, and the attitude was one of true devotion. But these are overwhelmed by repeated and authoritative condemnations that leave no room for "legitimate" image magic. Any verbal formula, written sign, or object suspended from the body used to some magical end was wrong and implicitly involved demons. Even if one were to assume the possibility that these had natural effects, the threat of powerful, intelligent, and deceiving demons was still always present. Further, magic was closely connected with superstition, paganism, and the sin of idolatry.

Subsequent authorities did not move substantially beyond these basic themes, although they developed more subtlety as they came into contact with the actual magic texts; Scholastic philosophers in particular concerned themselves with the specific nature of the processes involved. The penitential literature, which focused upon salvation for the laity, emphasized an active demonic role in temptation and insisted that nearly all magical sins involved collaboration with the devil.[21] As we shall see, there was a short period in the twelfth century when magic seemed to have achieved a foothold among the categories of legitimate knowledge, but it was short lived. A variety of reiterations of the Augustinian position, together with the profoundly influential statement of Hugh of St. Victor (represented in Vincent of Beauvais's encyclopedia by Richard of St. Victor), would overwhelm these notions.[22] While some subtle adjustments were made to discussions of magic following these early efforts, the new writers tended to repeat the earlier condemnations or echo their emphasis on demonic involvement. These blanket condemnations were even repeated—often very emphatically—by those who attempted to rescue certain kinds of magic as legitimate. The chorus of condemnatory voices thus seemed unanimous. At the same time, theories of magic were becoming increasingly sophisticated. An elaborate demonology was developing, especially in the context of monastic literature and ecclesiastical invective. Caesarius of Heisterbach, the author of the story that begins this part of the book, used elaborate stories about demons as a general *topos* for discussing temptation in his *Dialogue on Miracles,* a text that sought to prepare the novitiate for monastic life.[23] The vision of the Christian world under attack by demonic forces, manifesting themselves in the world as religious dissent, was also bound up with the emotional piety of the period. Scholastic discussions that focused on magic's physical processes responded to a significant, sometimes intellectually sophisticated, contemporary magic literature. The efforts by such men as Thomas Aquinas and the author of the *Speculum astronomiae* to discuss the issue of magic in the context of natural philosophy were particularly important. Their arguments (to which we shall turn presently) lent further credence to the belief that demons were the power behind most magical practices. The effect of this situation was that the literature on magic acquired an increased subtlety in its discussion of *how* demons might be involved in magic, but the threat of demons—a threat that resonated with the fear of idolatry and heterodoxy—remained the major theme in antimagic discussions. Augustine's unequivocal position thus retained its currency and remained powerful.

As Kieckhefer has suggested, the general conclusion one might draw from the antimagic material is that "virtually all types of magic might be demonic."[24]

Like the apothecary's priest, most no doubt tended toward the antimagic position of the authorities, who were quite unambiguous in their evaluation of all magic as implicitly demonic. Others, like the apothecary's friend Bonatti, sought out the small gray areas where some legitimacy might be accorded to certain magical practices on philosophical grounds. But in a period where the condemnatory voices were so unambiguous, and in which demons were a credible threat,[25] even the mind of one familiar with the philosophical discussions of natural magic must have been fraught with arguments, impulses, and voices in dramatic conflict with one another. Our apothecary was understandably filled with doubt.

Images and Natural Philosophy

The works on image magic considered in this study derive from a variety of sources, including Jewish and Greek traditions. But the overwhelming majority derive from Arabic sources. Although the texts vary greatly in the precise form of magic they describe, they are roughly unified by their astrological orientation. In most, it is clear what processes were understood to take place in the magical operations. They employ talismans constructed at suitable astrological moments, from suitable material, and often with some form of ritual action, such as suffumigation, incantation, or animal sacrifice. The goal of all of this, including the ritual actions, was to focus the powers of celestial influences or rays in a talisman for magical purposes.[26] Thus texts often treat images of a particular astrological category, such as images of Venus, the mansions of the moon, or certain fixed stars. Relatively few medieval authorities on medicine or astrology ever openly supported the idea that any kind of astrological image magic was legitimate. In fact, this magical literature could not be reconciled with the principles of Scholastic natural philosophy. Images, rituals, invocations, sacrifices, and gestures all strongly suggest the participation of a sentient being. Whether intentionally or not, the magical operator appears to communicate with this being, which almost certainly had to be a demon. Thus, if the operations worked, it would be the result of demonic intervention.[27] Nonetheless, as we shall see, works of astrological image magic were collected almost without exception with works of *naturalia,* seemingly supporting the view that they were legitimate. Moreover, they were not generally collected with works of ritual magic in which the authors explicitly conjured, and derived power from, demons and angels rather than from the stars. In other words, despite all the authoritative statements to the contrary, the scribes and collectors of these texts understood them to belong to the same genre of literature as other works concerned with the natural world, like medicine, experiments, recipes, and astrology. So how was it that until roughly 1500, despite the rarity of explicit support from authoritative voices, scribes continued to associate astrological image magic with the natural world and thus, implicitly, with the notion of "natural magic"?

Theories about magical images draw heavily upon the wellspring of late antiquity and in particular later Neoplatonism. The conviction that reason in itself could not provide access to the divine drove the development of theurgy. In this system of religious exercises, one could achieve this access through purgative practices, magical operations that manipulated hidden correspondences in the world (at the lower stages), and contact with increasingly higher levels of ethereal beings, ideally resulting in ecstatic union with the One.[28] The magical operations involved were not understood as commanding higher powers but rather as the automatic responses of one portion of the cosmos to another. The writings of Iamblichus, Proclus, and Synesius, which exerted a fundamental and direct influence upon the Renaissance mage Marsilio Ficino,[29] influence medieval natural philosophy indirectly. Among the works including extensive theoretical treatments of magic, only the *Picatrix,* an Arabic magical work, explicitly preserves something like the Neoplatonic combination of magical operations with the search for spiritual enlightenment, although in this case magical practices of a much more mundane nature take the place of theurgy.[30] The more common medieval point of transmission for Neoplatonic cosmological ideas were the synthetic works and commentaries of their Arabic heirs, whose reading of Aristotle was heavily Neoplatonic. For the sake of brevity, the discussion of this intellectual current focuses mainly upon the works that clearly framed and influenced the transmission of manuscripts, particularly those that had a significant manuscript presence of their own in the library of astrological image magic.[31]

De radiis stellarum (On the Rays of the Stars),[32] a treatise by the Arabic writer al-Kindī that survives only in its Latin translation, elaborates a credible natural explanation for many forms of magical practice, the use of magical images among them.[33] The work explains how the stars are responsible for all sublunary change, and how the "sage" may perform magic by manipulating these processes through his superior knowledge. Al-Kindī assumes a cosmos in which everything is linked by a descending emanation of reflected forms. The upper reaches are occupied by the real forms. Mimicking these, the stars create all sublunar things by transferring copies of the real forms to the sublunar world by means of rays. In this process, many forms come together or "pile up" to make up a "harmony," which results in some particular thing being created or some physical event taking place. Thus a blond-haired person might have a formal connection to the sun—the specific form of blondness having been projected through stellar rays in the moment that person's body was created. The same person would also contain numerous other forms, connected to other sorts of sidereal forms (e.g., tallness, strength, or a bad temper). The world is a vast web of corresponding forms connected by rays, which the magus may manipulate. The question is, how does the magus know how to do this?

Al-Kindī begins with a general discussion of the acquisition of knowledge, using Porphyry's introduction to Aristotle's *Categories, Isagoge* as his framework. He does this to demonstrate to his philosophically uninitiated readers how to discover universals. Certain people, specifically the sages of antiquity, were particularly good at identifying universals because they had been made especially perceptive in their examination of things and in the abstraction of knowledge.[34] The crucial step in this argument is his implicit assumption that these universals discovered by the sages are the forms that express themselves in the world through the influences of the stars. In this way, if you can identify a universal, you can also identify a particular kind of stellar influence and its sublunary effect. The *operatio* of each star is projected through rays into the world. All the stars' rays combine in various places to form a "harmony," which, as a whole, results in the production of all terrestrial things and the changes they undergo. In turn, every form existing in the world, either substantial or accidental, makes its own weaker rays in imitation of the sidereal form that produced it.[35] Thus all material things emit rays as well, rays that can also have effects on things. Since all material things emit rays that have effects, it is possible to conduct magic by using a wide variety of material things to produce specific kinds of lesser rays that have the desired effect. Forms in the imagination, in conjunction with faith, produce rays affecting bodily movement, which al-Kindī divides into muscular movement and the movement of speaking.[36] For the imagination to affect transitive movement, that is, to change a body not directly connected to the soul of the operator, some other additional cause is almost always required.

An example of such a cause is a word or formula (*oratio*), which al-Kindī regards as a form impressed upon air. There are two sorts of words, those of human designation and those having an ontological connection to the form they signify.[37] While both types of words have some effect, the latter are much more powerful and noticeable because they reflect their sidereal form directly. When one of these "forms" is uttered by an operator, who at the same time imagines the form with due solemnity and firm faith, the combination and consonance of forms can have the effect of producing rays (like those of the corresponding star), which in turn transmit movement (i.e., change) to another object. The final chapters repeat the same notions, using images and sacrifices in place of words as the "container" for the impressed form. In this way, by using special words, thoughts, and objects, one could produce a magical effect derived from the power of the stars and the ideal forms that lie behind them. Although the principal instance of al-Kindī's discussion involves magical words, his medieval European readers were more interested in magical images, and as numerous manuscripts attest, it was frequently in the service of images that this text was ultimately employed.[38] What was most important about this text was that it transformed books of magical instructions into potential repositories of information about natural causes and effects in which demons played no part at all.

During the period of translation, not only theories concerning magic but also the texts of image magic were transmitted into the Latin world. Magic works occur among the products of the early important translators, including Adelard of Bath and John of Spain. As they began to absorb the new learning, some scholars promoted the idea that certain kinds of magic involving images or words might be legitimate subsets of science, a position that ran counter to Augustine's blanket condemnation. In the early part of the twelfth century, Petrus Alfonsi identified a difference of opinion over whether the seventh liberal art was prophecy or necromancy. Somewhat later, Dominicus Gundissalinus suggested that "necromancy according to physics" (*nigromancia secundum physicam*) was part of natural science. Adelard of Bath similarly suggested that nigromancy (*nigromantia*) was a legitimate subdivision of natural science or "science of the stars."[39] Early in the thirteenth century William of Auvergne became the first to use the term "natural magic" in relation to talismanic magic. Somewhat later, Roger Bacon suggested that not only images but also words might have some kind of natural occult force connected with them. His position is carefully worded. He reserves the term "magic" for practices that are either ineffectual or demonic, and these he vociferously rejects. In so doing, he employs the standard antimagic position and appears to be highly orthodox. At the same time, however, he maintains the possibility that natural forces might be manipulated through the use of words of power or images.[40] Bacon's position exemplifies the ambivalence of thirteenth-century writers. For example, although he marks off the logical parameters of natural magic, he does not explain how to distinguish between occult effects derived naturally and those accomplished by the aid of demons. This ambivalence was also influenced by al-Kindī's *De radiis stellarum,* which circulated in numerous manuscripts and is mentioned favorably by medieval writers.[41] As we shall see, this work also occurs frequently in codices that include works of image magic.

As a whole, the scholarly community of the twelfth and thirteenth centuries was ill equipped to deal with the vast library of astrological and astronomical material it had inherited. Autobiographical accounts of scholars who later came to reject this literature often mention the seductive lure of astrology and magic in their early years as university students, and innumerable astrological manuscripts testify to the great number whose interest persisted into their mature years. The *Speculum astronomiae* (Mirror of astronomy) offered informed guidance through this astrological literature.[42] It provided the necessary bibliographic details for identifying the works involved, classed them into appropriate categories, commented upon their contents, and identified those counter to the Christian faith. If, as Paola Zambelli has observed, astrology was integral to the medieval worldview, magical images were at least as integral to astrology. The astrological library included a considerable number of magical works represented in hundreds of manuscripts, most of them derived from Arabic sources and concerned with the making of images. In addition, as we have seen, the argument, epitomized by al-Kindī, that magic derived from natural forces was common in both the literature and among scholars in the period. Thus it was incumbent upon the author of the *Speculum astronomiae* (hereafter Magister Speculi) to sort through the magical literature that claimed legitimacy as part of the science of astrology. Accordingly, chapter 11 of the *Speculum* treats the science of images (*sciencia imaginum*), which is included as part of the science of elections.

That the Magister Speculi includes a discussion of astrological images in this work by no means amounts to an approval of image magic. He identifies only one of three categories of images as potentially legitimate. The other two, which make up the vast majority of image magic texts, he condemns. The first and most abominable category

> requires suffumigations and invocation, such as the images of Toz the Greek and Germath the Babylonian, which have stations for the worship of Venus, [and] the images of Balenuz and Hermes, which are exorcized by using the 54 names of the angels, who are said to be subservient to the images of the Moon in its orbit, [but] perhaps are instead the names of demons, and seven names are incised on them in the correct order to affect a good thing and in inverse order for a thing one wants to be repelled. They are also suffumigated with the wood of aloe, saffron and balsam for a good purpose; and with galbanum, red sandalwood and resin for an evil purpose. The spirit is certainly not compelled [to act] because of these [names and suffumigations], but when God permits it on account of our own sins, they [the spirits] show themselves

as [if they were] compelled to act, in order to deceive men. This is the worst [kind of] idolatry, which, in order to render itself credible to some extent, observes the 28 mansions of the Moon and the hours of the day and night along with certain names [given to] these days, hours and mansions themselves.[43]

The Magister Speculi condemns the second category as well, which he considers only marginally better. These do not employ names but characters, which may represent planets or demons and which are exorcized "by certain names" (*per quaedam nomina*). Unbeknownst to the user, he warns, the names may represent things contrary to the honor of the Catholic faith.[44] He provides an extensive list of works and incipits that fall into each of these categories. In both cases demons are said to be responsible for making these forms of magic function. The author also reiterates the Augustinian position that God allows this magic to work as a temptation to Christians. In addition, however, he is concerned that the astrological trappings—the mansions of the moon in particular—will fool readers into thinking of this kind of magic as natural.

But the Magister Speculi did believe that a certain portion of the science of images might be legitimate. The third category of images are those that do not employ suffumigations, invocations, inscription of characters, or exorcisms but derive their effects only from celestial sources. These employ simple astrological images, constructed under specific astrological conditions that are clearly related to the intended function of the images.[45] He goes on to describe a detailed example of a legitimate astrological configuration for the engraving of an image of the moon and lists only two works as *apparently* legitimate: one of the translations of Thābit ibn Qurra's *De imaginibus* (Concerning images) and a work on images attributed to Ptolemy.[46] This tentative approval, however, is followed up with two qualifications. First, if the images in the work by Ptolemy were shown to be secretly necromantic, he would condemn them as well. Second, the penultimate chapter of the *Speculum*, which returns to this subject, makes clear that he does not recommend them but cannot condemn them on technical grounds:

I do not defend that section concerning astrological images on account of the nearness they have to necromantic images beyond what is said above in the chapter devoted to them, that they take their virtue from a celestial figure according to the ninth sentence of Ptolemy, . . . and except that nothing prohibits one from defending them in accordance with that which can be denied or defended. . . . Not that I recommend

them, but without any reason, it does not seem that they should carry
the iniquity of the other [type of images].[47]

Although it is clear that the author is trying to chip out a small area of legitimacy for natural image magic "in accordance with that which can be denied
or defended," he does so in a carefully worded manner, leaving plenty of room
for the reader to reevaluate the question on moral, legal, and even philosophical grounds. This tentative approval is hardly a ringing endorsement.

The *Speculum astronomiae* became a classic in the schools, although it
never became a standard schoolbook.[48] Its authoritative discussion of works of
astronomy and astrology provided an indispensable guide for those attempting to navigate this extensive and contentious literature. Figures as diverse
and significant as Nicole Oresme, Peter of Abano, and Jean Gerson can be
demonstrated to have employed the work in their discussions of the subject.
Ficino's use of the *Speculum* in his *De vita coelitus comparanda* toward the
end of the fifteenth century attests to its enduring influence. The most immediate effect of this authoritative discussion was radically to reduce the scope
of legitimate image magic. Earlier Latin writers such as Adelard of Bath had
accorded legitimacy to a much wider range of practices, such as suffumigation
and incantation. The Magister Speculi's rejection of these practices as indications of demonic involvement not only radically reduced the range of possibly legitimate practices; it also reduced the number of legitimate texts from
around forty to two. Even these two texts are accorded legitimacy only with a
carefully worded warning that they might be secretly demonic as well. As we
shall see, the *Speculum* also had a major impact upon the copying of works of
image magic. The vast majority of scribes appear to have followed the advice
of the Magister Speculi in choosing their texts, preferring those that he tentatively approved. However, most major authorities were much less tolerant.

Thomas Aquinas himself engaged in the debate over natural magic and
magical images in the *Summa theologiae* (2.2.96.2 and 4) and *Summa contra
gentiles* (3.105). He also treated the subject in a more extensive way in his
De occultis operibus naturae ad quemdam militem ultra montanum (Letter to
a Certain Knight Beyond the Mountains Concerning the Occult Operations
of Nature).[49] The central issue for Thomas was whether an artificially created
thing could have occult powers that extended in some way from its accidental qualities rather than from its substance. For example, could gold, a solar
metal, be made a more efficacious vehicle for solar properties (i.e., occult
influences) by being formed into a disk and carved with a solar image? Thomas agrees that it is possible for an occult influence to extend from a *naturally*
occurring substantial form (to return to our example, the form that made

matter gold, no matter what its shape or other accidents might be), and insofar as the heavens participated in the creation of the conditions for the reception of that substantial form, the occult influence would extend from or be
related to the stars.[50] He also allows that various individuals of a given species
might have greater or lesser powers, depending upon the disposition of the
heavens at the time they came into being.[51] However, he categorically rejects
the position taken by al-Kindī, and implicitly accepted by the Magister Speculi, that characters or signs, which are only accidental qualities or artificial
forms, could be efficacious in this way. Any such effect, he argues, would have
to arise from some external power.[52] Possibly referring to al-Kindī, Aquinas
also denies that human words can have any transitive efficacy derived from
a natural cause (i.e., the stars) and insists that such an effect would have to
derive from some separated substance (i.e., a demon). Analogous to something made by an artisan, words are merely a thing produced by human skill
for the purpose of expressing thoughts.[53] In themselves, neither words nor
images can produce magical effects.

Thomas clearly considered the problem of magical images significant
enough to produce an independent opuscule on the topic. It seems likely that
he was responding to pressure for discussion of the subject, and although in
most respects he answered with clarity, he did not do so uniformly. Eager
for some kind of foothold, subsequent readers who wanted to justify magical
images pounced on the ambiguities. In his treatments in *De occultis operibus naturae* and *Summa contra gentiles*, he used the term *figura*, by which
he meant a kind of abstract mathematical form, distinct from the illicit *lit-
terae* and *charactares*, which cannot have a natural occult effect. While close
analysis reveals that he regarded *figurae* as part of the process through which
things are created by nature and in the natural course of things, the meaning of the term was ambiguous enough that Aquinas's readers, particularly in
the fifteenth century, most notably Marsilio Ficino, employed this passage to
suggest that he believed that certain magical images could have a natural efficacy, one not associated with demons.[54] Although many readers may not have
understood precisely what Aquinas meant, these readings depended upon a
dubious distinction between different kinds of inscribed symbols (i.e., *figurae*
and *imagines*) and a wishful interpretation of Aquinas's works. Most readers
would justifiably have assumed that his position was unequivocally negative.

Vincent of Beauvais also includes magical images in his discussion of the
natural world, although without any of the associated theoretical apparatus.
His presentation is not a systematic or calculated one, since, as Thorndike
has noted, Vincent regarded himself not as an interpreter of the material he
reported but only as a compiler.[55] In this sense, his description is particularly

interesting as it gives a strong impression of the ambient ideas in the thirteenth century, presented without the rhetorical requirements of the moral writers or the systematic restrictions of the philosophical ones. As we have seen, Vincent maintained a relatively typical antimagic perspective by repeating the positions of Augustine and other church authorities, in which magic was by definition bad because, among other sins, it implicitly involved cooperating with demons. Although one section in the *Speculum doctrinale* includes a passage from Jerome suggesting that some stones and herbs may be used to ward off demons, that is as close to an approval of image magic as Vincent comes. Otherwise the cumulative position seems quite unambiguous. Any conceivable form of magic or divination was to be considered demonic or otherwise illicit.[56] Most of the proscriptions were drawn from legal sources, largely from Gratian, and focus upon various forms of divination. Chapter 121 rejects some written charms or characters, but chapter 122 contains one of Augustine's sweeping condemnations of magic, including magical images (*pictaciola*).[57] So there would appear to be no room for legitimate magic of any kind, much less image magic conceived as a natural and nondemonic operation. Yet this is precisely what we find in another volume of the *Speculum maius,* the *Speculum naturale,* Vincent's discussion of the physical world. Two sections discuss the powers of stones and include descriptions of a number of images carved on stones and their powers. The first includes astrological images engraved on gems. The second includes images drawn from a relatively common work of image magic ascribed to Thetel. The images are claimed to have been used by the "Sons of Israel" while they were in the desert.[58] Apparently, despite the unambiguous condemnation of any form of image magic in the *Speculum doctrinale,* this text was considered legitimate enough for inclusion in the encyclopedia. The seeming contradiction may be explained by the fact that this encyclopedia was not solely the work of Vincent but rather of a group of scholars working under his direction. Yet even if this situation were the result of the different interests or beliefs of two or more scholars, it can still be said that the work embodies the ambivalence with which magical images were approached in the later Middle Ages. Here, a single work presents magical images as potentially legitimate (and, if so, as nondemonic and part of natural philosophy), while elsewhere roundly and unambiguously condemning their use as sinful and their operations as demonic.

The discussions by Petrus Alfonsi, Gundissalinus, William of Auvergne, Roger Bacon, the Magister Speculi, and Thomas Aquinas demonstrate that the idea of natural magic was intellectually seductive enough to be convincing for many scholars. Of course, they did not uniformly affirm the possibility. Yet the idea was obviously widespread enough that Aquinas felt it necessary to address it several times. The final effect of all this discussion was less a uniform agreement that astrological images were a legitimate portion of natural philosophy than a consensus that the topic was a legitimate concern within natural philosophy and deserved independent philosophical treatment. It was not as simple an issue as Augustine suggested, and the compelling new philosophical arguments required fresh analysis. Bacon's arguments and the tacit position suggested by Vincent of Beauvais's presentation demonstrate that it was possible (if not philosophically consistent) to maintain a hard-line position on magic not unlike that of Augustine, while at the same time acknowledging that certain kinds of operations could be accomplished with words of power and astrological images. One way or another, twelfth- and thirteenth-century writers acknowledged that good magic, if there were such a thing, depended solely upon power derived from the natural world, in particular the stars. Bad magic, which probably meant all magic, derived its power from demons. While it is not always clear how the writers would distinguish good from bad images, many assumed that it was possible to do so, given sufficient skill in astrology and other occult sciences.

Valerie Flint has described the process by which astrology became an acceptable part of a Christian worldview in the Latin West as a spectacular and somewhat unlikely rescue.[59] While this evaluation may or may not be true of astrology as a whole, it is certainly true in the case of astrological images. To be sure, the philosophical reasoning that distinguished a legitimate astrological image from an image used for illicit worship or to enlist the aid of demons was relatively convincing, if not sound by Scholastic standards. But it must be regarded as significant that anyone would make such efforts to rescue this science in the face of the frequent and explicit condemnation of images and ligatures by the Bible, church fathers, and subsequent authorities. The condemnatory voices were matched by an equally powerful attraction to magic. A desire to rescue ancient learning, a curiosity about the unusual, a yearning for wealth, power, or control, or a fascination with the idea that these could easily be gained must all have motivated this rescue. It must also have been profoundly seductive for a learned elite, relatively powerless outside their studies or classrooms, to believe that these sorts of powers were available to them alone. Even those who roundly condemned learned magic gained something. By admitting that such magic, which was the preserve of the learned alone, was possible and potentially very powerful (even if it did involve demons), they granted a great deal of significance to their own learning, which could make such power available. They were also the greater for having chosen not to use it. The ambivalence of Bonatti's apothecary represents a complex and widely prevalent attitude in late medieval thought, and we must keep this in mind as we turn to those who collected texts of image magic.

2

SCHOLASTIC IMAGE MAGIC
BEFORE 1500

The idea of magic is inextricably bound up with the issue of representation in spoken words, visual signs, or physical gestures. In the sense that magical practices employ representations or apparent representations—and even divination may be said to enact the process of fate to predict a future event—all magic is image magic. Although pictorial representations ranging from written charms to necromantic circles appear in almost all late medieval magical practices, our discussion will be limited to a relatively specific library of magic texts that developed in the twelfth and thirteenth centuries. Their coherence as a group derives in part from their shared intellectual and cultural roots and their claim to operate within an astrological framework. Yet what unites this set of texts is not so much the precise details of the magical operations they contain, which can vary a great deal, but rather something that may be detected in how they were copied and transmitted: the way their scribes and collectors framed, understood, and analyzed them. These texts were regarded as potentially legitimate forms of magic according to philosophical and astrological standards; they were treated as texts in the genre of *naturalia;* and they were understood to belong to a certain kind of Scholastic debate or discussion. In this way they form a coherent library quite distinct from the collections of ritual magic discussed in the second part of this study, despite the fact that these collections also contained astrological images.

The Manuscripts

A typical example of image magic from the *Liber lune,* a text of Arabic origin, runs as follows. It is preceded by chapters outlining the nature of the twenty-eight mansions of the moon, suffumigations, and the names of planetary spirits:

> Said Belenus: Let an image be made in the first hour of the day to bind men so that, once it has been made, they may not say anything else concerning him, not even one bad word, ever. Accordingly, let an image be cast, of which half is of silver and the other half tin, to the measure of four palms, and in the likeness of him for whom you make it, and in the first hour of the day. Let the name of the lord of the image be carved on its head and on the chest the name of the lady of the first hour of the one for whose days it is made. Let there be written on the belly the name of the lord of the image; and those are the names of suffumigation with aloe and sandalwood. And wrap [it] in white and clean cloth. Afterwards, bury it in his doorway. And it is a binding prepared to bind all tongues.[1]

The reasons for referring to this genre as astrological image magic will be immediately apparent. The *Liber lune* concerns images that relate to the twenty-eight mansions of the moon; the images must be made in a particular hour of the day; and the names employed relate to astrological spirits or times. It should also be noted that specific metals are to be employed. Al-Kindī could certainly have regarded this as entirely natural. For a Latin interpreter, although the use of suffumigations might be deemed dubious, the rest might be acceptable. And, as we have seen, the idea that particular metals had powers that somehow derived from the heavens enjoyed a very wide level of acceptance.

The next example is drawn from a work attributed to Thetel concerning images to be carved on stones. Here is the first sentence of the two-sentence prologue and the first image:

> This is the most precious book of sigils, great and secret, of Cethel which the sons of Israel made in the desert after [their] departure from Egypt, according to the movements and courses of the stars. . . . If you should find sculpted in a stone a man seated above a plough, long bearded and with a curved neck, having four men lying in/on [his?] neck, and holding in [his] hands a fox and turtle-dove, this sigil, hung about the neck, has power for all plantings and for the discoveries of treasures. This is the artifice of it. Let him take pure undyed black wool, just as nature has produced it, and make from it a pillow which should be filled with wheat chaff, and a cushion similarly, which may be placed on top of the pillow. Let him sleep on [it] and he will dream of the treasures of the entire region where he is and how he is able to have them.[2]

Despite the complete absence of any astrological elements in the actual instructions, the introduction makes clear that the rings are to be understood as deriving their power from astrological conditions. The text then lists a variety of carved stones in precisely the same manner. The rings were also to be used in conjunction with certain things, like black wool. Although not explicit here, these also could have been understood by medieval readers as having astrologically derived (i.e., naturally occurring) occult properties.

The most commonly recurring texts of image magic in the Middle Ages are Thābit ibn Qurra's *De imaginibus;* Thetel's *De imaginibus*; a work on images ascribed to Ptolemy; another to Toz Graecus; a work on sculpted gems attributed to Marbodius; the *Liber lune;* and the two versions of the *De quindecim stellis, quindecim lapidibus, quindecim herbis, et quindecim imaginibus* (hereafter *De quindecim stellis*).[3] In these texts, the images were either small statues or representations engraved on disks, rings, or stones. To be effective, they had to be made under certain astrological conditions. Most of these texts are of Arabic origin, although some appear to be of late antique or even more ancient lineage.[4] Like most magic works, these texts do not make for exciting reading. They are systematic and lack long, fanciful, or theoretical introductions. They generally occupy only a few folios and typically describe a set of images corresponding to an astrological grouping or circuit (e.g., the seven planets or the twenty-eight lunar mansions). A short paragraph devoted to each image describes the material from which the image is to be made (precious stones, rings, or talismans), the necessary astrological conditions or times under which to carve the image (usually), and the effects of the image. Sometimes the instructions include angel names to be recited or inscribed on the ring, sometimes substances with which the image is to be suffumigated, and sometimes prayers that must be recited. Occasionally, they will take a slightly different organizational approach, giving a chapter each to astrological conditions, materials, suffumigations, images, and angel names. The effects of the images are often quite restricted—for example, the elimination of scorpions from a place. They also may be somewhat more general or abstract, such as images of "separation" or "destruction."

A superficial examination of the number of manuscripts and when they were copied demonstrates that image magic was well represented in medieval libraries. There are almost three hundred manuscript witnesses to this tradition dating between the thirteenth and the sixteenth centuries. These numbers indicate the considerable popularity of this literature, and some texts stand out as particularly well represented. For example, there are at least fifty-three surviving copies of the two translations of one of the more popular texts, the *De imaginibus* of Thābit. The peak of manuscript production appears to have occurred in the fifteenth century, as the vast majority of the surviving manuscripts of image magic date from before the end of the fifteenth century, and a very substantial number date from the fourteenth century or earlier.[5] The patterns in Britain are roughly the same as those found on the continent, with the exception that the peak in production appears to have come earlier. Two manuscripts date from before 1200, nineteen from the fourteenth century (including several imported around that time from the continent), sixteen from the fifteenth century, and nine from the sixteenth. This presents an interesting problem. Despite the popularity of Ficino's *De vita coelitus comparanda* and what is assumed to have been a renewed interest in image magic in the Renaissance, the tradition appears to have declined in the sixteenth century, at least if the copying of manuscripts is any indication. While this decline in copying raises some interesting questions about image magic in the Renaissance (a topic to which we will return in chapter 7), the matter is of direct significance to our current discussion, since sixteenth-century interests directly affected the transmission of earlier manuscripts.

The texts and manuscripts of image magic traveled along several routes.[6] A few translations were made in Italy in the eleventh century along with some lapidaries deriving from antiquity, but most texts of image magic derive from Arabic sources through Spain. The first wave of material was translated in the twelfth century, reaching England before the middle of the thirteenth. Among the important early translators was Adelard of Bath. A second wave of translations derived from the court of Alfonso and moved through the south of France around the beginning of the fourteenth century, particularly in Jewish and Christian medical circles in Montpellier. This material found its way into northern Italy and Brabant during the course of the fourteenth century. Works accompanying image magic texts suggest Montpellier as the major source for materials found in the library at the Abbey of St. Augustine's, Canterbury, during the fourteenth century. Paris was probably also an important conduit of transmission of this material as it passed northward. Manuscripts may have moved with scholars seeking a more liberal environment than was to be found in Paris after the condemnations of 1277. Although the literature of image magic flourished in France during the thirteenth century, as it did in England in the fourteenth, it spread through central and eastern Europe largely after the beginning of the fifteenth century. Monastic houses with large libraries, such as St. Augustine's Abbey in Canterbury and the Austin Friars' library at York, held significant numbers of image magic works as well as other works of occult interest, both theoretical and practical.

The relatively large number of manuscripts that survive provides a reasonably transparent window into the intellectual world of the collectors and scribes of image magic. It does not appear, for example, that they passed through a process of selection in which the surviving manuscripts were rendered unrepresentative of the original medieval library. Medieval manuscripts of image magic were, in large measure, preserved by sixteenth- and seventeenth-century collectors of medical, alchemical, and astrological works who had no particular interest in image magic per se. Very few surviving codices dedicate more than a fraction of their contents to image magic. Among the great seventeenth- and eighteenth-century collectors, such as Sir Hans Sloane, there is little evidence of any particular interest in texts of image magic. Although Sloane does appear to have been interested in magic, the codices dedicated entirely to magic that he collected are largely ritual magic texts, most of them copied in the sixteenth and seventeenth centuries. It is even possible that these magic texts were preserved only because they were copied or owned by medical and astrological practitioners such as Simon Forman. Only Elias Ashmole appears to have had a particular interest in talismans, but it is not clear that this in any way exceeded his interest in other forms of occult knowledge, such as ritual magic or alchemy. Thus these later collectors were probably relatively indifferent to the presence of a few short texts of image magic.

While there are a number of known sixteenth-century collectors, the most important for the preservation of image magic texts in Britain was Thomas Allen (1532–1594), from whose collection were drawn the 256 codices that Kenelm Digby (1603–1665) donated to the Bodleian in 1632. In Allen's massive collection may be found six codices containing works on image magic. There are also two copies of al-Kindī's *De radiis stellarum* not traveling with works of image magic, several collections of magic-oriented experiments, and a small part of an *Ars notoria* (a work of ritual magic).[7] Allen's strong interest in astrology can account for the presence of almost all of these codices. His associate John Dee also had a hand in the preservation of texts of magic, including three codices containing works of image magic.[8] Dee is particularly interesting because of his high level of engagement with various occult topics. Yet even in the case of Dee, whose marginal notes attest to his interest in magical images, there is no reason to believe that this interest was the dominant one, certainly not one that would have eclipsed his more general occult and scientific interests in the other texts in these volumes, which he also annotated. Thus, even in this rather unusual case, the image magic texts appear to have been preserved as much for the sake of the other texts that accompanied them as for their own sake. In comparison to other forms of magic, medieval image magic was not particularly popular among the dedicated collectors of magic texts in the sixteenth through eighteenth centuries, when increasing interest appears to have been paid to works of ritual magic. This is, in fact, fortunate. An independent interest in medieval image magic could well have driven a large number of copies into the hands of specialized collectors whose books ran a higher risk of not being preserved.

But if the selection process appears to be indifferent to the texts that *did* survive, can we make a case for a different kind of codex that might not have survived, one that either held no interest for collectors or was very interesting to specialists but was lost in the destruction of private collections? While this possibility cannot be entirely discounted, it does seem unlikely. We have numerous detailed records of the codices contained in medieval libraries, and there is no configuration of texts in the catalogues (e.g., no image magic bound with astrological works) that is not also represented in surviving manuscripts. There may, however, have been certain configurations that were *less likely* to survive. Codices containing the standard texts of astrological image magic and also works of explicitly demonic magic are relatively rare and usually contain only magic works.[9] It is possible that such volumes would have been destroyed at a higher rate owing to the absence of any redeeming works. But volumes of this kind appear very rarely in medieval catalogue descriptions, which suggests that if they once represented a larger portion of the library of magic works, it was not substantially greater than is represented in surviving witnesses. More than 90 percent of works known through catalogues or as surviving manuscripts do not follow this pattern. So there is little evidence that such volumes were numerous enough to seriously undermine the representativeness of the surviving manuscripts.

The only remaining factor that might have rendered the surviving manuscripts unrepresentative is the remote possibility that some may be forgeries. But the relatively lower level of interest in image magic texts after 1500 would have made them an unlikely target for forgery. In addition, most of these texts are quite short, often running to only a few folios, which means that they were generally transmitted with other material of less dramatic content. A forged codex of the usual accompanying literature, such as medicine, alchemy, or astrology, would be unlikely to waste precious vellum on extraneous material. In addition, unlike extended works of ritual magic, these treatises do not attribute magical qualities to the book itself. So there would have been no motivation to produce an old-looking manuscript in order to give it numinous qualities or make it appear more efficacious. As will become clear, most of the medieval collectors of this material would probably have ascribed a greater value to the accuracy of the transcription or translation, or to the authority of its author, than to the age of the manuscript. Finally, collectors from the sixteenth and seventeenth centuries tended to collect standard image magic texts with texts of ritual magic in their own notebooks. Collectors prior to 1500 very rarely did this. To produce a convincing forgery of a text of medieval image magic, it would be necessary to devote most of the codex to other topics, something that would make the forger's art quite uneconomical.

Scribes, Collectors, and Their Interests

The existence of a particular manuscript version of a work of astrological image magic tells us only that someone wanted a copy of it and that many others saw fit to preserve it. In itself this fact reveals nothing about why or by whom it was copied, what interests may have motivated preservation, or how any of those involved may have interpreted, categorized, or employed the treatise. The answers to these questions lie in a host of circumstantial evidence in the medieval books that contained them. The numerous works that make up most medieval volumes were seldom entirely random; most volumes represent many conscious decisions, often by several compilers, that sought to draw different texts together for some practical reason. As a result, a great deal can be learned about image magic by examining the works with which it was commonly collected and the interests these represent. Other internal evidence of scribal attitudes may also be found in the ways scribes organized and presented the texts on the page (including marginalia) and, more crucially, in the texts they chose and how they transmitted them. While single examples provide only fragmentary evidence, a coherent pattern of treatment does emerge through an examination of a large number of examples.

Nicolas Weill-Parot has argued rightly that, in philosophical terms, image magic could not be accommodated to Christian orthodoxy, particularly as articulated by authoritative Scholastic writers. In addition, he has shown that very few medical or astrological writers felt comfortable with the idea of promoting astrological image magic. Yet, as we shall see, this did not result in the ejection of this literature from the library of Scholastic *naturalia*. On the contrary, the most obvious general feature of the collections that include works on images is that, almost without exception, they also contain texts dealing with the natural world—that is, varying combinations of natural philosophy, astrology, astronomy, alchemy, medicine, secrets, recipes, and natural wonders. To be sure, there are a small number of exceptions to this rule before 1500,[10] yet the near ubiquity of this pattern of collection suggests two features of scribal attitudes. First, the scribes' or collectors' general interests lay in the direction of various aspects of the natural world and its processes. Second, whether they chose to ignore the philosophical problems and the relative rarity of authoritative sanction, to persist in believing that their text of image magic was legitimately nondemonic, or simply to regard astrological image magic as a subject that ought to be dealt with under the rubric of natural philosophy, most scribes and collectors still regarded image magic as a part of the broad subject matter of *naturalia*.

Three-quarters of the codices or parts thereof assembled before 1500 that include works on astrological image magic contain texts dealing with issues in astrology and astronomy.[11] Of these, all but one include works on the more "active" features of astrology of a nonmagic kind, such as discussions of judicial astrology, the casting of horoscopes, prognostication of one form or another, the use of astrological influences in medical treatment, or the detection of thieves. Digby 193 is a codex devoted largely to issues in astrology and astronomy and supplemented by works on mathematics. It contains two works on sculpted stones, one attributed to Marbodius, the other to Thetel, but is unique among the astrologically oriented codices in containing no other work with explicitly practical, physical applications. Texts like the *Theorica planetarum* (fols. 1–9) and Sacrobosco's *Tractatus de sphera* (fols. 17–22) make up the largest portion of the text. Yet even here, short discussions of good and bad hours (fol. 15) and the relation of celestial influence to the practice of medicine (fol. 36r) suggest the practical applications typical of all of the other codices. While the practicality of their companion texts need not denote the practical use of image magic, they do indicate that the scribes were generally interested in a literature with practical applications.[12] The same is suggested by a thirteenth-century continental example of a manuscript containing image magic in which the sections on judicial astrology are heavily annotated.[13] Works of image magic appear to have been widely considered one of a number of practical applications of astrological principles.

One group historically associated with the practical use of astrology and images, or at least suspensions, ligatures, and rings, is medical doctors. Medieval medical practice was inseparable from astrology, and ligatures, suspensions, and images appear frequently in medical literature. This historical association is also strongly reflected in British manuscripts. Seven codices betray an explicit interest in medical issues,[14] and an identifiable medical practitioner owned two additional codices.[15] Some might be as limited as a text in Digby 57, fol. 137v, which associates parts of the body with the signs of the zodiac. Some, like Ashmole 1471, contain a variety of medical texts attributed to Galen, Hippocrates, and Constantinus Africanus.[16] There are numerous similar continental examples.[17] John of London, one of the monks at St. Augustine's whom David Pingree has identified as having an interest in magical images and who also collected other works on magic, owned one codex containing the work on images attributed to Ptolemy and also a work on urine.[18] Medical texts fill twenty-three of his eighty codices catalogued at St. Augustine's.[19]

In addition to the circumstantial evidence provided by the occurrence of these medical texts, two collectors of image magic are identifiable as medical practitioners. London, Society of Antiquaries, 39 contains part of a collection by John Argentine, who was provost of King's College, Cambridge, in the late fifteenth and early sixteenth centuries. The magic texts in Argentine's collection appear in the same order, and supplemented with additional magic texts, in Ashmole 346, the early sixteenth-century collection of another physician, Thomas Scalon, a junior fellow at King's during Argentine's tenure as provost.[20] Both of these collectors are discussed in more detail below. For the time being, it need only be observed that both cases attest to an interest in magical images and that, in the case of the Society of Antiquaries manuscript, but for the concluding *quod Argentyn* we would have no idea that it was written by a doctor at all, since no medical texts appear in this collection. We thus have reason to suspect that medical doctors might have owned more of the codices. Even if we do not assume this, next to monks, medical practitioners remain the most commonly identifiable collectors of magic texts.

In alchemical collections, works of image magic blend in well with a host of similarly short alchemical works. Michael Northgate had a substantial amount of alchemical literature in his books, and two similar collections from Britain (Selden Supra 76 and Corpus Christi 125) include image magic. In all of these, at least some of the texts of image magic involve the use of engraved stones. Selden Supra 76 and Ashmole 1416 contain magic texts concerned with images engraved on gems. Corpus Christi 125 includes two works on images in addition to the tract on fifteen stars, fifteen herbs, fifteen stones, and fifteen images frequently associated with alchemical texts.[21] So, while interests in magic and alchemy do cross over, the attraction might also have something to do with a more diffuse interest in literature about stones. The alchemists' interest in symbols and symbolic language might also have attracted them to engraved images. Continental manuscripts combining alchemy and astrological image magic also exist.[22]

While most of the codices can be classified under the major categories of astrology, medicine, and alchemy, these interests flow together in most of the collections. It is rare that a single codex will not include texts from at least two of these categories, and a number of other identifiable interests also occur frequently. An interest in stones is found independent of alchemy; nonmagical lapidaries appear in four of the codices.[23] In Wellcome 116 the principal interest appears to be stones. In Cambridge, University Library, Ff. vi. 53, fols. 189–207v, two works on stones appear, one of them Thetel's text on engraved gems. Books of secrets, experiments, and recipes of various kinds appear frequently. The *Secretum philosophorum,* a book of experiments and tricks classed under the headings of the liberal arts, occurs three times.[24] The *Book of Secrets* attributed to Albertus Magnus occurs twice and the *Secretum secretorum* three times.[25] Corpus Christi 125 contains alchemical and astrological material but also other diverse material: texts on the properties of animals, recipes, various forms of divination, chemical experiments, secrets, and even a book on planting trees. At the same time, no single kind of text appears in every codex containing image magic texts. Astrological texts accompany them most frequently, but this rule is not without significant exceptions. In other words, while they were collected in the presence of a common interest in *naturalia,* texts of image magic should be considered a discrete interest. They were usually acquired independently, and their transmission did not depend upon another set of texts or an interest in any other specialized topic.

Because works on images often occupy a very small portion of the text—not least because many of these texts run to only a few folios—it is prudent to ask whether the works on images found their way into the collection purely by chance, by an association not of the scribe's conception, or by "piggybacking" onto another, nonmagic text.[26] In the case of Selden Supra 76, discussed above, a short text could easily be tagged on at the end of one of the irregularly sized booklets/quires to provide the right amount of text for a gathering that would otherwise end in one and a half folios of unused parchment—a kind of added bonus text. But this is not the case with Selden Supra 76, and I know of no instance where this could have happened. It is also conceivable that a magic text like Thābit's *De imaginibus* could have been included in a larger number of the same author's nonmagic works simply by virtue of having been written by the same author. Once again, this does not appear to be the case. Although Thābit's purely astrological works frequently travel three or four abreast, the *De imaginibus* generally does not travel in that company. As a rule, these magic texts are transmitted with other magic texts rather than with other works written by the same author, astrological or otherwise.[27]

It would be unwarranted to assume that any codex containing a single magic work represents a compiler or scribe with active and practical interests in magic. The text could simply have been copied as a curiosity or on a whim. However, the evidence suggests that the number of people for whom this was more than a passing fancy might have been relatively high. Of the twenty-six British codices containing works of image magic, all but eight have more than one work on magical images, and many have several. It appears that someone interested enough to copy or collect one work on image magic was likely to copy or collect others.

A final aspect of these texts is worth noting: their relatively high level of textual consistency. In comparison to works of ritual magic, which we will examine presently, the standard texts of image magic are far more likely to have been transmitted in a faithful way. Generally speaking, the texts are identifiable by a few standard incipits and do not vary a great deal in their contents. To be sure, some have muddy textual traditions, among them the text by Belenus, perhaps once independent, which generally travels as part of the *Liber lune.* Some have had additions made to them, such as the conse-cration formula for stones frequently found with Thetel's *Liber de lapidibus filiorum Israel.* Weill-Parot has noted an example of an image magic text that was developed from a version of Thābit's *De imaginibus.*[28] Yet it is still possible to identify the vast majority of these as belonging to a specific textual tradi-tion, whereas the transmission of ritual magic texts tends to be considerably less stable.

To summarize, works on images are not accidental parts of the collec-tions in which they are found and are generally transmitted in a more or less faithful manner. They constitute a genre that, within the broad category of *naturalia,* was not bound to a specific interest or group of texts. Everything about the codices examined so far suggests that the individual scribes did not stray far from the standard interpretations of astrological images discussed in chapter 1. They regarded magical images as a potentially legitimate part of natural philosophy, a practical extension of astrology, an adjunct to lapi-daries or alchemical works, or a feature of the natural world. The weight of circumstantial evidence in this regard is certainly considerable. Yet even more evidence that astrological images were regarded in this way may be deduced from the relation of this tradition of texts to those theoretical works tolerant of magical images, a subject to which we now turn.

Natural Philosophy and the Transmission of Image Magic

The *De radiis stellarum* appears eight times in the codices containing works of image magic or the collections of those who owned them, and several times in continental examples.[29] The *Speculum astronomiae* appears together with image magic only once in a British manuscript but frequently in continental ones.[30] Although it principally concerns the psychosomatic effects of images, the *De physicis ligaturis* of Qusta ibn Luca also appears twice in these collec-tions as well as in continental examples.[31] That such a large number of these theoretical works appear in these volumes indicates that they were considered important and that they formed a significant part of the interpretation of the magic material that they accompany. One can also reasonably assume that many other scribes of magic texts also made the connection, but either had access to one of these theoretical texts elsewhere (and so did not need to make a new copy) or would have copied one given the opportunity. This less visible influence of theoretical works may also be detected in other ways. In particular, the *Speculum astronomiae* can be demonstrated to have had a significant impact upon not only the interpretation but also the transmission of works of image magic.

That the *Speculum* appears so infrequently in British collections of image magic might be attributed to the work's relatively low degree of tolerance for the genre. The great number of continental examples, in contrast, suggests that the numbers from Britain are anomalous or due to chance destruction of key manuscripts. Yet the text's ubiquitous influence on the medieval magic library may be detected in other ways. Although the author considered it possible to have magical images that operated entirely by astrological mechanisms, he offered only two potentially legitimate texts, the work on images attributed to Ptolemy and the translation of Thābit's *De imaginibus* by John of Seville. Of the *Liber prestigiorum,* the bad or "necromantic" translation of the latter work by Adelard of Bath, only five copies have been identified as existing or once existing, none of them in British libraries or manuscripts. This stands in stark contrast to the fifty-three versions (forty-five written before 1500) of the "good" translation that can be identified, nine of them British. The other legitimate work, according to Albertus, the book of images attributed to Ptolemy, appears twenty-six times, ten times in British manuscripts. Of all the works of astrological image magic, the Thābit text is the most frequently copied and the Ptolemy text ranks second (though it is the most commonly copied text in Britain). The *De quindecim stellis* (both versions) and Thetel's *De imaginibus* were not mentioned in the *Speculum* and thus were not condemned. They appear twenty-seven times (seven in Britain) and twenty-three times (eight in Britain), respectively.

The works that the Magister Speculi condemned, on the other hand, were copied much less frequently, if they survive at all. As mentioned, the bad version of Thābit's work on images survives in only five versions. The *Liber lune* appears in four British and seven continental volumes. The *De imaginibus* of Belenus, whom Thorndike identifies with Jigris ibn al-'Amid, appears in two British volumes and two more continental ones.[32] A number of other manuscripts attributed to Belenus also exist that do not correspond to the incipit in the *Speculum,* but the total is less than twenty altogether. The *Liber imaginum Veneris* of Toz Graecus appears only three times.[33] The Hermetic *De imaginibus septem planetarum* appears twice. This may be the *De septem annulis de septem planetarum* condemned by the Magister Speculi, under which title one text appears in London, Society of Antiquaries, 39.[34] The *De quatuor annulis* attributed to Solomon appears twice.[35] These texts are all unified by their use of techniques that the Magister Speculi suspected involved demons. For example, the *Liber lune* involves suffumigations and incantations, and the *De imaginibus* of Belenus involves the use of angel names. The version of the *De septem annulis* that appears in Society of Antiquaries 39 is in essence astrological, although it also employs ritual features. The patterns of copying, which cannot be random, thus suggest two possibilities. First, the scribes may have employed the *Speculum* to assess the legitimacy of a text they were about to copy. Second, scribes may have applied the same kinds of standards that the Magister Speculi used when they evaluated and copied the texts. An examination of treatises that the Magister did not discuss can provide some insight into this issue.

Two tracts enjoyed relatively wide circulation and were not condemned or evaluated at all by Magister Speculi: the *De quindecim stellis* and the work on images by Thetel. The *De quindecim stellis* makes connections between astrological influences, particularly those of fifteen fixed stars, and related herbs, stones, and images. The work by Thetel makes similar claims. It begins, "In the name of the Lord, this is the precious book of the signs of Thetel, great and secret, which the sons of Israel made in the desert after leaving Egypt according to the motion and courses of the heavens."[36] The text more or less reflects the principle suggested by the title that the images derived their power from the heavens. It goes on to describe the talismans and their use, requiring no suffumigations, incantations, or other untoward ritual practices. The text even uses indirect language where the making of the image is concerned. Rather than counsel the reader to sculpt a particular image, the phrasing is "should you find" (*si inveniret*) such and such an image carved in a jasper. While the Magister Speculi might have objected to these texts on the grounds that the names of the fixed stars might refer to demons (as he had rejected the use of lunar mansions), the fact that only a simple symbol is used would tend to free the talismans from some suspicion. In addition, the texts do not include incantations, suffumigations, or other ritual procedures, a fact that would have made them even more acceptable. Finally, the structure clearly emphasizes the interconnectedness of the natural world and occult properties, something that would naturally suggest the theories of al-Kindī and the theoretical assumptions that underlie the *Speculum*. Their popularity may thus be accounted for both by the fact that they were not condemned and also by the fact that they loosely corresponded to the features of the legitimate texts.

There is also clear textual evidence for the influence of the *Speculum* on the transmission and understanding of image magic. One example, discussed in detail in chapter 3, is Digby 228. In this manuscript the marginal notes of a scribe of image magic make clear that he knew that the work of image magic he had copied was condemned in the *Speculum*. In another, much more explicit example, the scribe of a fifteenth-century manuscript introduces Thābit's *De imaginibus* as follows: "This book is listed among the natural, nonmagical and nonprohibited books" (*Iste liber est registratus in libris naturalibus et non mag-icalibus et pro[hi]bitis*). If this were not indication enough that the scribe was aware of the texts, the portion of the *Speculum* concerning magical images occurs in the same codex, copied by a contemporary hand.[37] Interestingly, this version of the chapter reverses the standard order of the three categories of images, placing the "legitimate" ones first.

Thus it is clear that the *Speculum astronomiae* had a significant and lasting impact on the transmission of image magic texts. The *Speculum* survives in almost fifty manuscripts dating from before 1500, so the chances are high that many of the scribes had access to a version, and, as we have seen, numerous versions were copied in conjunction with a work on image magic. It is also possible that scribes applied similar kinds of criteria without reference to the *Speculum* at all, but the patterns of copying of image magic texts make this unlikely. That the two works specifically deemed legitimate by the Magister Speculi should appear in such overwhelmingly greater numbers than those he condemned is powerful evidence of the lasting significance of this text. The great numbers of Thetel's *De imaginibus* and the *De quindecim stellis* appear to be due to their superficial similarity to those approved in the *Speculum* and to the tacit support of other authors. Finally, the fact that the *Liber lune* and the associated text by Belenus, which the Magister Speculi condemned both for methodology and for title and incipit as among the worst of magic treatises, survive in relatively higher numbers than others he condemned less forcefully suggests that his strong words may in fact have increased interest in them.

Even if the *Speculum* was not always used in the way I suggest, evaluations were still being made more or less in the same way that the Magister Speculi would have made them: by relying on the common assumption that certain forms of image magic could have natural effects and that those with demonic connections could be identified by their use of ritual, certain astrological deceits, or strange names. The translation of Thābit's *De imaginibus* made by John of Seville (prior to the *Speculum astronomiae*) lacked the dubious elements of the original, in particular the incantations. This text was approved by the Magister Speculi and was copied far more often than any other text of image magic. The translation by Adelard of Bath, on the other hand, which retained the incantations, was condemned by the Magister Speculi and survives in substantially fewer copies, by a factor of ten to one.[38] Scribes thus copied the texts of image magic most adaptable to Scholastic natural philosophy more often than any others and thereby transformed the library of magic texts.

Scholastic speculation clearly shaped the library of image magic in the later Middle Ages. Scribes and collectors clearly associated these texts with the natural world and with speculations about its occult processes. These collectors also betrayed almost no interest in the more dubious forms of ritual magic considered in the second part of this study. Instead, the collections in which these texts appear are almost uniformly composed of scholarly treatments of the natural world, which suggests that scribes understood them either as potentially legitimate or, at the very least, as an appropriate part of the library of *naturalia*. For these reasons I believe that we may justifiably describe these texts as "Scholastic image magic," despite the fact that most Scholastic authorities would have condemned them.

Doctors and Monks: Three Known Collectors

A considerable number of the scribes of Scholastic image magic can be identified and their collections analyzed. The most commonly identifiable professional groups are medical doctors and monks, and their interests generally follow the pattern I have already identified. But the peculiarities of their professional positions and the interests most often associated with these groups provide a more detailed picture of the variety of motivations and contexts surrounding the transmission of image magic.

Medical Practitioners: John Argentine and Thomas Scalon

John Argentine was probably born in 1442, entered Eton around 1454, and took the statutory oath at age fifteen, in 1458.[39] In 1461 he became a fellow of a college at Cambridge, where he earned a bachelor of arts degree by 1461–62 and a master of arts by 1465–66. At some point he appears to have become a doctor of medicine, and he was senior proctor of the university sometime in 1472 or 1473. By 1473 he was bachelor of divinity, although he was not a doctor of divinity until 1504. In 1470 he wrote a poem perhaps suggesting some disillusionment with the academic world,[40] and sometime between 1471 and 1476 a work on diseases that was never published, suggesting a return to medical practice.[41] He was ordained an acolyte in September 1473 at Lincoln and subsequently held several benefices, probably beginning in 1478, although he accepted his first recorded benefice in 1488.[42] While not in residence, he appears to have maintained a presence at King's College, remaining a fellow until 1478. He was physician to Edward V and his brother, Richard, Duke of York, until they were murdered in 1483, and he maintained his association with the court through the reign of Richard III.[43] In 1486 he was appointed physician to Henry VII's son, Prince Arthur, and dean of his chapel, which would have brought him frequently to Windsor until the prince's death in 1502. Argentine's distinguished career concluded with the post of provost of King's College, Cambridge, which he held from 1501 until his death in 1508.

London, Society of Antiquaries, 39 contains part of a collection by John Argentine.[44] The scribal identification "Quod Argentyn" provides the key piece of evidence for assigning ownership of this manuscript to him but is not sufficient in itself. The late fifteenth-century hand in which it is written makes it highly unlikely that the owner was Richard Argentine, writing in the mid-sixteenth century. But in itself the manuscript can tell us no more. Strong circumstantial evidence linking the text with John Argentine can be found in another manuscript. The same texts appear in the same order in the collection of another doctor, Thomas Scalon, master of arts in 1503 from King's.[45] Written slightly later, Scalon's manuscript is clearly copied from the Society of Antiquaries manuscript. Naturally, it is possible that at the time of copying the fragment was no longer a part of John Argentine's collection. Yet the common membership of these two men in the relatively small community of King's College makes contact probable. At a minimum, their contemporary residency at Cambridge suggests that the copying took place in that location and provides compelling evidence that the scribe of the original was in fact John Argentine.

Argentine's collection includes Thābit's book of images, images extracted from the *Secretum secretorum,* and the *De imaginibus* attributed to Ptolemy. The selection is intellectually conservative and certainly in keeping with the care that would have been required for Argentine's stellar political career. Two of the three texts in his collection were identified by the Magister Speculi as apparently legitimate. The third section on images (from the *Secretum secretorum*) contains little ritual material and so may also be counted among the most innocent of image magic texts. Interestingly, the manuscript contains no medical material; in the absence of the concluding "Quod Argentyn," there would be no evidence whatsoever that it was written by a physician. The other texts are perhaps indicative of a doctor's interest in astrology, including an astrological table and a work by al-Kindī on astrology and the weather. Although it is currently bound with a small fifteenth-century collection of ritual magic texts, there is no evidence of any early connection between these two parts of the codex.[46] Argentine's portion is written in a tight, controlled secretary on parchment, the other in a sprawling fifteenth-century cursive on paper.

In the rest of his books, there is no sign of interest in magic, with one significant exception. Argentine makes the only fifteenth-century English reference to the *Picatrix*, the infamous work of Arabic magic, which confirms that Argentine was actively interested in magic texts.[47] He was also evidently interested in the classics, and there is strong evidence that he had traveled to Italy and probably conducted his medical education at Padua.[48] Dennis Rhodes notes that his habit of signing his books in Italian,[49] not common in England at the time, suggests an Italian connection, if only through Italian booksellers. Rhodes goes on to say that his use of "zouan" for "Giovanni" suggests Venice.[50] Renaissance thinkers' attention to magical images, epitomized by Ficino, seems an obvious source of Argentine's interest. Yet given the consistent association of works of images with medical doctors, there is no reason to assume that Argentine's Italian sojourns had any influence on his thinking on the topic, except for one issue. His knowledge of the *Picatrix* might well have been derived from a continental source. No manuscript is known to have existed in England until sometime later, and Argentine makes the only known fifteenth-century English reference to the work.[51] Whether this knowledge influenced his thinking about magic is unclear. Another collector with Italian connections, John Typtoft, was for a time in possession of a codex containing a work on image magic. The codex, Corpus Christi 125, is of English origin, deriving from the collection of Thomas Sprot and Thomas Wyvelsburghe, monks at St. Augustine's, Canterbury. Although the texts may originally have come from Italy or other continental sources, there is no reason to believe that peculiarly Renaissance interests may be connected with English interests in magic.[52]

Argentine evidently felt no concern about identifying himself as the scribe of a text of image magic, and this suggests that he did not regard such texts as illicit. His early career suggests someone with ambition. His later career, especially the fact that he managed to maintain politically sensitive positions at court during the reigns of Edward V, Richard III, and Henry VII, suggests that he was politically astute. Had the copying or ownership of a text of image magic been considered dangerous in itself, Argentine would probably not have associated himself with such a text at any stage in his career. It is certainly unlikely that he would have set his name to the manuscript. The common appearance of works of image magic in catalogues where the original owner is freely identified also indicates that these works were considered acceptable in some manner. Although they may have been seen as superstitious, there was evidently no particular stigma attached to owning or copying them. In part, this must be attributed to English law, which distinguished between owning a book for purposes of study and possessing it for the practice of magic. Even so, several people close to the royal court had faced accusations of illicit astrological divination and magic practice in combination with charges of sedition.[53] Owning a magic manuscript was not without its dangers. Yet so long as one was careful, it appears to have been relatively safe. One is left to conclude that the association of this literature with the dominant intellectual discourse lent these texts a measure of acceptability.

As I have noted, the texts in Argentine's collection appear in the same order in Ashmole 346, the collection of another physician, Thomas Scalon of Haddiscoe, Norfolk. Scalon earned his bachelor of arts degree in 1499 and his master of arts by 1503 at King's College, during the early part of Argentine's tenure as provost. Although at this point no more is known about him, his manuscripts survive and indicate that he was an active medical practitioner through the first half of the sixteenth century. He had strong astrological interests, like most contemporary doctors, and employed astrology in his practice. Astrological nativities in his notebooks indicate that he was practicing at least until 1555. One of his manuscripts currently travels with material that had been owned by the famous late sixteenth-century medical practitioner and collector Richard Napier.

We are fortunate to have all 164 folios of Scalon's collection, made up largely of astrological and medical works but also including secrets and recipes. In addition to the magic material derived from the manuscript of John Argentine, Scalon collected two works of magic giving direction on finding thieves or stolen goods. If taking the trouble to copy from several sources is any indication, Thomas Scalon appears to have had considerable interest in the subject, although astrology and medicine dominate this and his other manuscripts. In Ashmole 340, fols. 64–85, Scalon's hand records astrological tables through twenty-two folios. Ashmole 391, fols. 1–16, includes another set of works in his hand, principally of astrological medicine, and the *Sompnia Danielis,* a work on dream interpretation with astrological dimensions (fols. 3v–5).[54] Nothing about these collections suggests practices that are anything but mundane astrological medicine, although tables of the kind contained in the first manuscript would have been necessary for the use of magical images. Similarly, article 2 of Ashmole 393 contains sixty-eight folios in Scalon's hand, mostly concerned with astrologically oriented medical topics, largely medical recipes of various sorts. In addition, a work on nonmagical experiments appears on fol. 33rv. The configuration of interests exhibited by Scalon's manuscript will be quite familiar by this point: medicine, astrology, divination, and other *naturalia.*

David Pingree has identified the medical center of Montpellier as a par-ticularly important location from which manuscripts of image magic were distributed. The tradition of using ligatures in medicine reinforced the strong association of medicine and magical images found in Arabic sources, as the theoretical work on images by Qusta ibn Luca attests. That magical images should be found in the collections of men with medical interests and train-ing should come as no surprise. Whether Argentine and Scalon had some personal contact remains unclear, although it seems likely. Certainly, a com-mon medical training would have formed an important context for personal contact. Perhaps most significantly, both men were products of the schools and were students of Scholastic natural philosophy, a fact that provides fur-ther evidence of the links between Scholastic discourse and the tradition of astrological image magic.

Michael Northgate and the Monks of St. Augustine's Abbey, Canterbury

If not the most common collectors of astrological image magic, monks are certainly the most *identifiable*. Unlike private secular collections, the cata-logues or inventories of many monastic libraries have survived and identify volumes belonging to individual monks, which generally became part of the larger monastic collections when they died. Books owned by other collectors would not have been recorded in catalogues with the same frequency, nor did they have the same built-in mechanisms for their preservation. In addition, monasteries provided a long-term intellectual context within which groups with common interests could develop. The number of monks at St. Augus-tine's Abbey at Canterbury who collected magic texts suggests such a situa-tion. Pingree has identified three monks of this abbey during the fourteenth and fifteenth centuries who collected texts of magical images and whose life-times would have overlapped.[55] The resources of this great intellectual center could only have encouraged such groups and interests.

Thomas of Wyvelsburghe and Thomas Sprot were both monks of St. Augus-tine's and owners of Codex 1277, now Oxford, Corpus Christi, 125. Sprot chronicled the history of the abbey. Some of the manuscripts of this history extend to the end of the thirteenth century. It seems clear that he lived into the early part of the fourteenth century. Wyvelsburghe, who next owned the codex, is mentioned in William Thorne's chronicle of St. Augustine's Abbey in a passage concerning the acquisition of the benefices for churches in Sturry and Kennington in the early fourteenth century.[56] The codex contains a diverse collection of material, principally alchemical, but also several works on image magic. It is preserved largely in the form in which it was originally catalogued.

John of London is more difficult to trace owing to his relatively common name. M. R. James identifies him with the John mentioned by Roger Bacon, a youth whom Bacon educated and sent with presentation copies of his books to Pope Clement IV in 1267. His expansive collection, which consists of almost eighty volumes, reflects Bacon's interests in math and astronomy but also in magic. More plausible is Wilbur Knorr's suggestion that the St. Augustine's monk was the same John of London who studied in Paris in the early decades of the thirteenth century. Knorr demonstrates that his books contain a large number of works by French, and specifically Parisian, authors and that these are consistent with this location and period.[57] As in the patterns of collection we have already seen, John's books indicate a high level of interest in medicine, mathematics, and astronomy. Three concern theology, twenty-three math and astronomy, twenty-three medical topics, ten philosophy, six logic, four history, three grammar, and one poetry. The remaining volumes are miscellanies.[58] Of this large collection, four volumes contain magic works or works of magic theory.[59] Codices 1140 (now Rawlinson C. 117) and 1166 (now Harley 13) both contain copies of al-Kindī's *De radiis stellarum,* devoting most of the rest of their pages to astronomical works. Marginal notes in John's hand indicate that he read it and understood the connections to his magic texts.[60] Codex 1161 contains a similar collection of astronomical material and Ptolemy's *De imaginibus.* Codex 1538 (1603), a miscellany, contains copies of the Solomonic *Ars notoria* and *De annulis Salomonis,* probably the *De quatuor annulis* condemned in the *Speculum astronomiae.* So, with the exception of the *Ars notoria,* addressed in chapter 4, the volumes follow the patterns I have so far described. Oxford, Corpus Christi, 248, once Canterbury Codex 1145, also includes a catalogue of astrological works evidently used in the production of the *Speculum astronomiae.*[61]

Of all the collectors at St. Augustine's, Canterbury, the most interesting is unquestionably Michael Northgate, who was active at the abbey in the early to mid-fourteenth century. It appears that he was educated at Paris at roughly the same time as John of London, although there is no evidence that their paths crossed. Most probably from Canterbury itself, Michael was ordained a priest in 1296 and became a monk in 1320.[62] His collection of more than twenty volumes, although modest in comparison to that of John of London, has a character of its own and, as James observes, affords insight into Northgate otherwise unavailable.[63] Six or seven of his volumes are devotional and three have to do with natural history; the other topics in his collection include surgery, astronomy, and alchemy. The large number of devotional works suggests a devout religious man, and everything known about Northgate's life supports this characterization. Northgate began his ecclesiastical career as a parish priest, and during his time at St. Augustine's he composed the *Ayenbite of Inwyt*,[64] a vernacular translation of a French work, *Le somme des vices et de vertue,* written by Laurentius Gallus in 1279 for Philip II of France.

Three volumes of the twenty listed under his name in the catalogue include works on magic: codices 767, 1166, and 1170 (which survive as Oxford, Corpus Christi, 221). As it would be very unlikely for this many magic texts to appear in his collection by accident, they suggest a strong interest in the topic. Codex 767 contains orations extracted from an *Ars notoria,* a matter discussed in chapter 4. Codex 1275 is largely a medical codex, although it includes works of *naturalia* such as Albertus Magnus's *Secretum secretorum,* a book on tree planting, the book of experiments called *Vacca platonis,* extracts from the *Kiranides,* and an alchemical work attributed to Hermes. Three of the medical works concern surgery. The works on images that follow are *De quindecim stellis* and treatises attributed to Aburabez, Belenus, Hermes, and Thetel.

That the medical material coincides with *naturalia* and magical images in Codex 1275 is understandable. It follows the pattern of collection already discussed at length, a pattern with a relatively high level of intellectual coherence. How this fits in with Northgate's wider interests is somewhat less clear. If the position on magic elucidated in *Ayenbite of Inwyt* is any indication, his view of magic was unhesitatingly negative.[65] His career as priest, monk, and translator of pastoral literature suggests someone well aware of the problems associated with magic practice and interests. It also suggests someone concerned with living an upright life in the pursuit of a more or less orthodox faith. It is perhaps enough simply to note the presence of these two facets of his intellectual life; it is also possible that an early interest in magic had waned by the time he translated the *Ayenbite of Inwyt.*[66] However, we have no evidence that this was the case. Further, if the magic books ran counter to Northgate's later beliefs, such a change of heart did not drive him to expunge or remove any of the magic sections, something that would have been relatively easy to do. So we must also ask whether there is some ground where his religious devotion and his interests in magic might have intersected in a noncontradictory manner. This line of questioning leads to some interesting possibilities.

Motivated by the same intellectual presuppositions held by medical doctors, men with explicit religious interests could draw upon a long-standing tradition of the use of the wonders of the world to direct attention to the divine. The well-known thirteenth-century Dominican encyclopedist Thomas of Cantimpré performed a valuable service for the preservation of magic texts when he included in his *De natura rerum* the entire text of Thetel's work on images.[67] He concludes this work with a short piece describing the blessing of a stone to return it to its prelapsarian—and thereby more efficacious—state.

Thomas's position was typically ambiguous, allowing for the possibility of natural (and therefore legitimate) occult virtues in stones. For Thomas, the text was not altogether trustworthy, nor were all sculpted gems to be regarded as effective. Although the form of the stones was to be honored for its virtue, "yet hope is not to be put in them but, according to what is written, in God alone from whom the virtue of stones is derived."[68] In other words, stones might be legitimate so long as one did not trust in them rather than in God, and so long as they were understood to derive their power from God. This position is very much in keeping with Thomas's rationale for writing *De natura rerum*. Should people not be moved by sermons of the usual kind, they might be moved to religious devotion by stories of the wonders of the natural world.[69] So the purpose of recording this information was certainly not to encourage the reader to sculpt gems for magical purposes but rather to provide a credible report of a wondrous facet of God's creation.

A similar project may have been at work in the assembly of Northgate's other volume, Codex 1170 (now Oxford, Corpus Christi, 221). The manuscript falls into two parts that evidently had separate histories before being bound together. The first includes extracts from another encyclopedia titled *De natura rerum* by the Carmelite John Folsham, in addition to another copy of Thetel, and a treatise on sculpted gems attributed to Marbodius. The remainder is taken up with recipes and medical notes. There is nothing out of the ordinary in this part of the codex or about a collector interested in recipes, medicine, and aspects of the natural world who also has a particular interest in sculpted gems. Both texts of image magic may have been deemed more tolerable, as they purport to derive from non-Arabic sources and lack the more dubious elements of sacrifices, suffumigations, and incantations. What is very interesting about this fourteenth-century collection is its second part, a twelfth-century collection that includes Gregory the Great's *Dialogues* and two saints' lives. The *Dialogues* are a classic discussion of the miraculous as evidence of God's active presence in the world. Saints' lives form another important portion of this form of devotional literature. The catalogue of the abbey's library records the codex, including Gregory's *Dialogues,* so it must have been assembled sometime before 1497, when the catalogue was written. The age of the binding plausibly dates its assembly and binding to the lifetime of Northgate.[70]

Circumstantial evidence further suggests that this volume was compiled with Thomas of Cantimpré's project in mind. Recently, Ron Baxter has suggested that St. Augustine's may have been the site for the programmatic promotion of the use of bestiaries as sermon *exempla*.[71] This position has been further confirmed by the identification of two additional volumes in the library that appear to follow this same pattern.[72] Northgate was interested enough in magic and the natural world to collect quite a number of works on both topics, and he was interested enough in devotional literature to write a vernacular work on the subject. His choices of profession and orders tend to confirm this interest. His collection of books is composed of approximately equal numbers of works on devotional subjects and works concerned with medicine, alchemy, secrets, astrology, magic, and natural philosophy. If Northgate did not regard his devotional and "scientific" interests as coherent in quite the manner of Thomas of Cantimpré, it nevertheless can be said that both of these interests are represented in Oxford, Corpus Christi, 221. More important, we have no reason to assume that Northgate was in any way vexed by this combination of interests.

The context of St. Augustine's also suggests that Northgate need not have regarded his interest in magic as antithetical to monastic life. As Pingree has demonstrated, from the late thirteenth century through the fourteenth, at least four monks were interested in magic at the abbey. That Codex 1277 (now Oxford, Corpus Christi, 125) was owned consecutively by two monks, Thomas Sprot and Thomas Wyvelsburghe, confirms that the common interests were more than a private matter and that a small community of interest in magic probably existed there. It seems likely that we may add a fifth monk to Pingree's list. Simon Maidstone, a monk at St. Augustine's in the fifteenth century, was probably the owner of Oxford, Bodley 951, a large folio copy of the Solomonic *Ars notoria* discussed in chapter 4. While his surviving works do not contain works on Arabic image magic, both John of London and Michael Northgate also owned works in the tradition of the notory art. So the community of monks was larger than Pingree has suggested, probably persisted for a longer period, and also had a wider common set of interests. Where the lifetimes of these known book owners may not have overlapped, making personal connections possible, continuity may have been provided by monks who did not own their own books, and certainly by the library, which in time absorbed most of the personal libraries of the monks. I say "most" because the spectacular manuscript Bodley 951 was not catalogued at St. Augustine's, which suggests that it may never have been absorbed into that collection. So additional copies of magic works may have circulated in that community that did not survive, were not catalogued, no longer bear the mark of an owner at St. Augustine's Abbey, or for some reason did not become part of its library.

A common interest in astrology, medical topics, and *naturalia* is the most plausible basis for this intellectual community of monks. A different dimension is suggested by the case of Simon Maidstone, whose books betray no interest in medicine but reflect only more traditional devotional interests.

John of London, Northgate, and Maidstone all owned copies of the *Ars noto-ria*. This suggests a different kind of interest in magic. As I demonstrate in chapter 4, the *Ars notoria* is a magic text of a much more explicitly religious variety, frequently collected with works that suggest a deep interest in affective religious devotion. Northgate's devotional and pastoral interests, which may well have formed a part of his interest in magic, thus may also have overlapped with magico-religious interests among the other monks of St. Augustine's Abbey.

In conclusion, our apothecary had every reason to be confused. As an intellectual exercise, astronomical image magic bridges a number of seemingly opposed discourses. It draws on a substantial theoretical tradition but clearly was considered to belong in the company of practical *naturalia*. It derives from a variety of largely non-Christian sources and yet could be, and was, integrated into pastoral literature as evidence of the presence of the divine in the world. It was commonly condemned by Christian authorities and intellectuals, but it was also studied and transmitted in the context of universities and monasteries. It involved practices such as suffumigation, incantation, and the engraving of unknown characters and words, which were commonly understood to indicate that it worked through demonic intervention. Yet its collectors persisted in regarding it as belonging to the category of *naturalia*. Many clearly believed, or wished to believe, that it was natural magic; most certainly regarded it as a topic framed by the larger Scholastic debates about the physical world and its processes. The process of transmission was informed by these tensions, and the texts of image magic were transmitted in a way that made them more like *naturalia* according to Christian standards. The *Speculum astronomiae* exerted a powerful influence upon which texts were copied. Those it tentatively approved as natural magic or that roughly matched its standards were copied much more frequently than those it condemned. The result was the first of the transformations of magic that are the subject of this study. The library of astrological image magic, and even the texts themselves, were streamlined, made more adaptable to Christian sensibilities as natural wonders, and made more like "science" and *naturalia*. A second, subtler transformation may also be detected here. Whatever their original intent, and in spite of the fact that their practices were not strictly reconcilable with Scholastic notions, Europeans came to understand this literature as part of the larger Scholastic library and discourse on the natural world.

3

SOME APPARENT EXCEPTIONS:
IMAGE MAGIC OR NECROMANCY?

In the preceding chapter, I described the common patterns of scribal interest associated with texts of astrological image magic. Scribes regarded these texts as belonging to the broad category of *naturalia,* and many evidently regarded image magic as a legitimate part of that library. Like the Magister Speculi, the scribes appear to have made a distinction between this sort of magic, which I have referred to as Scholastic image magic, and other kinds of magical practices that I will refer to as ritual magic. As we shall see, these texts involve the explicit binding, invoking, and employing of demons, the ritual engagement of angels or the Holy Spirit, the use of extensive Christian rituals, a heavy emphasis on the affective state of the operator, and a desire to engage directly with the divine or numinous. Prior to 1500, this genre rarely traveled with the standard texts of astrological image magic (at least not the ones commonly found in Scholastic image magic collections) and was almost never collected with works of *naturalia.* An interest in astrological image magic thus seems to have been quite distinct from an interest in ritual magic or the subcategory of necromancy. Two apparent exceptions to this rule deserve closer examination. First, some texts of astrological image magic closely resemble ritual magic in the operations they describe and are even sometimes referred to as necromantic. Did scribes actually think of image magic texts, including incantations or prayers, suffumigations, or the use of ethereal beings, as indistinct from ritual magic? Second, while it is usual for the Scholastic form of image magic to travel separately from ritual magic, two volumes in the collection of John Erghome present a major exception. Not only do they combine astrological image magic texts with works of natural philosophy and *naturalia* in the configuration I have demonstrated to be so common; they also include quasi-theurgic

works, like the *Ars notoria* and *Liber sacer,* and other works of explicit necromancy. How do these volumes bear upon our understanding of the more
usual pattern?

The author of the *Speculum astronomiae* designated as necromantic both
the texts of astrological image magic that he considered illegitimate and texts
of explicit demon conjuring. Yet, like him, the scribes of Scholastic image
magic generally regarded their texts as *naturalia.* Although they did not
copy them as often, scribes usually treated works of Scholastic image magic
involving more explicit ritual procedures, and even those condemned in the
Speculum, in the same manner as they did the approved works. In the Latin
West, true necromancy and other works of ritual magic explicitly claim to
derive their power through Christian rites from immaterial beings and, as we
shall see, are rarely collected with any form of *naturalia.* These texts of image
magic, however, cling to the library concerned with the natural world. The
coherent set of assumptions that surrounded the collection of the "legitimate"
works of Arabic image magic applied as well to those with more explicitly
ritual content.

The texts by Pseudo-Ptolemy or Thābit, which the Magister Speculi tentatively approved, contain little or no explicit ritual in their instructions for producing talismans, unless carving them or placing them in a particular place
may be considered ritual. Works like the *De imaginibus* of Belenus or the *Liber
lune* are quite different, as they prescribe the use of suffumigations or incantations. In addition, these works employ mysterious names, which are sometimes applied to certain astrological conditions or locations and sometimes
explicitly associated with ethereal beings. It was on the grounds of these ritual
practices and the potential presence of demons that the Magister Speculi condemned these works as necromantic. Although the *Speculum astronomiae*
appears to have had a wide-ranging impact upon the medieval library, those
texts that he condemns and that were copied in spite of warnings appear to
have been collected for the same reasons and by the same group of scribes
who collected those texts he did not condemn. Among those condemned
treatises may be found *De imaginibus septem planetarum, De quatuor anulis,
Liber lune,* Belenus's *De imaginibus,* the *Liber imaginum Veneris* or *Liber
Veneris,* and a work on images attributed to Aristotle, all of which survive in
British manuscripts.

Any individual text belonging to this group was copied with substantially
less frequency and tended to be the province of the bibliophile. Approximately one-third of British codices copied before 1500 that contain image
magic include explicitly condemned texts.[1] This might be taken to demonstrate that the influence of the *Speculum astronomiae* was not as profound as

I have suggested, or that more people were willing to copy condemned texts. However, the numbers are deceptive, as this group represents a larger variety of texts surviving in smaller numbers of witnesses. In addition, if we take the list in the *Speculum astronomiae* as our indicator, these texts represent only a small fraction of the illegitimate texts circulating in the thirteenth century. Of the forty magic texts the Magister Speculi identified, he approved only two. Although only a rough indicator, this would mean that the 5 percent of the available texts that were approved account for 66 percent of the witnesses, while the remaining 95 percent account for only 33 percent of the witnesses. Alternatively, the approved treatises were copied at a rate of 33:1 and the condemned ones at a rate of 0.34:1. In nonmathematical terms, the condemned texts were copied relatively rarely, and a significant number do not survive at all. The collections in which the condemned works appear tend to confirm their rarity. They were usually owned by collectors with substantial personal libraries, such as John Erghome, John of London, and Michael Northgate. These collectors would have had the resources to locate rare works and may have found it easier than others to justify their presence. They also tended to have collected several other works of image magic. This may have been a matter of raw probability (a larger collection would probably contain more such texts); it might also result from specialized interest in the area. All of this makes clear that the *Speculum* had considerable influence over the selection of texts and that, if not for the specialist or bibliophile, the works it condemned might not have survived at all. This forces us to ask whether the collectors of these condemned works had interests different from those who chose to copy less dubious material.

The short answer to this question is that condemned works were treated almost uniformly in the same manner as those approved by the Magister Speculi. For example, the medical collections of Thomas Scalon and John Argentine, discussed in the previous chapter, include images attributed to Aristotle.[2] A codex belonging to Michael Northgate contains medical material, alchemy, and secrets, in addition to Belenus's *De imaginibus*.[3] Royal 12.C.XVIII includes the same text with other works of image magic in a selection of largely astrological material.[4] Bodley 463 combines a work of image magic, the *De imaginibus,* with works on astronomy, stones, astrology, and natural philosophy.[5] By the sixteenth century and quite possibly earlier, the quires containing the *Liber lune* and other magical images in Harley 80 were bound together with astronomical and astrological material.[6] As shown below, the examples from the collection of John Erghome and Digby 228 confirm this as a standard configuration. A fascinating and strange Neoplatonic work on human interaction with spirits appears in Oxford, Corpus Christi, 125, together with the *Liber lune,* but it is essentially cosmographical rather than practical and, if a little strange, accords well with the overwhelming majority of texts in this volume, which concern the standard topics of *naturalia.*[7] So the more dubious forms of image magic—those condemned in the *Speculum astronomiae*—appear in substantially the same manuscript context as those that were not condemned, and their association with an interest in the natural world is not diminished by its author's suggestion that they are not natural.

Not only do the collections surrounding these texts betray their owners' interest in the natural world, but on some points they actually suggest a higher level of engagement with the available philosophical material on the subject of magic than what we find in the case of scribes of more acceptable image magic texts. Relative to their numbers, texts of this condemned group are more often associated with works of magic theory. Of British volumes including the *De radiis,* the *Speculum astronomiae,* and Qusta ibn Luca's *De physicis ligaturis,* half (five of ten) contain works of this more dubious nature.[8] This might support the argument that the condemned treatises were collected because of specialized and sophisticated interest in the subject. It could also be attributed to a high level of anxiety over whether these treatises were legitimate. A more detailed analysis of the only British version of the *Speculum astronomiae,* occurring together with a work on image magic, sheds some light on this issue as well as on the general question of scribal attitudes toward the more dubious forms of image magic.

The *Liber lune* and the Case of Digby 228

The *Liber lune* is a work of Arabic image magic attributed to Hermes. Like many other works in the library of magic, the text claims a more proximate author or editor, Belenus, who reports the wisdom of Hermes to us. (The text of Belenus's *De imaginibus* is in fact closely related to the *Liber lune* and may derive from it.) After an introduction, the text discusses the twenty-eight mansions of the moon, giving their names, number, associated planets, whether the mansion is good or bad, and the kind of image one makes in it. For example, the first entry reads, "When the moon is in Alnath, that is, in the first mansion, which is the face of Mars and a bad mansion, in that [mansion] you will make images of separation and discord."[9] The text then discusses the suffumigations used for good and bad images and provides a list of the names to be used when exorcising the images. A final preparatory chapter details the hours of the day and night, their names, and the kind of images to be made in them. The text then begins more specific instructions for the use of particular images, and it is from this portion of the text that Belenus's *De imaginibus* appears to be drawn, the preparatory chapters having been dropped. To bind someone's tongue, for example, an image must be made of tin and silver in the likeness of the victim and marked with the names of the "lord" and "lady" of the relevant hour, commonly understood as celestial spirits. It must then be suffumigated with aloe and sandalwood and, presumably, exorcized. The other images follow the same pattern; their purposes range from simple tricks, to having a woman do your bidding, to mass destruction.

To distinguish this text from the works of necromancy on the basis of content is a technical and somewhat abstract matter. Here is a complex array of ethereal beings, images, and incantations that employ strange names. The ritual features of the processes, beyond the carving of the image, receive a considerable amount of attention. If the major concern is the presence of strange names and rituals, then the fact that the *Liber lune* employs a different medium for making images (metal rather than parchment) and that it (like some ritual magic texts) omits any overt reference to the binding of demons, does not constitute a major difference. In short, we should not wonder that the Magister Speculi designated this text necromantic. However, the codicology of this version of the *Liber lune* is very much like that of other works on images and, as we shall see, entirely unlike that of most necromantic texts.

Digby 228 is a late fourteenth-century codex of seventy-nine folios, written on parchment by three main scribes. Contemporary quire marks suggest that the codex is complete to quire "h," the end of the extant codex, although it is possible that they indicate the reassembly of an earlier codex that might have contained additional quires. Like most medieval books, it betrays several levels of accretion. The first hand (mid-fourteenth century) began in what is now the fifth quire and ran to the ninth. The second hand (later fourteenth century) filled in sections at the end of the original quires and added three quires to the beginning of the volume. A few other subsequent scribes also inserted material, such as the sixteenth-century chart on fol. 2v. The volume evidently began with the first scribe copying the *Computus* of Robert Grosseteste (an astronomical work concerned with the calculation of feast days, notably Easter), a collection of secrets, and a variety of other astrological material. To this the second scribe added more astrological material, such as a short commentary on the *Sphere of Sacrobosco* and a text that explains the astrological significance of being born on a particular day. There follow a commentary on Ptolemy's *Centiloquium*, a tract on comets, the *Flores astrologiae* of Albumasar, a copy of the *Secretum secretorum*, and a host of other astronomical and astrological material. Finally, the second scribe added texts at the end of quires largely filled by the first scribe. At the end of quire 7 was enough room for him to include part of the *Liber lune*, but for some reason he stopped copying in the middle of the text, not even using up all available space on the last folio. He also filled in the text of the *Speculum astronomiae* at the end of quire 9. The third scribe, also late fourteenth century, included a variety of astrological material, including a text on the twenty-eight mansions of the moon. But the relationship of this portion of the codex to the rest is more nebulous. This means that we can treat the *Speculum astronomiae* and *Liber lune* as direct indications of the second scribe's interests, since he copied them, and the original material to which he added (written by the first scribe) as a supplementary indication of his interests.

Digby 228 also includes the standard array of astrological and theoretical works, which we have demonstrated to be the usual company of image magic, and this volume appears very much like any other volume of astrological texts that include image magic. If this predictable array of subjects were not enough to indicate the general direction of our scribe's interest, the second scribe copied the *Speculum astronomiae,* which confirms that he was very much interested in astrology and, potentially, magic. In the eleventh chapter (discussed above), which seeks to divide good works of magical images from bad, the *Liber lune* can be clearly identified as one of the "bad" texts, not only because the Magister Speculi cited its name and incipit but also because he condemned the category of images that it employs. After condemning the texts by Hermes and Belenus, the use of the names of angels said to be subservient to the images of the moon, as well as incantations and suffumigations, he concluded, "This is the worst idolatry, which, in order to render itself credible to some extent, observes the 28 mansions of the Moon and the hours of the day and night along with certain names [given] to these days, hours and mansions themselves. May this method be far from us, for far be it that we should show that [sort of] honor to the creature which is due [solely] to the Creator."[10] Next to this passage, either the second scribe or some relatively contemporary annotator has drawn a *manicule* (a hand with a pointing finger). Thus the scribe or a later owner was very much aware of the significance of this passage to the *Liber lune.* Given that the same scribe wrote both the *Liber lune* and *Speculum astronomiae,* the presence of these two texts in the same codex can hardly be deemed coincidental. One way or another, the *manicule* makes clear that the connection was certainly clear to either the scribe of the texts or a subsequent reader.

It is not clear at all whether this interest was practical or theoretical, or in fact whether the material was collected as part of *anti*magic interests. The third scribe, who recorded additional technical information on the lunar mansions, appears to have been more deeply involved in speculations about magic; the case of the second scribe is rather less clear. Whatever the case may be, the second scribe chose to approach the material through a work of magic theory and in conjunction with astrology. This fact firmly separates this case from the codices containing necromantic material, where such interests in theory are very rarely represented. Among British volumes, the *Speculum astronomiae* appears once[11] and the *De radiis stellarum* of al-Kindī appears eight times in the manuscripts containing works on magic or in the larger collections of their owners. In no case, except Erghome's *codices superstitiosi* (discussed below), does it appear in a codex with ritual magic texts. Among works of magic involving the conjuring and binding of spirits, there is very little evidence of an interest in theory until the sixteenth century. I know of only two continental volumes that combine explicit ritual magic with a theoretical work.[12] So if, on the basis of its rituals and use of spirits, we were to include the *Liber lune* in the category of necromantic magic, as the Magister Speculi did, Digby 228 would be an unusual codex. Classified in terms of the scribe's approach and other interests, and in comparison to the usual patterns of manuscript compilation, the codex unquestionably belongs in the company of collections of Scholastic image magic.

As a codex in the tradition of the Scholastic image magic collection, Digby 228 is entirely unexceptional, if not a definitive case. Astrology is as fundamental to most works on images as hierarchies of demons and angel names are to works on conjuring. So it is logical that the theoretical works appear here and that the second scribe should have an interest in the astrological works written by the first. Moreover, the *De radiis* is Arabic, and the *Speculum astronomiae* refers to the tradition of images that is largely Arabic. These works also tend to be associated with speculations that certain forms of magic are allowable on the grounds of being "natural." This is an explicit argument in the case of the *Speculum* and implicit in the *De radiis*. The theoretical grounds for the "natural" functions of an image are fundamentally connected to the theories about occult properties. So the first scribe's copies of such texts of *naturalia* as the *Secretum secretorum*, which concerns occult properties, can be seen as part of a coherent set of interests.

The question remains whether to include the *Liber lune* in general, and this version of the text in particular, under the umbrella of necromantic magic. It would be folly to attempt to categorize it purely on the basis of content, following the Magister Speculi. After an extensive analysis of the astrological inheritance of western Europe, we would ultimately have to conclude that it was a matter of interpretation whether the angels in this text were real, simply various flavors of stellar rays, or in fact demons. If we wish to understand this copy of the work as a medieval Latin artifact, we must classify it according to scribal attitudes and interests. As a text in Digby 228 and in the context of the tradition of Arabic astrological image magic, the *Liber lune* belongs to a group of texts with a markedly more innocent agenda. Its collector understood the work in its theoretical context and may have had no practical interest in the subject at all. On reflection, he may have decided that the *Liber lune* was indeed bad magic, and not attributable to astrological mechanisms despite what al-Kindī may have said. This we will never know. We do know that it cannot be taken as evidence of an interest in *necromantic* or ritual magic. Every aspect of this compilation suggests that the scribe understood this condemned work of image magic as related to the investigation of the natural world and as a subject to be approached through the literature of astrology and natural philosophy. The scribe's interests lay more in the direction of natural wonders rather than what Richard Kieckhefer has described as the "flamboyantly transgressive" features of ritual magic.[13]

If the circumstantial evidence of the direct influence of the *Speculum astronomiae* and other theoretical material on the scribes of astrological image magic were not strong enough, the scribe's *manicule* makes clear that he considered its relationship to the *Liber lune* significant. What he and the others may have decided about the *Liber lune* remains unclear, but as steady as it might be, the finger in the margin pointing to the condemning passage in the *Speculum astronomiae* does not suggest confidence. That the second scribe evidently broke off in the middle of copying the *Liber lune,* leaving it incomplete, could be the result of an imperfect exemplar. Yet almost a full page of blank parchment follows it, suggesting that the break may have been unplanned and perhaps motivated by doubt or caution. So, while this codex strongly confirms the usual patterns in which image magic and the natural world are associated, the overwhelming final impression is not one of confidence but rather of careful scholarly consideration, caution, or even ambivalence.

Michael Northgate's Codex 1275

The case of Northgate's codex 1275 of the library of St. Augustine's Abbey, Canterbury, is particularly interesting, given the apparently devout nature of Northgate's life and his other intellectual interests. Donated by Northgate, this codex was largely medical in orientation, although it included works of *naturalia* such as the *Secretum secretorum, De plantacionibus arborum,* the book of experiments *Vacca platonis,* extracts from the *Kiranides,* and an alchemical work attributed to Hermes. Three of the medical works concern surgery.[14] The works on images that follow are *De quindecim stellis* and works on images attributed to Aburabez, Belenus, Hermes, and Thetel. The Magister Speculi condemned at least two of these, those by Belenus and Hermes.[15]

As in the case of Digby 228, the scribe of this condemned material has provided a theoretical work that might explain, and perhaps even justify, the copying and use of these condemned works. Another of the medical texts, Qusta ibn Luca's *De physicis ligaturis,* forms a link between the largely medical content of this codex and the relatively extensive collection of image magic that follows it. This work discusses ligatures (i.e., things bound to the body for medical reasons, a term often meaning talismans) and other apparently magical operations. It concludes that while the ancients might have been correct in attributing power to ligatures, images, and incantations, the psychological effects of believing in them are sufficient to explain their effects. The examples recommended by the ancients that Luca cites are not of magical images but suspended stones, or stones set in rings.[16] Another text by the same title attributed to Discorides, which directly precedes it, is probably a collection of various medical ligatures not involving magical images.[17]

There is no evidence that the scribe considered the works of image magic medical. But it is clear enough that the works were directly connected with, or understood in relation to, medical literature, and in particular the evaluations of Qusta ibn Luca. The arguments he gives in no way justify the use of talismans, but they do examine and evaluate image magic in the context of natural philosophy or the practice of medicine. That the scribe (not inconceivably Northgate himself) saw these interests as part of a larger interest in the natural world is amply demonstrated by the works of *naturalia* with which the text is also collected.

John Erghome's *Libri superstitiosi*

The collection of John Erghome became a substantial part of the library of the Austin Friars at York sometime in the late fourteenth century.[18] Among the approximately three hundred books that the library catalogue lists as having belonged to him, seven notices contain works on magic, including two containing only a copy of the *De radiis stellarum.*[19] None of these seven has been identified with any surviving manuscripts. Most of these entries follow the usual patterns described above. Erghome catalogued one of the volumes containing the *De radiis stellarum* (A8 452) under the general heading of extraneous authors and philosophers (*Auctores et philosophi extranei*). Another volume containing the *De radiis stellarum* (A8 385) and two volumes containing works on image magic (A8 375 and 383) he catalogued under

Astronomia et astrologia. These latter two volumes, among other works of astrology, astronomy, experiments, mathematics, and recipes, contain a large number of works on image magic, including quite a few of those condemned by the Magister Speculi.

Closer examination of one of his volumes confirms that Erghome may have regarded image magic as a topic in natural philosophy, if not a genuinely legitimate part of that discipline. In A8 375, the presence of the *Liber lune* and five other works on magical images appears to have been as relevant to classifying this volume as astrological and astronomical as the other works it contained. The only other explicitly astronomical or astrological works are two short works by al-Kindī, listed as *De impressionibus* and *De subradiis planetarum.* The treatise *Philosophia* by William of Conches includes astrological topics but might better be described as cosmographical.[20] The other treatises are the *Pronostica Socratis basilei,* a divinatory work, experiments, and some biblical material.[21] In short, the bulk of the astrological material is magical as well. Thus it seems possible that Erghome did not consider magical images particularly problematic, at least not of sufficient concern to warrant classifying this volume as superstitious. In this way most of his books and the way he categorized them follow the conventional patterns. Yet these familiar patterns are not repeated in two other volumes that Erghome did identify as "superstitious."

Volume A8 362 contains a collection of magic works unparalleled in size and in the variety of its contents (see below). To my knowledge, no existing codex contains so complete a collection of the magic works available in the fourteenth century. What is significant for our purposes is that this codex contains not only the standard configuration of Scholastic image magic (e.g., *Liber Veneris, Hermes de imaginibus,* and *Liber imaginum Aristotelis*) and astrology/astronomy and magical theory (al-Kindī's *De radiis*) but also a substantial number of works of ritual magic and explicit necromancy. Erghome lists a *Liber Honorii divisus in 5 tractatus* which is undoubtedly the *Sworn Book of Honorius,* a work of ritual magic. It also includes numerous texts of what is probably explicit spirit conjuring, such as the *Vinculum Salomonis, Liber rubeus qui aliter dicitur sapiencia nigromancie, Tractatus de penthagono Salomonis, Tractatus ad inclusionem spiritus in speculo,* and *Tractatus ad habenda loquelam cum spiritu et effectum eternum.* The volume also includes the *Ars notoria* and *Ars notoria nova completa,* texts of ritual magic that call upon angels for spiritual and intellectual gifts. Several works, like *Tractatus de nominibus angelorum ordine forma et potestate et mansione,* are more suggestive of the practices of the *Liber lune* and perhaps occupy a middle category. It should be no surprise that this volume was collected under the heading

Prophecie et supersticiosa, given the inclusion of numerous works of explicit demonic and angelic magic, practices that make no pretense of having "natural" mechanisms.

The second book in this category (A8 364) presents more difficulties. If the rest of his collection is any indication, Erghome appears to have had a high level of tolerance for astrological image magic and theories concerning it, specifically those of al-Kindī. Yet here we find a fairly standard collection of astrological image magic works classified as superstitious, which suggests that he was not tolerant of them. The entry includes the *Liber lune,* al-Kindī's *De radiis stellarum,* another work on images, a *Liber prestigiorum* attributed to "Alkanus the philosopher," which is probably the work of the same title by Thābit translated by Adelard of Bath, also known in its other translation as the *De imaginibus.*[22] However, the classification of the volume was most probably related to the last work, identified as *Liber sacratus Petri Abellardi,* a title that does not suggest any known works of astrology or image magic. Instead, it is almost certainly the *Liber sacer* or *sacratus,* also known as the *Sworn Book of Honorius* (*Liber iuratus Honorii*), one of the most significant works of ritual magic circulating in this period, which also appears in Erghome's other volume of "superstitious" material.[23] Most surviving versions of this work were copied in Britain, so there would be nothing unusual about two copies appearing in this collection. Since the entries in catalogues typically record the title and author as they appear in the volume, the peculiar title does not suggest that the cataloguer did not know what the work involved. Moreover, the first few pages of this work are unambiguous about its purposes and make clear that it employs angels in its largely ritual operations and that it has a tolerant attitude toward necromancy. The prologue also takes an explicitly antiestablishment position by claiming that the church's negative attitude toward magic was unjustified and the result of demonic deception. The British version of this work (generally referred to as the London Honorius) is a shortened version of the original but remained a substantial text, usually occupying an entire volume. The *Sworn Book* would probably have taken up a considerable portion of this codex, certainly far more than the relatively short works on images. Its size, transgressive contents, and explicit nature thus easily account for the classification of this volume, and we need not assume that the astrological image magic was involved in the decision.

Erghome has no other volumes outside the class of superstitious works that contain texts of necromancy or elaborate ritual magic like the *Sworn Book of Honorius.* As no works of this kind appear elsewhere in his collection, it seems likely that a volume with any such lengthy work of ritual magic was simply classified among volumes of superstitious works. It might also be that the condemned contents of the *Liber lune* and *Liber prestigiorum* may have encouraged this classification, but since the *Liber lune* appears elsewhere in "scientific" settings, this explanation is less convincing. Given the breadth of material commonly found in individual codices, a cataloguer who had to classify an entire codex under a single subject heading would have had to make a decision based on a general impression of the book's contents, the relative importance of the included texts, or perhaps the first text in the codex. As it stands, we can regard the classification of this codex only as an indication of what Erghome thought (or wanted others to assume he thought) about magic in general. This cannot be taken as an indication that Erghome assumed that there were no differences between the texts in the volume. He could well have regarded Thābit and al-Kindī as belonging to a category quite distinct from the *Liber sacer,* as the scribes of most of Erghome's volumes that include magic works appear to have assumed.

Yet it remains the case that Erghome may well have had a hand in *assembling* these volumes. He would have been one of very few with the resources to compile such a collection of magic works from such disparate traditions, and if he did not collect each piece individually, he may have combined several volumes in a single codex. As we don't know how the books were structured (e.g., where the quire divisions might lie), it is difficult to offer a convincing argument for why a certain text might have ended up in a certain codex on codicological grounds. Even so, a structure, if not the physical structure, may be inferred from the contents. It is likely that a bibliophile such as Erghome would have been ill at ease splitting up a set of gatherings if it would mean breaking up one of the texts. So it is likely that any volumes he acquired would have remained as a single unit. Close examination of the manner in which the texts in 362 and 364 are organized reveals a clustering of related topics. This evidence in turn suggests how the volumes might have been physically assembled. It also reveals the same patterns of collection that characterize works of astrological image magic.

Humphreys's entry for 364 runs as follows. (I include in parentheses some of Humphreys's suggestions. Square brackets indicate works I consider solidly identifiable.)

a. *Liber ymaginum lune* [*Liber lune*]
b. *Liber ymaginum veneris* [*Liber Veneris*]
c. *Liber radiorum* [more than likely al-Kindī, *De radiis stellarum*]

d. *Liber prestigiorum Alkani philosophi* [probably Thābit, *Liber prestigiorum* (*De imaginibus*), trans. Abelard of Bath]

e. *Liber sacratus Petri Abellardi* [more than likely the *Sworn Book of Honorius*]

Items a through d relate to magical images and would constitute a fairly standard collection of Scholastic image magic. A plausible scenario for the assembly of this volume is that these texts were assembled separately and that the volume was originally split between items d and e. Al-Kindī's work was probably not separable from the collection and so could not be easily removed, even by taking apart the original binding. In this way, we can account for the fact that Al-Kindī's *De radiis* appears elsewhere in Erghome's collection in "scientific" volumes, and although Erghome might have considered it *incorrect* natural philosophy, there is no evidence to suggest that he regarded it as superstitious. That the Magister Speculi condemned all the remaining works of image magic as demonic might well have pushed them into the category of superstition for Erghome or the cataloguer. This explanation would also work if we were to assume that Erghome was responsible for the assembly of the volume. In any event, the image magic in this codex is clustered together and reflects the same patterns of collection we have seen elsewhere.

Although much more complex, the case of 362 is similar (see table 1). Once again, works on images, works on magic theory, and works that are usually collected with them tend to appear together. Items a through i are very much like standard collections that include image magic. The piece on judicial astrology (item b), the letter of Thomas Aquinas on occult virtues (item e), the work of dream interpretation (item a), and the associated theoretical work by al-Kindī (item d) indicate an interest in *naturalia* and natural philosophy. The genre of dream texts to which item a belongs is commonly found in collections of *naturalia* reflecting Scholastic interests in physical and somatic processes.[24] In addition to these, one of the geomantic texts (item i) appears to have a theoretical portion. A very similar set of texts that include geomancy, judicial astrology, and magic theory may be found in A8 385, catalogued as *astronomia* and *astrologia*. Items n through s also appear to be of a piece: all of them are concerned with image magic. Finally, items ah through ao also appear to be related. Among them we find the *Secretum philosophorum* (item ah), a text sporting rather innocent tricks and sleights of hand, which hardly qualify as superstitious in the sense that the *Vinculum Salomonis* might. In this instance, once again, the patterns of collection common with image magic texts are evident.

TABLE 1 York, Austin Friars A8 362

Shaded sections indicate portions of this codex that clearly correspond to the characteristic divisions between astrological image magic and *naturalia*, on the one hand, and ritual magic, on the other.

Ritual Magic	Other	Naturalia/Divination	Astrological Image Magic		Catalogue Entry	Bibliographical Information
		X		a.	Liber sompniarii Ybin Cyrin' in 8 partibus et pars in cifra	Humphreys identifies this as Achmet (Ahmed) ibn Sirin, *Oneirocriicon*, prob. trans. Leo Tuscus, as in Oxford, Bodleian, Digby 103; *HMES*, 2:291–93.
		X		b.	lïber qui intitulatur de iudiciis astrorum	Humphreys suggests that this may be a work by al-Kindī.
			X	c.	9 ymagines extracte de libro veneris	*Liber Veneris*. Lucentini and Compagni, *I testi e i codici di Ermete nel Medioevo*, 86–89.
		X		d.	brevis tractatus quatuor capitulis de sompno et visione	Humphreys identifies this as Al-Kindī, *De sompno et visione*, trans. Gerard of Cremona.
		X		e.	tractatus de operibus et occultis actionibus naturalium	Humphreys suggests Thomas Aquinas, *De occultis operibus naturae*.
		X		f.	liber Hermetis de celo et mundo distinctus in 6 partes	

		X		g.	theorica artis magice in 56 capitulis	Al-Kindī, *De radiis stellarum*.
		X		h.	flores coniunctionis veritatis geomancie distinctus in theoricam et practicam	
		X		i.	introductorium ad geomanciam docens terminos artis	
X				k.	tractatus de penthagono Salomonis	Possibly *Pentaculum Salomonis*, a title that recurs frequently in necromantic collections. See, for example, *Signum pentaculum*, found in Sloane 3851, fols. 31v–53r. *HMES*, 2:280.
X				l.	tractatus ad inclusionem spiritus in speculo	See *Ad includendum in speculo spiritum*, in Sloane 3884, fols. 57v–61r.
?	?			m.	opus capitis magni cum aliis capitibus pertinencibus	
			X	n.	tractatus ymaginum secundum mouimentum planetarum et operacionibus eorum	Humphreys suggests Belenus, *De imaginibus septem planetarum*.
			X	o.	tractatus ymaginum Gyrgit filie Circis de opere ymaginum distincus in theoricam et practicam	

(Continued)

TABLE 1   York, Austin Friars A8 362 *(Continued)*

Ritual Magic	Other	Naturalia/Divination	Astrological Image Magic		Catalogue Entry	Bibliographical Information
			X	p.	Hermes de ymaginibus	Belenus, *De imaginibus diei et noctis*? Lucentini and Compagni, *I testi e i codici di Ermete nel Medioevo*, 76–78.
			X	q.	idem in alio tractatu de ymaginibus	
			X	r.	tractatus Hyllonii de arte ymaginibus	
			X	s.	tractatus de nominibus angelorum et effectubus eorum	Possibly Paris, Bibliotheque nationale, MS 17178, fol. 37v. Incipit: Omnia angelorum et planetarum sunt haec. Saturni: Marthir Machanasen Prothemphares Gaymsuucils Abroth.Also possibly Thetel (Zael), Nomina angelorum planetarum, Vat. lat. 4085, fol. 105r. Incipit: Nomina angelorum planetarum secundum Zael es in libro de ymaginibus sunt hoc. Saturni: Chathir.
X				t.	vinculum Salomonis	This is a common title in necromantic collections. For a sixteenth-century text by this name, see Wellcome 110, fol. 36.

?		?			u.	tractatus de valeriana	
?		?			x.	tractatus de spiritu cibile	I.e., sibille.
			X		y.	tractatus de capite Saturni	*Speculum* astronomiae lists same title with incipit: Quicumque hoc secretissimum (sacratissimum in other versions of the *Speculum*).
X					z.	liber Honorii diuisus in 5 tractatus	*Sworn Book of Honorius*
X					aa.	tractatus ad habendam loquelam cum spiritu et effectum eternum	
X					ab.	aliud opus preciosum ad magnum effectum	
X					ac.	liber rubeus qui aliter dicitur sapiencia nigromancie	Possibly *Practica nicromancie*. London, Society of Antiquaries, 39, fols. 15v–17v.
?		?	?		ad.	experimentum bonum sortis	
			X		ae.	tractatus Fortunati Eleazari de arte euthontica ydaica et epytologica	Humphreys identifies this as Eleazar of Worms or Salomon, *De quatuor annulis*; the latter seems more likely. The incipit to this work appears in *Speculum astronomiae* 11.76–78 as "De arte eutonica et ydaica . . ."
?			?		af.	tractatus de nominibus angelorum ordine forma et potestate et mansione.	

(*Continued*)

TABLE 1   York, Austin Friars A8 362 (*Continued*)

Ritual Magic	Other	Naturalia/Divination	Astrological Image Magic		Catalogue Entry	Bibliographical Information
X				ag.	tractatus de Floron	Possibly a text on the demon Floron. See München, Bayerische Staatsbibliothek, Clm 849, fols. 38r–39v. Incipit: "Hic incipit speculum Floron, et alio modo quam supra sit notatum. . . . Fac fieri speculum de puro calibe, ad mensuram palme vnius in rotundo, ethabeat manubrium ad tenendum, et sit illuminatum et ludicum vt ensis."
	X			ah.	tractatus qui dicitur secretum philosophorum diuisum in 7 partes secundum quod pertractat 7 artes	
		X		ai.	liber veneris in tres partes diuisus	*Liber Veneris*. Lucentini and Compagni, *I testi e i codici di Ermete nel Medioevo*, 76–78.
		X		ak.	liber ymaginum Aristotelis	

			X	al.	tractatus Hermetis de ymaginibus	Belenus, *De imaginibus diei et noctis*? Lucentini and Compagni, *I testi e i codici di Ermete nel Medioevo*, 76–78.
		X		am.	alius tractatus ymaginum	
	X			an.	exceptciones horarum a Ptholomeo descripte	
		X		ao.	fforme ymaginum in singulis signorum faciebus	
X				ap.	ffinis artis notorie veteris	
X				aq.	ars notoria noua completa	
?	?			ar.	multa experimenta	

Separate from these blocks of texts are known works of necromancy and ritual magic, in addition to other items apparently involving ritual magic. These sections also reflect the usual patterns of collection in ritual magic texts discussed in the second part of this study, which is to say that they are rarely collected with any texts other than other texts of ritual magic. Items k and l both suggest ritual magic practices. The first is clearly from the Solomonic tradition of ritual magic and is probably the *Pentaculum Salomonis*. The second text, "To enclose a spirit in a mirror," is clearly a work of explicit spirit binding, a practice not characteristic of the astrological image magic tradition, and similar practices, such as the trapping of spirits in mirrors or vials, also occur in other ritual magic collections. Finally, item m has the nebulous description "a work of one great chapter with other pertinent chapters." This, naturally, could refer to practically any text but suggests the longer works of ritual magic rather than the shorter works of image magic. Items ap and aq are two standard texts of the notory art and would have been fairly substantial texts. The "many experiments" that follow (item ar) could be of the innocent variety, but since these experiments lack the adjective "good," used to describe a divinatory experiment above (item ad), one is led to speculate that they are of the bad kind, meaning necromantic experiments.

Items t through ag present more difficulty. Several major texts of ritual magic pepper this section: the substantial *Sworn Book of Honorius* (item z); the *Vinculum Salomonis* (item t), a text of widely varying contents common to ritual magic collections; a work on the demon Floron (item ag), a spirit commonly associated with captoptromantic processes; and two works evidently concerned with communicating with spirits (items x and aa). These are supplemented by a section (item ab) identified as "another precious work of great effect," which implies subject matter similar to that of the preceding work on communicating with spirits and by its ambiguity gives the impression of a work of ritual magic. Item u discusses the herb valerian. This may be an unusual intrusion of *naturalia* but cannot be regarded as significant. It is just as probably a discussion of valerian's use in ritual magic, although hyssop is more common. It is also not unusual for ritual magic texts to include scattered recipes or charms, and this text might also be of that nature. The works on image magic, however, appear less often in these sorts of volumes; in fact, the more common texts of astrological image magic, particularly those approved in the *Speculum astronomiae,* almost never do. Nonetheless, such image magic texts as those that appear here sometimes do occur in the company of ritual magic texts, as in the instance of London, Society of Antiquaries, 39, discussed below. Both *De capite Saturni* (item y) and *De quatuor anullis* (item ae) belong to the second category of magical images from the *Speculum astronomiae:* texts associated with exorcisms. The latter, in particular, claims Hebraic roots and employs substantial ritual practice in addition to an exorcism. So, although less common, these would not have been at all out of place in the company of ritual magic texts. The text on angel names and their astrological context (item af) could also be found in a more dedicated ritual magic text, such as Society of Antiquaries 39.

Far from being exceptions to the rule that Scholastic image magic and ritual magic tended to travel separately and were understood and treated in different ways, Erghome's volumes generally confirm the pattern. The portions of the text given over to image magic and theories of magic betray precisely the same kinds of interests as other collections we have seen. The presence of theoretical works on magic cheek by jowl with image magic texts further demonstrates the association of image magic with theoretical interests. The only portion of the text in which ritual and image magic are intermixed is dominated by ritual magic interests. Even if, for the sake of argument, we were to assume that Erghome saw no differences between these texts, the clustering of topics suggests that whoever assembled the volumes or the exemplars for these manuscripts did. The portions of the text that I have identified, particularly items a to g and ah to ao, could well represent volumes or sets of gatherings that originally were physically separate.

That said, Erghome's attitude toward these texts is by no means clear. If Erghome assembled A8 362, his classification of it among the *libri superstitiosi* would have to be understood to apply to both works of image magic and works of ritual magic. He unquestionably regarded ritual magic as superstitious, for no other works of ritual magic appear under other classifications in his collection. His position on image magic remains less clear. That codices devoted in large part to image magic were classed as astrological suggests that he regarded them as a potentially legitimate part of that discipline, or at least as legitimately associated with that part of the library. This would not prevent him from regarding them as superstitious as well, or potentially so. The texts of Scholastic image magic were accordingly understood differently from those of ritual magic, but their precise relation to legitimate natural philosophy remained ambiguous.

The Apothecary's Dilemma Revisited

The works of image magic described here form a distinctive genre owing in part to their contents but also to how they were understood, treated, and transformed. The scribes of image magic tended to be interested in issues relating to the natural world. Their codices reflect concern with such topics as alchemy, natural philosophy, astrology, and astronomy. Other interests included mathematics, secrets, experiments, recipes, lapidaries, and other assorted *naturalia*. The scribes understood and interpreted magic texts with the tools available to them, in particular works of natural philosophy. One important theoretical work in this regard, al-Kindī's *De radiis stellarum,* often appears together with works on image magic, even though it is devoted to incantations in addition to images. The *Speculum astronomiae* appears less frequently in the codices containing works of magic but seems to have had considerable influence upon what texts were chosen for copying. The function of magical images was generally understood as potentially connected to the natural world, and many scribes clearly assumed this. This was apparently so even in the case of codices containing texts condemned by the Magister Speculi and displaying features strongly suggestive of demonic involvement.

But it is not clear that the scribes regarded this material *without qualification* as scientific. The picture presented by the manuscripts consistently associates image magic with medieval scientific discourse. At the same time, the manuscripts consistently give no clue as to whether the scribes or collectors regarded them as *unambiguously* legitimate parts of natural philosophy. A defining feature of medieval attitudes toward these works lies precisely in this ambiguity, that is, in the fact that it was not always clear to the scribes or collectors themselves that image magic was legitimate. A codex is the record less of an argument than of a purposeful association of a certain group of texts. After all, the "purpose" might be as simple as collecting stray and otherwise unassociated texts. So we should not regard the presence of a work that discusses or justifies the use of astrological images as in any way indicative of a practical interest in magic. Rather, such a codex suggests that image magic was a topic of concern, and that the selection of materials was guided by the pursuit of a particular interest or line of reasoning. In this sense, the codices containing theoretical works suggest doubt. The Digby scribe may well have decided that the *Liber lune* was bad magic and rejected it on that ground. The evidence suggests as much. Although John Erghome appears to have regarded image magic as having some legitimate astrological status, in two significant codices he also classified such texts as superstitious works, casting into doubt the association of image magic with legitimate astrology. At least a portion of the codices thus appears to have been the work of scribes or collectors who were not sure about the status of works of image magic.

In the other examples, there is no evidence to suggest that the scribes and collectors regarded texts of image magic as *without qualification* legitimate natural philosophy. Neither conceptually nor in practice did the categories of "natural magic" or "secrets" or "experiments" bring this kind of literature about the natural world clearly and unambiguously within the ambit of accredited scientific or philosophical inquiry. When the Magister Speculi suggested that Ptolemy's work on images might be legitimate, he added the qualification that if the work possessed some secretly necromantic features, they would be illegitimate. In the end, the Magister Speculi himself was not sure. That this ambivalence occurs in the most influential positive evaluation of image magic accords these works at best a middling status or associate membership in natural philosophy. The liminality of astrological image magic is further attested by its manuscript history, which was distinct from texts of natural philosophy or astrology. Texts of image magic were commonly transmitted in groups and traveled back to back in most codices. In most cases they were not intermixed with other texts in such a manner as to suggest that the scribes regarded them as simply another variety of astrological treatise. In all probability, a scribe would have had to make a special effort to find them. Thus, while texts of image magic commonly traveled with books of astrology, their relationship to the astrological codex and the larger medieval library makes clear that they had a distinct status. This applied equally to their relationship to volumes of other sorts of *naturalia*.

Thus manuscripts offer no evidence that the scribes regarded the relation of image magic to natural philosophy as unproblematic; in fact, ambivalence appears to be the most common feature of scribal attitudes. Perhaps driven by concerns about what might lurk behind apparently legitimate images, or by the possibility that the legitimate features of the art would be rejected because of the apparently illegitimate ones, scribes tended to transmit the texts in such a way that the library became standardized. Their content was adjusted to orthodox standards by removing certain ritual features, such as incantations, or by not copying the texts that contained them. They were set on the page in the company of, and in like manner to, works of *naturalia*. They were selected for copying with reference to philosophical standards as set out in the *Speculum astronomiae*. Yet the ambivalence remained. It had to: image magic was attractive precisely because of its ambiguous status.

Thomas of Cantimpré, for example, was interested in magical images because the mechanisms that drove them were hidden and their effects were out of the ordinary. Without these surprising qualities, the value of much of this material would have been negligible. Of what practical worth, in Britain, was a text that provided instructions for an image that would rid a place of scorpions? Its value clearly lay in the fact that the result and the processes used were "wonderful." In this sense, magical images are like material in books of secrets, recipe collections, or works on experiments. Interest in them is driven by a desire to know the unknown and control the uncontrollable. But the practice of image magic involves much more profound oppositions than does the broader literature of *naturalia*. Its operations are much more powerful, and it draws directly upon higher powers. At the same time, it promises, if only implicitly, not simply access to these hidden powers but also an understanding of them. The potential dangers and sins associated with the practice of image magic were much more extensive and extreme than those associated with recipes, secrets, or the less dubious kinds of experiments. Not only did image magic involve the threatening possibility of demonic involvement and numerous forms of sin, it often explicitly employed some form of rite. At the same time, a substantial philosophical literature offered Christians the chance to practice this powerful form of magic legitimately. So the essential factor in the success and independence of these texts lies precisely in the apothecary's dilemma: the tension between the frightening, sinful, and mysterious, on the one hand, and the controllable, blameless, and knowable, on the other. Scribes and collectors of image magic were particularly interested in magic that was *also* science, magic that fell within the compass of controllable, identifiable mechanisms while still maintaining its dubious status. Accordingly, we must not read "scientific" when we see "natural magic." These terms are not synonymous. Regardless of what Bonatti might have told the confused and impoverished apothecary, and despite his assurance that the effects of his image were entirely natural, no solution could be offered to the apothecary's dilemma, because there was none.

PART II | BROTHER JOHN'S DILEMMA

Do not believe or acquiesce lightly to all visions, but by council of the Saviour, try the spirits whether they are of God, and seek discernment from the Holy Spirit in prayers.

Brother John of Morigny thirsted after enlightenment.[1] But its pursuit by necromantic means filled him with dread and fear for his soul. He unburdened himself to Jacob, a doctor friend, who suggested that the *Ars notoria* was his best alternative, since it employed angels instead of demons. Through this art John might achieve intellectual gifts and complete knowledge of the arts and sciences. After a program of prayers and meditations, the Holy Spirit would infuse him with these gifts. The suggestion launched John, who from an early age had been given to visions that filled the sky and shook the earth, upon a lengthy exploration of this art. Some of the resulting visions he believed legitimate, but toward others he was ambivalent, for they were frightening, puzzling, suspicious. John learned a great deal from the spirits, including information about magical practices, and he employed the art to understand the meaning of his visionary experiences. He assisted two others in practicing the art as well. His younger sister used it with great success to learn Latin but was plagued by terrifying visions. Another monk, who had persuaded John to instruct him, was ultimately warned in a vision that the art was without spiritual value. John also had visions warning him against his practices. In one, an angel demonstrated that the prayers of the Solomonic *Ars notoria* he was using had been imperceptibly woven together with necromantic incantations. Unknowingly, he and his associates had been calling upon demons for assistance, not angels.

So John gave up all hope of practicing a good form of magic and, despite his fears, began dabbling in necromancy. He became so proficient that he began, and, by his later account, finished, a book on the subject. But he was already being plagued by a new set of visions. In one, an angel delivered John over to a demon to be killed; in another, Christ himself appeared and convinced John that he should abandon his explorations in magic altogether by having him beaten severely. When John finally renounced all of these magic arts, his visions no longer involved demons but rather the Virgin, angels, saints, and even Christ on the cross. Instead of filling him with dread, they suffused him with joy. He was sure that the divine had inspired these visions. He was no longer plagued by the terrifying and explosive appearances he had experienced before. Yet this did not stop him from desiring knowledge from spiritual sources. In the short term, he continued to use dreams to seek answers to questions. In the end, John asked the Virgin for permission to compose a new book of thirty simple prayers that would provoke the infusion of knowledge of scripture, the arts, and the sciences, a book that would destroy and supersede the old and evil *Ars notoria:*

> And lo, that wooden image was transformed into the human likeness of the same undefiled virgin, and she spoke with me, saying, as though unwilling and heavily, and as though she tired herself by speaking, "It pleases me that you should compose such a book as you have asked for." And I said to her, "Hey, my lady, how will I recognize it and be able to compose it?" And she responded: "When you do it, I will give you such eloquence that you will fashion it well."[2]

John then wrote and compiled the *Liber florum celestis doctrine*. The autobiographical stories recounted here are drawn from its prologue, the *Liber visionum*, the title of which has hitherto been applied to the entire work.[3]

The apothecary with whom we began this book could interpret the operation of a magical image in two ways. One was morally neutral and legitimate because, like any other tool or natural force available to human beings, it could be used by bad and good alike and could be judged as bad or good only on the basis of how it was used. While most authorities argued that such "natural magic" was not possible, the traditions of Arabic astrology and the influence of the *Speculum astronomiae* were evidently enough to give some hope that it was. The other option, drawing on a considerable range of authoritative statements extending back to Augustine, asserted that *all* magic involving images operated by inherently evil processes that involved demons. The majority of medieval scribes of image magic evidently assumed that it was natural, potentially natural, or belonged to the library of natural philosophy, with the result that the library of astrological image magic was modified to look more legitimate, according to scientific standards, and was commonly collected by those interested in *naturalia*. Brother John's position was slightly different, and so was the effect it had upon the works of magic he encountered.

If the history of religious dissent is any indication, religious conviction or direct experience of the numinous can give one the courage and assurance not only to do and say unconventional things but even to face persecution, torture, and death. To connect these emotional resources with ritual magic is not to eulogize its practitioners but to recognize the powerful forces that their interests, practices, and desires could, and frequently did, bring into play, and the effect of these forces on practitioners who wrote down and transmitted their art. As writers and users of ritual magic collected, wrote, and practiced magic, they drew deeply upon their religious sensibilities and direct experience of the numinous for sanction, inspiration, and discernment. A more or less uniform set of basic religious beliefs and practices in Europe, particularly the liturgy, provided the central elements of their practices and gave them a certain consistency. Often also using elements from Hebraic and Arabic sources, they produced a significant body of texts self-consciously Christian in orientation, arguably the largest body of illicit magic works original to the Latin West. Eventually, a set of texts regarded as standard appeared, having passed through a process in which they were edited, supplemented, and/ or reorganized. Although some of these texts settled into a relatively stable textual tradition, they often traveled in the form of extracts or fragments, as a result of which the integrity of the original text was lost. They also gave rise to entirely new texts that emulated them in the same way that the originals had emulated Jewish and Arabic texts. This impulse to create new texts was fueled by the principle that each magic operator needed to engage personally with the text and that the text was a means to acquire knowledge from the divine, not a source of knowledge in itself. That they additionally sought knowledge from encounters with the numinous introduced an anarchic influence that fueled the perpetual transformation of the available texts, creating a comparatively chaotic written tradition. Readers interested in this sort of magic were thus faced with the difficult task of discerning truth in inconsistent or corrupted texts without the explicit guidance of authoritative writers, and since they were already disposed to seek access to the numinous, they sought out that truth in its mercurial resources—in visions, dreams, and other forms of divine guidance. To illustrate this process, let us reexamine the story of Brother John.

John's autobiography can be read as an account of how a single user transformed two written traditions, the *Ars notoria* and necromancy. The *Ars notoria* existed in at least two versions by the time John employed it. If we take him at his word, he was brought by divine intervention to the realization that it was secretly demonic. His subsequent transformation consisted in part of stripping out the sections containing *verba ignota*, that is, the long prayers written in what is purported to be transliterated Greek, Hebrew, and Chaldee. To remove such unknown words and replace them with thirty simple prayers would move the text a good deal closer to what might be regarded in Christian terms as legitimate or even genuinely good.[4] Yet the transformed text required justification, particularly since it followed the form of a book of magic that, by John's own admission, contained demonic elements. Unlike image magic, which stood or fell on scientific grounds and could draw upon positive evaluations from a few significant writers, ritual magic had no such toehold. In order to lend authority to his new text, John drew upon the same resource that the original version of the *Ars notoria* had claimed to employ: divine revelation.

The full title of the *Liber visionum*, the autobiographical prologue, or first book, of the *Liber florum*, is the "Book of Apparitions and Visions of the Most Blessed and Undefiled Virgin, Mary Mother of God, which Mary Graciously Obtained and Revealed with the Permission of the Supreme God." The first chapter of this prologue describes the educative goal of the work, emphasizing the prayers and how knowledge will be transferred to the operator through "unheard" angelic words, or, in accordance with the operator's merits, through direct visionary experience of the Blessed Virgin. In the subsequent two sections, John argues that he cannot keep the light of his experiences under a bushel and describes his book as the end result of Mary's efforts to snatch him from the jaws of perdition. In fact, he fashions it as an offering, memorializing her efforts on his behalf. When he finally presents a narrative of his life, John begins with a vision of the Virgin that he had at age fourteen, predating his interests in magic. Thus in a narrative, rhetorical, and literal sense, the text begins with divine revelation. He seeks to establish its validity by carefully locating it in the story of a sinner saved by divine intervention. In honor of the Blessed Virgin and with divine sanction, this sinner has produced a work that will lead people to divine truths. In all of this, John draws heavily upon the rhetorical approaches of mystical writers[5] and the long-standing Christian principle that the truth could be revealed to the most humble of believers in visions or dreams. Having produced the volume with divine inspiration or guidance, John draws his autobiography to a close. He has achieved what he set out to achieve and seems convinced that he has produced a work of Christian intellectual magic that deserves, as he says, a place among the "Apocrypha of the Faith." However, the fortunes of his book were far from assured, and John is uncomfortably aware of this fact.

Unlike the author of any work of astrological image magic of which I am aware, John expresses concern in the *Liber florum* about changes that might be made to the work by subsequent scribes or practitioners. "Note that you ought to reduce or change nothing in all that we have written," he warns, "as in the prayers so in figures, imaginings, and instructions, unless from God or the glorious Virgin there has been a prior divine inspiration, that is, a revelation."[6] John expresses concern about the possibility not only of scribal errors but of substantial reductions in the length of the text or of intentional alterations to its contents. His own story discloses a wide range of reasons for fearing such a possibility. One such reason lies within this very injunction: the inherently slippery nature of visionary experiences.[7]

The vision presents problems for John. He frames his autobiographical prologue around his spiritual journey from sin to redemption, a journey that includes his increasing abilities in discernment. For a time he truly believed that the visions produced by the *Ars notoria* were divine, and that it was not his vague doubts about them but divine intervention that saved him from sin. John was shown that the *verba ignota* it contained were secretly necromantic. He was also advised and chastised by the Virgin and even beaten by angels. As he emphasizes, these interventions were undeserved. Yet he makes clear that without them he could not have extracted himself from the life he was leading. It also would have been impossible for John to learn how to discern good from evil in his visions. If he was sure in the end that he had acquired the ability to distinguish true visions of the divine, he was not convinced that his readers would be able to do so, at least not without help. The autobiographical details are clearly intended (among other things) to educate the reader about the nature of visionary experiences. In addition, the final chapter of the prologue discusses at length the nature of his visions of the Virgin and provides three points on distinguishing demonic from divine visions.[8] The concluding words of the prologue, quoted in the epigraph above, emphasize John's concern that his readers be attentive and seek spiritual aid in discernment: "Do not believe or acquiesce lightly to all visions, but by council of the Saviour, try the spirits whether they are of God, and seek discernment from the Holy Spirit in prayers." Despite his desire to present the vision as a stable basis for establishing truth, then, John's story argues equally for the fundamental instability of this medium.

To trace the instability of this tradition, however, we must turn to the texts themselves. While the texts of astrological image magic are not without divergences, the written tradition of ritual magic is far more complicated. Like those of image magic, many ritual magic texts and practices draw upon non-Christian traditions. The idea behind the *Ars notoria* probably extends from Hebraic sources.[9] Necromantic texts draw upon a variety of Hebraic, Greek, Arabic, and other ancient sources. Unlike image magic, their transference into a Christian context was not accompanied by an extensive written literature that a scribe might employ to justify them and that might direct how they should be treated or understood. The tremendous variety of written texts and the instability of the written tradition of ritual magic can thus be explained partly by their many non-Christian sources and the lack of a single convenient justificatory mechanism. The result was a far greater variety of highly distinctive and individual productions. The *Liber florum* added yet another tradition of texts to the library of ritual magic. And despite the fact that the *Ars notoria* presented itself as Christian, John was evidently aware of its non-Christian roots when he described his transformation of the text as despoiling Egypt of vessels of gold and silver.[10]

Another key aspect of John's story is the highly individual nature of his intellectual journey. He claimed primacy for his text over the other texts in the tradition. Despite his rhetorical claims to modesty, John had no difficulty regarding himself as somehow special. As one privileged with visionary experiences, John clearly understood himself as meritorious.[11] Even if we do not regard it as narcissistic, John's authorial presence absolutely dominates the work; his particular set of experiences is fundamental to justifying the work and providing instructions for practicing its art. This individualized approach is part of a larger culture of individualism in this tradition. As a magic operator, John's individual merits are important, but so are the practical abilities he acquires. John reports that he learned the practice of necromancy through visions provoked by the *Ars notoria*.[12] He became so proficient that he was in the process of writing his own book on the subject.[13] He describes how he worked with the *Ars notoria* for a long time and eventually figured out how to make it work.[14] Similarly, the *Liber visionum* plots his increasing ability to discern good from evil in his visions. As he emphasizes, these are learned skills and derive not from a text but from practical experience and the assistance of the divine. Successful use of these operations is as much a skill or art as it is a set of procedures. Ultimately, having gained abilities in this area, John completed his journey with the composition of yet another book. In this way, the individual-centered nature of the practices drove the fracturing of the tradition into a variety of personalized versions.

The visions and other experiences of the numinous (however they were understood to take place) play a fundamental role in this process. When John originally used a corrupt text, the Solomonic *Ars notoria* secretly woven together with necromantic incantations, he did not recognize its flaws. Only divine instruction made it possible for him to construct the ideal form of intellectual "magic." Although John may have had merits and abilities in magic operations, despite his repeated claims of humility, it was only with divine assistance that he was able to discern the truth in the texts. When he finally composed the *Liber florum*, his lack of ability and eloquence was overcome by the divine infusion of these gifts from the Virgin. To complicate matters even more, even the divine itself need not be a static standard for judging truth: what it has established, the divine may change. John is emphatically convinced of the authenticity and divinely sanctioned goodness of his text; were it to be changed by subsequent scribes, it would no longer be an authorized version. However, it attests to John's ingenuousness that he should effectively undercut the potential integrity of his text by openly affirming that it could be altered as a result of the subsequent visionary experiences of others. How, then, were subsequent readers to be sure of the authenticity of the text before them? Had it been changed since John wrote it? Did the Virgin support the version they had? In effect, the status of *any* version of his work was fundamentally precarious, and therefore its "truth value" had to be established by individual revelatory experience.

John's struggle to discover the truth in the texts of ritual magic, and the manner in which he found it, epitomizes the experiences of scribes across the whole spectrum of ritual magic. The text John originally employed did not suit his purposes because it appeared to be demonic magic. His awareness of authoritative teachings no doubt informed his concerns, but his story dramatizes a far more fundamental spiritual struggle with his own religious sensibilities, concerns, and visionary experiences. It was in vision, prayer, and ritual that John found some certainty. In short, he appealed once again to mechanisms that had previously resulted in some very frightening experiences, the numinous areas of human experience. His own deception by demons and his efforts to help his readers avoid the same pitfalls emphasize the problems inherent in this approach. Unlike the case of the *Speculum astronomiae* and astrological image magic, John's personal attempt to create an orthodox version of the *Ars notoria* could not appeal to any textual authority, however badly conceived. It follows that his efforts to revise it required an original formulation, one specific to him. This only added to the confusion of voices characteristic of ritual magic. Moreover, the way he transformed his experience into the *Liber florum* legitimizes not only further visionary confirmation but even further textual elaboration by later users. In fact, subsequent scribes did substantially alter or abbreviate John's text.[15] And so it went.

Ritual magic was also an acquired inner discipline, not something that could simply be performed by anyone, as if following a recipe. One might need a text to begin with that established certain parameters and recommended techniques, but the magic could be learned only in practice. In this sense, a ritual magic text only potentially points the reader to the correct practice or discovery of truth. In part, this approach derived from the nature of the magical practices involved, which emphasized that truth was to be discerned in the ambiguous world of the numinous. The "mystical technologies" employed, such as skryers, reflective surfaces, smoke, flames, crystals, and dreams, could provide richly evocative but unstable results, the veracity of which was understood to supersede the text. In part, this approach also derived from the inherent frailties and insufficiencies of the written word.[16] Once you found the correct form of practice or the means to acquiring the truth, how could you pass it on? As in the case of mystical writings, how can you communicate the incommunicable, those things that are valuable precisely because they cannot be communicated but only experienced? And not only are written texts not sufficient to the task; they are easily corruptible. Put simply, this is Brother John's dilemma: should he enter into a never-ending hermeneutic spiral in an attempt to reconcile the irreconcilable, the oppositions between divine truths, the written word, and human experience? And yet, if he has discovered divine truths, how can he not do so? It subsists in a tradition that insisted that truth needed to be found in the experience of the numinous and was suspicious of its own texts, yet used texts to communicate that truth. If texts can be corrupted, how can you find truth in them? Once you find truth, how do you pass on techniques and experiences that may be inexpressible? And if you manage to do that, how can you keep these records from being misunderstood or recorrupted?

The first tradition we will examine is a body of works sometimes referred to as *theurgic*.[17] Although this term lacks precision—connoting a set of practices and assumptions associated with late antique paganism and later Neoplatonism—it may be used in a more general sense to designate practices through which the operator contacts and achieves enlightenment from higher beings for personal spiritual benefit through religious rites and exercises in purgation. The tradition of the *Ars notoria*, including the revisions of John of Morigny and others, forms the largest body of medieval Latin literature of this kind. In this context we will also examine a text known as the *Liber iuratus Honorii* (*Sworn Book of Honorius*). The following chapter deals with the case of necromantic collections, many of which also have theurgic elements but form a distinctive tradition of their own.

4

THE *ARS NOTORIA* AND THE
SWORN BOOK OF HONORIUS

The *Ars notoria*

The *Ars notoria* ascribes its authority to Solomon. It elaborates upon the account in 2 Chronicles 1:9–12 and 2 Kings 3:5–14, where God appears to Solomon in the night. Among other things Solomon has asked for, he is granted *sapientia, scientia et intelligencia*. That a wider group of people might expect such gifts from God is suggested by Daniel 1:17, in which God endows Daniel and the four young men with skill and wisdom. Daniel is additionally given insight into visions and dreams. Similarly, in Luke 21:15 Christ promises to endow certain Christians with the gift of wisdom. A story in the *Dialogus miraculorum* of Caesarius of Heisterbach in which a priest is given the gift of preaching in his sleep (and which refers to the biblical story of Solomon) attests to the currency of these notions in the later Middle Ages.[1] In a similar way, the *Ars notoria* seeks the acquisition of knowledge and/or other special gifts, such as rhetorical skills, through a program of prayers, rituals, and meditations that employ the inspection of complex figures inscribed with prayers. It is from these figures, or *notae*, that the art derives its name.

As with all works of medieval ritual magic, the textual history of the *Ars notoria* is complex. It first appears in the late twelfth or early thirteenth century, but the early version evidently lacked sufficient clarity, particularly if a potential practitioner did not have the guidance of a master who had figured it out. As a result, by the fourteenth century the work had more than doubled in size through expansions to the original text and a substantial explanatory gloss. An additional text also appeared at this time, the *Ars nova*. This version may have been intended as a simplification of the text and as an autonomous work, but significant ambiguities remain. Although the *Ars nova* may be performed as an independent operation, it has also been incorporated into the operations of the larger text. A final set of prayers may also be added to the main body.[2] That we can see something of an ordered process in the development of this text testifies to the skills of its modern editor, Julien Véronèse, more than it does to any textual stability. As we shall see, the individual texts circulating in medieval libraries differed substantially from one another.

What did one do when one wished to practice this art? The differences among circulating versions of the text make any description of the actual practice something of an abstraction. Nonetheless, Véronèse's outline of a fourteenth-century manuscript in the Bibliothèque nationale, which I summarize here, provides a crucial starting point.[3] The art begins with a fifteen-day operation to determine the spiritual worthiness of the seeker that concludes with the drinking of a specially prepared concoction of water and leaves inscribed with angel names. The process involves fasting and reciting prescribed prayers. A worthy candidate will subsequently have a dream indicating that he may proceed and telling him what to expect to gain from the art. Once confirmed as worthy, the operator must pass through a series of four-month rituals, each corresponding to the form of knowledge he wishes to acquire. Each ritual builds in intensity toward the end, requiring higher levels of prayer and fasting, and concludes with a month during which the operator must sequester himself, engage in more intense preparatory rituals, and finally inspect the *notae* in a contemplative manner. To complicate matters, in addition to observing lunar months, the operator must ideally also observe certain astrological restrictions, seeking certain forms of knowledge at propitious times, although this may not be necessary, depending upon his worthiness. Véronèse suggests that it would probably take several years to complete the entire program if one were to observe the guidelines strictly. If we take seriously John of Morigny's claim that you had to learn how to practice the art, it may actually have taken a good deal longer to achieve any results.

The "tool kit" of the *Ars notoria* includes a variety of elements. The operations are divided into "generals" and "specials." Generals seek to have a broad impact on the condition of the operator in terms of such skills as augmenting memory or developing eloquence. The same operations also have secondary efficacies to be used for other purposes, and these usually respond to the circumstances of everyday life, such as the need to determine the outcome of an illness. The specials seek the knowledge of the seven liberal arts, philosophy, and theology. Each is accompanied by prayers and at least one, but sometimes as many as five, *notae*. The notes are usually complex figures with interconnecting geometric shapes in which the prayers are written. Formulaic sorts of graphic elaborations and sometimes figures of angels accompany them.[4] Some of the prayers are in Latin, but a significant number are purportedly written in transliterated Greek, Hebrew, and Syriac. These, the text advises, may not be translated because the words would lose their efficacy. As the fasting and abstinence in the rituals make clear, the moral disposition of the operator was a crucial part of successful operation. Ideally, the operator would live an entirely chaste and religious life, but certainly it was essential to maintain ritual purity throughout the operations. The language of the prayers and instructions also continually reinforces the sense that the operator's attitude must be humble and reverent.

Whether these tools were regarded in themselves as sufficient causes of the infusion of spiritual gifts is a question that has plagued this art almost from its inception. Both medieval critics and modern interpreters have asked whether the results of the art were understood to be automatic, even something like the sacraments. Aquinas's critique of the art addressed this issue, and there is no question that the *Ars notoria* seems to verge on this sort of assumption.[5] Yet the evidence remains ambiguous. The Solomonic version employs the term "sacramental" in reference to itself. But the implications of this term were not entirely clear at the time that it was written, potentially meaning only that the rituals have the quality of a divine mystery. One way or another, the text seeks to leave in God's hands the decision whether a seeker might practice the art, implying that the results were not automatic but depended upon divine permission. This emphasis upon divine discretion also persists in John of Morigny's version.

If we take the genre as a whole, including its various emulations and reworkings, its defining feature is not so much the use of angels or *notae* as it is the goal of spiritual and intellectual enlightenment. The genre was generally confined to more innocent contexts and does not involve the use of demons. But some necromantic emulations of the *Ars notoria* also exist, in which demons instruct the operator, and one sixteenth-century necromantic manual includes a Solomonic *Ars notoria*, suggesting that John of Morigny's excursion from it into necromancy was not singular among its users.[6] While John of Morigny clearly wanted to work with angels rather than demons, his original Old Compilation text included a vastly greater number of figures than the original. These figures were criticized by certain unnamed "barking dogs" at Sens for appearing "too much like necromantic figures," prompting a reduction and simplification of the images and a complete revision of his own (divinely confirmed) *Liber figurarum* in 1315.[7] As we shall see, some versions of the Solomonic text include only the prayers, and some shorter emulations include only short prayers to bring on dream visions.[8] The necromantic emulation mentioned above does not employ notes. Even the analyses and condemnations of this form of magic tend to focus on the reception of spiritual gifts. They may regard the art as secretly demonic, but they do not confuse it with necromancy or image magic. Rather, they tend to focus on whether it is possible and appropriate to acquire knowledge or skills through prayers, fasts, and figures.[9] So the defining feature of these texts appears to be as much the "theurgic" goals as the means by which they are sought.

The scant attention the *Ars notoria* received until the past decade or so is quite out of proportion to the large number of surviving manuscripts. For example, E. M. Butler's discussion of ritual magic makes no mention of it, and Lynn Thorndike's discussion runs to only a paragraph.[10] Nonetheless, Véronèse identifies almost fifty manuscripts from the fourteenth through six-teenth centuries. Eight of these are of British origin or provenance.[11] British medieval library catalogues tell a similar tale: the *Ars notoria* is listed almost as many times as all other texts of more explicitly ritual magic combined. To date, I have found five notices, for a total of thirteen either known or surviv-ing versions.[12] The continuing significance of the art in the sixteenth century is attested by numerous manuscript versions written in that century. In the seventeenth century it appeared in print in a Latin edition and in an English translation.[13] It was also incorporated into the *Lemegeton*, a collection of Solo-monic ritual magic texts also known as the *Lesser Key of Solomon*.[14] In time, more manuscripts may surface, either having been catalogued as works on notarial abbreviations (the cataloguer having confused *Ars notaria* with *Ars notoria*),[15] or, as in the case of some John of Morigny manuscripts (includ-ing McMaster University Library MS 107), having been classified without much description among liturgical works, devotions to the Virgin, or prayer formularies.

While the *Ars notoria* is not among the works of magic frequently men-tioned in literary texts, it was often discussed or condemned by intellectuals, and its considerable manuscript presence is paralleled by a large and inde-pendent presence in medieval descriptions and discussions of magic.[16] It was also condemned by name in the indices of Milan and Venice of 1554 as a category parallel to necromancy.[17] The frequency with which writers in the later Middle Ages discussed it indicates its currency in late medieval concep-tions of magic. Current scholarship will certainly do a great deal to correct the unjustifiably low level of attention received by this genre, but this scant attention is worth considering, as it may have affected its transmission in the first place.

Modern scholars' limited attention is no doubt the result of the art's low profile in medieval literature, its general absence from court records, its relatively harmless intents, and its perceived lack of "scientific" merit. We have few records of prosecutions for using or possessing it,[18] as compared with the considerably more frequent instances of court cases involving the possession of works of necromancy. This is not surprising. The *Ars notoria* posed no threat to anyone but the operator, except insofar as it might be heretical or might encourage interest in other, more dubious forms of magic. In addition, its practices lacked the prurient appeal that made other forms of magic so attractive in romances or proscriptive literature. This, no doubt, explains why it did not find its way into literary and artistic representations of magic practice, which are concerned almost entirely with demon conjuring. Representations of necromancers provided a colorful and dramatic context for discussing human foibles, hell, the devil, demons, and the immanence of evil. From the perspective of literature, the *Ars notoria* is essentially invisible. Finally, modern historians of science, such as Thorndike, have focused their attention on more classic topics, such as occult properties and the extensive related literature in natural philosophy, leading to an emphasis on such magic traditions as books of secrets and astrological image magic.

The relatively large number of witnesses may also be explained by the fact that they survived at a higher rate than other forms of ritual magic, making them appear more prominent relative to other forms of magic than they actually were. Like short necromantic experiments, short versions of the art commonly survived because they were written on a spare folio of a larger collection. Such is the case in a number of examples in this survey.[19] Among the volumes dedicated solely to magic practice, it seems likely that larger manuscripts of the *Ars notoria* had a higher chance of surviving than similarly large necromantic volumes. In part, this has to do with their generally higher quality as manuscripts (i.e., quality of materials, production, etc.). Survival would also have been made more likely by the relatively innocuous nature of the art. The operations involve angels, not demons, and they seek no transitive effects but only effects upon the operator. Their frequently beautiful and moving prayers also belie the more instrumental features of the texts, so that they were sometimes included in prayer formularies, discussed more fully below. This is not the case with necromantic experiments, which are easily identifiable by the presence of magic circles or other figures and by initial phrases such as "Coniuro vos spiritus maligni." The relative harmlessness of the art would also have made it less worrisome to cataloguers, hence the large number of medieval notices. For a wide variety of reasons, then, the *Ars notoria* stood a better chance of being recorded in a catalogue, or of surviving in manuscript, than a necromantic collection. It follows that we cannot assume that the larger number of survivals indicates that this practice was overwhelmingly more popular than any other form of ritual magic. At the same time, fifty manuscripts of any text, particularly one that still stood a good chance of being destroyed as an illicit text, constitute a significant presence in the medieval library, so the importance of the *Ars notoria* cannot be questioned.

In summary, the *Ars notoria* was evidently popular in the learned world of the later Middle Ages. Its fusion of learned and spiritual goals, of the practices of university learning and highly ritualized contemplative exercises, no doubt appealed to the sensibilities, self-conceptions, and desires of those in the orbit of the university. These features, as well as its foundation in biblical precedent and its relatively innocuous goals, meant that it did not attract the same level of negative attention that necromancy did. Instead, it had the quality of a stealth weapon, making it invisible in literary sources, enabling its manuscripts to survive at a higher rate, and ultimately helping it escape the attention of modern scholars.

Manuscripts of the *Ars notoria*

It appears that the original text or texts have Hebraic roots and connect themselves with Solomon.[20] It was the Solomonic version that first occupied John of Morigny, and it was in relation to this text that he composed the *Liber visionum*. A number of abbreviated, adapted, or entirely new versions also exist, most of them from the sixteenth century. These are treated in Part III of this study. Among medieval witnesses, some, like Sloane 3008 and the version found in Sloane 513, the collection of the monk Richard Dove,[21] are quite short, running to only a folio in length. In general terms, like the longer versions of the art, these concern the acquisition of knowledge or intellectual capacities such as memory. Like other works of ritual magic, they tend to be freely adapted or modified and often bear little direct relation to the original. Although generally considered separately, the *Sworn Book of Honorius* may also be considered a part of this textual tradition, as it contains material pillaged from the *Ars notoria* and pursues similar spiritual and revelatory ends.

Among British manuscripts, these shorter versions tend to travel in company similar to that of image magic: astrology, alchemy, natural philosophy, mathematics, and in the case of the collection of Richard Dove, monk at Buckfast, physiognomy and chiromancy. At the same time, the art rarely travels with works of necromancy prior to 1500.[22] Yet there is comparatively little astrological content in any of the collections I have described here, from which it might be inferred that the scribes did not associate the art with ideas about natural magic, as they did in the case of works of image magic. Certainly the Magister Speculi's criterion that the images used must be of an astrological variety could not be used to justify the use of *notae*. Given that al-Kindī's theories were developed principally to justify the effectiveness of magical incantations, in particular words putatively derived from pristine languages, they might be regarded as applicable here. The *verba ignota* of the *Ars notoria* were certainly understood as inherently powerful, but they were also clearly understood to be prayers, and thus quite different from al-Kindī's words of power, which could achieve an instantaneous and automatic effect. While it is not impossible that these texts were conceived of in terms similar to those of image magic, this seems unlikely. In addition, when the Solomonic *Ars notoria* advises that the astrological features are not absolutely essential, it makes clear that astrological preparations merely support the ritual and contemplative exercises, and this makes them qualitatively quite different from works of astrological image magic. A more credible interpretation of the evidence is that these versions of the *Ars notoria* interested a group of people similar to those who were attracted to image magic. For example, the *Ars brevis* that appears in Sloane 513 may have been collected as part of a larger interest in divination. It is also possible in the case of small versions not appearing with other magic texts that their small size allowed them to be included as a novelty.

Whatever may have motivated the scribes to collect them in the first place, the shorter versions of the art have survived for reasons that relate to the codices that contained them, not to the texts themselves. Among British manuscripts, two of these shorter versions survive, Sloane 513 and 3008, along with only one longer version that can be connected with a medieval British collector, Bodley 951. This strongly suggests that the smaller versions are overrepresented in this sample, owing to higher survival rates. The most convincing evidence, however, may be found in medieval catalogues. The three, perhaps four, references to manuscripts of the *Ars notoria* in medieval British catalogues all appear to refer to the longer sort, and none of these versions survive.[23] Thus the longer versions were probably much more numerous than the current survivals reveal.

The transmission of these works was also not neutral, and, as with other forms of ritual magic, the textual tradition is somewhat chaotic. The art grew from a single text; two major traditions of the longer version are represented in medieval books, and a host of other versions have emerged in their wake. Among the versions in British sources from before 1500, both Sloane 513 and Sloane 3008 are radically shortened and modified versions of the art. British manuscripts of the sixteenth century attest to what was probably an earlier tradition of rewriting in this genre. They include texts such as *De arte crucifixi* and *Ars memorativa*.[24] Finally, volume 767 in the catalogue of St. Augustine's Abbey at Canterbury contained a section identified as prayers extracted from the *Ars notoria* (*Bartholomei de Rippa Romea oraciones extracte de arte notoria*). Turning to the continent, where John completed his reworking of this tradition, we find similar projects. A fifteenth-century German manuscript contains a necromantic version in which, rather than entreating the divine for angelic assistance, the operator acquires knowledge through conjuring demons.[25] Several versions of the *Liber visionum* were also adapted to other purposes.[26] So John of Morigny's impulse to rewrite, extract, or reconfigure the art was acted on frequently by other writers.

The most dramatic surviving example of a Solomonic *Ars notoria* in circulation in late medieval Britain is Bodley 951, a fifteenth-century large-folio manuscript running to twenty-one folios. The text is not complete. The first quire contains the beginning of the text in a two-column format with a formal framing gloss. The size of the document and the gloss give it an impressive, authoritative, and sophisticated appearance, especially in contrast to the small, scrawled necromantic collections of the period. The gloss is a legitimate one, with *lemmata* preceding commentary on the text. A catchword at the end of the first quire does not match up with the following page, suggesting at least one lost quire. "Notes" for all seven liberal arts, philosophy, and theology may be found in the following gatherings. Paleographic elements suggest that the manuscript may be Germanic in origin. The dramatic size of the manuscript is matched by the fabulously complex figures in the second half. These are executed in color and frequently fill the entire large folio pages. The notes are perhaps superficially similar to necromantic figures of the kind used in conjuring, but unlike necromantic figures they take the form of a formalized presentation of a prayer. The notes are also considerably more complex and require a high level of skill to execute. In one instance, a prayer is written in a thin line of text that spirals outward from the center of a circle to span a diameter of more than twelve inches (fol. 9r). In other cases, the prayers are written in complex, connected globes resembling cabbalist trees. Considerable time, effort, and attention were required to design the pages and to match the prayers to the size of the various shapes that were to contain them.

While this manuscript is singular in its size and complexity, there is another lengthy version of the *Ars notoria*, Sloane 1712, which is also continental in origin and accompanied by complex color images. Michael Camille has analyzed the illustrations in two similar volumes, Turin, Biblioteca nazionale, E. V. 13 and BnF lat. 9336.[27] Bodley 951 is now a solitary traveler and, given its size, probably always has been. Sloane 1712, which contains two works on the art, is also now unaccompanied by other texts, although there is no indication that it was always thus. What is clear from all of these manuscripts is that a great deal of time, effort, and possibly money was devoted to their production, an indication that they were taken very seriously. It is interesting to observe that one of the grounds cited for the condemnation of John of Morigny was his excessive concern with the production of the book and the potential cost of such a production.[28] Certainly, few manuscripts of magic texts I have examined, other than those of the *Ars notoria*, took as much time and care to produce.

John of Morigny evidently was acquainted with a deluxe volume, and Thomas Aquinas probably had access to one as well.[29] So this relatively higher level of manuscript quality is apparently not only a common feature of the manuscripts of this genre but a particularly important one. The requirement that the figures be used for contemplative purposes might promote such a presentation. A monastic setting might have furnished the resources for the production of this kind of manuscript, and the monastic tendency to associate scribal activities with devotion probably provided additional impetus. The appearance of the text was clearly regarded as an important feature of its numinous properties. The visual power of such a manuscript is also considerable, if only because of its impressive size. Finally, the sense of danger in owning such a self-consciously executed volume, whose contents would be relatively easily identifiable, might imbue the work with a negative aura of power as well. That all of these features associated the volume with the numinous was no doubt the scribes' intention.

The *Ars notoria* and the Monks at St. Augustine's Abbey at Canterbury

A fifteenth-century hand in Oxford, Bodleian Library, Bodley 951, says simply "Maideston." For a variety of reasons, it seems likely that the owner was Simon Maidstone, a monk of the Abbey of St. Augustine at Canterbury whom we encountered in chapter 2. We know that Maidstone was a book collector because of the numerous books listed as once his in the medieval catalogue, although none betrays any interest in magic. One of these books contained Maidstone's copy of a gloss on Paul's Epistle, a *Summa* from his own pen, together with what is probably a pastoral work, *Aurea biblia, Repertorium biblicum,* or *Figurarum biblie* by Anton Rampigollis.[30] The argument that Maidstone was the owner of this volume is supported not so much by his own collection as by the occurrence of the *Ars notoria* among the collections of two other monks of the same abbey. At least two versions of this text also appear in the collections of John of London and Michael Northgate. All of this suggests that the transmission and perhaps even the use of this text was supported by a scholarly community of monks. While one might be tempted to assume that the contemplative and mystical features of the text would have appealed strongly to such collectors, and while the bulk of the evidence supports such an assumption, some ambiguities remain.

As we have seen, both John of London and Michael Northgate collected standard texts of image magic as well, and this raises the question whether the same interests that drove the collection of image magic also drove the collection of the *Ars notoria*. The transmission of image magic was very heavily informed by tentative suggestions about its potential legitimacy and by theories of celestial influence that supported them. Astrological elements in the *Ars notoria* form only minor parts of the procedures, and certainly no major theologian or philosopher had suggested that its practices might be legitimate. The complex figures, lengthy and incomprehensible prayers, and very extensive ritual activities would make it impossible to justify according to the Magister Speculi's astrological criteria. At the same time, some of the volumes containing the work, such as this one owned by John of London, suggest an overlap:

de miraculis beate marie virginis [Miracles of the Blessed Virgin Mary]
Item quedam extrauagancia de papis [Compilation of papal decrees]
Item de sermonibus quedam [Sermons]
Item ars notoria Salomonis [Solomonic *Ars notoria*]
Item liber de anulo Salomonis [Ring of Solomon]
Item tractatus de lepra et cura eius [Lepers and Their Cure]
Item Ciromancia in Gallico secundum iij translationes cum omnibus caracteribus et varietatibus figuratorum pictis [Chiromancy in French][31]

In this volume we find both the *De anulo Salomonis* and works on medicine and divination, topics that commonly appear in collections containing image magic. The treatise on rings was possibly one that the Magister Speculi regarded as belonging to the less detestable of the two varieties of image magic. However, surviving manuscripts of works by this title take the form of astrological image magic in some manuscripts but explicit necromancy in others.[32] Given that the necromantic version appears in a much later manuscript, it may well be that the Magister Speculi was referring to the astrological version. This in turn could suggest that the scribe saw some commonality between the magic of astrological images and that of the *Ars notoria*. The following two texts, a medical work on lepers and a work on chiromancy, suggest the broader interests in *naturalia* characteristic of image magic collections. At the same time, like Erghome's volumes of superstitious works, this volume falls into two obvious parts, bridged by the *Ars notoria*. The first part of the volume is taken up with texts that give quite a different picture of the scribe's or collector's interests. The collection of sermons strongly suggests that the collector had an active religious vocation involving preaching. The miracles of the Virgin may have been used as a supplementary text for preaching or perhaps served the devotional interests of the scribe. The third text, a compilation of papal decrees, suggests broader religious concerns. Similar patterns of collection that combine devotional works, works of *pastoralia*, and the *Ars notoria* may also be found in the continental manuscripts.[33] In other words, the scribe may well have collected the art in the presence of devotional interests. In the final analysis it is not clear. The same cannot be said of our next example.

Michael Northgate, as we have seen, was the owner of Oxford, Corpus Christi, 221, a volume that I have argued may indicate a link between pastoral interests and magical images. For the most part, his collection reflects the usual combination of image magic with scientific and medical topics. The Library of St. Augustine's catalogue also records Codex 767 as once his, which includes prayers extracted from an *Ars notoria*:

Liber catholice fidei editus a beato Augustino anglorum apostolo qui vocatur Manuale et in eodem libro [A book on the Catholic faith, Pseudo-Augustine][34]
Stimulus amoris [A devotional work by James of Milan or Walter Hilton][35]
Angeli[s]ca [ieromancie] ierarchie [Brackets indicate James's editorial exclusions. Possibly Pseudo-Dionysius, *Celestial Hierarchy*][36]
Barth[i] de Rippa Romea Oraciones extracte de arte notoria [Prayers extracted from the *Ars notoria*]
Oratio ad spm scm et incipit *veni creator* [Prayer to the Holy Spirit]
Memoria passionis dominice [Remembrance of the Lord's Passion]
Oratio missa a beata Maria sancto mauricio parisien' episcopo [Prayer to Mary, possibly by Maurice of Sully, 1120–1196][37]
Oratio ad sanctam appolloniam pro dolore dencium [Prayer to Saint Apollonia for toothache]
Orationes spirituales [Prayers]
Confessio generalis [General confession]
Quod homo debet preparare se ad recipiendem corpus x[i] et [That people ought to prepare for receiving the body of Christ]
liber de confessione nouiciorum [Concerning the confession of novices][38]

One need not analyze this codex in detail to recognize its generally devotional nature. It includes a variety of devotional and religious works in addition to prayers and a prayer compilation. This sort of context for the *Ars notoria* is consistent with continental examples and strongly suggests that the text was regarded as bearing some relation to religious or devotional material.[39]

Before examining this relationship in more detail, we must first consider the possibility that the text was simply hidden in this codex because it was an unlikely spot in which to find a magic text, rather like a flask of brandy hidden in a false book. Several facts make this unlikely. First, the simple fact that the work was catalogued indicates that the monk who owned the book was not squeamish about its contents, for he allowed it to pass into the monastery's library. If we assume a scenario in which the monk *was* squeamish about it but the transfer somehow occurred anyway—say, he died suddenly—the cataloguer evidently had no overwhelming concerns about recording it and allowing the work to pass into the library intact. Second, the simple fact that the cataloguer was able to identify the source of the prayers and the name of the extractor indicates that this section of the manuscript began with a clear title. Had the scribe or owner wished to disguise it, he could simply have left out or expunged these identifying marks. Finally, the numerous similar examples would demand that we assume a rather unlikely scenario: that a large number of scribes chose to "hide" their copies of the art in the same kind of book while forgetting to expunge the title. It seems far more likely that these volumes indicate either a general set of interests of which the *Ars notoria* was a part or a more purposeful juxtaposing of works that the scribes regarded as related.

That the prayers are extracted could indicate that the original magical purposes of the text were no longer present. For the most part, the prayers of the Solomonic *Ars notoria* are very orthodox in appearance. In fact, if one were to encounter them independent of their original magical context, they would be indistinguishable from any other Christian prayer. For example, Sloane 3853 contains prayers extracted from the Solomonic version of the text, one of which ends as follows:

> And you, who are my God, who, in the beginning, created the heavens, the earth, and everything from nothing, who formed everything in your spirit, fulfill, restore, and heal my soul, that I might glorify you through every work of my thoughts and words. God, Father, confirm my prayer and augment my intellect and my memory to undertake your blessed vision with my little living body and to perceive your more than lofty and eternal essence, you who live and reign forever.[40]

A prayer of this flavor, as a conventional cobbling together of commonly used liturgical phrasings, would be quite at home in Northgate's codex. It highlights the combination of spiritual and intellectual goals characteristic of the *Ars notoria* and, since it is framed as a request, could hardly be considered problematic. Even highly instrumental prayers were a common part of late medieval piety. We need only recall the biblical precedent of Solomon praying for wisdom. Yet Sloane 3853 also contains prayers written in *verba ignota*, making it easily identifiable as a version of the *Ars notoria* and a magic work. We cannot know if these more dubious prayers appeared in Northgate's volume. Even if no prayers in unknown languages were found in that volume, the catalogue openly cites the source of the prayers as an *Ars notoria*. It is unlikely that they appear here simply because they were nice prayers.

A number of features of this collection suggest more involved interest in magic. A general confession was an integral part of most forms of ritual magic because one could succeed only in a state of spiritual purity.[41] The presence of the work on confession for novices makes this interpretation less likely, although it could have been included in the codex in the same gathering as the general confession. The prayer for a toothache similarly suggests a collection with more instrumental purposes than an ordinary devotional collection, although charms for toothache are very common indeed. Finally, the name Bartholomeus de Ripa Romea is often associated with magic topics. A collection of works on magical stones and images that is usually attributed to Albertus Magnus appears in Wellcome 110 under his name, and he is cited in the sixteenth century on this topic.[42]

The apparent presence of the *Celestial Hierarchy* of Pseudo-Dionysius in the same codex argues much more powerfully that it was concerned with the instrumental features of angelic magic or devotion. The first three chapters of this work concern human and heavenly hierarchies. In particular, the work deals with enlightenment, which is passed down from God through the spiritual hierarchy in order to uplift all to the imitation of God.[43] A particularly interesting facet of this work is its recommendation of the use of apparently incongruous images as the most appropriate means to begin contemplation of the divine.[44] The parallels between these ideas and the angels of the *Ars notoria* who communicate heavenly gifts following meditative exercises are obvious. Even Pseudo-Dionysius's discussion of images could be seen as bearing upon the *notae*, so it does not appear coincidental that they occur side by side in this volume. If the unedited title given in the catalogue, "Angelisca ieromancie," does not refer to the work by Pseudo-Dionysius, then the word *ieromancie*, or *heiromancy*, strongly suggests the "theurgic" practices of the *Ars notoria*, the whole perhaps meaning something like divination involving angels through divine practice, priestly operations, or perhaps sacrifice. In that case, we may have here the record of two works of the art.

Another work, the *Stimulus amoris* by the Franciscan James of Milan, also suggests that a coherent set of interests drove the collection of works in this volume. Nicholas Watson has compared the meditative exercises of this work to the *cogitationes* that John of Morigny prescribes in the *Liber visionum* in place of the *notae*.[45] John advises the reader to meditate upon these *cogitationes* in much the same way that the original text requires meditations on the *notae*.[46] The commonalities in technique suggest that this copy of the art was collected by someone with an interest in seeking spiritual gifts or meditative states through the more conventional practices of affective piety. The volume could even conceivably represent a project similar to John of Morigny's, in which the *notae* were stripped out and replaced by *cogitationes*. As the *Ars notoria* was relatively well-known, it is unlikely that the text was copied in ignorance of the contents of the complete work. So the volume evinces some considerable coherence in subject matter.

The compiler's interest in the *Ars notoria* appears to have been woven together with affective mystical piety and situated in the presence of considerable devotional interests. In fact, Michael Northgate may well have regarded his interest, or his active involvement if he had any, as defensibly orthodox. As we saw in chapter 2, Northgate had collected enough volumes, including works on image magic, that the presence of a version of the art in his collection cannot be interpreted as coincidental. It is entirely feasible that he was responsible for compiling it, and while the codex cannot be used to demonstrate that Northgate was practicing the art, it definitely suggests that he had a serious interest in the topic. The presence of a classic work dealing with angelic mediation between God and humanity, and another involving meditative techniques of the kind employed in the *Ars notoria*, does not seem coincidental. As a whole, the collection gives the impression of a careful and engaged examination of the text under the rubric of affective piety and mysticism, or at least the assumption that the *Ars notoria* belonged in the company of such works.

The *Liber Iuratus Honorii* or *Sworn Book of Honorius*

Like the *Ars notoria*, the *Sworn Book of Honorius* passed through a complicated set of redactions, emendations, reorganizations, and rewritings. Two surviving traditions testify to an earlier base text, probably originating in Spain in the early fourteenth or even late thirteenth century. Berengario

Ganell drew heavily upon it when he wrote his *Summa sacre magice* in the fourteenth century, an early attempt to systematize a wide variety of magic literature circulating in Spain at that time.[47] A second tradition of texts, which extracted, reordered, and supplemented portions of the original text, survives solely in manuscripts of British origin.[48] Given that this study begins with British manuscripts, our examination will focus upon the latter of these two traditions, the "London Honorius." Although less successful as a coherent compendium of magic, the London Honorius reveals the difficulties inherent in the transmission process and the creative responses of its transmitters. More important, its author evinces an awareness of the knot of problems I have referred to as Brother John's dilemma.

After a brief prologue and table of contents, the volume begins with detailed instructions for the performance of two magical ceremonies. The first concerns the construction of a sigil of God (*sigillum Dei*) and a set of rituals that seek nothing less than a vision of God. This operation for the *visio Dei* is remarkably complex and takes up the bulk of the text. It advises that a potential operator must be governed by some general rules of conduct. He must keep his clothing clean, live in an upright manner, and avoid women and wicked people. As with the Solomonic *Ars notoria*, he must begin with an operation that seeks divine permission to proceed with the rest of the ritual. This involves a regimen of fasting, confession, penance, and a repeated cycle of prayers spread over three days and culminating on a Sunday, at which time an angel will appear in his dreams and indicate whether he may go on or not. A slightly modified regime, involving almsgiving and prayers for mercy, follows for those deemed unworthy but still seeking permission.

For one who succeeds and may move on, the first stage of the operation takes thirty-two days. It begins with a cycle of nine prayers at matins, tierce, nones, and vespers on the fourth day after a new moon and every four days afterward through the thirty-second day. A second cycle of three prayers (often repeated as many as three times each) must be said on the first day of the new moon, the third day, and every third day after that through the fifteenth day, once again at specific hours throughout the day. A special regime of prayer is designated for the eighteenth day, and a different set of prayers is to be recited on any days not taken up with the rituals so far described. Following this, a twenty-day ritual begins during which the operator should say a series of prayers at all hours except prime. In addition, he must go to Mass each morning saying a series of nine prayers. A priest must be engaged to sing matins, prime, and tierce and to say the Mass of the Holy Spirit, inserting numerous prayers from the *Sworn Book* into the liturgy. During communion, the priest should also pray for the operator's success. The final period then begins, again covering twenty days. First, during a twelve-day fast on bread and water, he must continue with the preceding regime. Special operations must then take place on the thirteenth day, which must be a Thursday, after which the operator should go into isolation. An intensive regime of prayers and the recitation of divine names follows and continues day and night until the following Thursday. On the final Thursday, the operator must say the same cycle of prayers and then prepare his room. A bed of straw must be surrounded by ashes in which he must write the hundred names of God. He must then bathe, praying while he does so, and don a hair shirt and black clothing. Following more prayers, the recitation of divine names, and a concluding prayer, he must observe complete silence until he goes to sleep. In his dreams he will behold the "celestial palace," the majesty of God, the orders of angels, and souls of the blessed.

The second portion of the text turns to the invocation of spirits of the planets, air, and earth and seems like a strange turn away from the mystical orientation of the first. However, there is considerable continuity between them. These operations are built upon and slightly modify the prayers and rituals already described, and they employ the sigil of God described in an earlier chapter. They give more evidence for the fluidity between "theurgic" and "necromantic" magic that we have seen in the story of John. Because they are built from the same elements (prayers, purifications, going to Mass, etc.), the preparatory rituals are practically identical, if somewhat shorter than what we have already seen. The final portions, however, differ substantially in location, equipment, and rite. Special conjuring sites must be made. The circle for spirits of the air, for example, must be constructed on level ground that has been cleared of any debris and consecrated. It must include three concentric circles, the largest being nine feet across. Within these, various angel and divine names must be written, and in the center a heptagon must be inscribed. On the second day, the operator must attend all seven canonical hours before returning to the circle, where he erases seven divine names and suffumigates the circle with a censer. He makes a first call to spirits of the wind, restores the divine names, and prays. If he is successful, he should notice stillness and clouds around the circles. The following day after church he must return, carrying a variety of equipment, including a hazel wand, seven swords, a specially constructed whistle, a censer and incense, a candle of virgin wax, the seals of god and of the planetary spirits, and wine. Associates may be needed to carry the equipment and should have stools to sit on so as to avoid wiping out portions of the circle.

A complex operation then follows, involving further prayers and calls. Enclosed in the circles and surrounded by swords stuck into the ground at certain points of the compass, the operator performs a ritual suffumigation while reciting prayers and holding the seals. He then conducts nine more suffumigations while he invokes the spirits and strikes the swords with his wand. Following another prayer, he must again invoke the spirits and then walk around the circle striking the swords and saying further invocations. Further prayers must then be said at each point of the compass, and he must finally call the spirits, standing in the center of the circle and holding the seal of God. At this point the spirits may attempt to frighten his associates out of the circle or lure them with attractive visions. At his command and by virtue of the seal, the spirits will stop their trickery and will ultimately appear in unfrightening form to perform the tasks he sets them. The operation for planetary spirits is slightly less complicated and involves a stone circle with a circular mound in the middle. The operation for spirits of the earth is similar and involves a concave circle dug into the earth. While these operations with spirits make the *Sworn Book* qualitatively different from the *Ars notoria*, they are similar to that work, and inextricable from the operation for the vision of God, in their use of common ritual elements.

The instructions for achieving the *visio Dei* take up two-thirds of the text and were clearly regarded by the redactor of the London Honorius as a crucial element. In fact, internal evidence suggests that the ritual was intentionally shifted to the beginning from its original location, disrupting the logic of the text.[49] This emphasis on experience of the divine and on the religious nature of the exercises infuses the whole section. The ritual elements of fasting, prayer, confession, contrition, attendance at Mass, and giving alms all draw upon conventional Christian devotional practice. The operator follows a program structured largely around the canonical hours and including the Mass and the cooperation of a priest. These aspects, taken together with the necessity that the operator be a Christian (and even a chapter that details exactly what orthodoxy is),[50] suggest that the authors did not see this as alternative to conventional practice but rather as flowing logically out of it and even as dependent upon it. Astrological elements are present, particularly in the second portion of the text, but they are swallowed up in an overwhelming sea of Christian rites. Rather than use planetary times, the text divides the day by the canonical hours. Even the use of lunar months (although singled out by the Magister Speculi as problematic elements in image magic texts) could well have been understood as liturgical owing to their use in the church calendar. Finally, like the *Ars notoria*, the *Sworn Book* may often appear to regard the mechanisms upon which it depends as automatic, but at the same time it maintains that none of them will work without divine permission. So, arguably, they do not represent a limitation on divine freedom.

The explicit focus on the operator and his interior state that characterizes ritual magic (as opposed to simple gestures, materials, or ambient conditions) is reflected here in the requirements of physical purity, pure spiritual condition, and an assessment of "worthiness" by the divine. In addition, the practices of ritual magic explicitly require an attitude of attentiveness. They require not only that the operator be Christian but that he engage in the reflections necessary for confession and contrition and be attentive to his moral condition. Many of the preparations also powerfully engage his senses, something that probably helped to provoke subjectively convincing experiences. He must bathe in cold, clear water, wear clean clothes or a hair shirt, and engage in circuits of fasting followed by eating regularly and drinking wine. He must also attend to his senses. His dreams are crucial channels of communication with the divine; he must look for signs during the ritual processes, such as stillness, clouds, or signs of spiritual presence. All of this ritual was no doubt compounded by the fact that such exercises and their goals attracted those already fascinated with the idea of experiencing the numinous directly—people like John of Morigny. And finally, such a wearying program of prayer, ritual, and fasting could certainly render the operator suggestible and achieve some dramatic and subjectively convincing results. As in the case of the *Ars notoria* and late medieval affective piety in general, the rituals of the *Sworn Book* engage the senses and sensual imagination in ways that in all likelihood had a significant impact on the psychological state of the magician. Whether they actually might involve the divine is a matter for the theologians.[51]

The London Honorius also reveals significant features of the transmission and transformations of magic. Some of the changes it underwent resulted from a lack of crucial knowledge by the editor or from struggles with a fragmentary source. Certain elements make clear that its roots lie at least in part in Jewish traditions of magic. While the original text was probably a good deal more sophisticated in its knowledge of Jewish traditions (for example, in its treatment of the Shemhamphoras), the author of the London Honorius lacked the requisite knowledge to transmit this material intelligently, which resulted in a number of ham-fisted textual errors.[52] Evidence also suggests that the editor of the London Honorius struggled with fragmentary sources and that this may lie behind some of its more confusing features. As Veenstra has demonstrated, what is presented there as a table of contents (but bears little relation to the operations that follow) actually derives from another portion of the original text and was a kind of grocery list of potential applications to which the *sigillum Dei* could be put. If this list occurred on a loose folio, the mistake might be understandable.[53] It might also be that the editor knew that his text was fragmentary and was doing his best through this reorganization to suggest what originally had been part of it. Perhaps the most dramatic alteration to the text is the replacement of the original series of prayers with prayers from the *Ars notoria*.[54] Once again this appears to have been the result of a fragmentary original that lacked the discrete section devoted to prayers.

While we might be inclined to regard all the changes as deriving from ignorance or fragmentary manuscripts, many of them reflect a genuine desire to change the text, most significantly the relocation of the operation for the *visio Dei* to the beginning of the book. While this could conceivably have been the result of a disordered original, it seems just as likely that it was an intentional change of emphasis. The editor includes a brief discussion of the theological legitimacy of the idea of the "beatific vision," making it clear that this was a matter of some concern to him. One way or another, the result was that the explicit connection between the vision and the preparation of the *sigillum Dei* was lost, making the work somewhat harder to understand.[55] For some reason, the London Honorius redactor also reduced the evidentiary requirements of some of the rituals by not demanding thunderbolts and earthquakes as marks that the ceremony might progress. One wonders if the editor was attempting to increase the text's chances of success, thunder and earthquakes being much harder to imagine than stillness, the approach of spirits, or the appearance of clouds. The London Honorius redactor also made particular efforts to differentiate his operations from those of the Jews, whereas Ganell (living in Iberia) understandably concerned himself with their differences from Islamic magic.[56] That Ganell's text is itself a significant reworking of the original that incorporates material from several other texts also makes clear that the impulse to transform the texts, based on an editor's knowledge, circumstances, or sensibilities, was common.

Although it is perhaps already clear, it is worth emphasizing that such transformations and adaptations would have been encouraged by the text itself. No critical reader could have regarded the London Honorius as anything but fragmentary. The table of contents has little correspondence to operations found in the book, and the relationship of the *sigillum Dei* to the operation is not entirely clear. A reader familiar with Jewish traditions might have been aware of the text's failings on this point. In response to these inadequacies, one would have to engage in some creative reinvention in order to use the text or understand what it was originally all about, and, as we shall see, subsequent scribes did have to do this. The text also encourages adaptation by itself adapting prayers or rituals to various purposes. As in the *Ars notoria*, many prayers or rituals are used for multiple purposes, changed only by the replacement of a few key phrases. As we shall see, these sorts of adaptations were common in necromantic manuals, where conventional liturgical forms were altered slightly to suit magical purposes. And since the text was so emphatic about its revelatory potential, it should come as no surprise that a reader might turn to visionary experiences to supplement or correct the inadequacies of the text, as John of Morigny did with the *Ars notoria*.

In light of these facts, the prologue of the text is quite remarkable. The London Honorius begins with a myth about its own origin that pits humans, and in particular a brotherhood of magicians, against the assaults of demons. It describes how demons deluded the high churchmen into believing that they should persecute the magicians. It then quotes a forged but reasonably credible papal letter, which condemns the arts of magic and orders the church to root them out. Having been forewarned by God of the great persecutions to come, the masters of magic—described as having a host of spirits under their command—decide to compile their art into a single book rather than destroy their enemies. A council of eighty-nine masters is called, and Honorius of Thebes is chosen to work for them. With the counsel of the angel Hocroel, Honorius excerpts knowledge from magic books, retaining the "flowers" for the magicians and leaving the "husks"' for others.[57] Then, still under angelic guidance, he distills the *Sworn Book* from these. The church authorities then satisfy themselves with burning trifles (by implication the husks), while this volume survives, the core of a sacred and divinely sanctioned magic. The prologue ends with rules for transmitting the text, to which any owner of the volume must swear compliance. Only three copies can be made at a time, and they cannot be given to a woman or a minor but only to a godly man who has been tested for one year. The practitioners must not reveal their secrets, even at the cost of their own lives, and must aid one another in the spirit of love and brotherhood. Finally, should the "master" be unable to pass the work on to a suitable disciple, the work must be buried with him. The owner of the manuscript is to swear to uphold these regulations in order to get a copy, and this is the basis for one of its titles, the *Liber iuratus*, or *Sworn Book*.

We find here many of the same elements found in the story of Brother John's dilemma, and they eerily echo the realities of the text's history. The author of the London Honorius speaks plainly about its unorthodox status and the increasing chorus of antimagic voices in the institutional church in the early fourteenth century. In response to church pressure, the author emphasizes the book's holy origins—not, curiously, by employing the myth that the text was transmitted fully formed to humans but claiming instead that Honorius composed it through a complicated mix of editing and divine consultation. The texts he confronted, if not corrupt, were full of extraneous materials. One might expect that Honorius, as the greatest living magus, would be entirely in command of his art, and he may well have been. Yet in order to sort through his source texts and epitomize them, he employed angelic guidance, and it appears from the story that this was regarded as the appropriate approach. Precisely what the author meant to imply when he says that Honorius left "husks" for others is not clear. It may be that he wished to imply that Honorius intentionally left behind corrupt, false, or partial works to confuse the ignorant and satisfy those who burned them. One way or another, the prologue makes clear that the library of magic texts was full of these kinds of works both before and after Honorius's efforts. Given that the author evidently *did* confront a partial text and had to collect materials from different sources, it seems reasonable to suggest that the prologue contains at least a grain of autobiographical truth and reflects the struggles of the redactor himself. Whether he truly felt that he had received divine guidance in creating his new book, or whether the prologue is merely an expression of wish fulfillment by someone in a cloud of uncertainty, makes very little difference. His message was that magic texts were not in themselves sufficient conduits of reliable knowledge, in part because they had been corrupted, and that divine guidance was necessary to decode or purify them.

The prologue also reflects significant concern over how the text should be transmitted, and this reveals further aspects of Brother John's dilemma. A brotherhood of disciples led by a master safeguards the text, bound by an oath to abide by the rules governing its transmission. Predictably, they must maintain a high level of moral purity, but, more important, they must also swear not to make the book available to the ignorant and to make no more than three copies. In order to pass the text on, the master must evaluate the potential recipient, the implication being that only a master should ever have possession of the book. This restriction emphasizes two important features of magic texts. First, they were vulnerable to corruption by the ignorant and/or immoral, although it is not clear whether corruption meant alteration, misuse, or merely misinterpretation. Second, the way to safeguard these texts was to ensure that the master's experience, knowledge, and code of behavior were passed on to the disciples. The culture of secrecy thus involved a negative aspect, in which access to the text was limited, but also a positive one. The recipient had to be of good character, and the transmission had to be accompanied by the passing on of experience from master to disciple. Again, it is tempting to see these ideas as expressions of the author's desire for guidance in his struggle to create a workable magic text from incomplete fragments and mysterious Jewish elements. At the very least, it makes clear that he regarded the text in itself as an insufficient form of transmitting wisdom. The master's experience and wisdom were crucial elements in the survival of the truths the text contained.

The Manuscripts of the *Sworn Book*

We have already said a good deal about the transmission of the *Sworn Book*, but we will close with a brief examination of the manuscripts themselves. Two surviving witnesses date to before 1500, and we know of two additional versions once held in the library of John Erghome. Sloane 3854, fols. 112–139, dates to the early fourteenth century, and Sloane 313 to the second half of the fourteenth century. The latter volume contains only the *Sworn Book*; the former, although now bound with a large collection of other magic texts, is unrelated to those texts. Although it took place later, the collection of this text with other magic works is a common pattern. Both volumes of superstitious works owned by John Erghome include a copy. Another of the later witnesses, Sloane 3885, fols. 58–96, was bound with other magic works and was copied by the scribe of the preceding work (fols. 26r–57r), a work of necromantic magic known as the *Practica nigromancie*. A sixteenth-century English translation of the work, Royal 17.A.XLII, is also solitary. None is related to the matrix of interests commonly gathered around works of astrological image magic.

The evidence for scribal attitudes yielded by these volumes is not as rich as in the case of image magic or even the *Ars notoria*. That a significant number of these manuscripts are solitary travelers may well be due in part to the fact that they did not ally themselves comfortably with conventional wisdom. By self-consciously opposing themselves to the institutional church and declaring themselves unorthodox (at least in practice), they might well have guaranteed their codicological isolation. Such texts would be better preserved in discrete private volumes. For the same reason, other works of magic would make reasonable companions, given that they were similarly illicit. The general tendency for later scribes to collect the *Sworn Book* with works of ritual magic seems to be reflected in Erghome's volumes, where it was accompanied by a wide variety of such works. Given the shift to spirit conjuring in the second portion of the *Sworn Book*, it is not surprising that the text might ultimately be collected with necromancy.

The individual manuscripts yield few further details about how the texts were transmitted or the struggles the scribes and interpreters faced. Only Sloane 3854 is a complete version; all the others are fragmentary. So readers of these versions would have been faced with challenges in their use and interpretation in addition to those already discussed. The effort to use the text is reflected in the marginalia of Sloane 313, including cross-referencing, which Hedegård suggests seems to have been produced by an engaged user. This version also includes a variety of small additions to the text. Efforts to correct the text are also evident in the sixteenth-century English translation, which has been reorganized and supplemented by passages from Cornelius Agrippa's *De occulta philosophia*. So, although these versions were not subjected to the more substantial transformations of the London Honorius base text, textual instability and efforts to overcome the text's inadequacies continued to be a part of how it was transmitted.

Conclusion

Some of the manuscripts containing an *Ars notoria* contain works similar to those commonly collected with image magic. This is particularly the case with the shorter versions. Some of the collectors who were interested in image magic, in particular John of London and Michael Northgate, were also interested in the longer versions of the art. The occurrence of these longer versions in their collections was certainly not coincidental, nor does it seem likely that it was considered a novelty. Northgate's codices also illustrate how he or a previous compiler understood the work in ways different from image magic. The *Ars notoria* occupied a codex separate from those containing image magic texts. Northgate's codex, Corpus Christi 221, understood astrological image magic as a feature of the natural world. If my suggestion is correct, it had a place in his religious thinking as evidence of the wondrous nature of God's world and as an element in the pastoral project of Thomas of Cantimpré. On the other hand, Northgate collected the *Ars notoria* together with prayers, sermons, works of affective devotion and meditation, and the *Celestial Hierarchy* of Pseudo-Dionysius. The perspective involved in the examination and performance of image magic is that of the audience or analyst: one heard about it, reflected on how it could work, or watched the wondrous event occur. The perspective involved in the practice of the *Ars notoria*—as in the practice of affective devotion—was one of participation. The magical event occurred within or around oneself. One immersed oneself in the experience of the numinous.

Very much like image magic in relation to Scholastic thought, the *Ars notoria* and *Sworn Book* have an ambiguous relationship with conventional piety. Considerable evidence suggests that scribes and collectors believed what the *Ars notoria* itself claimed, that the art contributed to the religious life of the operator and was itself a form of religious devotion. Northgate's codices certainly provide evidence that he recognized its commonalities with devotional and mystical texts. We also have every reason to take at face value both the sincerity of John of Morigny's devotion and the desire for a powerful vision of the divine represented in the *Sworn Book*. At the same time, more dangerous elements lurk in the shadows of these texts. The prologue to the *Liber iuratus* makes the standard heretical argument that its adherents practice orthodox Christianity and that the apparently orthodox definitions of the institutional church were false. The necromancers are the holy protagonists, battling to survive the onslaught of demonically inspired persecution. From this perspective, the author and anyone who took the prologue seriously would have to be regarded as religious dissenters or heretics. The story of John of Morigny's sometime interest in necromancy and the approving evaluation of necromancy in the *Liber iuratus* suggest considerable fluidity between necromancy and theurgic magic. It is not so much that the theurgic material was any less serious about its religious focus. We may rather wish to follow Richard Kieckhefer's suggestion that we may distinguish these texts from more conventional mystical devotion by their overwhelming fascination with both the holy and the unholy, a fascination that drew upon the effects not only of wonder but also of fear.[58]

Central to this study is the treatment of the texts and manuscripts. The scribes of both the *Ars notoria* and the *Liber iuratus* reflect similar habits in their treatment and transmission of texts. In general, they show a willingness to rewrite, extract, or transform the texts. In this respect, John of Morigny's story illustrates many of the details common to the scribes of this literature. The *Ars notoria* was commonly transmitted through personal connections, and the *Sworn Book* regarded this as the ideal. It seems clear, however, that they were both also transmitted in a purely textual form and without a community that might pass on an understanding or interpretation of the texts. Both also reflect the textually unstable nature of the ritual magic tradition. Two principal versions of the Solomonic *Ars notoria* were subject to considerable elaboration over the years. If there is some consistency within these textual traditions, the *Liber visionum* and the other spin-off texts demonstrate the impulse to rewrite or reinvent. In a similar way, the *Sworn Book* is itself one of two redactions of an earlier text and appears to have been built from a fragmentary copy. In the process, the redactor included materials pillaged from the *Ars notoria*. Later scribes supplemented it and reorganized it as well. In both cases efforts to rewrite were in part driven by problems with the written word; either the manuscripts were fragmentary or the original text was not clear enough and needed to be supplemented.

Given their illicit status and complete lack of authoritative sanction, it is remarkable that the London Honorius and John of Morigny do not simply claim divine origins. Instead, both authors claim they had divine *assistance* in a complex editing process in which they picked out the flowers of truth from a library of texts polluted with problematic materials. The Blessed Virgin and

angels aided John in the composition of the *Liber visionum* and in his engagement with the *Ars notoria* and the necromantic traditions. Honorius wrote
the *Liber iuratus* with angelic guidance, sorting the wheat from the chaff as
he did so. Perhaps no other feature of this tradition suggests so strongly that
the transmission of these texts was surrounded by a culture that saw them
as problematic vehicles for divine truths and assumed that they needed to
be corrected or supplemented, either with divine guidance or through direct
experience of the divine. It certainly reflects the realities evident in surviving
manuscripts: practitioners consistently dealt with ambiguous and fragmentary texts.

The authors and many or most of the scribes were aware of the resulting
fluidity of texts, and they dealt with the problem by sanctifying features of the
book and its transmission. The striking appearance of *Ars notoria* manuscripts
suggested mysterious and divine origins, as it was no doubt designed to do.
If scribes of the *Liber iuratus* did not as consistently seek to lend authority to
their text with similar visual strategies, the text itself does so in more explicit
ways. It insists that it be transmitted by a sanctified brotherhood of wise men
who will preserve the book and its wisdom, and it provides complex rules
governing the text's transmission and copying to which they must swear. In a
similar fashion, John of Morigny enjoins his readers not to alter his book. In
another sense, these works present themselves as works that somehow transcend the problems inherent in other texts. The *Ars notoria* and *Liber visionum*
promise to render the operator learned by a direct process of infusion, without all the trouble of reading books, which are naturally less accurate reflections of divine truths than the Holy Spirit. The *Liber iuratus* offers its reader a
similar direct exposure to divine truths. Of course, if these works were driven
by a desire for solidity and systematization in a chaotic library, they ultimately
failed, because their abbreviated and reinvented remains contributed further
to the very confusion of flowers and husks from which they arose.

5

THE MAGIC OF DEMONS AND ANGELS

By the vertu of all the holy masses & goddys devyne seruyce &
prayeris said & song in euery holy place vniuersall.
—Rawlinson D. 252, fol. 148v

Necromancy is one of the more peculiar progeny spawned in the rich, turbid waters where Jewish, Greek, Arabic, and other ancient literature flowed together in twelfth- and thirteenth-century Latin Christendom. Its manuscript children often give the impression of Frankenstein's monster, stitched together from whatever varied and improbable parts came to hand. Yet despite the unlikely parentage and wild appearance of this tribe—or perhaps because of them—necromancy achieved a high level of notoriety in the Latin West and survives in one form or another to the present day.[1] Like the theurgic magic we have just examined—but unlike Arabic image magic—necromancy was a very Christian art. Despite its instrumental, self-centered, and even puerile goals, its practitioners were deeply concerned with creating or performing rituals of an explicitly Christian nature. Unlike scribes of image magic, who tended to copy their texts in much the same way that they would a work on natural philosophy, scribes of ritual magic tended to transform the ritual content of their non-Christian sources into an explicitly Christian form, making them much less transparent witnesses to earlier traditions. As we shall see, the sometimes unsophisticated nature of these transformations could result in odd combinations of practices, poised somewhere between seemingly incompatible traditions. In most cases, for all intents and purposes, the works were original creations of Christian authors whose impulse to transform their source texts lay not only in a desire to "plunder the Egyptian treasure" for Christian use but in an intellectual culture that was highly individualistic, emphasized individual experience, and valorized transformations of texts on the basis of personal experience or divine guidance, whether fictional, imagined, or real. Their transformations took the form of extracting elements from existing texts, synthesizing those elements, radically reordering or rewriting texts, or creating entirely new works. By its very nature, the practice of necromancy produced a remarkably rich and diverse, some would say chaotic, written tradition. And, as in the case of Brother John's operations, the practice of necromancy was intimately bound up with the process of interpretation of texts in an unstable world of ritual magic works, personal notebooks, dreams, and visions.

Although the precise origins of much of this literature remain unclear, certain elements can be identified. The structure of rituals for exacting service from an otherworldly being (i.e., preparation, prayer, invocation, constraint, manifestation, petition, and dismissal) was fixed in custom in ancient times.[2] The Hebraic tradition offered complex hierarchies of angels and their names as well as elements from kabbalism. The Arabic writers offered a tradition of "astral magic," which often involved a high degree of ritual performance that frequently involved astrological images and planetary deities or spirits.[3] The Christian tradition provided the crucial elements that made the magical practices at once powerful, convincing, titillating, and dangerous for Christian practitioners: namely, the liturgy and various other programmed practices of the church, exorcism in particular.[4] For this reason the terms *exorcizatio* and *coniuratio* are used interchangeably in necromantic treatises. The Christian tradition holds that an upright Christian could invoke the power of God to cast out a demon.[5] One had only to refer to the liturgy to find out whether one could cast out a demon *and how* to do so; it was only a short logical step to the idea that one could command a demon to do other things as well. A few minor elaborations upon this tradition, a few selective borrowings from Greek, Arabic, and Hebraic magic, and a certain lack of judgment or caution were the only elements necessary for the birth of necromancy.

In addition to these ambient and homegrown elements, a number of texts involving the conjuring and binding of spirits circulated in Europe from the late thirteenth century and evidently flowed from earlier traditions. The *Clavicula Salomonis*, a text with only one surviving medieval witness that probably appeared in Europe sometime in the late thirteenth century, appears to have Greek roots.[6] A text on the magical uses of the Psalms deriving from a Hebrew original, which commonly travels with ritual magic texts in full or extracted form, attests to Hebraic influence on the tradition. The angel invocations of the *Liber Razielis*, originally a Hebrew text, no doubt influenced the tradition and certainly did so in the sixteenth century.[7] The *Sworn Book of*

Honorius, which includes conjuring, has Hebraic roots. The *Almandal*, a text on communicating with angels that circulated in the thirteenth century, is probably of Arabic provenance and possibly derives from a Sanskrit original. However, the heavy-handed editing of its medieval Christian transmitters for the most part obscures its origins.[8] A variety of other such texts are mentioned in the *Speculum astronomiae*.[9]

A final influence upon the traditions of necromantic magic stems from the social and intellectual context in which it was born, shaped, and transmitted. The worlds of the monastery, the university, and the secular church overlapped in complicated ways from the twelfth century onward. Necromantic magic was not limited to any of these contexts any more than their members were, but, like any other intellectual tradition, it flowed through all of them and into any context where their members might sojourn. The practices of necromantic magic certainly suggest clerical sensibilities. The texts often demand an extensive and wearying program of fasts, purgations, sexual abstinence, prayers, confession, communication, and attendance at Mass. A clerical calling thus may well have helped not only in practical ways, such as the time it afforded, but because of the clergy's direct, regular involvement in religious matters. The demands for the participation of a priest in the rituals, the required familiarity with the liturgy, not to mention the prerequisite ability in Latin all suggest this group.[10] The regular clergy strove for generally similar ideals and would have had intimate familiarity with the liturgy as well. Examples of monastic necromancers, fictional and real, are common.[11]

The element that united all of these professions was education. One had to have some facility in Latin in order to read the texts; even in the fifteenth century, when they begin to appear regularly in the vernacular, literacy was essential and knowledge of Latin remained almost indispensable. The sensibilities and pretensions of the learned also unite necromantic practitioners. Necromancy allowed the basest ambitions considerable latitude for expression, if not the promise of fulfillment. At the same time, it affirmed the corporate identity of the learned, particularly the "control" over the numinous associated with clerical offices. It mythologized ideals that educated men commonly held, such as moral purity, regular participation in church rituals, celibacy, and emotional or sexual self-control, and it attributed significant power to their practice. Many necromantic texts represented their learned transmitters as following a divine calling to protect and preserve the revealed truths these texts contained.[12] Necromancy also accorded considerable power to learning in a world that, on both the individual and corporate levels, was still very much governed by brute force. And if attaining learning (and the quasi-clerical status that went with it) was not a satisfying badge of manhood, necromancy held out the promise—unavailable to the ignorant—of wealth, power, love, knowledge, and influence. By reinforcing two very appealing prejudices, necromancy even offered something to those among the learned who eschewed its practice: learning was a very powerful thing, and clerical status involved great spiritual influence. Those who chose not to practice this art were implicitly that much more noble for having forgone the power it offered, while their learning still remained potent and worthy of respect. For who, in the end, could defeat the necromancers and their demon allies if not the learned?[13]

Two general features of medieval Christianity shaped the tradition of necromancy: an intense interest in ritual and a fascination with demons. First, the deep concern in the Latin West with the precise, appropriate, and uniform performance of Christian ritual would logically be reflected in its magic traditions. As in the case of liturgical performances, much attention was given to small details, such as the days when a ritual could be performed, the modes of preparations (often including a specific Mass), gesture, the direction in which the operator faced, the kinds of clothing worn, the tone of voice, and the prayers said. Sometimes the services of an ordained priest were also required. Second, the great significance that Christianity granted to demonic forces accorded necromancy a special status as a window into that dark world. The morally neutral portrayal of necromancers in many late medieval sources may be related to the rather useful role they played as literary devices. They could offer interesting, credible, and colorful details about the nature of evil, demons, the devil, and hell.[14] In this sense, necromancy should be understood as part of a wider medieval fascination with otherworldly visions.

The notion that someone could mediate between the living and the dead was an ambient part of both popular and learned culture, and this also probably bolstered the credibility of necromantic practice. Among the colorful figures that appeared before the inquisitor Jacques Fournier was a man who mediated between deceased members of the community and their families. Claiming to be able to see the spirits of the dead, he offered advice with regard to the status of departed relatives. For example, he would suggest the acts necessary to free a soul from purgatory.[15] A necromancer played a similar role in a Franciscan chronicle, when he called up from hell the soul of a departed bishop for the pope.[16] In a story from Caesarius of Heisterbach, demons dragged a living man directly to hell, and a necromancer was able to assist in retrieving him. Although it might have been difficult to justify in theological terms, the story suggests a certain fluidity between the living and the dead into which the necromancer had insight and over which he might exercise some control.[17] In this case, the necromancer, as the unfortunate man's advocate, even had some limited influence over his fate. As we shall see, practical exercises for mediating between the living and the dead occasionally occur in the texts of necromantic magic.[18] The tradition of communicating with the dead through a medium thus may also be counted among the popular sources of necromancy.

One final feature of necromancy, which no doubt made it attractive to some, was its explicitly rebellious or transgressive character. The negative views of necromancy, in particular concerning its use of demons, undoubtedly dissuaded most people from practicing it. Yet these features may have added to its appeal for others. Certainly, anyone compulsively driven to rebellion or transgression would have found it attractive, and some of those brought to trial for necromantic practice seem to have been driven by such self-destructive tendencies. But its success may also lie in a more private attraction to its "shock value" among people who had no intention of making a public spectacle of themselves. R. I. Moore has discussed the power that heretical leaders could gain by virtue of their confident and wild transgressions.[19] The shocking inversions of orthodox religious practices, the strange interplay of holy and unholy, and the necromancer's inordinate claim to power were certainly analogous to the dramatic transgressions of such leaders.[20] The allure of necromancy as a literary device, if not as a practice, may thus also be attributed in some measure to its "bad attitude."

General Features of Some Classic Texts of Conjuring

Before examining the manuscript evidence, let us begin with a brief discussion of a few representative examples of the identifiable texts for summoning demons and angels that circulated in the later Middle Ages, and their reflection of the general features of ritual magic discussed in the previous chapter. Although many of the texts (and certainly many of the known users) may have lacked the sophistication of the *Ars notoria* and of practitioners like John of Morigny, they nonetheless betray very similar sensibilities. Necromantic operators regarded the text as only part of what it took to discover the truths to which it might lead, and they often emphasized that divine guidance was needed to understand the texts fully. Some even encouraged their readers to seek knowledge themselves directly from angels. They were acutely aware that the text had been transmitted from scribe to scribe over a long period of time and may have been translated from other languages, they valorized the intellectual communities that preserved it, and they acclaimed those who edited and passed on the wisdom it contained. In this way they implicitly encouraged in their readers individual interpretation, editing, reconfiguration, or even authorship. The *Almandal, Liber Razielis, Liber Theysolius, Clavicula Salomonis,* and *Thesaurus spirituum* form the basis of this discussion.[21] The first three works concern the summoning of angels, a very common part of necromantic texts. The last two are explicitly concerned with the conjuring of demons.

The varied sources of these texts give a sense of the cultural melting pot that lay at the roots of necromancy. The *Clavicula Salomonis* appears to have Greek roots, the *Almandal* probably derives from a Sanskrit original by way of the Arabic world, and the *Liber Razielis* and *Liber Theysolius* stem from Hebraic sources. In most cases the texts are explicit about being translations or redactions of more ancient originals, a feature that later texts of conjuring seem to have emulated. The *Thesaurus spirituum,* although seemingly a native European text, claims to have roots in Alexandria, and in some sixteenth-century versions is attributed to a Turk. All of these works claim (or, in the case of the *Thesaurus spirituum,* imply) an ancient lineage. The *Liber Razielis* was revealed to Adam by the angel Raziel, and Solomon wrote the *Almandal* and *Clavicula.* The *Liber Theysolius* claims to have been written by a Greek philosopher of the same name. The *Almandal* was also said to have been translated by none other than Saint Jerome.

The *Clavicula, Almandal,* and *Liber Razielis* claim to be founded upon divine revelation, a quite common element in the mythology of ritual magic texts, as we have seen. If not exactly redemptive in the sense of the crucifixion, the *Liber Razielis* presents itself as a kind of consolation or aid for Adam in his fallen state.[22] The *Almandal* also implies that success in its magic is a fruit of salvation, if not the cause of it.[23] The profound spiritual truths these texts putatively contain implicitly demand that they be preserved and passed on. Simultaneously, the need for secrecy is emphasized so powerfully that it creates an inherent tension with the simultaneous need to preserve the text by copying it. The possessor of the text was required to keep it secret, away from the corrupting influence of the ignorant and impious, a duty that Solomon took so seriously that he had the *Clavicula* buried in an ivory box in the hope that a worthy owner would one day find it.[24] One of the major effects of this tension was probably to feed individualistic or even grandiose impulses in the reader.

At the same time, it is worth emphasizing that the text was not simply given to a single person but was entrusted to a particularly pious subsection of one social group, the learned. Those who preserved this text were, ideally at least, a community. According to its prologue, when Saint Jerome set about translating the *Almandal* he could not understand it and turned to a group of Greek masters, who directed him.[25] Rupertus Lombardus implicitly suggests that he attended some sort of school of magic at Alexandria, where he learned the art he writes down in the *Thesaurus spirituum*. The prologue of Alphonso's translation of the *Liber Razielis* mentions a text that the king of Babylon sent to Solomon accompanied by two wise men. Further, as Sophie Page has suggested, this prologue presents Alphonso the Wise as parallel to Solomon, a transmitter of ancient wisdom through his patronage.[26] This was clearly intended to establish the work, produced in a community of scholars he supported, as part of *his* legacy. We thus need to be careful how we interpret the role of an individual author, interpreter, or transmitter of a text. Although the *Liber Razielis* is not explicit about it, even the Old Testament kings and patriarchs who passed on the knowledge from Adam to Solomon are similar. They are a group not of solitary people but of men whose lives overlapped in time. Moreover, one would have good reason to assume that authors and readers alike would have understood a king's text to be held, interpreted, and transmitted by a community of the learned at his court. Very much like the master and his brotherhood of magicians in the prologue of the *Sworn Book*, protocol was not breached unless the text was given to someone of weak morals. The secrecy of these texts is thus more like a guild secret, literally controlled by a master, or the privileged knowledge of a priestly and learned class, than something necessarily held in strict secrecy by a single person. Such a group ensured that the proper interpretation and understanding of the text might be preserved.

If an intellectual community could not pass on the wisdom in the text, it could be attained in two other ways. As we have seen with John of Morigny, who had to figure out how to make the *Ars notoria* work, experience also served as the basis of knowledge. The prologue to the *Thesaurus spirituum* emphasizes Rupert's long experience in the art as the basis for his ability to write the text, and the experience of the Greek masters was essential to helping Jerome understand the *Almandal*.[27] But another form of experience might be necessary. The divine wisdom hidden in the texts could also be discovered through direct spiritual guidance, as in the case of Honorius and Brother John. A spirit guide assisted Toz in understanding and transmitting the *Clavicula Salomonis*, and the *Liber Razielis* not only recommends the use of a spirit guide in order to understand the text but provides instructions on how to get one.[28] The angel conversations of John Dee are only the best known of such enterprises in evidence throughout necromantic literature, as we shall see.

Once he understood a text, a sage could translate and sometimes reorganize, epitomize, or supplement it. Despite their pretensions to revealed status and the requirement of secrecy, all of the texts are quite self-conscious about the translation and editorial process through which they have passed.[29] Some, like the *Clavicula Salomonis* and *Almandal*, imply that the texts have remained (more or less) unchanged. The *Liber Razielis*, translated by Alphonso, is not only literally a compilation of available texts but makes this clear by including texts like the *Liber Theysolius*, attributed to other authors. The *Thesaurus spirituum*, like the *Sworn Book*, openly describes itself as extracted (*quasdam conclusiones extraxi*). Very much unlike the Bible, which is certainly not explicit about its own transmission process, these texts discuss that process openly. Perhaps because the texts were noncanonical, because their status as divinely revealed texts was not self-evident, their authors felt obliged to provide their lineage. Nonetheless, discussion of the transmission process remains a remarkable and quite common feature of ritual magic.

Although it is outside the scope of this chapter to describe the operations in these texts in detail, they generally demand the same sort of attentiveness as the theurgic practices already examined. Initial observances, including fasting, baths, special clothing, and shaving, have a highly sensual quality, and throughout these preparations the user must attend to his internal state, assuring moral purity. Long prayers, compulsory confession and communion, special masses, and the observance of canonical hours orient the user's mind to the affective states associated with religious devotion. The requirement that the operator observe atmospheric conditions and particular times (planetary hours, hours of the day, phases of the moon, etc.), and that the stultifyingly long prayers and ritual performances be performed precisely, deepens the need for attentiveness. Finally, these works tend to seek experience of the numinous in various ways, whether in the conjuring circles of the *Clavicula Salomonis* or the eerie smoke rising through a specially constructed table in the *Almandal*.

One side effect of the emphasis on personal experience, on spiritually guided writing or interpretation, and on the precious contributions of transmitters of texts is a tendency to valorize individual human agency. The human heroes of these stories are either great men deemed virtuous enough to receive a great revelation themselves, or divinely guided editors and transmitters of holy truths. Truth originates in, and is consubstantial with, the divine, but the mythologies connected with these texts are as much about a kind of perennial discussion with the divine by many people over time as they are about singular, never-to-be-repeated revelations. A revelation to Adam or Solomon was not the end of the story but only the beginning of repeated appeals to the divine for assistance in understanding it. Any user would naturally be disposed to fantasies of worthiness to participate in such a discussion. It would hardly be surprising, in other words, if this mythology were to encourage either pretended or genuine convictions of prophetic status among its enthusiasts, and in turn to encourage the creation of new texts or the reformulation of old ones.

General Features of the Manuscripts

Unlike texts of image magic, the codicological presentation of which was usually more formal and scholarly, a significant portion of the conjuring literature appears in less formal notebooks, where the constituent texts are frequently not identifiable by bibliographic means. Like recipe literature, many of these collections have fluid and largely anonymous contents, the lineage of which would be very difficult to trace. Therefore, an adequate study cannot be accomplished from a reading of texts identifiable by standard bibliographic tags (title, author, incipit, etc.). Further, many of the texts of late medieval necromancy never found their way into print.[30] This may have been due in part to the small supply of larger coherent and systematic treatises. Although commonly based upon medieval antecedents, either textual or practical, or the mythologies associated with them, most of the modern printed volumes of ritual magic were produced after the seventeenth century. For example, the early nineteenth-century *Grimoire du Pape Honorius* contains medieval elements such as the "Pentacle of Solomon," a common title in medieval collections, and an apparent reference to the *Sworn Book of Honorius* in the title, but the text is largely modern in composition. The *Clavicula Salomonis* had become the single most common text of conjuring in manuscript in the eighteenth and subsequent centuries, but its internal coherence and scope is unusual among surviving medieval manuscripts. So an accurate picture of late medieval necromancy can be painted only by examining the manuscripts of individual necromantic collections.[31]

Unlike the *Ars notoria* and astrological image magic, the early history of necromancy is fragmentary. Manuscript lists, condemnations of specific texts, and catalogues all attest to a robust manuscript tradition, but surviving manuscripts of conjuring, particularly from before 1400, are relatively rare. Some early British fragments suggest necromantic practice. A thirteenth-century recipe collection includes some processes reminiscent of necromancy, but these form a very small portion of the collection itself.[32] Two apparently magical images appear on fourteenth-century fragments. These lack any explanatory text and are relatively ambiguous, particularly as they cannot be directly associated with any other text.[33] The earliest catalogue references to works of necromancy in Britain are found in the two volumes of superstitious works in the fourteenth-century record of Erghome's collection, examined in the previous two chapters. Among them we might list the *Sworn Book of Honorius*, in that its second section contains conjuring operations, but given the central concern with the beatific vision in surviving English manuscripts, it is not clear that its transmitters were interested in the necromantic portions.

An entry found in the indenture of the Merton College Library dated 1483 mentions a "book of necromancy," although this could conceivably have referred to other kinds of magic.[34] In some other fifteenth-century examples, an isolated, anonymous necromantic experiment occurs among other nonmagical material.[35] The earliest surviving British dedicated necromantic collections are two parts of Rawlinson D. 252, Sloane 3849, fols. 17–19, and London, Society of Antiquaries, 39, fols. 1–17, all written in the fifteenth century. Similar circumstances prevail on the continent, where few manuscripts of this kind predate the fifteenth century.

It would be an understandable but erroneous assumption that works of medieval ritual magic might be prone to forgery by scribes of the seventeenth century or later. The texts of ritual magic of principal interest in that era, such as the *Clavicula Salomonis*, actually survive in very few medieval witnesses. In any event, their value lay not in being medieval but in being putative witnesses to a much earlier tradition of magic. The forger's time would thus have been better spent on more lucrative projects. As we shall see, a few sixteenth-century scribes used anachronistic hands, some of which have resulted in misdating. For now we need only observe that these scribes sought not to deceive the reader but to produce a mysterious, archaic, or powerful-*looking* book. Because the use of an intentionally anachronistic hand was not meant to deceive, the scribes of these works left a great many obvious signs of the book's true age. The few works that might be considered forgeries, then, are not. This fact, combined with the poor quality of most of the surviving manuscripts, makes it very unlikely that any are forgeries and more likely that they represent the realities of medieval conjuring.

In one respect, however, surviving manuscripts probably do not reflect the original library. Of the twelve fourteenth- and fifteenth-century manuscripts of ritual or necromantic magic examined here, two do not survive, and six were probably not preserved because of an interest in necromancy. Two pastedowns or flyleaves preserve necromantic figures.[36] A fifteenth-century hand has recorded a short anonymous necromantic experiment on the last leaf of a fourteenth-century codex containing a text on geomancy and Chaucer's *Conclusions of the Astrolabe*.[37] An experiment for seeing angels in a boy's nails also appears in the *Commonplace Book of Robert Reynes of Acle*, in the company of charms.[38] Finally, a necromantic experiment occurs at the end of a short collection of instructions for achieving a woman's affections, mostly sleights of hand and the like, and not actually in the least necromantic.[39] Thus accidental survivals constitute half of the surviving examples of necromantic magic from Britain before 1500, a percentage that would be higher if we included the necromantic portions of the *Sworn Book*. There were much better reasons to preserve a commonplace book, or a work by Chaucer, than to save a poor-quality, wretchedly executed collection of necromantic magic lacking in any redeeming features. Further, there were good reasons—personal if not legal—to hide a dedicated necromantic collection or to destroy it if one's interest in the subject waned. If it passed into someone else's hands, it also ran a high risk of being destroyed. So concrete and circumstantial evidence suggests that significantly more necromantic and ritual magic collections existed in the Middle Ages than the number of surviving manuscripts suggests.

The way in which these texts entered modern collections suggests similar patterns of transmission. The Rawlinson collections (Oxford, Bodleian Library, Rawlinson D. 252) did not appear in a major library until the eighteenth century, when Rawlinson acquired them. They were donated to the Bodleian in 1752 with the other 5,205 volumes of his library.[40] Even in this massive collection, this significant manuscript is one of only three such examples, the other two deriving from sixteenth-century England (Rawlinson D. 253) and fifteenth-century Poland (Rawlinson liturg. D. 6).[41] The survival of Rawlinson D. 252 seems to have been more a matter of chance than the result of any occult interests on Rawlinson's part. Although the Sloane collection preserves a large number of necromantic or ritual magic collections, most of these derive from the sixteenth and seventeenth centuries. Only one manuscript from this collection, Sloane 3849, contains material written in Britain during the fifteenth century.[42] This volume and many others in the Sloane collection appear to have been preserved because of their connection with medical doctors, not as a result of their contents. Similarly, the Society of Antiquaries manuscript was probably not preserved owing to the portion dealing with ritual magic. According to the description inside the front cover, the volume was in private collections until 1807, by which time its survival could be accounted for purely by its antiquarian value. Earlier, its survival probably had to do with the vellum portion, including works on images, which had been written by John Argentine. The portion that contains ritual magic is written in unattractive scrawled cursive on paper. Only a collector interested in the occult might have seen fit to preserve the manuscript for the sake of this part, but, as noted above, the interests of occultists after 1650 shifted away from such texts. It is just as likely that purely antiquarian interests drove the preservation, and that the second section was of principal interest. All of this suggests that most major book collectors and occultists showed little interest in medieval necromancy between 1600 and 1800, and that the attrition rate for ritual magic collections was very high and the likelihood of forgery low.

The following discussion is based on the necromantic collection, as opposed to the isolated occurrences of necromantic experiments in larger, nonnecromantic codices. This approach requires some justification, as it departs significantly from the approach taken with astrological image magic texts. The hundreds of examples of the latter make it possible to discern coherent patterns of collection, whereas too few necromantic texts accompanying nonmagical material survive to suggest the collectors' probable intent. They may have been recorded merely as curiosities. Further, only one of these (Reynes's miscellany) was written by the primary scribe of the codex. The necromantic experiment in Sloane 121 is part of a small collection of tricks and sleights of hand designed to impress a woman. Taken as a whole, the collection is not a necromantic work, and it constitutes only a small part of a larger codex, a circumstance that makes it difficult to discern the reason for its presence.[43] In Sloane 314 a later scribe added the short necromantic text on some blank vellum. Finally, because of their shortness, it is difficult to develop a coherent sense of the attitude of the scribes of these works based on the texts themselves, so these examples tell us little about how necromantic texts were regarded. Necromantic *collections*, by contrast, despite their smaller numbers, provide a much richer and more dependable source for our purposes. If I am correct that there was a high attrition rate among manuscripts of necromancy, collections of conjuring texts would have been the more frequent context for the transmission of this material, despite the fact that they account for only half of the surviving manuscripts.

In examining these collections we find that the manuscripts of necromancy and Scholastic image magic are very different from each other. One significant general feature of the collections of necromantic ritual magic covered in this study is a lack of interest in astrological literature (independent of the practice of magic), alchemy, books of secrets, natural philosophy, and other *naturalia*. In short, they generally do not reflect the interests that usually accompany the standard texts of astrological image magic, especially prior to 1500. In addition, although such texts were widely available, there are few examples where one of the works commonly occurring in Scholastic image magic collections appears in a ritual magic collection before 1500. To be sure, other works concerned with magical images do occur in this context. Usually, however, such astrological material seems to have been absorbed under the broader umbrella of ritual magic practice in such a way that the original technical details of astrology may not have survived or are not a central concern. These two sorts of magic collections are also transmitted in fundamentally different ways. Whereas the standard texts of image magic were more often translated with an eye to preserving their original form, or at least their technical integrity as works of astrology, image magic texts in ritual collections were often altered in ways that indicate greater concern with creating magic rituals of an explicitly Christian nature.

Furthermore, the collectors of ritual magic texts were frequently less concerned with preserving the text as a whole or with mentioning the author or source, tending instead to extract short sections. Another significant feature of ritual magic collectors, one also in evidence among enthusiasts of the *Ars notoria*, was a tendency toward innovation and synthesis. Scribes modified, enhanced, or synthesized the existing material in order to make it more efficacious or acceptable or to adapt it to different purposes. The knot of assumptions, impulses, and textual problems I have described as Brother John's dilemma drove these transformations. In short, not only were these texts understood in different ways, but the way they were written, transmitted, and collected was also very different. Despite some overlap in subject material, these two genres of illicit magic, Scholastic image magic and necromancy, tended to run in parallel but separate streams of transmission that reflect fundamentally different intellectual cultures. To illustrate these differences, let us turn to two late medieval collections.

Society of Antiquaries 39: Astrological or Ritual Magic?

London, Society of Antiquaries, 39 is composed of two discrete fifteenth-century collections. The second, a standard collection of Scholastic image magic already discussed, was owned and written by John Argentine, but there is no evidence that Argentine had any connection with the first seventeen folios. If his scribal practices were at all consistent, his controlled, even severe hand is altogether different from the sprawling fifteenth-century cursive that records the texts in the first collection. The first section is written on paper, the second on parchment, and the earliest indication of the date when the two were assembled is a foliation of the entire codex dating to no earlier than the mid-sixteenth century. The scribe of the earlier portion is usually accurate yet frequently does not bother with abbreviation marks if the meaning is clear without them. The three magic treatises that make up the collection may be distinguished from one another with some effort, but the standard writing technologies for distinguishing between chapters and texts are carelessly applied, making it difficult to do this at a glance. The collection was clearly intended for personal use. As the three existing texts do not break off unnaturally and as no internal quires are missing, the collection may be complete in its current form. On the other hand, an early foliation begins on the first folio at seventeen, so it seems to have included two more quires at one time, and these could have been written in the same hand. Similarly, the termination of the last text at the quire division may be entirely coincidental, and further quires may have been lost.

The first text concerns the construction of magical rings, although little remains of the introduction, which might have made it possible to identify it with one of the texts condemned by Albert. The remainder of the text is regular in its organization and appears otherwise complete. The first chapter begins after two mutilated lines, which reveal nothing about the text. The chapters give instructions on making rings in each of the twenty-eight mansions of the moon. They are divided by lines drawn across the page but are identifiable only by the number of the mansion listed in the first line. The text is complete insofar as it treats each of the mansions. The instructions are quite formulaic, making it possible for the scribe or author to abbreviate the later chapters considerably. A single chapter will thus suffice to give a good impression of the text and the techniques it promotes:

> To make battling armed knights appear: In the third mansion let a concave gold ring be made. In its hollow put undefiled parchment, on which is written in human blood these names: denetica alibiat stablacctis virciseri. With the ring thus completed, on the following day at dawn, hold it at the entrance to any field and suffumigate it with the [blood?] of a dead man and say this prayer, on bended knee facing the field. "Lord God Omnipotent, who, from the remotest heaven, looks upon the abyss, who made man in his image and likeness—through which abundance of mercy the living live and the dying die—I entreat that as I touch the ring with my saliva, on whatever day or hour, those very spirits whose names are enclosed should make battling, armed knights appear before the eyes of whomever I wish." In so doing, touch the ground with the ring while making this sign 🜍. Afterward, wrap it in black cotton and keep it very clean. When you wish to operate, say, touching the ring with your saliva, "O you spirits whose names are enclosed, I conjure you through him, to whom you chiefly must yield obedience, that you accomplish what I desire." Having said this, you will see wondrous things.[44]

Each chapter instructs the reader to write figures and spirit names on parchment and to enclose them in a ring. The first chapter identifies the spirits as angels (fol. 2r). These actions are to be performed in a given mansion of the moon, accompanied by prayers and ritual practices. In each case the power of the ring is invoked by touching it with one's saliva. Presumably the operator is intended surreptitiously to touch the ring to his tongue or a moistened finger—spitting on it would seem a rather messy, though dramatic, alternative. The names, figures, suffumigations, and substances used for writing vary from section to section. Although the prayers remain substantially the same, they shift slightly so that the biblical references have something to do with the power of the ring. A ring to make an illusory river appear requires a prayer that refers to the stories from Exodus, in which Pharaoh's army was drowned in the sea and water flowed from the rock struck by Moses.[45]

Many aspects of this text are similar to those used in the standard works of astrological image magic. Rings are employed, although in this case the names and figures are inscribed on parchment, not on the ring itself or the stone it holds. Simple figures and angel names are used, and the rings are suffumigated with various substances. The rings are constructed in the twenty-eight mansions of the moon, much like the images in the *Liber lune*. Finally, like the standard works on image magic, the text is relatively short and systematic in its presentation. Here, however, the similarities end.

Closer examination of the rituals reveals practices much more akin to necromancy. Among the works of image magic examined to this point, binding rituals, if present at all, are only implicit. The author of the *Speculum astronomiae* argued that astrological connections could be simply a disguise for necromantic activities, that is, attempts to force spirits to do one's bidding. If he is correct, the disguise is such that the binding is not an obvious feature of texts in most Scholastic image magic collections, particularly in the more common works of the genre. In the text quoted here, binding is explicitly represented by enclosing the spirits' names in rings. A prayer invoking God's aid in achieving this end duplicates the necromantic practice of invoking a higher power to bind a lower one. Although some of the words commonly used in conjuring texts to refer to this process (*constringere, vinculum*, etc.) do not appear here, the meaning of *coniuro* (I conjure) is clear enough. Necromantic texts employ a combination of good and evil powers to bind demons, but they also regularly employ prayers to God or the names of God to the same end. If somewhat simpler than most works of conjuring, the text bears all the marks of a necromantic treatise and would certainly have deserved condemnation for that reason.

The final verbal formula is not a prayer at all but directly commands the spirits by the power of God. This makes somewhat peculiar the claim that the spirits employed are angels. The use of the word *angelus* as synonymous with *spiritus* is relatively unusual in necromantic literature, which generally recognizes that, while it is not improper or impossible to compel a demon, an angel's help may be requested only in prayer. Technically, the text may have meant *angeli mali*, that is, demons, where it simply says *angeli*. Once again, this is not generally the term used in the necromantic literature for demons, where they are more often referred to as *spiritus* or *spiritus maligni* or *demones*.

The conflation of angels with particular stars or astrological conditions is read-
ily understandable. The name of each angel used in the *Liber lune* corresponds
to one of the mansions of the moon; other texts have similar structures. As
noted above, the combination of simple images, names, and suffumigations is
also common to Arabic material. Michael Swartz has examined similar kinds
of techniques in medieval Jewish magic, where amulets are used to invoke
angels though God's power.[46] So the use of angel names, in addition to these
other features, suggests either Arabic or Hebraic sources. The use of explicit
binding rituals and extensive prayers is less common in Arabic literature, at
least in the material that appeared in the Latin West under Arabic names.
Prayers like the one quoted above, which refer to the Old Testament, might
conceivably be Hebraic in origin, and the use of these kind of *historiola* was
also common in Jewish amulets. Certainly, the techniques correspond more
closely to the second category of illicit images discussed in the *Speculum
astronomiae*, which David Pingree has described as Solomonic, noting their
apparently Hebraic origin.[47] But one prayer in this text, referring to the miracle of the water transformed into wine (John 2:1–10), clearly identifies the text
as Christian, at least in part.[48] It seems, then, that we have a text or practice,
Hebraic or possibly Arabic in origin, that has been reworked in an explicitly
Christian form. As we shall see, whatever the origin of this text may have
been, this Christianizing process is one of the features common to collections
of necromantic magic.

The next text in the collection identifies itself as *Tractatus de sigillis septem
planetarum et anuli*, quite possibly the text on seven rings text attributed to
Hermes and condemned by the Magister Speculi.[49] It appears to be the same
text that occurs in a Vatican manuscript attributed to Hermes.[50] Although our
version attributes authorship to one Philos, the fact that the text describes
the use of sigils as the "first philosophy" might suggest Hermes Trismegistus.
Each of the first seven chapters discusses one of the planets and its sigil, angel,
and ring. The subsequent chapters concern the use of the rings or sigils. One,
for example, which employs the sigil and angel of the sun, seeks to provide
the operator with a magic horse.[51] Unlike the first, this text is more explicitly astrological and does not involve ritual binding or explicitly Christian
ritual. The beings involved are said to be angels, not demons. Although less
systematic than a text like the *Liber lune*, it is in every way consistent with
the material from Arabic sources. Finally, there is no question that this text
would fall among the Magister Speculi's condemned texts. It involves not only
angel names but the far more dubious ritual practices of fasting and animal
sacrifice. This raises the question of why this particular text is included in this
collection. Given its more explicitly astrological nature, might this text reflect

interests commonly connected with the more mainstream texts of Scholastic image magic? Trithemius not only regarded it as problematic but listed it among the works of explicit conjuring in his bibliography of magic texts.[52] But only an evaluation of the whole collection can give us a clear idea of what interests may have driven the collector.

At first glance, the astrological beginning of the third text in this collection, *Preceptualis ars magice*, appears to suggest that this collection may be something like a Scholastic image magic collection. It sets out in systematic form the astrological conditions and hours in which various kinds of "experiments" should be conducted. It explains how, for certain operations, one must take care to observe the astrological conditions and their humoral qualities. Yet these experiments are not of the variety generally found in the collections of image magic. Rather, the text explicitly describes them as *ex arte exorsizationi*, that is, experiments in the conjuring of demons. This would have automatically excluded it from the category of legitimate texts according to the *Speculum astronomiae*. In fact, the text is the *Practica nigromantiae*, a work usually part of the *Thesaurus spirituum*, the text of explicit demon conjuring discussed above. No explicit necromantic operations are included in this extract. So, although it follows the usual pattern of textual transmission for ritual magic, one might be led to believe that the collector was not interested in necromantic magic. Internal evidence, however, suggests otherwise. The text begins with a set of rules for operation characteristic of ritual magic, including shaving, washing, the wearing of clean clothes, and the avoidance of sin. The ritual preparation of the operator does not typically figure in astrological image magic collections. In ritual magic, by contrast, it is a fundamental element.

More significantly, Society of Antiquaries 39 emphasizes the inherent power of Christian ritual. While the Christian scribes of astrological image magic no doubt assumed the superiority of their religion and its rituals, and occasionally adapted their texts in explicitly Christian fashion, here we find a much more complicated integration of Christian ritual elements. A few folios later, we find two chapters concerning the hours of the day and night appropriate for operations: "Also note that anyone can exorcize well in any hour of the night, excepting the hour of matins, or in which matins are sung, for many spirits fear to come while the hours are sacred, because the divinity of God expels demons, and on that account, that hour is not good to begin an exorcism."[53] In fact, the discussion of necromantic operations in the hours of the day and night throughout this chapter takes into account the canonical hours: "Note that four principal kings cannot be bound in any hour of the day, except in the darkness of night. Likewise the spirits called kings cannot be bound except before prime. Likewise the princes, from terce up to midday, and from sext to vespers, or to compline. Next mich<...>es [text mutilated] from sext to compline or from compline to the setting of the sun of day."[54] According to a note in the *Speculum astronomiae*, the four kings are important demons in charge of the four regions of the world; they also recur in necromantic rituals as principal demons.[55] These highly ritualized operations involving demons, then, are to be performed at particular hours. Some of the instructions require that the times for operation be governed by astrological rules, and these could be explained with reference to al-Kindī's ideas about rays and changing astrological conditions. But the canonical hours are harder to accommodate to an astrological frame of reference and are not at all characteristic of image magic texts.

John of Seville's translation of the work on images by Thābit ibn Qurra did not include the incantations.[56] Its lack of untoward elements made it attractive because it could cling to the Scholastic dream of natural magic. The alteration brought the image magic text closer to astrology and natural philosophy as understood in Christian circles. By accepting the suggestions of the *Speculum astronomiae* and choosing this text to copy, scribes changed the complexion of the medieval library of astrological magic. The opposite process occurred with texts appearing in ritual magic collections. Rather than emphasize the astrological features of the texts (and downplay the ritual ones), the authors or translators of ritual magic texts explicitly employed binding rituals to achieve the aid of demons or angels. Rather than strip out the incantations and other ritual practices, the scribes or authors translated them into Christian ritual. The alterations made to the rituals in the first text also translate the ritual into a Christian form and might arguably have made it worse by Scholastic standards. Rather than simply preserve the astrological features, which translated relatively easily, scribes endeavored to translate the ritual features into a form understandable to and resonant with the sensibilities of the Latin West. In this case, the process involved prayers of a Christian variety and *historiola* drawn from the New Testament. Despite the ubiquity of astrology in these texts, attention to Christian rites and myths is thus clearly central to the way in which the material was transmitted and transformed.

If any common feature of the texts in this collection might explain why they came together as they did, it would not be a common interest in *naturalia*, as in the case of collections of Scholastic image magic. Rather, all of these texts concern themselves deeply with ritual in the practice of magic and have been transformed accordingly. Both the first and last texts involve the explicit ritual binding of spirits and the observation of hours of the day and night pertaining to Christian rituals. The first employs Christian *historiola* and prayers. The middle text does not involve the same kind of explicitly necromantic ritual but employs suffumigations, food prohibitions, and animal sacrifices. But these blend in seamlessly with the other works, and, ironically, the intent and spirit of the original text may be better preserved here than it would have been in the more characteristic Latin context for image magic. The astrological elements are common to all works in the collection but do not form the backbone of necromantic operations, and so can be considered an important element but not a defining feature. We can also see that, as a whole, this collection makes no pretense to being natural magic, nor does it attempt to accommodate the concerns raised in such theoretical works as the *Speculum astronomiae*. Rather, it explicitly does precisely what illicit works of magic were assumed to do, that is, by the illicit use of ritual, it employs or conjures demons and angels. Unlike the traditional collection of astrological image magic that clings to natural philosophy as an analytical framework or a means of demonstrating its legitimacy, these works either rejected the orthodox view of necromancy as wrong or simply persevered in the face of it. Rather than imply the idea of occult powers of nature, they invoke the numinous powers of Christian ritual.

At the same time, Society of Antiquaries 39 does not contain the usual sort of rituals for conjuring demons, such as magic circles and complex invocations. Perhaps this is because other portions of the collection did not survive, but assuming that this was not the case, we might wish to describe this collection as astrological necromancy. It certainly demonstrates the diversity of ritual magic practice preserved in Latin manuscripts. Kieckhefer's perceptive discussion of the psychology of the necromancer refers principally to works that concern the actual summoning of demons, where the operator is actually supposed to see the demon appear.[57] While the texts in this collection do involve the binding of demons or angels, they do not seek to summon them. Only the last treatise suggests this kind of operation, and it provides only the correct times to carry out the operations. It is certainly possible (and would be consistent with the form of other contemporary conjuring manuals) that other texts of explicit conjuring were once part of this collection. But it is also possible that its rules were used only in pursuit of the kind of magic described in the preceding two texts. There is certainly no firm evidence that the collector was interested in the direct conjuring of demons. Thus the complex dynamics involved in the fearful relation to the numinous that Kieckhefer has called "visionary necromancy" may not apply in this case. The magical operations described here involve a somewhat more distant relation to demons and angels and involve no fearsome or explosive appearances. The more "mystical" necromancers, whom we will encounter in the next text considered here, were attracted by such dramatic and numinous features. They may well have been less than satisfied with this collection, in which the scent of brimstone is not so strong.

Various additional aspects connect Society of Antiquaries 39 with the larger tradition of ritual magic. In addition to its containing Christianizing transformations, the transformations are more dramatic than those in Scholastic collections of image magic, where the Latin texts tend to be more transparent witnesses to the originals. The collection also includes an extract from a larger text on conjuring, which reflects the excerpting tendencies of ritual magic. This last text includes rules that center upon the physical and moral condition of the operator and encourage close attentiveness to times, feelings, and moral condition. Finally, the scribe clearly wrote down the text for his own private purposes and exhibits little concern for any subsequent reader. This not only demonstrates the generally recondite nature of necromantic collections but also suggests the more individualistic nature of the endeavors they represent.

The Rawlinson Necromancers: Rawlinson D. 252

The Texts and the Practice of Magic

In Rawlinson D. 252, a fifteenth-century necromantic collection, two informal hands have copied into two personal notebooks at least seventy separate items of widely varying magic content. One fifteenth-century English scribe wrote the bulk of the volume, and a second scribe of the same period wrote quires seven through nine (fols. 63–80). Because the two collections occupy their own sets of gatherings, it is impossible to ascertain which was written first and whether one of the scribes took over the collection from the other. Although they are in roughly contemporary hands, they could have been joined as late as the seventeenth century, the date of the earliest surviving foliation. The fifteenth-century part of a table of contents at fol. 98v (quire 11) makes no mention of the texts in quires seven through nine. This could be explained by the fact that this table refers only to the larger or more significant texts on conjuring in the first six quires, with the result that the scribe might simply not have bothered to record any of the texts in quires seven through nine. But this seems too coincidental to be plausible. It is more likely that quires seven through nine were originally a separate collection and were inserted by the scribe of the first section or by a subsequent owner. In what follows, I treat them separately as "Rawlinson B." Unless I refer specifically to section B, it may be assumed that I am speaking about section A.

A lack of explanatory detail on many of the items and a general informality in presentation suggest that these collections were intended for personal use only. Both hands are in a relatively informal cursive and, beyond section markers, the notebook uses only rudimentary textual aids, sometimes leaving it unclear where one text ends and the next begins. As mentioned, the table of contents, which appears about halfway through the codex, lists only the major works of conjuring in the volume, excluding a wide assortment of smaller texts. These smaller texts, often no longer than half a page, are scattered throughout the volume in no obvious order. In most cases it is not immediately obvious that various texts were employed in conjunction with each other. The scribe will end a set of instructions without so much as a title that might indicate the next step in a ritual performance. At one point, the complete text of the first chapter of the Gospel of John appears, with no indication about where or how this may have been used in magical operations.[58] This is only one of perhaps thirty such small and apparently unconnected texts scattered throughout the codex. Even many of the longer operations consist only of a set of conjurations, with no indication as to what actions might be performed in conjunction with them. It seems likely that the scribe knew what he had to do, so there was no point in recording it.

Numerous details suggest a greater coherence in the volume than first meets the eye. In particular, the scribes evidently combined various texts to produce the ritual they desired, a technique that is a logical extension of what we have seen in the *Sworn Book* and *Ars notoria*. In some cases, one text refers to another. For example, one conjuration ends with the instruction that the reader should now employ the *Vinculum Salomonis*, a conjuration used in the case of a spirit who refuses to appear. Although the scribe does not give a folio reference, this text appears elsewhere in the volume.[59] The *Vinculum Salomonis* would have been applicable only in certain circumstances, circumstances that might arise in the performance of any conjuration, so it makes good sense for it to travel separately. And this was not an isolated case. The title of another section (fol. 37r) betrays a similar pattern of use: *Oraciones dicenda* [sic] *in omni operacione* (Prayers to be said in all operations). And two further texts, the *Coniuracio licentialis* (about which more in a moment) and the *Liber consecrationum*, which gives instructions for consecrating a magic book, are similarly discrete texts to be used in certain circumstances.[60] In fact, most of the conjurations in the manual provide a blank space in which to insert the name of the particular demon to be invoked and so could be used in this flexible manner as well. Most of the operations lack the usual initial purification rituals, but this does not mean that the scribe did not perform or recommend them. Rather, since general instructions do appear in other places in the collection, the practitioner probably applied them in each case rather than copy out the same rules again and again. For example, a section devoted to *regula inuocationis* (rules for invocations) gives preparatory prayers for any conjuration (fol. 120v).

The annotations of a seventeenth-century scribe, who evidently added them to the volume in order to make it useful, beautifully illustrate the complex way it was used. In Rawlinson A, for example, at the end of two conjurations (fols. 40v–47v and 48v–59r), this hand refers to fol. 36v, a text called the *Coniuracio licentialis*. This is to be said following a magical operation to get the spirit to depart peacefully and to ensure a peaceful and subservient return when the spirit is conjured again. So the seventeenth-century operator (and presumably the original user) would have completed each conjuration with this concluding formula. The multiple prayers and psalm verses, which also appear scattered throughout the volume, would probably have been used in the same way. Cross-references in this same hand fill the book. All of this suggests a much greater level of sophistication in this personal collection than is immediately obvious from the disordered presentation. In fact, the lack of explicit organization could be taken as evidence that the collection was not copied as a whole (i.e., from another identical notebook) but compiled. One way or another, the evidence suggests an intentionally synthetic approach to creating magic rituals in which the scribe or earlier collector chose a variety of material he considered potentially useful.

Although other manuals of the fifteenth and sixteenth centuries may be less chaotic, they regularly contain a variety of purpose-built texts with independent textual lineages. For example, the *Vinculum Salomonis, Pentaculum Salomonis*, and *Liber consecrationum* appear in a variety of collections across Europe, and these are only the most common such texts.[61] The *Ars notoria* and *Sworn Book* took a similar approach when they made use of a single set of prayers for a variety of purposes. Although perhaps articulated more radically in necromantic collections, the combinatory approach was thus widespread and common to ritual magic in general. Unlike astrological image magic texts, where the complete operation was generally understood to be contained within one text (and very often one part of one text), the Rawlinson collections and other European necromantic texts assembled materials from a variety of sources, and in practice a single ritual might be compiled from several of them. The boundaries between texts were far more permeable and their interrelations situational and changeable. And since there was no single right way to do it, there would also have been less direct correspondence between what was written in the handbook and what was actually performed.

The operator may have arranged the elements in response to circumstances arising in the magical procedures, such as the need to intensify a conjuration or reconsecrate a book.

The freedom that scribes of ritual magic felt to rewrite or edit their texts is amply attested in this volume as well. Many of the texts of the Rawlinson manuscript exist in no other collection, making it conceivable that at least some of them may be original to its scribes. The tendency to alter texts may also be seen in those few instances where texts with numerous other (apparent) witnesses can be found. The *Vinculum Salomonis*, for example, occurs several times in European manuscripts, and some surviving versions bear vague resemblances to one another. The version in the Rawlinson manuscript has the same incipit as a sixteenth-century witness, but after the first few words the texts correspond only roughly, and eventually all similarities dissolve. The later version seems to have been employed for treasure hunting and shifts into conjurations of "Barach," whereas the Rawlinson version is employed in the usual way as an all-purpose conjuration for recalcitrant spirits. Only the concluding pentacle remains in both versions. Its relation to a fifteenth-century Italian witness seems even more distant.[62] In another example, a work on the magical uses of seventeen psalms appears in section A of the Rawlinson manual. This was evidently extracted from some relative of a similar late fifteenth-century witness in Florence. The Italian version includes all of the psalms and somewhat more extensive directions for their use, including characters to be inscribed on amulets, suffumigations, and other such operations. The Rawlinson version is not only an extract but also a considerably abbreviated version lacking any magical characters.[63]

In some instances, traces of similarity between texts in necromantic manuals suggest an even more distant textual relation. An exorcism in the Rawlinson manual that follows instructions on making rings of Mercury and Jupiter begins with words very similar to a passage in a Copenhagen manuscript that also follows instructions for rings. Both echo the formula for the liturgical exorcism of salt and employ more or less the same angel names, but after fifteen or so words, the tantalizing similarities disappear altogether.[64] There is no correspondence between the instructions for the rings at all. Did the similarities derive from a common original text? If so, it was evidently fundamentally changed and connected with different tracts on rings. In many cases, however, no such textual link can be made with other manuals. One is once again driven to surmise that many of the texts in the Rawlinson collections are, at least in part, the original work of the scribe.

But to what extent were the scribes of necromancy aware of the instabilities of their texts? A similar example, the *Liber consecrationum*, provides some insight on this issue. It may be found in a number of manuscripts, including the Rawlinson collection, and in two versions in the Munich handbooks (Clm 849). In his edition of this volume, Kieckhefer has listed the two texts in parallel columns for easy comparison.[65] The texts are clearly related throughout, but the differences are substantial and far more than a matter of mere scribal correction or rewording. It is particularly interesting that the Munich handbook's scribe was clearly aware of the textual divergences, because he copied both versions. A similar text occurs in a seventeenth-century British manuscript. It employs the same rituals for consecrating books and magical circles but shifts to an altogether different text in the second half.[66] The text in the Rawlinson collection is not immediately visible, beginning with the declaration that whoever desires salvation must before all else hold to the Catholic faith. The text goes on to provide the Chalcedonian trinitology, the Nicene Christology, the litany of the saints, and assorted prayers.[67] It concludes with three of the prayers in the Munich version by which one may consecrate one's magic book.

The author of the Munich handbook was aware of the textually fluid nature of his source texts, but, as Kieckhefer has argued, the flaws in a manuscript may not have been of great concern to the necromantic operator. The requirement (which we see in this passage) that a book be consecrated in order to be effective suggests that the contents could somehow lose their efficacy. The prayer asks that the book be consecrated, blessed, and confirmed in order to obtain the power to perform the magical operations it contains.[68] The attribution of numinous power to a book may indicate that the scribe attributed tremendous power to the written word. From another perspective, however, such attribution recognizes the limitations of the text and emphasizes the central importance of the operator. The efficacy of the volume resides as much in the operator's ability to consecrate it as in the book itself, as much in the specific time and place that the magician consecrates the book as in an ongoing textual tradition. Efforts by scribes of the *Ars notoria* to lend a powerful and numinous appearance to their manuscripts may be regarded as a comparable effort to enhance the text or to emphasize that its supratextual qualities are the most important things about it.

I began this section with a heading that implies a separation between the texts and the practice of necromantic magic. In comparison with Scholastic image magic, the collections so far examined betray a very different relationship between the compiler and the original text and between the operator and the written text. Like many other features of ritual magic collections, the habit of editing, rewriting, or reformulating a work suggests that collectors were not concerned with reproducing the original text exactly as received. Even if a text was not altered, the uses to which it was put in different settings could vary a great deal. The "free-form" system of organization and the permeable boundaries between texts had the further effect of deemphasizing the importance of the written book itself, in the sense that there was no direct correspondence between the organization of text on the page and the ceremony that might be developed from it. The ritual performed could vary substantially according to circumstance. When John of Morigny rewrote the Solomonic *Ars notoria*, he was far less concerned about the source of the original material than he was about the authenticity of his new work. The Rawlinson collections suggest a similar pattern of transmission, one seen in the Society of Antiquaries collection. Texts have been extracted, rewritten, or recombined in ways that can make them quite different from their source. Were material from a text of Scholastic image magic to appear here, it would probably be broken into bits and pieces, with no introduction or mention of the author. Whereas manuscripts of image magic almost uniformly identify the author or source of the text and usually strive to preserve the letter, the Rawlinson scribes seem more concerned with conveying the correct spirit.

The Practice of Necromantic Magic

The vast bulk of the Rawlinson collection is devoted to conjuring, and it includes illustrations of pentagrams and other magical figures, lengthy prayers, incantations, and successive operations for summoning, binding, and dismissing demons. But precisely how many of the rituals may have been conducted remains conjectural. Taken as a whole, the book employs a variety of ritual performances, such as fasting, preparation of materials or tools, wearing of special clothes, suffumigations, consecrations, exorcisms, conjurations, and prayers. The operations seek a variety of ends, among them finding treasure or stolen goods, detecting a thief, getting spirits to do one's bidding, creating illusions, discovering secret information, or gaining wisdom. The collection also includes a certain amount of necromantic magic, employing astrological conditions that might be classed as "astral magic," although, as we shall see, this astral magic has been largely incorporated into necromantic practices.

One of the principal techniques employed by the scribe of section A is the conjuring of spirits with the use of a young boy, although other divinatory devices are also used.[69] Typically, the ceremonies involve the conjuring and binding of demons in much the same way as would occur without the use of a young boy. After the usual dramatic prayers, suffumigations, gestures, and creation of magic diagrams, the child was supposed to be able to see demons or spirits in some object, usually a mirror or crystal. The technique is an old one. John of Salisbury mentions that a priest attempted to use him for this purpose when he was a boy, but that he could see nothing.[70] The conjuration that Benvenuto Cellini witnessed in the Coliseum was also accomplished with a boy medium and serves as a good example (but perhaps tongue in cheek) of the dramatic results that could be achieved with a suggestible or imaginative child.[71] The boy saw demons in the smoke and darkness and managed to thoroughly terrify the adult participants in the ceremony. The fact that this technique endured may well be attributed to the more dependable results it returned. In an age when every living adult believed in the immanence and power of demons, a child involved in the complex and evocative rituals recorded here might easily be convinced that he could see something. He might also discover that he had a marvelous ability to attract adult attention or favor by *pretending* that he could. Either way, the results for the operator could be equally effective and satisfying.

The Rawlinson A collection devotes many of its pages to treasure hunting, identifying thieves, and finding stolen goods.[72] Much less dangerous than efforts to inflict harm by occult methods or to curry favor in politics, these practices addressed common concerns and may have enabled a practitioner to make something of a living. Many of these practices correspond with what we know about professional necromancers and cunning folk in England in the premodern period.[73] At the same time, other aspects of this collection suggest broader interests and a closer affiliation with the theurgic traditions of learned magic: operations for wisdom and discernment, for example. The scribe's familiarity with the liturgy also suggests a clerical rather than secular scribe, although the latter possibility cannot be discounted. It is difficult to make any firm claims about the identity of the scribe or the nature of his interests.

The unifying element in these collections is not a theoretical or cosmological framework but rather a belief in the power of Christian ritual practice. The scribes and authors of this material evidently considered contemporary orthodox rituals, and more or less credible elaborations upon them, as particularly powerful or desirable in magical operations. A formula for confession, for example, concludes with a section that has been added explicitly for the protection of a necromancer. A ritual on fol. 125 for those with a malady of the eyes (*dolorem in oculis*) would seem out of place in this volume except that it involves the use of a psalm (perhaps a kind of analogue for a "secret" of nature in a volume interested in image magic). An interesting section mentioned above demands that whoever desires salvation must hold to the Catholic faith and provides the Chalcedonian trinitology, the Nicene Christology, the litany of the saints, and assorted prayers. Psalms appear at various points, sometimes with no explanation, sometimes interspersed between prayers in magical operations. The text usually gives only the first line, evidently in the assumption that the user would be able to recite them from memory.[74] The first chapter of John, which the scribe of section A has included for ritual purposes, was recited at the end of every Mass in late medieval England.[75] Its use in the Mass and also in exorcism, not its philosophical tone, may explain its significance to the scribe. Certainly, its use in orthodox ritual lent it powerful ritual significance. This biblical text is assumed to have magical power in its own right, in the same fashion as the various invocations or orations. Since the passage is not contained within one of the constituent treatises on conjuring but stands on its own, the practitioner appears to have incorporated contemporary religious practices into his own magical operations.

A tendency to emphasize experience and an attitude of attentiveness characterizes these collections as well. The first paragraphs of a conjuring operation may yield very little by way of instructions for operation. Some give no instructions at all; others insist upon at least a three-day period of abstinence followed by confession of sins. During this period, the operator must avoid any kind of pollution, so a relatively high level of personal monitoring was presumably necessary, and the donning of clean clothing prior to operation was also recommended. The conjurations that follow commonly run to several folios and would have required long periods of intense concentration to perform. If, as I have suggested, these operations also involved many of the other texts in the volume, a more complex picture of the operations emerges. Prior to any operations, one would have to perform a dedicated ritual to consecrate the book—and presumably, if one added material to it, one would have to repeat this ritual. A single operation might involve ensuring that the astrological and liturgical times were propitious, reciting special prayers for wisdom and discernment, or perhaps angelic protection, ritual bathing, shaving, and suffumigation, reciting a specialized prayer of confession to protect the operator, and reciting a dedicated series of prayers and psalms. Somewhere in the midst of this, the operator might have recited the first chapter of the Gospel of John. The sensuality of fasting, special clothing, suffumigations, bathing, and other bodily preparations would have enhanced the experiential aspects of the rituals, and these were supposed to lead to dream visions, waking visions of some kind, or vicarious experiences through the skryer and attentiveness to his reports. In short, although less onerous than the intensive preparations laid out in the *Ars notoria* and *Sworn Book*, necromantic operations still involved a high level of attunement to interior states, to the discipline of ritual performance, and to individual experience.

Astrology and Image Magic in the Rawlinson Collections

The common standard works of Scholastic image magic, such as the books of images attributed to Ptolemy or Thābit, the Hermetic *De quindecim stellis*, and even the less common ones like the *Liber lune*, are entirely absent from the Rawlinson collections, although raw probability might predict the opposite. This codex runs to 160 folios and includes approximately seventy separate items, each between a few lines and five folios in length. One might reasonably expect one of these image magic texts to appear here, especially as they were at least as numerous as necromantic texts and, given their presence in major libraries such as St. Augustine's Abbey and the Austin Friars at York, comparatively accessible. By the time this collection was assembled, they had been in circulation for perhaps two hundred years, making the probability that they might appear here that much higher. And since the texts are often quite short, they would have been easy to copy. Moreover, while a scribe might not include a text of conjuring in an astrological codex, as it might be prudent to hide such a conjuring text, there would be no reason to exclude a text like Thābit's *De imaginibus* from a conjuring collection if one were interested in such things. Nonetheless, the better-known and more commonly copied texts of image magic rarely appear in ritual magic collections before 1500, and this pattern remains the most common prior to 1600 as well. The only early exception in Britain is Erghome's collection of "superstitious" works, and this codex, as we have seen, follows the conventional division of ritual magic and image magic, probably because it was compiled by someone who regarded them all as problematic.

What makes this more interesting is that, as we have seen, some forms of astrological image magic do appear in necromantic collections. So it is not a lack of interest in that sort of magic that occasions the codicological separation. Rather, the two sorts of text often appear to derive from distinct sources, and if they were ultimately derived from the same sources, they have become different kinds of texts in separate and parallel streams of transmission. The straightforward work of astrological image magic that appears in the Society of Antiquaries collections is rare, and the other has been heavily edited in patterns more common to those of ritual magic. The Rawlinson collections betray the same patterns. Some of the techniques they employ are informed by astrology or structured around astrological conditions, but there is scant evidence of the kind of interest in natural philosophy or *naturalia* that informed Scholastic image magic.

A portion of Rawlinson A, containing several texts (fols. 29v–35r), presents material usually associated with images in a fashion reminiscent of works like the *Liber lune*. The texts furnish an array of astrological information, such as "the howses of the vii planetts" and "the natures and kinde of the xii synes perteynyng to the elements" (fols. 29r–30r). The lists of angel names, more astrological details, and suffumigations in subsequent pages further suggest the practices of Arabic image magic. As in the *Liber lune*, the text furnishes the material in a systematic manner. Each of the elements of the magical procedures appears in a separate section, organized according to the time of operation. But the text moves on immediately to instructions for conjuring demons: "When the sun is in a warm and dry sign, it is good to conjure infernal spirits; when in a warm and wet sign, aerial spirits; in a cold and humid sign, aquatic spirits; and in a cold and dry sign, earthly spirits."[76] Among the other magical activities listed in this section, we find speaking with spirits and finding stolen goods (*ad loquendum spiribus* [sic] *et furta habenda*). While the verb *coniuro* might conceivably be applied to the processes involved in standard image magic, speaking with spirits is much more commonly the province of ritual magic. Subsequent instructions also make clear that the instrument of conjuring was to be a standard necromantic circle, not a talisman: "Therefore see to it always that the air is clear before you begin to make the circle. But if clouds arise when you are making the circle, do not do any more. But if clouds arise after you have made the circle and completed it, then operate, since the sign is that you will have no impediment."[77] So the operations employ astrology in support of the explicit conjuring of demons, very much the province of ritual magic and necromancy.

At the beginning of the next section, the scribe returns to a discussion of astrology and once again includes many of the elements common to standard Scholastic image magic texts. Several tables in Latin link planets with hours. "There follow three tables correlating angels and suffumigations with the days of the week, which are, of course, listed by their standard planetary names" (fols. 31v–34v). In some instances, works of image magic also detail astrological conditions, appropriate hours for operation, and the suffumigations and angel names associated with them. Closer examination, however, reveals important elements quite unlike the standard works of image magic, which suggests that we are dealing with quite a different kind of text. To begin with, no descriptions of images appear here, and although it is conceivable that angel names could have been engraved or written on a ring or other object, no such instructions are provided. The angel names are Hebraic, not Arabic.[78] This could suggest a Hebraic source, or it could be that the Arabic names have been replaced in a Christian context, where the Hebrew names would have been regarded as more acceptable or efficacious. Although the materials are similar, the suffumigations do not correspond with patterns in Arabic sources. The discussions of image magic in the *Liber lune* and the *Speculum astronomiae* both hold that certain suffumigations are to be used for good purposes and others for bad. Rather than associate a suffumigation with the nature of the magical activity, the Rawlinson scribe links them to the days of the week and, most tellingly, assigns a final one to the operator (*Subfumigatio tua*)! Suffumigating the operator might well derive from the use of incense in the Mass, since Arabic magic characteristically only purifies or intensifies the effect of the image by holding it in the smoke.[79] The single short prayer included in this section is addressed to God and invokes the Trinity. This is a familiar pattern in ritual magic texts, in which Christian elements have been superimposed upon what appear to be practices or structures originally deriving from Arabic or Hebraic sources. Further, the prayer to God and the angels in this section includes the line "and you aforementioned glorious angels know the questions that I desire to ask, helpers and supporters to me in all my business."[80] Asking questions of angels, which appears to be at least part of the intent of this text, is well outside the bounds of the vast majority of Scholastic image magic texts.

Only one short section in the Rawlinson B collection cannot be demonstrated to have been motivated by an interest in conjuring or similar activities. Yet even in this case, involving the making of two rings, the astrology is unsophisticated and the practices are overlaid with Christian ritual. The second instruction for making a ring appears to be a composite text, more focused on making an image on goat skin than the ring that it initially discusses:

> The ring of Mercury ought to be made from copper, just like Mars, in order to have all knowledge and victory in every struggle with any lord, and that you will not be condemned by any judge. When you wish to operate, fast on the day of mercury (Wednesday) to the evening. That same night, make this character 🜿 and the name of the angel, which is Yparon, with the blood of a fox or cat on the skin of a he-goat. When you come before the judge or any other man, write this character on your chest or forehead with the name of the Angel. Hold the document in your hand, and he will not have the power to condemn you. Make the ring in day of mercury and his hour.[81]

Very much like some of the instructions in the Society of Antiquaries collection, the operation employs both a ring and a leather amulet, and it is conceivable that the parchment was supposed to be enclosed in the ring in a similar way. In the passage that follows, evidently meant to be connected with the preceding two passages, the scribe refers to the rings and, presumably, the leather amulet as "creatures of the planets" and says they are to be "exorcised" to make them effective. The spirits of the planets are said to have created the powers of the rings by the power of the angels Uryel, Salatiel, and Acoel. The prayer exorcises the planetary materials in preparation for their magical use, through the power of God, and seems to have been based upon the standard exorcism for salt.[82] A subsequent prayer to God, invoking the tetragrammaton, explicitly requests that the ring be effective. We have here the basic material for Arabic image magic, that is, an astrological image engraved under certain astrological conditions and a cosmology that conflates astrological influences with the planetary "spirits." The astrology is not sophisticated, however, referring only to planetary hours and days. The angel names are once again Hebraic, not Arabic. The use of leather amulets, more common in ritual magic collections, also seems to have Hebraic roots. Further, the processes involve a number of ritual performances drawn from the liturgy, including an exorcism, the invoking of higher powers, and Christian prayer. Finally, the ring has become only a part of the process, to a large extent displaced by the leather amulet. These features suggest not only that this text is at least a hybrid but that, as in the rest of the constituent texts, the scribe's central concern is to elaborate an authentic, or at least believable, Christian magical ritual. This situation, in which the authors or redactors have subsumed the astrological elements (and perhaps the original sources) in magical operations dominated by explicitly Christian and ritual elements, may be detected in other features of these two collections.

Neither collection contains a hint of interest in natural philosophy, theories of magic, or even *naturalia* in general, despite the presence of astrological material. Some portions of the Rawlinson notebook seek to provide general information, which could imply an interest in general cosmological structure. For example, the scribe provides general discussions of astrological conditions, the association of certain planets with certain days, suffumigations for each day, and days that are not good for magical operations (fols. 29v–35v). But none of this amounts to an abstract philosophical analysis of the processes that underlie the magical operations, such as were known to, or actually copied out by, the scribes of image magic. Finally, no texts of natural wonders, secrets, astronomy/astrology, alchemy, natural philosophy, or magic theory appear here, which might point to a common interest in these materials, if not a theoretical orientation. Some written charms appear, for example, "goode to bere upon a bedy for many causis." But the closest this volume gets to secrets, astrology, astronomy, or natural philosophy is a short table (fol. 62v) that identifies the usual shorthand symbols for the planets. Thus the texts of the Rawlinson collections contain magical practices that are superficially similar to those found in collections of Scholastic image magic. But, as in the case of Society of Antiquaries 39, fols. 1–17, scribes drew these practices from a generally distinct set of sources and then employed, understood, transmitted, and collected them in almost entirely different ways.

A few other aspects of these sections are worth mentioning. First, the lack of clarity on how one might use the tables and other instructions in these sections suggests the mix-and-match approach taken elsewhere in this volume and in the ritual magic tradition in general. Second, as we have seen elsewhere, the operations give the operator a central position. When the Jewish exorcists in Acts 19:13–17 tried to cast out demons by invoking Jesus, of whom Paul preaches, the demon answers, "Jesus I know, Paul I know, but who are ye?" Had they been good Christians, they would have been able to accomplish the task, the names would have been powerful, and *they would have been recognized*. In a similar way, the moral status of the operator is critical to the success of necromantic operations. Image magic is morally neutral and engages the operator's interior state only insofar as an image in the imagination or firm intent might aid the operation. Otherwise, the status of the operator is irrelevant. In ritual magic, baptism, confession, prayer, and masses together with fasting, abstinence, and silence protect and strengthen the operator. In a similar way, the suffumigation of the operator suggests both the apotropaic use of incense in the Mass but also an effort to ritually purify the operator. Astrological elements, whatever their derivation, have thus been wound together in a form more typical of Christian ritual magic.

Angels, Demons, and Hidden Knowledge

The author of the *Speculum astronomiae* doubted that angel magic was acceptable and regarded angel names as a poor camouflage for demonic mechanisms. Yet some, like John of Morigny, took the division between angelic and demonic magic very seriously indeed. So long as John felt that he was able to make the distinction, he avoided necromancy. Yet when he felt that this was not possible, he abandoned his hopes for good magic and for a period practiced necromancy. Two questions arise. How did practitioners of necromancy regard angel magic? And what are the commonalities between the two that might encourage John to choose necromantic magic as a replacement for his failed attempts at the angelic magic of the notory art? We have already discussed a number of principal features common to scribes and authors of ritual magic that help us to understand John's necromantic turn. They regard the operator as central to the magical process, attribute great power to ritual practice, feel free to rework or combine texts in various ways, and employ them in flexible and combinatory patterns. To these features we can add three more. First, angelic and demonic magic are, for the most part, inextricable in necromantic practice, making the dividing line between the two less than clear. Angelic assistance was regarded as crucial, particularly for protection but also for discerning the truth in books or the words of spirits. Second, the processes involved in working with these creatures are often quasi-theurgic and have no clearly predefined goals apart from some form of communication with spirits. Third, both angels and demons were employed to discover information that could then be applied to the practice of magic.

Broadly speaking, a common interest in visions and ritual links necromancy and the notory art. Yet the association goes deeper, in the sense that both angelic and demonic forms of magic were often practiced by the same people and in many cases were blended together. In magic collections of all varieties, we have seen the use of angel names in the construction of magical images. The *Ars notoria* involved purely angelic magic, but the London Honorius only largely so. Although their operations were more highly ritualized than the practices of the standard image magic texts, necromancers also employed angels in aid of magical images, sometimes as protection, sometimes even in binding rituals. In part, the similar cosmological status of planetary deities or spirits, angels, and demons meant that they could be conflated, especially where a translator of an Arabic or Hebraic text felt compelled to nudge a category like a planetary deity into Christian cosmology. The Society of Antiquaries collection is a good example of how ambiguous the resulting blend could be. While this confusion of categories appears to be more or less accidental, the divinatory use of angels in necromancy was not. There are strong liturgical traditions for devotion to angels that would logically have necromantic analogues. In addition, angels served different purposes from their infernal brothers.

The usual duty assumed by angels in the orthodox setting was to protect or to act as a messenger for God. In the late Middle Ages, angels were very much a part of popular affective piety. Litanies that included angels and cults dedicated to angels were both common.[83] So it is not surprising to find in the Rawlinson manual a prayer written by the scribe of section A that seeks the aid of a guardian angel to protect the necromancer from misfortune and evil demons (fol. 50). But the angel's messenger status, which allowed the angel to transmit information to select humans, also included the task of infusing wisdom. The acquisition of knowledge, particularly associated with the notory art, finds some analogues in necromantic practices. The first passage in the necromancer's manual edited by Richard Kieckhefer (Clm 849) is an interesting example.[84] Undoubtedly modeled upon an *Ars notoria*, it promises knowledge of the liberal arts, employs Hebraic-sounding angel names, and seeks to achieve its goals through dream visions. Instead of supplicating, however, the operator conjures; instead of *notae*, we have *circuli*. In short, the text is necromantic. But this direct emulation is not common and is not found in the Rawlinson collections, where the operations that employ angels tend to seek visions and knowledge more applicable to the goals and problems of necromantic practice.

In some cases, the Rawlinson scribes employed angels for treasure hunting or detecting thieves and stolen goods. The final folio in the collection (162r) contains a prayer for a dream vision (*Ad visionem in sompno*). Unfortunately, occupying the last folio of the original manuscript, it is badly worn. Although very short, it is similar to an *Ars notoria* in the sense that it seeks a dream in which an angel appears and reveals things. The initial prayer asks for information about "this thing," indicating that the reader is to fill in the specifics, but gives no clue as to what the thing might be (*ut doceant et respondeant michi rectam veritatem istius rei N.*). Employing the plural would have been more suggestive of the general kind of knowledge sought through the *Ars notoria*. Although otherwise badly mutilated, that last page contains a prayer, which evidently requests information concerning a treasure. One fragment of its text seems to imply that gold, silver, or gems are to be transferred from their hiding place.[85] Thus it appears likely that the "thing" mentioned in the first section was simply treasure, and unlikely that this was a figurative way of speaking about a storehouse of knowledge. But if angels could be employed in such instrumental capacities, is there any difference between how angels and demons were to be employed?

In fact, angels do seem to specialize not just in transferring information but also in the more engaged role of helping the operator to become wise. Most of the passages involving angels are unspecific about the kind of knowledge they seek. One example makes use of a magical image (a pentagram inscribed with the names of five angels) and an abbreviated prayer. The short passage, amounting to only a few lines, invokes several "good angels" in pursuit of answers to "my questions."[86] The nature of the knowledge is not specified. Another passage in the astrological material in section A describes angels as "helpers and supporters in all my business," but also as angels who "know the questions that I desire to ask."[87] Throughout the collection, then, angels play a particular role in providing knowledge, both in response to general or specific questions but also in the more engaged role of helper and supporter.

Another, more extensive passage bears the somewhat more evocative title *De sene barbato* (Concerning the old bearded man). The instructions purport to bring on a vision of an old man who will reveal things. After laying out extensive ritual performances, including prayers and the creation of a complex magical figure, the text concludes, "then take yourself to bed and an old bearded man will come to you who will respond to you concerning everything."[88] Although much quicker to accomplish, the technique is similar to that of the *Sworn Book of Honorius*. The use of dream visions also may be found in some versions of the *Ars notoria*.[89] While one is left to infer the identity of the old man, the prayer, addressed to God, refers to him as a messenger (*nuntius*) whom God is to send, so there is little doubt that he is supposed to be an angel. What knowledge the old bearded one might reveal to the sleeping operator is not specified. The modest size (one folio) and tone of the piece do not suggest the grand goals of the notory art. Certainly, no indication is given that the old man is capable of infusing spiritual or intellectual gifts; his function seems to be limited to the verbal communication of unspecified information.[90] Given the practical goals of many of the rituals, one suspects that a user's questions might be similarly practical and worldly, yet there is no mention of treasure or stolen goods here, and the nature of what the old man might reveal is quite open-ended.

Other passages that seek knowledge suggest that the information desired may have concerned the practice of magic itself. One contains a prayer in which the operator asks for divine and angelic aid. While this aid ultimately might have been employed in the pursuit of pecuniary or at least worldly goals, the intermediate goals and the language employed suggest otherwise:

Let irreprehensible memory, incomprehensible wisdom, undeniable power fill my consciousness. Let your wisdom, and the sweetness of your grace, fortify my mind. Let all your holy angels with all the powers of heaven desire to look upon and illuminate my face and heart without end. Let the wisdom by which you made everything, the intelligence by which you transformed everything, the enduring blessedness in which you established the angels, and the love and generous charity *through which you taught Adam all knowledge*, form me, fill me anew, instruct me, correct me, restore me, and make me anew *that I might be made wise in the mandates to be understood and received from your angels and in the vision and knowledge of spirits*, for the salvation of my body and soul and the salvation of everyone believing in your name which is blessed forever. Amen.

Therefore, I pray to you, undivided Father of all, and I trust in your complete pity. So hearken to my petition, you who mercifully hear those devotedly crying out to you. Grant me, I entreat, Lord my God, grace, wisdom, virtue, and power, that an angel or angels, that is, this one or those .N. [i.e., fill in angel name(s)] may appear benignly to me whenever I invoke him or them, just as they may avail to fulfill my truthful petition through your glorious majesty and holy name, blessed in eternity, you who live and reign, God through all ages. Amen.[91] (Emphasis added.)

Although it has been substantially shortened and modified, the first paragraph of the prayer derives from the *Ars notoria*.[92] This in itself demonstrates the fluidity between necromantic practice and theurgic magic, but this passage also demonstrates the textually fluid nature of ritual magic and the tendency of scribes to pillage material from prior texts and adapt it to their own purposes. The *Ars notoria* makes use of this prayer at a variety of points, sometimes for protection. But the original prayer also mentions the original science taught to Adam and his being "made new" in understanding God's laws. So, while the original version makes no specific mention of seeking understanding of the laws of angels and visions, the general intent of the passage and of the art, to seek enlightenment and spiritual gifts, persists in the Rawlinson version.

The reworked prayer falls into two parts. As is typical, the first section sets the tone, reminds God of past glories and mercies, and assures him of the operator's holy intentions. The second makes the specific request. But the nature of the "truthful petition" is unspecified. It is unlikely that the prayer is simply a kind of general request for God's aid in the pursuit of angelic and demonic magic, which might or might not involve visions. The prayer asks that the angels appear in a nonthreatening form, and this certainly suggests a vision. Further, as the operator is supposed to fill in the specific petition, the prayer does not appear to be a general prayer for success but rather an operation in its own right. Typically, the *historiola* in a prayer or incantation reflect the request. The operator's reminder to God of the wisdom given to Adam and the repeated references to wisdom, memory, and knowledge suggest that the goals sought in the second section have to do with acquiring knowledge. As in the examples from the scribe of Rawlinson A, the knowledge sought might be very specific, and there is no way of knowing what an individual practitioner might have done with the prayer, given its rather open-ended nature.

If we take the prayer literally, the knowledge it seeks has to do with becoming wise in "understanding and undertaking the laws of your angels and in the vision and knowledge of spirits." While this leaves quite a bit of room for interpretation, the operation plainly seeks knowledge about magic involving angels and demons. It also makes clear that, so far as the author is concerned, angelic and demonic magic are of a piece and not to be separated. But why would one seek this knowledge from visionary experiences, particularly since it would seem so crucial to successful operation? The consistent demands in demonic invocations that the demons speak truly or desist from mocking the operator underline the fact that there was considerable doubt that the rituals would provide the unassisted operator with the truth.[93] The prayer certainly seeks skill in discernment. But would it not be easier simply to write down "the laws of the angels" in an instruction manual? The request for knowledge of this kind implies that reading conjuring manuals was insufficient and that the magic practitioner had to become wise in other ways. This might come about through long experience in the art, as John of Morigny suggests, but the goal of the prayer implies that visions of the divine were the appropriate means of gaining truth and wisdom. In short, the operation seeks something very much like the divine guides of Brother John, Honorius, Toz, or the readers of the *Liber Razielis:* guides who assisted in the interpretation of texts or supplemented them where they were insufficient. The passage also implies that the received text was not the final word. The necromancer assumed that his magic was fluid and something upon which he could build with further operation. Its practitioners regarded ritual magic as a living process, not limited to the instructions provided in whatever texts they had acquired. In a tradition of this kind, it is no surprise that the scribes, collectors, and authors of ritual magic texts altered, extracted, and transformed them as freely as they did.

That necromancers regarded their activities as information-gathering exercises is also attested in the operations with demons. In a conjuring procedure described by the scribe of Rawlinson B, the information gained through visionary experience is directly connected with future magical practice. In particular, the scribe gives a list of questions to ask a spirit who has been conjured:

> When the spiryt is apperyd: What is thy name? Under what state and what dynite [i.e., dignity] hast thow? What is thy powyr and thy offyse? Undyr what planet and sygn art thow. Of what parte arte thow of the world? Of which element art thow? Whych is thy monyth? What is thy day and thyn owyr? What is thyne howre, day or nyght? Whych is thy winde? What be they caretes that thow abyst to? Whych is thy mansion and thy day? Which is thy sterre? Which is thy stone? Which is thy erbe? What is thyne offyse to do. What is thy metale? What is thyne Aungellys name that thow moste obeyst to? And in what lykenes aperyst thow? How many commyst thow wythall? (Fol. 65.)

The scribe of Rawlinson A records a similar passage following a conjuration: "And if [the spirit] appears, show him the pentacle of Solomon and ask him his name and his office and what his character is and under what governor he is and what his days, hours, and months are, etc." (120v). Evidently one did not always know what demon would appear, suggesting either that operations for a particular demon might go wrong or that some of the conjuring exercises were more like exploratory missions. One way or another, the open-ended nature of the operation made possible the acquisition of new knowledge not contained in the conjuring manual. The author (assuming he was able to achieve a visionary experience himself or employ an effective medium to have one for him) would be able to record new information to be used in subsequent operations. The same pattern, this time in angel operations, also appears at the end of the *Almandal*.[94]

Once this kind of information was attained, the scribe could employ it in operations like the general-purpose conjuration of any malign spirit (*cuius-cumque spiritus maligni*) (fols. 24r–28v). In this example, the operator was required to supply only the name of the spirit, but if more information was acquired, presumably it could also be employed to construct conjurations tailored to a specific spirit. These kinds of operations implicitly recognized that the knowledge contained in the texts was limited and could be supplemented through magical operations themselves. The general-purpose angel-summoning rituals could also be used for this kind of exploratory magic or to confirm information derived from demons. As the examples of John of Morigny and Honorius of Thebes indicate, angels would certainly have been far more dependable sources and aids in the composition of new texts. While we have only anecdotal evidence for this practice prior to 1500, there are numerous later examples. A mid-sixteenth-century manuscript—London, British Library, Additional 36674, fols. 47r–62v, discussed in chapter 6—purports to communicate with the divine and with spirits of the dead to acquire information and even books about magical operations. The best-known examples of these kinds of operations are the "angel conversations" of John Dee. The colossal volumes of obscure information received from the angels have in turn become an important part of esoteric traditions and sources in their own right.

At the beginning of this chapter I raised the question of how John of Morigny moved so easily between the world of the theurgic and angelic *Ars notoria* and demonic or necromantic magic. The transition appears even more dramatic given how powerfully John opposed the demonic magic he had once practiced to the good system of prayers with which he replaced it. Simply put, the answer is that the practitioner of the notory art, the necromancer, and the variety of practitioners between these two extremes share a good deal of common ground in how they operated, treated manuscripts, discerned truth, wrote books of magic, and mythologized these processes. These commonalities unite ritual magic practices and also point to a commonly experienced set of countervailing forces, which I have described as Brother John's dilemma, that formed the creative core of this tradition.

Necromantic magic explicitly employs demons, gives less emphasis to protracted periods of spiritual preparation, and in general gives more latitude for seeking worldly goals of one kind or another, but otherwise its mechanisms are very similar to theurgic or angelic magic. Ritual magic of all stripes employs angels for assistance, particularly to aid discernment, gain knowledge, and get protection from demons. Ritual magic practitioners commonly supported their practices with natural forces, such as the disposition of the heavens, or employed techniques associated with natural magic, such as astrological images. But because the operative core of their magic lay elsewhere, they exhibit no desire to associate their practices with *naturalia*, and in fact often appear to have no particular independent interest in it at all. In place of natural sources of power, they employ Christian liturgy, words of power, and biblical passages, as well as the power of Christian rituals or observances such as fasting, abstinence or chastity, prayer, exorcism, masses, and the sacraments themselves. Without baptism, success in this kind of magic was impossible. While these elements were naturally powerful in themselves, ritual magic operations additionally emphasize and draw upon the spiritual condition of the operator, a resource requiring constant attention. When the elements are combined, the magical event occurs in, around, through, and because of the master. The rites also employ mechanisms emphasizing his experience of the numinous (vicarious or direct) that have a reasonable chance of delivering subjectively satisfying results: dreams, skryers, affective states, contemplative exercises, fasting, and a discipline of attentiveness. And the emphasis on these sorts of mechanisms evidently attracted people interested in compelling or dramatic spiritual experiences. Whether conjuring demons or calling upon angels, then, ritual magic practitioners were interested in the same sorts of experiences and used very similar techniques, many of them drawing deeply upon interior spiritual resources.

The various forms of ritual magic also shared a common approach to the received text. Unlike scribes of image magic, who transformed the library of image magic into something more like the elusive ideal of natural magic, ritual magic scribes sought to wed their source texts to Christian ritual practices. The dramatic transformations this required were no doubt made more conceivable because scribes simultaneously recognized the fallibility of their often corrupt or fragmentary sources. Perhaps owing in part to the state of these texts, they also regarded magic texts less as containers of truth than as means of attaining it. Ritual magic had to be learned, not merely performed, and the knowledge crucial to understanding it had to be acquired by non-textual means, through practical experience, divine guidance, or instruction by an adept. The brotherhood that passed on the knowledge of the *Sworn Book* and the mages who instructed Saint Jerome appear to be more a matter of wish fulfillment by scribes who wished they had such guides, a further indication of scribal struggles with interpretation. At the same time, scribes did not hesitate to pillage earlier texts in order to create new ritual practices, and it is perhaps this culture of pillaging that led to the mix-and-match approach evident in necromantic manuals, where discrete texts were copied in the assumption that they would be used in a variety of contexts and when needed. The tradition thus tended to disassociate magic rituals or truths from the received texts. Scribes of image magic could (and did) refer to the standards articulated in the *Speculum astronomiae*. Lacking any such point of orientation, the scribes and authors of ritual magic texts turned back to their own techniques, both mythically and literally, and the revelations or divine guidance they offered. But finding the truth was not the end of the process. For Brother John, the logical result of his engagement with the texts and his practice of necromancy was a new book; the same logic also applied to his work with the notory art and the *Liber visionum*.

John's approach to authorship applied to both necromantic and theurgic texts because it was a logical extension of the techniques, myths, and psychological realities shared by both sorts of magic. The ritual magic operator was central to the magical processes, his attentiveness to himself and his surroundings crucial to their success, and his experiences crucial to discovering how to make them work. Ritual magic texts commonly promoted mythologies of their divine status, but they gave as much if not more emphasis to the divinely guided editing or translation process through which the text was transferred to the reader. The tradition also tended to emphasize personal merit, as in the case of Brother John and a host of other ritual magic authors, or accomplishment, as witnessed in the bragging sections of necromantic manuals. In a variety of ways they draw readers into fantasies of being similarly worthy or accomplished, particularly of being themselves part of the process of divinely guided transmission. It is thus hardly surprising that these mythologies are reflected in the practices of ritual magic scribes. They routinely extracted, epitomized, reorganized, recombined, and rewrote the texts with which they began. They created rituals designed to derive new knowledge about magic that could not be found in their libraries or perhaps in any other. And as they wrote new texts and practiced their magic, they prayed for divine protection and assistance in discernment.

All of these features united in dynamic tension in Brother John's dilemma. The incoherence or cultural otherness of the received tradition and the desire to make sense of it, systematize it, and use it drove a process of reinvention. This reinvention was justified through mythologies of divinely guided authorship or editing and even encouraged by the delusions of grandeur these myths could inspire. These myths also encouraged scribes to think of their texts as unstable and insufficient to contain divine truths, an idea that would have been amply attested by the experience of scribes struggling with fragmentary sources. The lack of an authoritative benchmark, however illusory, meant that any reinvention committed to the page, whether derived from the scribe's imagination or from some encounter with the numinous, would be personal, the sense of stability it inspired, fleeting. A new text only added to the multitude of voices claiming divine revelation or sanction. And so the tradition turned in upon itself again and again.

PART III | MAGIC AFTER 1580

While faith in natural magic and astrology, in sympathy and antipathy, and the like, may be seen as great and widespread during the period which we have just reviewed as in any preceding age, use of superstitious ceremonial and magical rite, of incantation, word and number, has fallen off markedly. Occult virtues and relationships in nature are still believed in, but magical procedure is largely abandoned. Thus the way is open for mathematical and scientific method.

—Thorndike, History of Magic and Experimental Science, 6:591

These words, which conclude Thorndike's volumes on the sixteenth century, epitomize a perspective on the historical relation between early modern magic and science from which later scholarship has not radically deviated. They also reflect a common assumption about the distinctiveness of the sixteenth century. Frances Yates has argued for the presence of a magical tradition that fueled the scientific revolution, variously styled "Hermetic" or "kabbalist and Hermetic" and heavily natural and mathematical in focus. Renewed by Ficino under the influence of the Hermetic corpus, the old natural magic was transformed into "astral magic." Under the influence of kabbalism and in the hands of later writers from Pico to Bruno, this tradition of astrological image magic, its assumptions about the relation of humanity to the world, and its increasingly mathematical focus formed the foundation for the new science. Yates's works have themselves been reevaluated by a new generation of scholars who argue for a middle course, insisting upon the importance of occultism as a feature of the sixteenth-century worldview without making it into a major motive force behind the scientific revolution. Yet throughout the debates, most participants have not taken issue with Thorndike's focus upon the medieval traditions of natural magic. Most assume that this is the principal area of continuity—or at least the most significant one—between the medieval and Renaissance traditions of magic. Most also assume that a break with the earlier magical traditions occurred sometime in the late fifteenth century.[1]

A tendency to regard the magic of the sixteenth century as the product of new currents of thought, and to accept Renaissance writers' disavowal of medieval magic at face value, has also led to a selective approach to the sources—a significant body of evidence has remained almost entirely unexamined. Historians have focused on the high points of sixteenth-century occultism, such as Ficino, Pico, Agrippa, and Dee, whose works may be demonstrated, with varying degrees of success, to promote natural magic. Those that do not correspond to the learned magic of the great Renaissance mages are summarily dismissed as remnants of a bygone era. In marked contrast to this assumption, we find a vast literature of ritual magic in sixteenth-century hands, the overwhelming bulk of practical magic literature in manuscript. In addition to the low magic of the necromantic tradition, this library continued to include the high magic of the *Ars notoria* and the *Sworn Book of Honorius* and continued to appeal to an educated audience. In addition, as in previous centuries, this literature treats natural magic as an adjunct or supplementary art, if it includes it at all. It may be that the reason so little work has been done on sixteenth-century magic collections is the limited amount of material in manuscript that confirms assumptions about the importance of natural magic, kabbalism, Hermetic sources, and Renaissance Platonism. To be sure, natural magic continued to be an important part of Renaissance discussions of occult topics, and perhaps the most significant topic in learned discussions of magic. With few exceptions, however, the records of those who actually practiced magic—those who were not merely employing magical ideas for rhetorical or philosophical purposes, not merely promoting or purchasing magical texts as a curiosity but engaged enough to copy texts and compose notebooks—tell a different story.

The collection of image magic in the old Scholastic modes examined thus far, and even the copying of texts associated with that form, virtually ends around 1500. The copying of ritual magic texts, by contrast, flourished. Medieval texts such as the *Liber sacer, Vinculum Salomonis, Clavicula Salomonis* (Key of Solomon), *Thesaurus spirituum*, and various versions of the *Ars notoria* continued to be copied and transformed throughout the century, and a number of new texts appear among the works of necromancy and angel conjuring. In Europe, including Britain, I know of three codices containing ritual magic that survive from the thirteenth century, nine from the fourteenth, twenty-two from the fifteenth, forty-three from the sixteenth, and forty-nine from the seventeenth.[2] Among British manuscripts, twelve manuscripts of ritual magic survive from the fifteenth century, twenty-two from the sixteenth, and even greater numbers from the seventeenth.

Interest in this kind of literature was also represented in printed works. Three editions of the *Fourth Book of Occult Philosophy* (a work concerning ritual magic that circulated under Agrippa's name) and a similar text called *Arbatel* were printed around the middle of the sixteenth century.[3] This is not to mention the multiple editions and translations of both Ficino's *De vita coelitus comparanda* (which, I argue, has extensive commonalities with medieval ritual magic and was used as a source for ritual magic practice) and Agrippa's *De occulta philosophia*.[4] Library records and copies made from printed volumes amply attest that these works were circulating in Britain.[5] The multiple publications of the *Beringos fratres* in seventeenth-century Lyon, the English translation of the Solomonic *Ars notoria* and the *Fourth Book of Occult Philosophy*, and other such printed works continued the pattern in the seventeenth century. Reginald Scot's *Discoverie of Witchcraft* was not intended as a *grimoire*, but it was certainly used in that way, and its publishers evidently reissued it at midcentury, having recognized this potential and the financial returns it offered.[6] In the end, censorship, destruction, the differences of print and manuscript production, and other variables make impossible any accurate numerical comparison of the popularity of ritual magic with other forms of magic on the basis of print and manuscript copies. At the same time, it cannot be denied that ritual magic was flourishing and was in no danger of diminishing in popularity in the sixteenth century. To recall Thorndike's words, an interest in "ceremonial and magical rite," far from diminishing, flourished in the sixteenth century, and with it the complex problems of Brother John's dilemma.

6

SIXTEENTH-CENTURY
COLLECTIONS OF MAGIC TEXTS

If we date the beginning of the "magical renaissance" to the publication of Ficino's *De vita coelitus comparanda* and Pico's *Oration on the Dignity of Man, 900 Theses,* and *Apology* in the 1480s, the new era they inaugurated does not appear to have had a significant impact upon the traditions of ritual magic. Although we may detect new influences and perhaps broader intellectual horizons in sixteenth-century ritual magic collections, neither the texts nor the way they were regarded and transmitted changed a great deal. The texts common in collections of the fifteenth century and other very similar material still populated the manuals of the sixteenth. Necromancy and the *Ars notoria* were evidently still the most prominent focus of ritual practices. In addition, scribes struggled with their texts and treated and transmitted them in the same sorts of ways as they had in centuries past. A focus on resonant ritual over precise transmission, a tendency to seek the truth in appeals to the numinous areas of human experience—these did not change. The transmission of texts remained a fluid and creative process. So also continued the concern with discovering the truth, both in the texts themselves and in the practical results they might produce. For an example, and before examining the broader nature of magic manuscripts in the sixteenth century, let us turn to two representative manuscripts.

A Necromantic Manual: Sloane 3853

Textual and paleographic evidence suggests that London, British Museum, Sloane 3853 was composed in the middle or latter part of the sixteenth century. The first part of the volume is written in a sixteenth-century British secretary hand (fols. 3–45 and 141v–174), and an italic hand fills in one section and completes the volume (fols. 138–141r and 176–266). Although the secretary hand could suggest a date considerably earlier, the scribe does what many scribes of ritual magic did after 1533: he refers to Cornelius Agrippa (fol. 53v). It is possible, but relatively unlikely, that the scribe had access to an early manuscript version of Agrippa's *De occulta philosophia* (completed by 1510). The balance of the evidence, however, suggests that the manuscript must be dated to after the printed edition of *De occulta philosophia* in 1533. The scribe refers to one of his own texts as "De occulta philosophia." The borrowing of the title of Agrippa's magnum opus suggests an even later date, when Agrippa's renown had spread sufficiently to encourage such emulation. Other paleographic evidence also suggests a later date, in particular the italic hand used to set off sections like the table of contents from the rest of the text.

Like many other sixteenth-century scribes, the writer of Sloane 3853 endeavored to impress the reader with the appearance of the manuscript. One of the first features one notices is the crude cipher used to disguise certain words in the headings. The scribe replaced each vowel with the consonant that follows it in the alphabet. While a little startling at first, the cipher would not deter or fool anyone of normal intelligence, especially since it is applied only to certain significant words that can be inferred from context. For example, *coniuratio* is rendered *cpnkxrbtkp*. (My first reaction, since the word was obvious, was puzzlement over what appeared to be a sudden combination of rather odd letterforms. Why does that O have a tail? What a peculiar I!) Clearly, the practice was intended to lend a certain air of mystery to the codex. This kind of self-conscious production of a book that *looks* magical may also be seen in Royal 17.A.XLII, a parchment manuscript containing a translation of the *Liber sacer* composed in black letter, a hand characteristic of higher-level manuscripts of the preceding centuries. The mock frontispiece for Sloane 3847 (fol. 2r) also has the effect of loudly advertising the contents of the volume. While the texts of fifteenth-century magic could involve self-conscious efforts to impress the reader visually, only scribes of the *Ars notoria* had expended this much energy on design in order to make an ordinary page *appear* magical. The kinds of overt attention to the design of magic texts evident in the sixteenth century may be a response to an intellectual environment more tolerant of learned magic, or to the vogue magic enjoyed in this period. As with the late medieval manuscripts of the *Ars notoria*, these scribal affectations may have been an attempt to make the manuscript appear more efficacious to impress a reader or potential purchaser. But, like the earlier examples of that work, these efforts may also be a private affectation reflecting either the desire to associate the text with the numinous or the conviction that it *was* powerful and magical.

With a few possible exceptions, the content of the collection in Sloane 3853 does not differ a great deal from that of the fifteenth-century collections we have examined. It begins with the *Thesaurus spirituum*, which, as we saw in chapter 5, also travels in an extracted form as the *Practica nigromantiae*. At forty folios (5r–45v), this is a relatively extensive single work on conjuring. The introduction claims that the work records the practices of Roger Bacon and a certain Turk, and there follows a set of seven rules for operations. These operations are indistinguishable from what we have seen in the Rawlinson collection, combining angelic and demonic magic. They involve the binding and deploying of demons, the standard set of purifying preparations, the construction of magic circles and a magic room, the composition of a magic circle and its consecration, and the use of characters and sigils. Among the instructions we find the characteristic open-ended rituals, such as an unguent that allows the operator to address and converse with spirits (*ungentum preciosissius ad cotidie aloquendum et colloquendum spiritus*) (fol. 30v). The various versions of this text correspond roughly to one another, but their significant divergences witness the typically fluid nature of ritual magic texts. For example, the version in Sloane 3853 corresponds more or less to the text of the same work in Sloane 3885 for the first four chapters. Although the general sense of the texts corresponds, there is little word-by-word correspondence between the two even to this point. By the time we reach chapter 5, the correspondences begin to break down and then disappear altogether. Sloane 3885 may have been interpolated with large new sections or the text reordered. It is also possible that Sloane 3853 substantially simplified an earlier version represented in Sloane 3885. In any event, these versions of the text evince the usual unstable nature of the textual transmission of ritual magic.

The remainder of Sloane 3853 records similar material, reflecting not only the collecting patterns of preceding centuries but also the scribal habits of extracting and synthesizing. The second text claims to be the *Sephar Raziel* but appears to be a small extract from the *Liber Razielis* concerning the names of angels related to particular months, beginning with March.[1] Various necromantic figures follow, along with planetary characters extracted from Agrippa (fol. 53v). An operation very much like the Rawlinson crystal operations using a young boy promises information and instruction in all matters desirous to the operator (fols. 54–59v). This is followed by a wide spectrum of conjurations, materials for the performance of angelic magic, and consecrations. Later, we find another work for conjuring the "four kings," a practice mentioned from time to time in the medieval magic literature.[2] Another passage records a "devin sell [i.e., divine seal] of God broght from heven be and [i.e., by an] angell to king Salomon." The description of the seal, some of the introductory material, and most of the prayers in this section are drawn from the *Sworn Book of Honorius*. These prayers are used as part of a ritual for angel invocation that does not appear in the *Sworn Book*. The sixteenth-century hand concludes with a further and more extensive extract from the same source.[3]

A particularly interesting operation on fol. 74v suggests the same kind of engagement with traditional forms and texts of Christianity that we saw in the Rawlinson collections. Although it appears to be an exorcism (rather than a conjuration, as it calls itself), its context clearly suggests that it was used in conjuring. This is also suggested by the text itself. The operator begins by reading a selection of five passages from the four Gospels that appear to be original to this collection. Matthew 2:1 (he gives only the incipits) begins the account of the three wise men; Luke 1:26, the angel Gabriel and the annunciation; Mark 16:14, the appearance of Christ to the apostles after his death (when he tells of the gifts of the spirit, including exorcism); and Luke 4:31, the account of Christ casting out a demon in the temple. He also includes the incipit for the first chapter of the Gospel of John ("In the beginning was the word") that we have seen associated with exorcism and necromancy. Although exorcism and the power that Christians may exercise over demons in Christ's name are the most prominent themes, the other passages make clear that the intent was to establish a kind of biblical justification for ritual magic. The story of the magi has nothing to do with exorcism as such; its appearance here is clearly motivated by the implicit recognition that pre-Christian magic traditions could determine universal truths and might even somehow be legitimate as a result. The motivation for including the annunciation is less clear, but it appears to be due less to Mary than to the presence of the intermediary angel. The passages are thus all linked by their associations with the basic elements of ritual magic, and their assembly here reflects the ongoing creative nature of the tradition.

The texts of this codex tend to be longer than those of the Rawlinson collections. In this way, it is more akin to other fifteenth-century manuals, like Clm 849 or the ritual section of London, Society of Antiquaries, 39. Yet this does not indicate a higher level of textual integrity. Those elements for which we have other witnesses, such as the *Thesaurus spirituum*, differ substantially from them and attest to the high level of fluidity in this tradition. It might be argued that the presence of a portion of the *Liber Razielis* reflects a new interest in more explicitly Hebraic material, but given that the source is a medieval magic text, this interest can hardly be regarded as new. Similarly, although ritual magic manuscripts, on the whole, may have *looked* more magical in the sixteenth century than they did earlier, the self-consciously produced magic work was not new to the sixteenth-century collection. Necromantic practice continued to constitute the greatest portion of the collections and to be mixed freely with angel magic. The continuing presence of texts like the *Liber Razielis*, *Thesaurus spirituum*, and *Sworn Book of Honorius* demonstrates the continuity in magic traditions from the later Middle Ages through the sixteenth century. Nor do these texts remain fixed. Rather, they are extracted, reformulated, and employed in a variety of new ways that may or may not reflect the original intent or usage in the text from which they were drawn.

Harley 181: The *Ars notoria*

The frequency with which the *Ars notoria* was copied was probably declining somewhat in the sixteenth century, but the manuscripts nonetheless suggest a lively engagement with it throughout the century. Véronèse lists eight surviving manuscripts from the thirteenth century, fifteen from the fourteenth, thirteen from the fifteenth, and fourteen from the sixteenth.[4] One could reasonably assume that manuscripts from earlier centuries stood a higher chance of being destroyed, and so the stable number of survivals suggests that this particular form of ritual magic had been in gentle decline since its peak in the fourteenth century. At the same time, unlike Scholastic image magic texts, the manuscripts reveal both continuing scribal transformations and continuing struggles with the textual tradition. In short, we see only the most minor changes in this portion of the library of magic and the way scribes related to it. The old habits and struggles of ritual magic continued through yet another century.

Harley 181, a manuscript of the late sixteenth century, contains three texts in the tradition of the *Ars notoria*. The first begins, "If thou wilt be perfect in phisik and surgery. Thou must begyn this arte in a frydaye in lent in the waxinge of the Moone."[5] The text that follows provides instructions for the performance of ten sets of orations and preparatory exercises, mostly drawn from the second part of the full *Ars notoria* text, the *Ars nova*.[6] Despite the introductory words, nothing more is said about medical skills. The gifts that the text promises—clarity of mind, good manners, virtuousness, and understanding—might be seen as contributing to the practice of medicine. But they are among the goals of the standard *Ars notoria* and are not specific to the practice of medicine. It would appear that we have a rather simple adaptation, perhaps for the purpose of selling the book to a specific person, perhaps reflecting the particular interests of the scribe. It is also conceivable that this reflects either an increasing interest in magic in the medical community or an increasing association of magic with medical practitioners. The second portion of the manuscript (fols. 18r–74v) contains other incomplete fragments of the *Ars notoria*.

The third and final text in the collection is another variation on the *Ars notoria*, titled *De arte crucifixi*, a fifteenth-century text that also appears in another sixteenth-century manuscript.[7] The operator is instructed to fashion a wooden cross, to consecrate it, and to put it in a secret room under certain ceremonial conditions. After a program of prayers, the operator will receive a dream vision in which Christ will provide a wide array of information:

> And if you proceed well in this operation and do it regularly, there will appear to you, sometimes even when not asked for, the crucified Christ, and he will speak with you, face to face, just like one friend to another, instructing you concerning the truth in many matters, from which you will be able to know the truth of every uncertain question either for you or for someone else. For through this art the past present and future, the counsels and secrets of kings, the rites of spirits, the sins of men, the status of the dead are known. We [*sic*] will even be able to know hidden thoughts and their actions, the outcome of future things, a hidden treasure, a thief, a robber, health of a friend or enemy. Through this experiment you will easily attain the fullness of the arts, alchemy, medicine, theology, and the remaining sciences and arts, minerals, powers, virtues, the power of stones, the bindings of words, the offices and names and characters of spirits, good and bad, the properties of creatures, and other things in the world that are knowable.[8]

It is interesting that Christ will appear even when not called upon. This qualifying phrase suggests that the author or scribe of this passage did not expect to have control over his visionary experiences. The phrase may have been a self-conscious effort to emulate the experiences of more orthodox mystics, few of whom had any control over their visions. It is also possible that it may express the real experiences of the author, who, like John of Morigny, found himself plagued by unrequested and frequently undesired visions. In either case, apart from facilitating contact with the numinous, the text has no predetermined goals.

Although the introduction gives the impression that one could seek any sort of information one could imagine, the text does emphasize certain kinds of knowledge in particular. The suggestion that the operator might seek information concerning the rites of spirits and binding words reflects a continuing flirtation with necromantic magic by users of the *Ars notoria*. Seeking the powers of stones suggests an interest in the broader traditions of magic. The arts of alchemy and medicine also figure very prominently, suggesting that the mention of "phisik and surgery" in the first text was not a passing whim. The *Ars notoria* had always claimed to introduce the reader to all arts and sciences, including the more dubious ones, so these should be understood as reasonable elaborations on the earlier traditions. At the same time, it is worth noting that the scribe emphasized the use of magic in acquiring magical and alchemical knowledge. These features, as well as the open-ended process and the complete dedication of the collection to ritual magic, are all congruent with the patterns of earlier ritual magic collections.

Ritual Magic and the Quest for Knowledge

Late in the 1560s, Humphrey Gilbert, John Davis, and most probably Humphrey's brother Adrian conducted a series of necromantic operations over the space of three months. Gilbert, the second son of a powerful Devonshire family, had close connections with the court of Elizabeth I that preceded her ascension to the throne, and held a number of significant military commissions afterward. He also led several exploratory voyages to North America and founded the first English colony at St. John's, Newfoundland. A proposal he brought to the queen for a new royal academy, a kind of combined research institute, college, and national library, also survives, although the academy never came to fruition. He was, in short, a minor but well-known player in the world of Elizabethan politics and a major one in exploration, in which capacity he visited John Dee's home at Mortlake. His one known accomplice in conjuring, John Davis, was a teenager at the time of the operations but would later become the most skilled navigator of his age and a sea captain in his own right. In later years Davis was a regular companion of Adrian Gilbert, and the two men evidently engaged in magical activities of one form or another, an interest that took them to Mortlake in 1583, at which time they were evidently familiar with Dee and his former skryer.

The record of their operations survives in a codex of magic material collected in the seventeenth century and is remarkable for several reasons. Predating the surviving records of John Dee's operations by more than a decade, it is the earliest known set of notes recording the visionary results of ritual magic exercises. Earlier accounts of visions, such as those of John of Morigny, were well digested and were written sometime after the experiences themselves. Although the surviving notes of Gilbert's operations appear to be copies of what must have been less formal originals, they nonetheless seem to have been composed either during the operations or immediately afterward. Beginning with the time of the operation and the astrological conditions, they record in intricate detail what John Davis claimed to have seen in the crystal stone.

Like the notes of John Dee, the records are clearly not works of fiction except insofar as they sprang from the imagination of the skryer and the questions of the master. They record what the skryer and possibly his associates saw or claimed to see, including a wide variety of bizarre details that any contrived account would have been likely to omit. A short passage from London, British Library, Additional 36674 gives a strong sense of the text.

> Seene by H.G. and Jo. on the 14 daye of marche anno domini 1567 at the sonns sett, or a little after, I knowe not perfectlye. It was aboute 7 of the cloke. First I, and my skryer sawe a rownde fyer in the west, which sodaynly vanished and came agayne. There apered annother with hym which I beheld very well, and from them there went a greate blacke cloud under them, which went from the west, by the north to the east pointe. And ouer that cloud there came an extreme number of fyer[s], and in the place where the first fyers were there was a greate quantitye that was marvelous red, and the which turned into gold. And some parte of the fyer went towards the south, soe that god of a great miracle shewed it to me and my skryer. Also the fyer was marvelous greate and bright, and tourned into gold as before. And sodainly casting my eye asyde, there was a great blacke cloude, which gathered into a sharpe pointe, into the west, and spreade very brode into the top towards the East, being maruelously inclosed with fyer, hauing .6. sundry points of blacke, having under ech bundle on the south side, a longe streyke of gold, very bright, which were in closed with greate fyer. And after the litle streike there apered aboue them 2 greate bundles of golden streiks, which stoode aboue ech of the golden strikes, but the bundle yat stoode vppermost, was not soe bright as he that stoode below. There was a greate blacke clowd betwene these 2 bundles and about the topp of this maruelous thinge, there was a greate quantitye of greene as before apereth. And betwene of the .6. blacke clowds as before, there was a greate number of fyer betwix eche of them as before you see. Also there apered on the south syde of yt, uppon the nether most bundle of gold, a square golden hyll with .4. corners, with 4 ang[el]s standing about yt, at ech corner one, whose names were Mathewe, Marke, Luke, [and] John, being barefoted with bookes in there hands, ther being a greate tre[e] of bloud in the middle of the golden hyll. Also there passed by vs 2 doggs running on the grounde, which were spirits comming from the south towards the northe. The first of them was white, red and blacke, and

went lering away apace which had noe tayle. Then followed the other
dog which was all blacke, with a long tayle. And when he was right
against me and my skryer, he loked first on the miracle before drawen,
and then on me, and then on it againe, and soe passed awaye. These
dogs had little legs, and greate brode feete, like unto horses. All which
things aperith to vs with in one howers space. And when I went from
the place, all things vanished awaye.[9]

Whatever one might make of the accounts or the evident credulity of the
operators, one feature of these descriptions cannot be dismissed: the attention to the details of the skryer's visual experience, including a variety of very
strange and seemingly irrelevant elements. Although, in principle, only he
actually saw the visions, this passage suggests that both men saw it, and the
writer clearly seeks to duplicate that experience as closely as possible. Even
if one regarded this attentiveness as an entirely rhetorical construction, the
message would nonetheless be the same: a magician must attend to the senses.

Several details betray the fundamentally medieval nature of the operations.
The necromantic manual they wrote employs standard medieval rituals, such
as conjurations for the four kings, the demons governing the cardinal directions. These follow the usual structure and rhetorical conventions of earlier
conjuring manuals. Gilbert and his associates also began their operations
with a conjuration of the demon Azazel to gain access to the spirits of the
dead. Such operations were in circulation in the fifteenth century and appear
in other sixteenth-century manuals.[10] All of this suggests that they had some
kind of late medieval conjuring manual at their disposal when they began.
After conducting the ritual, they sought to speak with the spirits of Adam,
Job, Solomon, Roger Bacon, and Cornelius Agrippa. This remarkable geneal-
ogy of magic connects the relatively current magic of Agrippa not with figures
like Hermes Trismegistus, Zoroaster, Iamblichus, or Proclus, but with Bacon,
the Scholastic philosopher and pseudonymous author of medieval works of
magic, and with Adam and Solomon, the great magicians of the *Ars notoria*,
Liber Razielis, and other medieval necromantic works.

As may be seen elsewhere in the sixteenth century, Protestant sensibilities account for many of the changes to the medieval practices. For example,
rather than employ the virgin boys or girls required in medieval texts, Gilbert
used adult skryers; Mary and the saints are conspicuously absent from the
conjurations; and in place of the complex ascetic preparations of the medieval works, he preferred simple ones.[11] The theological supports for regarding chastity as spiritually powerful had evaporated in Protestant contexts, so
the virginity of a skryer or the ascetic preparations of a magician were often

not considered crucial. But these transformations amount largely to removing material or simplifying the operations, rather than creating entirely new
ones. In other words, they transformed the medieval material in a predictably
Protestant but essentially superficial fashion.

Elements of the visions suggest that Gilbert and his associates sought
information about Gilbert's future, but information about magic was the first
order of business. They began the operations with a prayer addressed to God,
requesting knowledge that had "not been revealed to no man."[12] The spirits
certainly seemed willing to assist in this endeavor, and titillating visions of
holy books of wisdom appear early in the records:

> Jo[hn] sawe a greate woods, having a greate howse in the middle of yt
> with a little house by it most strongly buylded, hauving an Iron dore,
> with 9 keyholes. These being written vn the dore, thes caracts following
> [numerous sigils]. And in the house he sawe a chamber richly hanged
> with gold, in which chamber there was a tre of christale which was writ-
> ten upon very well, hauving many branches, with a dore on hym, as it
> were with 7. keyholes, which had the charact[er]s written on yt. Within
> therewith there ware many bookes, whereof one had a christall cover
> and another with the heary syde of a skyn outward, with divers other
> goodly bookes. (Fol. 59r–v.)

The knowledge they were to receive was thus a divine gift and was described
as a kind of primordial library. At the same time, receiving divine wisdom
turned out to be a good deal more complicated than merely getting hold of
one of these books.

The way Gilbert and his friends received knowledge from the spirits and
what they did with it closely resembles the spiritually guided editing process
of medieval ritual magic practitioners. Of the two associated manuscripts
discussed here, one might well assume that the conjuring manual predates the
visions and was used to provoke them. However, the authors evidently wrote
this manual during the period of the operations, working from medieval prece-
dents and making alterations based upon information gleaned from the visions.
For example, a spirit advised Gilbert to employ a different form of crystal stone
engraved with certain figures, and they added this method to the manual. The
spirit of Solomon also dictated a new prayer to be used at the beginning of
the operations. They not only employed this prayer but included it on the first
page of the manual.[13] While the careful record keeping that makes it possible for
us to see this process might be a sixteenth-century innovation, the process of
innovation itself and the mythology that supported it were far from new.

It should go without saying that John Dee, one of the foremost British intellectuals of his day, regarded his angel conversations as central to his life's work. The discomfort many of his biographers have felt with these practices has only recently begun to be overcome, and the decades he dedicated to these practices are only now being treated as an important element in Dee's intellectual life.[14] Whatever interest he may have expressed in traditional forms of natural magic or astrological image magic—he certainly wrote on the subject, collected manuscripts of this kind, and annotated them—the form of magic he most avidly practiced was his own variation on medieval ritual magic. Like all the ritual magic practitioners we have examined, Dee was more than just a magical operator. His worthiness was a fundamental element in the success of the operations. Following patterns we have seen in the *Ars notoria*, the London Honorius, and Humphrey Gilbert, he sought a kind of fundamental and universal knowledge of the world and framed his operations in religious terms. Like other medieval ritual magic practitioners, he employed skryers to inspect some kind of reflective or translucent surface to establish contact with angels. These magical exercises offered powerful sources of information, and, as we have seen in both the mythology and the practice of ritual magic, they could also be used to correct, supplement, and even supersede the received texts of magic.

Dee's angel operations have been discussed at length elsewhere, but a brief summary of his activities is a useful point of departure. Dee employed a series of skryers, most notably Edward Kelly, in operations that extended over at least twenty years. Most of his skryers were adults (his attempt to employ his son Arthur was evidently unsuccessful), and with varying degrees of success they transmitted crucial information to him, putatively from angels. Following long-standing conventions, the operations were required to take place in clear atmospheric conditions, principally during the day. He used a polished, oval-shaped piece of obsidian in place of the similarly shaped show stones traditionally made from crystal, such as the one Gilbert employed. The stone was placed on a specially constructed table inscribed with various characters and resting on four magical seals. Angelic instructions directed him in its design and also required that he employ a variety of other accoutrements, such as a breastplate, no doubt modeled upon the Old Testament ephod. After brief initial prayers, the skryer would begin to report what he saw in the stone and act as an intermediary between Dee and the angels.[15]

As Deborah Harkness has argued, these conversations must be understood as a fertile interaction between Dee and his skryers, particularly Kelly. Dee's vast and eclectic learning, long study of the traditions of magic, and evident tendency to grandiosity were crucial elements in this process. In his role as master, he was the intended recipient of the angelic messages, he directed the conversations through his questions, and he interpreted the results. Kelly's quick mind, knowledge of occult traditions, imagination, and opportunism helped him to produce both a subjectively convincing experience of a conversation with an angel and also compelling results in the form of mystical information. Between them, Dee and Kelly developed a substantial body of detailed records of the conversations, in addition to new volumes containing materials transmitted by the angels and written in angelic language. Dee never penetrated the mysteries of these texts, which have themselves entered the library of Western occultism as sources of knowledge about magic. Motivated initially by his desire for knowledge of the natural world that would supersede fallible worldly doctrines, the conversations led Dee to believe that God had selected him to play a crucial role in the magical restoration of a decaying nature. The information communicated to him and, crucially, interpreted by him was supposed to form the foundation of this renewal of creation.[16]

The texts produced by his operations, the mythology he spun around himself, and the theories through which he supported his practices are certainly remarkable and original. But the nuts and bolts of the operations, *what he actually did*, had not changed substantially from the practices of preceding centuries. His use of techniques from the medieval conjuring work the *Liber consecrationis*, and of the sigil of God from the copy of the *Sworn Book* in Sloane 313, makes clear that these similarities are not coincidental.[17] In his note taking, he also preserved the old discipline of attentiveness, although in what appears to be a peculiarly sixteenth-century form. Dee focused less on visual particulars than Gilbert did, but he made detailed notes of his conversations. The fantastic complexity of the tables in the *Liber Logaeth*—acrostics containing thousands of letters and numbers—similarly evinces a tremendous attention to detail. And as Harkness has so eloquently argued, his operations with angels brought about not the passive reception of information but engaged and involved conversations during which Dee probed for details and sought to overcome any lack of clarity.[18]

Perhaps most important of all, the way Dee transformed the tradition also follows the patterns we have identified in medieval ritual magic. Some of these transformations were minor, such as those motivated by his religious sensibilities. Dee's rituals reflect his Protestantism, and, as in the case of Gilbert, the resulting changes amount to little more than deletions of problematic elements.[19] Many of them were considerably more complex. During the course of his operations, Dee developed new forms of magic, such as the equipment he used and the original magic texts he produced on the basis of angelic instructions. Finally, the entire process, in both literal and systematic terms, took the form of a conversation. On one level, it was a conversation between

Dee and Kelly; on another, a complex interaction between Dee's broad knowledge of magical, philosophical, kabbalist, and other traditions and the "numinous," as represented by Kelly's imagination and his own knowledge of occult texts. Magic also involved discernment and interpretation. Even after the books written in angelic language were completed, it still remained for Dee to decode them. As with his medieval forebears and Gilbert a decade or so earlier, his magic was in significant measure a spiritually guided transformation of earlier traditions.

Another product of the conversations was their sustaining mythology. That Dee had a special role in God's plan to bring about the restoration of nature, and that this role involved the practice of magic and required spiritual guidance, did not spring fully formed from Dee's imagination. Rather, these things developed over time in the fertile relationship between Dee and Kelly. But what is important for us is less their originality than the patterns they repeat. These myths also bear remarkable similarity to those in medieval works of ritual magic. Knowledge of magic, understood as a kind of foundational knowledge of the cosmos, was said to spring from a singular revelation to a prophetic wise man. It might also be preserved or elucidated by such a man through spiritual guidance. To put it another way, Dee's grandiose self-conception closely resembles the mythologies of the London Honorius and other authors of ritual magic.

As the previous two chapters demonstrated, there is a long list of medieval magicians, mythical and real, who employed interactions with the numinous to understand existing traditions and/or to reconfigure them. Moreover, the associated myths of magic glorified these personal interactions with spirits, and the authors of ritual magic texts claimed to have produced their divinely sanctioned texts through them. Perhaps most crucially, the Rawlinson collections demonstrate that magic rituals dedicated to acquiring information about the practice of magic itself were part of the magician's tool kit. Viewed from this perspective, Dee's project should be regarded not only as an elaboration upon the techniques and traditions of medieval ritual magic but also as a full flowering of the revelatory and self-transforming potential of this tradition and its techniques.

Some Sixteenth-Century Developments

We have seen how medieval scribes of ritual magic adapted, modified, extracted, or re-created existing texts from a range of magical and liturgical sources; these habits continued in the sixteenth century. At the same time, scribes not only continued to transmit the medieval ritual magic corpus but also preserved the fundamental characteristics of the associated intellectual culture. While this study emphasizes the continuities between the Middle Ages and the Renaissance, particularly in the tradition of ritual magic, it cannot gloss over the real changes that did occur. Some of these changes, such as the erasure of explicitly Catholic elements or the development of note taking, we have already discussed; a few others deserve brief but direct attention.

Increasing Use of the Vernacular

Like Harley 181, an increasing number of the texts of ritual magic were written, at least in part, in the vernacular. Already a feature of such fifteenth-century collections as Rawlinson D. 252, this habit became much more common in the sixteenth century, perhaps reflecting the transmission of ritual magic to a broader audience that was less comfortable with Latin. The majority of sixteenth-century manuscripts include at least some English, especially for the headings or introductions. It is also much more common to find English translations of such larger works as the *Ars notoria*, *Clavicula Salomonis*, and *Liber sacer*. For example, Ashmole 1515 contains an aborted attempt to produce an English translation of the *Ars notoria*, and Royal 17.A.XII contains a translation of the *Liber sacer*. These manuscripts demonstrate the continued active interest in medieval ritual magic through the century. At the same time, many of them reflect the older magic traditions by maintaining the original language of the incantations or prayers. Prior to the end of the fifteenth century, texts of ritual magic tended to employ prayers in Latin, particularly if they were originally derived from the liturgy or the Bible. This may be explained by the fact that, for the practitioners, the language of traditional religious ritual was deemed more efficacious. They may also extend common assumptions in magic traditions that some words or languages were inherently powerful.[20] In short, the associations with religious ritual and mysterious, primordial power could be valued more highly than whether the operator understood what was being said. Some sixteenth-century manuscripts include passages transcribed by scribes who clearly had little or no Latin at all, who could not expand abbreviations, and who followed English scribal habits by liberally adding the letter "e" to the end of words in Latin, a language in which word endings are crucial to their meaning.[21] So, in fact, incomprehensibility might well have increased their perceived power. But this is not always the case.

Sloane 3849 is a particularly interesting example in which the use of the vernacular is of a more radical nature than in most manuscripts, since almost all of the biblical passages *and prayers* appear in English. The Latinity of the scribe may have been limited, as is suggested by the occasional phonetic spelling (e.g., *meserere* for *miserere*), which could explain his preference for English. On the other hand, as the previous examples suggest, this did not prevent others from employing Latin. Evidently, the scribe or translator regarded English as an appropriate language for the operations. Certainly, the work was produced for use by people more comfortable with the vernacular than with Latin and for whom the vernacular was as good as Latin had been for prior practitioners. By the time this text was written, sometime around the middle of the sixteenth century, the vernacular had been used in the liturgy for a significant period of time.[22] Many of the texts it employs, like the Psalms, had been circulating in English translations for centuries. This manuscript thus marks one of two transitions. Its scribe may have considered it more magically efficacious to *understand* the prayers than to recite them in their original language, possibly reflecting Protestant ideas. But it is more likely that this change indicates that the vernacular texts had been in use long enough to accrue the necessary numinous associations desirable in magical practices—a process that took only one generation. Either way, the text was modified in a way that coincided with larger changes in religious practices and sensibilities.

The Birth of Learned Fairy Conjuring

The trappings of Prospero's magic will be very familiar to us by now. Prospero has an ancient library, and one book in particular is a book of magic that appears to have its own numinous power. The magical creatures are summoned and bound like demons. The saintly and wise practitioner stands above the morality of ordinary men, exhibits a tremendous level of self-control, and is learned, even to a fault. His celibacy may have been occasioned by circumstance but is not unnatural to him. His triumph over the evil witch who had dominated the island, her child, and her spirits emphasizes the masculine nature of his power and the rectitude of his magic. In short, Prospero epitomizes the ideal magus as envisaged by the authors of medieval ritual magic texts. Were it not for his solitary tendencies, one could almost imagine him leading the brotherhood of practitioners described in the *Sworn Book of Honorius*. Likewise Ariel, whom Prospero conjures, has many of the features of a demon: he is gleefully deceptive, frightening, powerful, ethereal, sexually ambiguous, and was once the servant of a witch. Yet he is a fairy, not a demon. While this might be attributable to Shakespeare's playful habit of combining classical and contemporary imagery, such as the combination of witches and the three fates in *Macbeth*, this instance seems rather to draw upon contemporary magic traditions and marks a curious change in conjuring practices.[23]

The same kind of substitution also sometimes occurs in sixteenth-century British conjuring manuals. In the Middle Ages, conjuring rituals dealt exclusively with demons, angels, and spirits of the dead. Starting sometime in the middle of the sixteenth century, British practitioners occasionally substituted fairies for demons in standard formulae for conjuring.[24] In fact, the demon Oberion, who appears in fifteenth-century conjuring manuals, is possibly related to Oberon in *Midsummer Night's Dream*.[25] Shakespeare's choice thus appears to reflect a wider shift in ritual magic, but the reasons for this development are far from clear. Interestingly, popular fairy magic was increasingly understood to have been in decline in the later sixteenth and seventeenth centuries.[26] Fairies may have been regarded as a kind of morally neutral spirit between demons and angels, making possible a kind of powerful necromantic magic that was a little less dubious and dangerous. In a period when religious controversies were constructed in national terms, they might have been regarded as a peculiarly British sort of spirit, and perhaps even less Catholic than demons. Their appearance might also reflect a growing tendency to seek out popular traditions of magic ultimately expressed in the recipe collections of the seventeenth century.

The Influence of Printed Works

The story of the influence of printing on the traditions of learned magic has yet to be written. The work of Owen Davies and William Eamon has documented the transmission of learned traditions of magic and books of secrets to a wide reading public beginning in the sixteenth century. Eamon demonstrates how a group of learned authors became "cultural brokers," making available both the learned traditions of secrets and the knowledge of crafts. Davies shows how works containing descriptions of the practice of learned magic appear during the course of the sixteenth century, founding the tradition of the printed *grimoire* and transforming the practices of cunning folk who now increasingly incorporated the traditions of learned magic. But how this may have qualitatively transformed the learned traditions themselves, even in the sixteenth century, remains unexamined, and the scope of this study allows us to discuss only one aspect of this circumstance, the use of printed sources by enthusiasts of magic. Whatever the long-term impact may have been, we can certainly see an appetite for ritual magic material represented in the regular extracting of materials from printed books.

Numerous works concerning ritual magic were available in print in the sixteenth century. Three editions of the *Fourth Book of Occult Philosophy* (Pseudo-Agrippa), another work on ceremonial magic attributed to Agrippa, and a similar text called *Arbatel* were printed around the middle of the six-teenth century. A work on ritual magic entitled *Heptameron* and attributed to Peter of Abano also appeared in sixteenth-century editions.[27] The first edition of Reginald Scot's *Discoverie of Witchcraft* contains extensive examples of mag-ical operations, and the second, almost sixty pages of necromantic operations drawn largely from unknown, apparently medieval sources.[28] Most influential of all are the multiple editions and translations of Agrippa's *De occulta philos-ophia*. Copies from these texts attest to the importance of the printed volumes as additional sources for occultists. Many of the manuscript collections of ritual magic works include handwritten extracts from printed volumes.[29] For example, London, British Library, Sloane 3850 contains copies of the *Fourth Book of Occult Philosophy* (fols. 3r–13r) and *Heptameron* (fols. 13v–23r).

If collections of magic are any indication, Cornelius Agrippa's *De occulta philosophia* was the most commonly consulted printed book on magic in the sixteenth century. This is hardly surprising, given its encyclopedic scope and the depth of Agrippa's learning. Even today, any occult bookshop worth its salt will carry copies of the seventeenth-century translation of this work. I have given numerous examples of extracts from Agrippa in my discussion of Sloane 3854 above. In Sloane 3853 the scribe uses the title *De occulta philos-ophia* in place of *Thesaurus spirituum*, an obvious form of emulation of Agrip-pa's work. Further, a note on fol. 53v refers to Agrippa as either a source for information or a point of comparison. Similarly, the scribe of Royal 17.A.XLII drew directly from the *De occulta philosophia* to supplement his version of the *Sworn Book*, and the scribe of Sloane 3846 quoted the same work in a discussion of angels.[30] Others simply mentioned Agrippa by name.[31] Still other manuscripts contain extracts from the spurious *Fourth Book of Occult Philosophy* or references to it.[32] Many of these references, copies, emulations, and additions or corrections to manuscripts occurred within fifty years of the publication of these two books. The speed with which Agrippa's work became the standard reference can be attributed not only to the synthesizing genius of the work itself but also to the wider need for an orientation point in an otherwise chaotic tradition.

Curiously, a second important source for magic was Reginald Scot's *Dis-coverie of Witchcraft*. As a way of demonstrating the irrational nature of Catholic beliefs, Scot collected examples of both magic and Catholic religious practice together on the same page, mocking and refuting them while rhetori-cally collapsing them into a single category. Often understood as an example of a developing skepticism toward magic, the work borrows its critiques almost entirely from prior sources.[33] At the same time, it no doubt served in important ways to shape Protestants' views of their own theology as rational and scientific. While ostensibly a work of anti-Catholic invective wrapped in quasi-scientific or rationalist arguments against witchcraft, within years of its publication the work also became a sourcebook for practitioners of magic and even a sort of Catholic primer. Scot's strategy of providing extensive examples of magic and Catholic practice to expose their superstitious qualities may have convinced some; for others, it provided a rich sourcebook with unimpeachably Protestant camouflage.

A good example of this is Oxford, Bodleian Library, Bodley Additional B. 1., a curious little manuscript written on scraps of parchment, offcuts from the margins of a destroyed liturgical manuscript. Writing shortly after the publication of the *Discoverie of Witchcraft*, the scribe of this curious little handbook copied passages from a variety of sources, including a number extracted from Scot. The passages of explicit magic that he extracted include material on conjuring, an interest supplemented by conjuring rituals he gleaned from other sources. Many of the other passages from Scot might better be described as charms or short magical operations. In some cases the scribe filled in lacunae in Scot, such as the insertion of a variety of divine names. He also commonly altered Scot's wording, referring to the passages not as "charms" but as "prayers." All of this suggests that some of Scot's readers were part of a process of reenchantment, in spite of his efforts to the contrary.

Another interesting aspect of this volume is its blend of magic and what might be described as "old religion." The scribe cannot be regarded as Catholic, and certainly not recusant. For example, he copied a passage from Scot that refers to the pope as an arch-conjurer without hesitation and without correcting the text, as he had done elsewhere. At the same time, he included numerous passages that Scot had drawn from pre-Reformation English Catholic primers. These could only be described as magic using anachronistic and Protestant views of Catholic popular religion. Yet his use of Scot as a kind of combined primer and *grimoire* challenges us to reconsider the possibility that the old religion and magic were allied, if only in the minds of some scribes of magic texts. It may also be that this eliding of boundaries between magic and religion by a credulous practitioner was less a feature of contemporary sensibilities about magic and religion than one of the unexpected results of Scot's rhetorical strategy.

The "Decline" of the Scholastic Image Magic Collection

The most important change in the library of illicit learned magic deserves separate treatment and relates to the texts commonly transmitted in Scholastic image magic collections. Sloane 3847, a magic collection from the third quarter of the sixteenth century, is largely taken up with the earliest British version of the *Clavicula Salomonis* and another work on images attributed to Solomon, *De quatuor annulis*, with the explicit conjurations, Christian formulae, and long prayers of ritual magic. A more significant feature of this volume relates to the two short works appended to it: *De quindecim stellis* and *Liber imaginum Zebel*, two standard works of Scholastic image magic.[34] As we have seen, despite the wide availability of Scholastic image magic texts, volumes that combine them with ritual magic are quite rare prior to 1500. For example, among the very numerous copies of the last two image magic works, *none* appears in medieval ritual magic collections. That the pattern of collecting such texts with ritual magic became common in the seventeenth century suggests that this manuscript is not an anomaly but part of a more general change.[35] It might be argued that these texts appear here because the scribes of ritual magic had developed a new an interest in natural magic. The instance of a sixteenth-century version of the *Ars notoria* promising information about natural magic, discussed above, might confirm this line of reasoning. However, the only hint in Sloane 3847 of the *naturalia* that characteristically accompanied Scholastic image magic in the fourteenth and fifteenth centuries is a single recipe entitled "An excellent medicine for the stone" (fol. 82) and a list of "Egyptian days" (fol. 99r).

A second change in the library of magic is the increasing copying of the *Picatrix*. Often described as a classic of medieval magic, the *Picatrix* makes its first appearance in British sources in a short extract in the late fifteenth-century commonplace book of John Argentine, and two more substantial versions can be dated to the latter part of the sixteenth century.[36] The text had been in circulation on the continent centuries earlier, but its relatively late appearance in England is not as strange as it first appears. Unlike any other text of Arabic image magic, most copies of the *Picatrix* were made after 1500, suggesting that interest in it may have been growing and that it was perhaps less a classic of medieval magic than has been commonly assumed. It could also be that the scope of this work discouraged copying. The full text of the *Picatrix* could occupy an entire volume, while the traditional texts of Arabic image magic are tiny and quick to copy. Unlike these smaller texts, it also proposes a variety of kinds of magic, not merely astrological image magic, so a lack of focus could conceivably also have discouraged copying, particularly since the wide variety of practices it contained would have fit less comfortably into the relatively focused Scholastic debates about natural magic. But this does not explain why the text was suddenly copied more frequently.

The transmission and treatment of the *Picatrix* follow the patterns of Scholastic image magic in most respects. The image magic of the *Picatrix*, as in the other Arabic works we have examined, includes significant ritual features. In addition, some of the operations invoke entities, such as planetary deities, commonly assumed by most Latin authors to be demons. So, like most of the Arabic texts, the magic it proposes was tricky to justify according to Scholastic standards. Nonetheless, it was commonly treated in a fashion identical to other works of astrological image magic. Prior to 1500 it was commonly associated with *naturalia*, a tendency confirmed by its appearance in the commonplace book of John Argentine, a medical doctor with an interest in *naturalia* and other texts of image magic. Also like more dubious texts of image magic, it appears in very few medieval witnesses. After 1500, however, British scribes tended to collect it together with ritual magic interests in much the same way that astrological image magic texts were collected. This may have been encouraged by Ficino's covert use of the text. But such a possibility must be considered together with a third shift: the sudden decline of the Scholastic image magic collection.

In Britain, the peak in the production of the standard texts of astrological image magic appears to have taken place in the fourteenth century, and a steady production took place through the fifteenth. Of the manuscripts of image magic surveyed in this study, sixteen may be dated to the fourteenth century, ten to the fifteenth, and only two to the sixteenth century. A survey of a considerably larger set of manuscripts of continental origin suggests that a similar situation prevailed on the continent, where the production of Arabic image magic texts also drops off dramatically in the sixteenth century, although it appears to have peaked in the fifteenth century rather than the fourteenth.[37] In all probability, these numbers mask an even more dramatic decline in copying in the sixteenth century. Manuscripts from earlier centuries would have stood a higher chance of destruction (particularly after the dissolution of the monasteries in Britain).[38] Hence it is reasonable to assume (even given that these trends can be taken as no more than rough indicators) that a relatively high level of production took place in the fourteenth and fifteenth centuries and that the sudden drop in the sixteenth may be even more dramatic than it first appears. This peak in the fifteenth century bears out Weill-Parot's claim that there was a great interest in this literature at that time, perhaps encouraged by an increased level of tolerance.[39]

To summarize, the sixteenth century saw the appearance of volumes that combined texts classically transmitted in Scholastic image magic collections with ritual magic works. It also saw an increase in copying of the *Picatrix*. These changes occurred at the same time as the near disappearance of the Scholastic image magic collections, which had been so popular and so common in the previous century. Before attempting to interpret this situation, a number of factors must be examined in more detail. First, how might the availability of printed versions of astrological image magic texts have affected the number of manuscript copies made? Second, might the political and religious upheavals of the sixteenth century have affected the frequency with which these texts were copied? Third, does the nature of codices containing image magic change over time, and could this change explain what was happening?

Works of astrological image magic were available in sixteenth-century printed books, many of them taking the form of medieval collections, and this might account for the drop in manuscript copies. A scribe who could purchase a printed version would hardly feel compelled to go to the trouble of copying it. Ficino's *De triplici vita*, which passed through numerous sixteenth-century editions, contains sections on astrological image magic and reflects many of the elements we have seen in Scholastic image magic collections. Presented as a medical work, it explicitly draws upon Scholastic natural philosophy and combines the use of images with a range of other natural concoctions. The *Speculum lapidum* of Camillus Leonardus concerns the properties of stones and also contains a large section on magical images carved in stones, most of which was more or less directly transcribed from the circulating manuscripts, including the standard authors Raziel, Thetel, and Hermes. It too belongs to the tradition of Scholastic image magic insofar as it is concerned generally with stones and begins with a theoretical discussion of natural magic. Two Latin editions were printed in the early part of the sixteenth century and one Italian translation in 1565.[40] The first book of Agrippa of Nettesheim's *De occulta philosophia* concerns natural magic, such as the occult properties of things, and the second is centrally concerned with magical images extracted from a variety of medieval sources (see above). An edition of the Hermetic *De quindecim stellis* may be found as an unsurprising addition to an edition of Ptolemy (Venice, 1549). Finally, Thābit's *De imaginibus* was published independently at Frankfurt in 1559. All of this demonstrates that the literature of astrological image magic, much of it in the old Scholastic trappings, had broad popular appeal. It might also be argued that the availability of these printed editions would make it unnecessary to make manuscript copies.

Yet far from accounting for the decline in manuscript copies, these printed editions actually make it seem even more dramatic. The acquisition of a collection of astrological image magic solely through printed works would have required the purchase of many volumes. Some, like the edition of Ptolemy's works, would have been relatively costly, not only because printed books were very expensive but because one would have to purchase a large volume for the sake of only a few pages of text. In addition, Ficino and Agrippa were justifiably circumspect and did not provide detailed practical instruction. So printed versions were neither the most cost-effective nor the most dependable sources of information on the practice of image magic. A significant number of those who might have an interest in this literature would not have had the necessary financial resources and would logically have been driven to making their own copies. The classic works of astrological magic are short, quick to copy, or inexpensive to have copied by someone else. Moreover, if sufficient practical information was lacking in some printed works, the manuscript versions could have been copied to fill in the gaps. Finally, only a small portion of the literature on astrological images is represented in printed editions, and a serious enthusiast would necessarily be driven to consult manuscript sources. Almost every aspect of the situation thus suggests that, as in the case of ritual magic, one could reasonably expect *more manuscript copies* (rather than fewer) to have been produced owing to the availability of printed editions. Yet no large-scale copying took place—in fact, it dropped off radically—and thus we are even further from explaining the situation. In the century in which Ficino's *De triplici vita* was a "runaway best-seller," this would seem very puzzling indeed. However, a closer look at the other two other changes mentioned at the beginning of this chapter can shed some light on the situation.

If other sorts of texts including image magic were declining in popularity, the *Picatrix* was not. The tendency of ritual magic scribes to include works once solely the province of Scholastic image magic collections was also on the rise. Of the manuscripts including image magic texts in the sixteenth century, almost half occur in codices together with ritual magic. This configuration of magical interests appears to peak at this time, making it the only kind of collection including astrological image magic that increased in number in the sixteenth century. In previous centuries, the standard pattern of image magic collection included no ritual magic in the vast majority of cases (more than 85 percent in the fifteenth century). Some of the sixteenth-century codices continued the standard pattern of most surviving manuscripts of the fifteenth and prior centuries.[41] But a very large portion reflects a new pattern in which image magic texts traditionally associated with works of *naturalia* (and belonging to an essentially separate stream of transmission) are now more often included in collections of ritual magic. In Britain, this appears to happen late in the century, but continental sources suggest a steady increase from the fourteenth through the sixteenth century. In some cases, like Sloane

3822, a collection that combines image magic texts with rituals for confession and exorcism, the overall direction of the scribe's interest is not clear. In most cases, however, and in increasing numbers where image and ritual magic are combined, the predominant interest of the collector appears to be in ritual magic.[42] At the same time, the number of codices that reflect the usual medieval pattern associating image magic with *naturalia* plummets radically in the sixteenth century. In other words, scribes continued to copy the classic texts of astrological image magic and evidently employed them in their largely ritual magic operations, but they no longer collected these texts in the form of the Scholastic image magic collections so popular in the preceding centuries. Curiously, the only evidence for the *practice* of astrological image magic lies outside the period of this study, surviving from the last years of the sixteenth century and the early decades of the seventeenth. The notes of Simon Forman and Elias Ashmole make clear that they were experimenting with astrological talismans, but their notes make no mention at all of the sources for the images.[43] Very much unlike fifteenth-century scribes who took care to preserve the original text, Ashmole and Forman evince little or no interest in source texts for the images (which they do not even cite), focusing instead upon the discovery of practical effects.

To make sense of the strong presence of image magic in printed books, a crude but useful distinction may be made between the printed volumes and the sixteenth-century handwritten collections. To seek out an exemplar and copy a work by hand indicates a strong personal interest in magic, something not necessarily required with a printed edition of image magic. In order to be economical, printed books had to have mass appeal, and it would appear that many of the books on images were produced to benefit from the sixteenth-century hunger for books of secrets.[44] Perhaps more significantly, it is unclear how many of the purchasers were interested in astrological image magic in itself. With the exception of the edition of Thābit's *De imaginibus*, none of the printed works were concerned solely with magic, much less magical images. The small number of sixteenth-century personal manuscript copies strongly suggests that the specialists were simply not as interested in them, or in the Scholastic debates that they historically implied. When scribes of ritual magic collections were interested in this literature, they made manuscript copies despite the availability of printed versions. Moreover, printed versions of ritual magic works did not reduce the number of ritual magic manuscripts. In fact, if they did not bring about an increase in the numbers of manuscripts, they certainly introduced a range of new texts to the manuscript tradition. So there appears to be a qualitatively different relationship between the sixteenth-century readership and these two magic traditions. A workable explanation of this situation would be that many printed volumes containing works on image magic were purchased and employed as entertainment or reference books. They may also have been employed as illustrations of the popular Renaissance notion of the world as filled with, and united by, natural correspondences. What this will not explain is why interest in these texts of image magic may have fallen off among the more dedicated enthusiasts of magic and why the Scholastic configuration of collections almost disappears.

One explanation might be that growing skepticism toward astrology in the sixteenth century drove its more suspect subdivisions, like image magic, out of the canon of astrology, where they formerly belonged. It has been suggested that the twelfth through fifteenth centuries may be regarded as a period of integration, and that a growing chorus of criticism of astrology culminated in the sixteenth century.[45] Ultimately, the separation of astrology from astronomy and of science from metaphysics led to the destruction of astrology late in the seventeenth century. These long-term changes certainly help to account for how the treatment of magic changed over these two centuries. Yet these changes were gradual and complex. Astrology itself was still relatively vibrant in the early part of the seventeenth century. Many of the constitutive elements of the medieval theories explaining the functioning of magical images survived well beyond the sixteenth century. The edition of Ptolemy containing the Hermetic *De quindecim stellis* is an example of this continuing tradition. In the sixteenth century, an occult property—a property that could not be explained with reference to the object that possessed it (e.g., a magnet, an electric eel, etc.)—was frequently assumed to be derived from astrological influences, and this notion survived well into the seventeenth century.[46] Thus, while the fortunes of astrology and the commonly associated ideas about occult properties may account for the long-term transformation of astrological magic, they cannot account for the dramatic short-term changes around 1500.

Changes in taste may have contributed to this shift. It has been suggested that the Renaissance interest in classics initially resulted in a turning away from medieval scientific sources, sometimes in the vain belief that a new science, purged of medieval accretions, could emerge from the classics. The sixteenth century also saw a decrease in interest in the medieval and Arabic commentators.[47] The lukewarm reception of this literature may thus be accounted for by the largely Arabic derivation of the texts and its association with Scholastic and Arabic thought. That manuscripts of the *Speculum astronomiae* and al-Kindī's *De radiis stellarum* (texts that connected astrological image magic with natural philosophy) also fall off sharply in the sixteenth century tends to confirm this line of reasoning.[48] Further, the manuscript copies of Arabic image magic texts that had once almost exclusively traveled with *naturalia* begin to travel with ritual magic, suggesting that the old Scholastic association of natural philosophy and image magic was no longer so central a feature of scribal interest. On the other hand, the printed editions including works on image magic demonstrate that there was a considerable market for the literature—very much in the form of the Scholastic image magic collection—despite its Arabic sources and Scholastic associations.

A final explanation might be that the institutional disruption produced by the dissolution of the monasteries meant that works were simply not available or known to copyists who might have been interested in them. The personal connection was the most significant factor in the transmission of ritual magic material. Whether it was information about a text passing to John of Morigny from his doctor friend, or written material passing from Simon Forman to Richard Napier, ritual magic depended upon personal connections, as it was less likely to be preserved and transmitted for purely academic reasons. Image magic, by contrast, as a more or less legitimate feature of the literature of *naturalia*, was transmitted and preserved in monastic and university libraries. No doubt, it was often preserved as a part of a larger, more legitimate interest in astrology and natural philosophy. Thus the dissolution of the monasteries meant that a significant context for transmission of image magic texts in England had disappeared, which in turn might account for the lack of new copies. However, the production of Scholastic image magic texts on the continent, where there was a much lower level of disruption to monastic institutions, also fell off sharply in the sixteenth century, so the dissolution alone cannot account for the situation. And, of course, even after the dissolution in England, the secular intellectual community and university context remained significant arenas for interest in both ritual and image magic (as may be witnessed in the interests of John Caius and John Dee). In fact, John Dee acquired several volumes containing works of Scholastic image magic from St. Augustine's (e.g., Oxford, Corpus Christi, 125). So the texts continued to be available to occultists despite the dissolution of the monasteries.

To summarize, the decline in interest in image magic among specialists and the near disappearance of the Scholastic image magic collection remain difficult to explain. The growing skepticism toward astrology, a lack of interest in material of Scholastic or Arabic origin, the availability of Scholastic image magic texts in print, and (at least in England) the dissolution of the monasteries may in part account for a decline in manuscript production. But these forces do not account for the sharp decline in the copying of astrological image magic texts, the almost complete disappearance of the Scholastic image magic collection in manuscripts, or the increased transference of typical

Scholastic image magic texts to collections of ritual magic. This decline is particularly dramatic when set against the backdrop of ritual magic, where manuscript and print production flourished and where the medieval traditions were preserved in the construction and practice of magic. In the next chapter we turn to sixteenth-century occultists to attempt to understand this shift in interest and, in particular, the induction of Scholastic image magic texts into the canon of ritual magic.

7

MEDIEVAL RITUAL MAGIC AND
RENAISSANCE MAGIC

Surviving sixteenth-century manuscripts of illicit magic betray no dramatic changes in ritual magical traditions following the publication of works by Pico, Ficino, and Agrippa. The few changes that the library of ritual magic underwent in the sixteenth century were, in almost every way, natural continuations of transformations already under way during the fourteenth and fifteenth centuries. How, then, do we account for the apparent disjuncture between the interests of the famous Renaissance proponents of magic and those represented in the surviving manuscripts? How is it that the traditions of Scholastic image magic, so strongly represented in Renaissance writers, could suffer such a drastic decline in popularity among specialists? It seems counterintuitive that sixteenth-century scribes would choose to copy a poorly transmitted, disorganized, sprawling work of ritual magic written in poor Latin, rather than a work of reasonably well-written and ordered astrological image magic. But, as we have seen, after 1500 ritual magic texts *were* chosen far more often by those who copied magic texts, and when the classics of Scholastic image magic were copied, it was increasingly by those interested primarily in ritual magic.

Ritual magic might have been inherently more attractive to Renaissance or humanist sensibilities. Charles Nauert has suggested that an enthusiasm for antiquity may have made more acceptable a tradition that "claimed to stem from ancient Persian Magic, the sages of Egypt, and the Hebrew elders." Since it "expressed the divine power in man," the tradition of medieval magic also connected with Renaissance conceptions of man as microcosm and as mediator between the mundane and the divine. Finally, Nauert sees the magician as standing outside rationality and an ordered universe; his magic defies bounds and disrupts order.[1] To put it another way, man is the hero in the story of magic, as he is in the mythology of the Renaissance. While there may be some truth in Nauert's ideas, the situation is much more complex than what he describes. The suggestion that medieval magic disrupted the order of the Scholastic universe is problematic since, as we have seen, it was precisely the possibility that magic was natural according to Scholastic standards that made it attractive to most of its medieval scribes. Even demonic magic, which certainly lay outside the conventionally defined moral order, was not external to the natural order. Demons were quite natural and had characteristics and powers that could be defined and discussed in philosophical terms.[2] An enthusiasm for antiquity may have encouraged the copying of medieval ritual magic texts attributed to Solomon. Yet it evidently did not do so for Thetel's work on the images carved by the "Sons of Israel" while in the desert, or for the Hermetic *De quindecim stellis*, both of which appear in drastically reduced numbers in the sixteenth century. Finally, while the Promethean aspects of magic, and especially of ritual magic, might have been attractive to Renaissance writers, these cannot explain the pattern of copying. The desire for literature in which man, or more specifically a magus, was the hero might have recommended ritual magic texts to readers, but it would not have driven scribes to neglect Scholastic image magic. So we must push beyond Nauert's suggestions.

The pattern of manuscript copying suggests that an anti-Scholastic attitude could have been an important feature of the way in which the texts were vetted: all else being equal, a humanist scribe might prefer a text not associated with Scholastic thought. More to the point, he might be less inclined to browse a codex containing medieval natural philosophy in the first place than a volume dedicated solely to ritual magic. Assuming that the scribe was in a position to choose between the two, he might opt for ritual magic precisely because it often explicitly positioned itself outside the mainstream of medieval thought and ran counter to Scholastic sensibilities. This scenario does not entirely match up with the evidence either. Many image magic texts claimed great antiquity, usually predated Scholasticism, and, although supported by a certain portion of the Scholastic tradition, did not explicitly appeal to its authority themselves. In short, an anti-Scholastic attitude could just as easily have driven interest in image magic. Aquinas, along with most authoritative Scholastic writers, rejected magical images as demonic. In Catholic territories, Aquinas's corpus formed the core of moral theology in the sixteenth century and, even for humanists, was very much the standard by which orthodoxy was measured. Even assuming that a sixteenth-century scribe might pass over codices of Scholastic natural philosophy on principle, he would have no reason to do so with many others that contained astrological image magic. As has been demonstrated, image magic often traveled separately from explicitly Scholastic works in the company of other texts of *naturalia*. These volumes certainly reflected the Scholastic assumption that image magic had to do with natural processes, but most were not explicit about this connection and contained texts that remained popular in the sixteenth century. Further, if an anti-Scholastic attitude was sufficient to drive scribes away from the standard texts of image magic, why did such texts and other similar sorts of material appear in the works of Agrippa and Ficino and in ritual magic collections? In the end, none of these explanations seems entirely adequate.

Although a complete exploration of this question is not possible here, we will examine Renaissance magic through two of its most important exponents, Marsilio Ficino and Cornelius Agrippa. The influence and popularity of these writers may be justification enough for this focus, but there are other reasons as well. To a significant degree, the magic of Ficino and Agrippa may be said to flow, respectively, from the traditions of Scholastic image magic and medieval ritual magic collections. An examination of these two figures may thus shed some light on the broader fortunes of ritual magic and astrological image magic in the Renaissance, and on the question of the apparent disjuncture between the manuscripts and the great Renaissance mages. The approaches of Ficino and Agrippa are unquestionably original and specific to their period. Both writers also brought an entirely new set of sources to bear upon the idea and practice of magic, so it would do them a disservice to argue that they were merely part of the medieval tradition. That said, we may still recognize the ways in which their ideas and approaches were, *or were perceived to be*, continuous with the existing ones. My discussion of their works begins by sketching out the broad structural similarities between these thinkers and their medieval antecedents. That Agrippa may be seen to stand firmly in the tradition of medieval ritual magic may come as no surprise, but Ficino is a different matter. His magic is commonly, and rightly, understood to represent a dramatic Neoplatonic turn in the tradition of Scholastic astrological image magic. In significant ways, however, his formulation has far more in common with medieval ritual magic, a fact that was not lost on subsequent occultists like Agrippa. Ficino and Agrippa also directly confronted and sought to deal with what I have called Brother John's dilemma. This complex problem involving the individual, truth, text, and the divine, which formed the creative core of medieval ritual magic, also powerfully informed Renaissance magic.

Ficino's *De vita coelitus comparanda*

The *De vita coelitus comparanda* was not the Hermetic manifesto that Frances Yates wished it to be. Yates was nevertheless correct in her view that

Ficino's approach played a fundamental part in establishing magic as a topic of intellectual vogue. Published in 1489, the work became something of an underground classic, weaving together Neoplatonic ideas with the theories of medicine and magic current in the medieval West. It was by no means the only contemporary work on magic and was only part of the watershed of the 1480s, the beginning of the magical Renaissance. In particular, Pico's *Oration on the Dignity of Man, 900 Theses,* and *Apology* introduced a new form of learned magic that employed kabbalist and Neoplatonic ideas and united them with the goal of a broader contemplative or mystical ascent.[3] Pico's work is tremendously important, but he limited himself primarily to theoretical discussions, and his works are far from accessible. Ficino, in contrast, paints a relatively explicit and accessible picture of at least some of his magical practices, which may in part account for the popularity of the work. In this way, he also had a demonstrable if slight influence on the textual traditions of ritual magic in Britain, where some of his practices were employed.[4] He also explicitly employed magical images and reconfigured the classic theoretical formulations of the Middle Ages. Thus Ficino's work can serve as a useful benchmark for understanding not only Renaissance attitudes toward illicit magic practice but the ways in which the Renaissance transformed image magic. Despite his use of magical images, the magic of *De vita coelitus comparanda* resembles medieval ritual magic traditions far more closely than it does astrological image magic, as understood by most of its late medieval scribes. This in turn suggests that the decline of the classic Scholastic image magic collection was part of a more general reorientation in magic ideas in the late fifteenth century.

Ficino believed that the ancients and their Muslim and Christian commentators spoke with a more or less unified voice on the subject of magic. In an effort to revive the magic of the ancients, he sought to demonstrate the harmonies between a diverse range of Christian and pagan sources. Ficino's debt to Neoplatonic and Scholastic philosophy in the *De vita coelitus comparanda* has been well documented. He justified the use of astrological images through a synthesis of arguments from Aquinas's *De occultis operibus naturae* and Plotinus's fourth *Ennead*.[5] While one might question Ficino's interpretation of Aquinas, his reading is founded upon long-standing theoretical tradition, extending from Neoplatonism through al-Kindī and Scholastic figures like Albertus Magnus, whom he regarded as the author of the *Speculum astronomiae*. Unlike the works of Arabic image magic, which did not generally seek to justify themselves with extensive theoretical or mythical prologues, the *De vita coelitus comparanda* begins with a substantial theoretical discussion. In a rather clever interpretation of Aquinas, Ficino vindicated the practice of magic as orthodox. By synthesizing that interpretation with ideas from Plotinus, Ficino situated it within the fashionable Platonic ideas of the Renaissance. Because of his medical training, he was able to weave this theoretical material into an otherwise traditional medical framework. Like many of his medical predecessors, whose manuscripts suggest that they might have employed astrological images or amulets in their treatments, Ficino included images as part of the therapy one could pursue, though not a necessary part. He also called upon a wide range of classical sources to locate the origins of his magic in a pristine past. In this way, Ficino had one foot in each world. He drew upon and reformulated the classic Scholastic formulations but at the same time actively integrated aspects of the newly available corpus of Platonic literature. His arguments provided a powerful defense for the practice of magic, but, like Pico, he achieved this by creating the impression that a coherent body of magic philosophy from the past lay buried, scattered like gold, in a variety of intellectual traditions.

Much of what Ficino intended is not visible in the *De vita coelitus comparanda*, but he is explicit about the more obviously medical levels of his system. In order to live a happy life, he argues, we need to fit ourselves to the heavens. Our individual natures predispose us to receive certain kinds of influences from the heavens, and these may have good or bad effects upon our health and the quality of our lives. By the use of magic or even simple medicines, we may balance bad influences with good or draw positive influences in lieu of bad ones. Among the magical methods he espouses, which include movements, songs, and suffumigations, Ficino devotes the greatest amount of space to astrological images, which suggests that he might have regarded these as particularly powerful or efficacious. As we shall see, other elements of his magic may well have been more problematic, so it is not impossible that his discussion of images is something of a red herring. One way or another, images are certainly the most obvious and most explicitly magical element in the work, and Ficino followed his Scholastic forebears in his assumption that image magic could reasonably be included in a discussion of medicine or the natural world. His efforts to defend it as a legitimate part of contemporary natural philosophy also followed Scholastic precedent. In other ways, he pushed the usual limits.

Had Ficino merely listed the images without defending them, he might well have flown under the radar of the guardians of orthodoxy, but he tempted fate by explicitly theorizing about the subject and by broadening considerably the array of ancient authors who he believed supported their use.[6] Astute readers would have been aware of his unacknowledged debt to magic texts like the *Picatrix*,[7] or his proposed use of a magical room that may well derive from medieval ritual magic practices.[8] Although he fashions them as *dae-mones*, suggesting thereby that they were not inherently evil, he also gives demons an explicit role in the magic he describes, and not in a roundabout manner. He mentions them seventy-two times in this book alone![9] His style of argument, which could easily be interpreted as evasive, may also have been a red flag for his critics. Using an approach he habitually took when following potentially unorthodox lines of argument, he fashioned this work as a commentary.[10] To complicate matters, Ficino was not a systematic metaphysician, and his imaginative, poetic, synthetic, or intuitive style could make his writing seem maddeningly vague or inconsistent, an approach that has earned him the epithet "philosophaster."[11] Modern commentators from Kristeller onward have been more tolerant of his approach and have argued that his writings are best understood, at least in part, as almost contemplative exercises full of allegory and metaphor, an approach he arguably had to adopt in order to subsume the full richness of pagan polytheism under a Christian rubric.[12] Nonetheless, the sense that he was covering theurgic or necromantic magic with flowery metaphor no doubt encouraged suspicion about his intentions, and quite predictably the text did come under attack.[13]

Any suspicions that Ficino was treading on dangerous ground would have been amply justified by what we can discern of his practices. As we have seen, occult powers, either in astrological image magic or in other sorts of therapies, had long been associated with the practice of medicine. So when Ficino set images in the context of a wide variety of therapies for receiving "gifts" from the heavens, he was drawing upon a long-standing tradition. At the same time, the practices he suggested went well beyond what was commonly considered legitimate by Scholastic standards:

> Since the heavens have been constructed according to a harmonic plan and move harmonically, and since they bring everything about by harmonic sounds and motions, it is logical that through harmony alone not only human beings but all lower things are prepared to receive, according to their abilities, celestial things. In the preceding chapter we distributed the harmony capable of receiving things above into seven steps: through images (as they believe) put together harmonically, through medicines tempered with a certain proper consonance, through vapors and odors completed with similar consonance, through musical songs and sounds (with which rank and power we wish to associate gestures of the body, dancing, and ritual movements), through well-accorded concepts and motions of the imagination, through fitting discourses of reason, through tranquil contemplations of the mind.[14]

In addition to the demons he mentions so frequently as the vehicles of the influences, a superficial reading of the elements mentioned in this passage— the images, suffumigations, ritual actions (in the form of gestures, songs, or music), imagination, and the manipulation of contemplative states—suggests not only the more reprehensible forms of image magic but the sorts of practices we have seen in ritual magic collections. The passage also presents the magic not as a set of scattered and unrelated operations but as a series of seven progressively higher operations culminating in the transfer of immaterial "gifts" to the soul, which suggests something very much like theurgy. Ficino certainly took great pains to argue that the influences derived from the heavens through these sources did not determine human action, and that material preparations could not affect the immaterial soul, and he made some progress in overcoming Scholastic objections to image magic.[15] But even if one were to allow that this made some of the elements legitimate, one would still be left with the question of how ratiocination or contemplative states might work into the magic (since these were activities of the soul), or what role demons might play in it, since the orthodox view of demons was considerably less nuanced than the Neoplatonic one.[16] While some Scholastic writers had discussed the value of the operator's intent in performing image magic, this level of emphasis on spiritual creatures and psychic states in magic had parallels only in the more elaborate mystical technologies of ritual magic. Certainly, for a sixteenth-century reader the most obviously similar sort of magic would be ritual magic.

In fact, both his written work and his personal practice make clear that Ficino flirted with the theurgic practices of the later Neoplatonists, although it is a matter of conjecture just how far he got into the water.[17] In the *De vita coelitus comparanda*, he speaks openly of his experimentation with an image on a lodestone.[18] In other commentaries he theorizes about how "star souls" can influence our own, and about how demons can communicate through mirrors.[19] Ficino was the first to reintroduce the West to the notion of the four *furores*, an idea with obvious affinities with the ecstatic, visionary, or prophetic states sought in ritual magic. Kaske and Clark have suggested that Ficino wished to create a legitimate form of theurgy and used *daemones* in his quasi-theurgic magic in a conscious effort to avoid the much more problematic involvement of supercelestial gods found in the original practices.[20] D. P. Walker has compared his musical performances on the Orphic lyre to enraptured psalm singing or religious rites.[21] Drawing together a variety of threads from Ficino's commentaries and contemporary reports of his musical performances, Michael Allen has elaborated considerably upon this suggestion. He speculates that Ficino regarded his Orphic magic as one way to get into an enraptured state in order to be a "perfect instrument or medium for the divine presence," and that his performances took place in an air hung heavy with incense, a medium in which *daemones* might fleetingly appear.[22] There seems to be little doubt that his magic was intended as a powerful instrument of meditation. While it might be sufficient to observe that Ficino's magic was essentially a form of ritual magic, bearing superficial similarities to medieval traditions, a few crucial aspects deserve closer examination, in particular the sensuality of his magic, the individual-centered nature of his system, the attitude he encouraged toward foregoing traditions, and his self-conception as the revivifier of ancient magic.

The strong magical, astrological, and medical contents of the work have tended to dominate our understanding of the *De vita*, and this has led to numerous misreadings of Ficino. For example, scholars have noted that Ficino seems credulous of astrology at one point and skeptical at another.[23] Ficino's position has never been regarded as determinist, but the *De vita* has often been taken as an indication of his apparent acceptance of a fairly mechanistic model of astrology. More recent studies have worked to correct this view by pointing out the nondeterministic aspects of the work, its emphasis on the dignity of man, and its psychological complexity. Ficino's perspective on astrology became increasingly complex as he interiorized and psychologized astrological ideas. He recognized that humans are significantly circumscribed by their natures, including their astrological makeup, but he expressed a tempered optimism on their ability to overcome their limitations. Astrology could be employed as a hermeneutic of introspection to gain self-knowledge, knowledge that could release individuals from their "inward zodiac," which he regarded not only as a limitation but also as a resource upon which they might draw.[24] A close examination of Ficino's use of astrological methods in the *De vita* further confirms this position. It also highlights important similarities to medieval ritual magic in his methods, in his attitude toward the techniques and literature of astrology, and in his emphasis on the importance of the individual to magical operations.

Ficino titled the twenty-third chapter of the *De vita* "To live well and prosper, first know your natural bent, your star, your genius, and the place suitable to these; here live. Follow your natural profession."[25] In this chapter Ficino developed one of the central features of the book. In order to fit yourself to the heavens, you must first know yourself; without this knowledge you may well pursue a life not only lacking assistance from the heavens but actually in conflict with them:

> Whoever is born possessed of a sound mind is naturally formed by the heavens for some honorable work and way of life. Whoever therefore

wants to have the heavens propitious, let him undertake above all this work, this way of life; let him pursue it zealously, for the heavens favor his undertakings. Assuredly for this above all else you were made by nature—the activity which from tender years you do, seek, play-act, choose, dream, imitate; that activity which you try more frequently, which you perform more easily, in which you make the most progress, which you enjoy above all else, which you leave off unwillingly. That assuredly is the thing for which the heavens and the lord of your horoscope gave birth to you. . . . Therefore anyone having thoroughly scrutinized his own natural bent by the aforesaid indicators will so discover his natural work as to discover at the same time his own star and daemon. Following the beginnings laid down by them, he will act successfully, he will live prosperously; if not, he will find fortune adverse and will sense that the heavens are his enemy.[26]

After a discussion of the ways in which one might use this knowledge, Ficino notes three methods by which one can determine one's demon or genius, mentioning the approaches of Porphyry, Julius Firmicus, and the Chaldeans. He concludes this discussion as follows:

Therefore let us first of all search out the inclination of our nature and of our daemon—*whether by that experiment and careful attention which we narrated above, or by the astrological art which I have just now recounted.* We will judge a person to be unfortunate who has professed no respectable employment; for he who does not undertake respectable work does not in fact have a daemonic guide in his profession, and he scarcely has a daemonic guide for his natural self either, for it is the duty of the stars and daemons (or guiding angels divinely stationed on guard) to act always, excellently, and on a grand scale. Still less fortunate is the person who, as we said above, subjects himself, by a profession contrary to his nature, to a daemon unlike his Genius.[27] (Emphasis added.)

In other words, in order to arrange oneself to receive favorable influences from the heavens, one must determine one's astrological makeup. To do this, the reader may employ any of four methods, one of them an informal process of self-reflection. Ficino gives no indication, here or elsewhere, that such an open-ended approach is problematic. If anything, the attention he devotes to the process of self-reflection suggests a preference for the less formal approach.

It should come as no surprise that the core of Ficino's magic should rest upon personal choice or self-reflection. This sort of response was no doubt second nature to a thinker concerned with human dignity and self-determination. That this should form the basis upon which an astrologically based magical system should function is an interesting twist. Rather than worry about the diversity of possible readings—which diverse methodologies will naturally render—Ficino has directed the reader to what we might call a supratextual or supratechnical way of discovering the truth. The operator should begin by employing astrological methods and symbols as a complex hermeneutic for self-discovery in which interior reflection and self-knowledge determine their truth-value. In this way, he manages to subsume and transcend the differences and inconsistencies in this literature. To return to the question of Ficino's attitude toward astrology, we may conclude that, while he took astrological influence for granted, his use of astrological methods and source texts was nonrestrictive and even playful. More important, the use of these methods and the interpretation of their results hinged on personal choice or reflection. In this sense, his approach is very similar to what we have found in medieval ritual magic texts and practice, where the problems of interpreting obscure, corrupt, or incomplete texts and ambiguous visions or dreams were resolved through nontextual means, by recourse to reflection, contemplation, vision, and divine illumination or guidance. In both cases, the "truth" could not be found recorded in the text or unambiguously achieved through a particular technique—these merely assist the operator in discovering that truth—but rather through a more complex process of discernment.

A second important feature of the magical processes Ficino describes is that the operator stands at the center of the process. Unlike image magic, in which the magical event may have little to do with the operator (except insofar as he arranged it), Ficino's magus is *himself* the magical image. His gestures, ritual actions, thoughts, and contemplative state constitute central elements in the magical processes. In fact, without the operator's "inward zodiac" and self-reflection, there can be no Ficinian magic. To use Scholastic language, the operator is not only the efficient cause but also the final, material, and formal causes. When Ficino's operator seeks to balance the astrological influences in his life, the magical event occurs around, through, because of, and within the operator. His state determines its nature and he also performs it. Further, the goal of discovering one's intended way of life and employing this kind of magic is not only a practical matter but a moral one. It is a way in which the operator may give the greatest possible expression to the gifts given by God. Image magic has thus been subsumed under a much broader project in terms of both its mechanisms and its goals.

Just as we have seen in ritual magic, Ficino's magic also requires a high level of attentiveness, particularly to the operator's own interior condition.

In part, this had to take place in the process of self-reflection just described, but his method also involved attention to the effects of the magical processes. Ficino's magic was profoundly sensual. A practitioner seeking benefits from the sun might wander in pleasant sunlit locations wearing yellow clothing, drink white wine (rubbing a little on the temples), make solar motions, associate with solar people, and sing solar songs. At one point Ficino even associates odors, tastes, and foods with planetary influences. He also clearly sought personal experience of ecstatic states and perhaps even visual experience of demonic presences. This emphasis on experience and attentiveness was also a crucial part of the performance of magic. For example, he describes an experiment he undertook with an image on a lodestone in which he found that the effect on him was not beneficial and decided to discontinue using it.[28] If his own practice can be taken as a model, the practice of magic involved an ongoing process of self-reflection, experiment, and attentiveness to the results. As John of Morigny suggested, one had to *learn* how to perform this magic. Ficino's system thus followed the ritual magic tradition in its emphasis upon attentiveness, experience, and learning.

But was it ritual magic? Ficino would probably have argued vociferously and justly that it was not, at least insofar as such a claim might associate his work with necromancy. However, subsequent readers evidently believed otherwise. Cornelius Agrippa's *De occulta philosophia* was divided into three parts. The magic of the first two books is commonly connected with Ficino's magic because it employs natural and celestial things, that is, material things from the world and formal or abstract things such as astrological images. But crucial elements of Ficino's magic also appear in the third book, which is dedicated to ceremonial and ritual magic and, as we shall see, employs techniques and seeks ends practically indistinguishable from those of medieval ritual magic texts. Here (3.21) we find copied almost verbatim the passage just discussed on finding one's genius. Agrippa included it there because attention to the nature and state of the individual operator forms a fundamental part of his ceremonial operations. Confirming the importance of the individual to ritual magic and demonstrating how Ficino's magic could be understood as intimately related to that tradition, Agrippa's version of this passage was subsequently extracted in a sixteenth-century ritual magic manuscript (Sloane 3846, fol. 21) in which genius was conflated with the late medieval idea of the guardian angel.

Pico della Mirandola's discussions of magic disclose ideas similar to Ficino's insofar as they emphasize contemplative and interpretive processes. Under the influence of the kabbalist tradition, particularly the work of Abraham Abulafia, Pico regarded legitimate natural magic as an extension of contemplative or exegetical magic. While he saw natural magic as possible and its performance as potentially valuable in its own right, it was not his central concern. Instead, Pico focused upon mystical experience, and natural magic assumed a secondary position. He regarded natural magic as part of a larger process of mystical ascent attained through a contemplative and "exegetical" approach to the natural world, philosophy, and scripture. Once the operator achieved a state of mystical rapture, he could act upon nature at will as a result of his purified and deified nature. Natural magic is legitimate only insofar as it aids or results from this larger project.[29] Although different from what Ficino proposed, there are striking similarities. The interpretive process through which the operator must pass, the use of contemplative states, the operator's central position, and the seeking of ecstatic states are features of both Pico's and Ficino's approaches. More important, both of these seminal figures in Renaissance magic regarded the material exercise of natural magic as an extension of a larger individual, self-reflective, interpretive, and contemplative project.

One final aspect of Ficino's magic is worth considering. In many ways, his self-conception, self-fashioning, and the *De vita coelitus comparanda* itself reflect the self-focus and even grandiosity that I have suggested are part of the pathology of the ritual magic author and the mythologies of divinely guided editing that they associated with themselves. As Kaske and Clark have observed, the book is largely autobiographical, a commentary on Ficino's own attempt to redeem his Saturnian horoscope and melancholic temperament.[30] In this way, it is much like the *Liber visionum*, in which John of Morigny binds instruction together inextricably with self-reflection and self-disclosure. Perhaps more crucially, Allen has argued that Ficino also represented himself and was understood by others as divinely selected to bring about the rebirth of Platonic philosophy in his age. Given his ideas about demons, any great act, such as his project to revive ancient Platonic philosophy, would require consonance with the demons of birth and profession—and thus literally would be divinely intended if not guided.[31] That demons might not only aid but explicitly guide the operator is attested in Ficino's letters, where he speaks explicitly if playfully about being guided by demons.[32] Although far more sophisticated (or perhaps roundabout) than the myths of the divinely guided authors of magical texts, there is a good deal of common ground here.

Ficino's magic thus bears close resemblance to the traditions of medieval ritual magic for a number of reasons. It was highly sensual in that it demanded a discipline of attentiveness to experience and interior states. Ficino reinterpreted past traditions in an effort to revive the magic of the ancient world, and he regarded this as a divinely guided project. He did not merely repeat old ideas about magic images but absorbed them under the rubric of a more expansive project involving not just natural processes but also the immaterial processes of the soul itself. The magic he developed was operator-centered, not only because its subject and object were identical but because it required attentiveness to interior states and a kind of self-analysis. In this process, the traditions of astrology served as vehicles for self-reflection, not as necessary containers of truth themselves. In fact, Ficino might be said to have solved Brother John's dilemma by making the determinant of the truth he sought in texts entirely individual. These formal similarities may owe a greater debt to the medieval ritual magic tradition than has usually been recognized. More important, however, if we may take Ficino's *De vita coelitus comparanda* as representative of a Renaissance approach to magic or of the tastes of Renaissance scribes, the broader interest in ritual magic is entirely understandable.

Cornelius Agrippa's *De occulta philosophia*

As we saw in the previous chapter, in the late 1560s Humphrey Gilbert employed the demon Azazel to call up the ghosts of a select group of magicians: Adam, Job, Solomon, Roger Bacon, and Cornelius Agrippa. A mere three decades after his death, Agrippa had attained a position next to the greatest reputed magicians of the ancient and Christian eras. If the calling up of Agrippa's ghost is a little surprising, the estimation in which Gilbert held Agrippa is not. Among the second generation of Renaissance writers on magic, he is unquestionably the most influential and colorful. His great work on magic, *De occulta philosophia*, became an instant classic in the library of occult learning. The work won him a place on the indices of Venice, Milan, and Rome in 1554, as well as in the processes of the Holy Office at Fruili.[33] More telling, however, is the shadow he cast in the library of magic. Within twenty years of Agrippa's death, his restless ghost was already present in the form of pseudonymous works printed under Agrippa's name. His notoriety and influence in the world of sixteenth-century occultism are also well attested in manuscripts of magic: as we have seen, no other Renaissance occult writer was quoted, extracted, or cross-referenced with such frequency. Agrippa's project is therefore central to our understanding of magic in the sixteenth century.

The extent of Agrippa's influence resulted from a combination of brilliance, esoteric style, and the ambitious and encyclopedic nature of his project. Agrippa sought nothing less than a kind of humanist reconstruction of ancient holy magic from the remaining shreds scattered through the body of occult literature and its attestations in ancient literature. That he was reasonably successful is a testament to Agrippa's brilliance, but his value for contemporaries had as much to do with more mundane features of the work. In the tradition of the great medieval hexameral encyclopedias, Agrippa structured the work on cosmological principles, although he employed the kabbalist threefold division of the cosmos rather than the six days of creation. Each book was further subdivided into rationally ordered chapters, making it easy to assemble not only information about a particular image or technique but also a host of references from ancient literature that supported it or attested to its use in the ancient world. In short, if you knew what you wanted to do and more or less how to do it, Agrippa could almost invariably enrich your operations. So it is not surprising that scribes regularly employed his work to correct or supplement other works of magic. In fact, modern occultists and scholars of magic continue to employ *De occulta philosophia* as an unparalleled reference tool. At the same time, its success may also be attributed in part to what it does not say. Although the outlines of his larger project are clear enough, Agrippa systematically avoided speaking directly about exactly how one would employ this dizzying battery of knowledge, and the resulting mystery was doubtless attractive as well.

Perhaps the most important reason for the magnitude of Agrippa's influence was that, although he presented it in a new guise, his magic was still very familiar in form. He took the existing traditions and reformulated them in a distinctly Renaissance fashion by incorporating kabbalistic and Neoplatonic elements, and he constructed the whole within the frame of Renaissance literary expectations. The package was understandable, at least in outline, and related directly to the practical literature available. The goals, techniques, and religious assumptions remained substantially what they had been in medieval ritual magic. Had this not been the case, it is unlikely that Agrippa would have been so influential, but his work made immediate sense to a large sixteenth-century audience that, if it had magical interests, still worked very much within the traditions of late medieval ritual magic. When Gilbert imagined a lineage of great magicians whose ghosts he would contact, he did not include Hermes Trismegistus, Neoplatonic writers, or any authors associated with Arabic image magic, but rather a line characteristic of medieval ritual magic and its largely Jewish sources, culminating in Agrippa.[34] In short, from the perspective of practicing magicians, Agrippa did not represent a break from medieval ritual magic but was its greatest sixteenth-century proponent.

In accordance with a kabbalistic cosmological division derived from Reuchlin,[35] Agrippa divided the *De occulta philosophia* into three parts: the elementary, the celestial, and the religious. A brief summary of the first two books of the work provides a fair impression of the daring breadth of its subject matter, and the way in which Agrippa worked to uncover a coherent structure in the vast library of occult learning.[36] The first book deals with the elemental world and the magical properties of physical objects. Agrippa's examination runs from plants, animals, and the magical properties of humans to the question of how the virtues are distributed from the heavenly bodies. The second book concerns the celestial or mathematical world, that is, the various forms of abstract representation. These are more powerful than the substances from the elemental world because they more closely approach the divine. Topics here include the art of astrological images, geomancy, planetary names used in incantations, Chaldean numbers, magic number squares and associated seals, musical harmony and the harmony of the human physique, and images and faces of the zodiac. As one would expect, Agrippa gathers together a good deal of the practical and theoretical literature of the image magic we have already seen in the medieval sources. Much of this section takes the form of extensive charts that plot the interrelations between numbers, Hebrew letters, angel names, sigils, celestial influences, and the like. All of this was very much the stuff of astrological image magic, except that Agrippa subsumed it into a larger structure.

Much more so than in the case of Ficino, Agrippa's reader is practically drowned in possible techniques and approaches. The first encounter with *De occulta philosophia*, now as in the sixteenth century, is often marked by frustration, bewilderment, or dismay. To complicate matters further, Agrippa's skeptical work (to translate the full Latin title) *Declamation on the Uncertainty and Vanity of Arts and Sciences and the Excellence of the Word of God* (*De incertitudine & vanitate scientiarum & artium, atque excellentia Verbi Dei, declamatio,* hereafter *De vanitate*) appears on the surface to reject all magical practice but was clearly intended as a tacit clarification of his position on magic.[37] This has made difficult any attempt to identify what kind of magic Agrippa was actually practicing or promoting. The profusion of approaches and techniques in the *De occulta philosophia* may, however, be the best point of departure for understanding the nature of Agrippan magic and its influence. Agrippa presents the materials of occult philosophy as a vast library of overlapping and even contradictory information through which only long experience could carve a path. The result is a relatively open-ended set of techniques and information that throws readers back on their own resources. In addition, the plethora of examples he cites can be taken in two ways: as concrete indicators of the magic he intends for his readers, or merely as analogous practices intended to assist the reader in understanding, in demonstrating the efficacy of a particular practice, or in attesting to its use in the ancient world. Agrippa's style is also esoteric: if there is a single way to read him, it is not at all clear what that might be, and he explicitly states that he cannot speak openly about his subject. As a result, the *De occulta philosophia*, like medieval ritual magic manuscripts, forces readers to make choices and construct their own approach. It drives them into a hermeneutic spiral involving his works and the vast library he cites.[38] More important, it appears that Agrippa was (or had been) engaged in just such a hermeneutic spiral himself, and, as in so many other cases in the ritual magic tradition, a high level of autobiography is implicit in the text. To understand more, in particular how this spiral could be resolved or closed, we must turn to the third book of the *De occulta philosophia*. Here we may see how Brother John's dilemma lies at the heart of Agrippa's magic.

Agrippa begins the third book by framing his entire magical enterprise as a quest for divine truths through religious exercises. This goal is not only the pinnacle of magical operations but an indispensable element in *any* magical operation. Having filled two substantial volumes describing natural magic of the kind commonly found in Scholastic image magic collections, Agrippa now warns that its practitioners may be deceived by evil demons:

> Now it is time for us to turn to higher matters, and to that part of magic which teaches us to be skilled in and to understand the laws of religion, how we ought to arrive at the truth by divine religion, and how rightly to cultivate our spirit and mind, through which alone we can comprehend the truth. . . . But whoever relies on natural things alone, leaving religion behind, is most often wont to be deceived by evil demons, but contempt for sin, cure of sin, and protection against evil demons are born from the understanding of religion, since none is more pleasing and acceptable to God than the man perfectly pious and truly religious, who surpasses other men as much as he himself stands apart from the immortal gods. Therefore, having first been purged, we ought to offer and entrust ourselves to divine piety and religion, and then to await that divine ambrosian nectar, our senses being asleep and with a quiet mind . . . praising and adoring that supercelestial Bacchus, greatest of the gods and priests, the high-priest, the author of regeneration, whom the old poets sang as twice born, from whom rivers most divine flow forth into our hearts.[39]

While this position on natural magic appears very similar to that of the Magister Speculi, it is not. Unlike the author of the *Speculum*, who suggests that some magic may be legitimate if the right techniques and processes are employed, Agrippa regards *all* natural magic practices as involving the threat of demons. To deal with this situation, he employs the same strategies found in medieval ritual magic. First, pious and religious behavior can protect the operator from demons, which are a ubiquitous threat. Second, pure magic cannot be accomplished by regulating technique (such as avoiding unknown words) but only by discovering the truth through divine illumination. Third, divine illumination not only helps the operator to discover the truth (and presumably to arrive at appropriate techniques); it is also an end in itself and the central goal of high magic.

Even so, natural and celestial magic, which Agrippa regards as middling magic, remain indispensable. The operator must use them to prepare for religious magic, which in turn protects the operator from demonic deception and bears him to divine experience and works:

> Thus it should be known that, just as something is often produced through the influx of the first agent without the cooperation of middle causes, so also something may be done solely by the work of religion, without the application of natural and celestial virtues. But no one can work by pure religion alone, except he who is made totally intellectual. But whoever, without the mingling of other virtues, works only through religion, if he persists long in the work, will be swallowed up by the divine power and will not be able to live long.[40]

Just as it may be possible to conduct natural magic without being deceived by demons, it is also possible to conduct religious magic without natural magic. In both cases, however, there are risks. The purpose of the magic of the first two books is to support the more elevated practices in the third by preparing and strengthening the operator. In the sense that Agrippa makes an explicit distinction between natural and religious magic and insists that the former is necessary, he is different from medieval ritual magic practitioners. On the other hand, medieval ritual magic was the only contemporary magical tradition involving both astrological and ritual elements in combination with religious assumptions. As we have seen, ritual magic typically employed various forms of magical images (astrological images, magic circles, or *notae*), angel names, magical squares, suffumigations, rings, and various physical articles. These materials were commonly employed in combination with, or directly in support of, magic that employed and sought experience of the numinous and claimed to pursue religious goals. If Agrippa's magic was different from medieval ritual magic in other respects, on this fundamental level its assumptions and structure were very much the same.

Following this introduction, the third book of the *De occulta philosophia* provides a more concrete sense of what Agrippa means by religious magic. There follows a long discussion of mystical theology incorporating Neoplatonic and kabbalist material as well as Orphic hymns. Agrippa then addresses a range of interests: divine emanations, divine names, seals, intelligences, spirits (including evil spirits), how good spirits preserve us against or help us overcome evil ones, kabbalistic methods for calculating angel names, and how evil spirits can be bound. In the next section he deals with the nature of humanity, the meaning of being made in the image of God, the structure of the human composite, and the powers of the soul, mind, reason, and imagination. He includes here a lengthy chapter on discovering one's genius, which he supplements with a long (practically verbatim) extract from Ficino, the precise passage considered above. Once again drawing on Ficino, Agrippa concludes with diverse kinds of contact with the divine in the forms of "frenzy," prophecy, oracles, and the preparations one must make to receive them. These include various forms of common religious observance, purifications, suffumigations, and ceremonies, although Agrippa is not precise about these.[41] In these descriptions, Agrippa refers to a host of classical, biblical, patristic, and philosophical sources, but he does not provide any explicit instructions on how these states might be attained.

If we take Agrippa at his word, his compendium of magical practices somewhat resembles angelic necromancy, or perhaps the *Sworn Book of Honorius* cast in a kabbalist and Neoplatonic mold. Frances Yates's summary of Agrippa's third book highlights his use of Orphic hymns, kabbalism, and Pseudo-Dionysius.[42] That synopsis, however, concentrates almost entirely on the first ten chapters and devotes little attention to the following forty-seven, especially those chapters that deal with necromantic practices. Christopher Lehrich has proposed at least as plausible an outline of Agrippan magic that reflects a very standard set of medieval techniques. He lists, in order of operation: purification of place, construction of ritual space and a magical circle, inscription of seals, recitation of verbal formulae of a religious nature, some form of "sacrifice" (which might be a Mass), consecration of ritual objects, and words of command.[43] To this we must certainly add rituals and activities that purify the operator. If Lehrich is correct, or if Agrippa's magic ultimately became a more simplified form of angelic magic seeking prophetic states or divine inspiration, most of the standard techniques of medieval ritual magic are nevertheless represented in his book. Agrippa proposed to communicate with the divine in order to seek information, build upon his knowledge of the occult world, receive spiritual and intellectual gifts, and even achieve direct experience of the divine. Also like his medieval forebears, Agrippa believed it possible to create a system of intellectual and religious magic in which it

would be not only permissible for a Christian to participate but also of fundamental spiritual value to do so.

One central feature of ritual magic is its emphasis on the centrality of the
operator, and we have already seen how Agrippan magic reflects this emphasis by seeking direct experience of, and illumination by, the divine, and how it
takes great care over the physical and spiritual state of the magician. We have
also seen that each of the preparatory elements that make possible safe, effective, and good magic (many of them common elements of natural magic and
the stuff of Scholastic image magic collections) is also "operator-centered."
Finally, we have seen how Ficino's discussion of genius remained compelling
not only to Agrippa but to subsequent scribes of magic. That Agrippa includes
this discussion in the third book is significant for our reading of Ficino, since
at least one important reader has understood it to be an essential element in
the higher reaches of ritual magic. Evidently regarding it as an important element in ritual magic practice, the subsequent sixteenth-century scribe who
copied it from Agrippa conflated the notion of genius with the late medieval guardian angel. The examples of Agrippa and Ficino certainly demonstrate how important the nature of the operator was to effective magic. To
this reader, at least, the passage was centrally important, and his idiosyncratic
reading of it suggests that he saw here not only "operator-centered" magic but
magic involving a kind of intimate and personal connection with the divine.

In what is perhaps the most famous passage of the *De occulta philosophia*,
Agrippa gives another important example of the centrality of the operator:

> Therefore our mind, pure and divine, burning with religious love,
> decorated by hope, set in order by faith, placed in the height and top
> of the human mind [*animus*], draws the truth. Suddenly comprehend-
> ing, it observes in the divine truth itself, as if in a certain mirror of
> eternity, all the stations, reasons, causes and sciences of things both
> mortal and immortal. Hence it comes about that we know things above
> nature while constituted in nature, and understand all things below,
> and continually receive as oracles not only those things which are and
> have been, but also things that will come about presently and long in
> the future. Furthermore, not only in sciences and arts and oracles does
> the mind claim for itself divine power of this sort, but also it assumes
> miraculous potency in all sorts of things that can be changed at its com-
> mand. Hence it comes about that though established in nature, yet we
> sometimes govern over nature, and bring about works so wonderful,
> sudden, and difficult that evil spirits obey them, stars are disordered,
> heavenly powers are compelled, and the elements enslaved. Thus men

devoted to God and raised up by these theological virtues command the elements, drive away mists, incite winds, cause rain, cure diseases, and raise the dead.[44]

In Agrippa's conception, the operative capacity of high magic is consubstantial with immersion in the divine. When the wonder-working magus has grasped the entire frame of reality, he does not return to a normal state in which he moves mountains with the magical information he has acquired. Rather, he is made powerful by his devotion to God; because he has been *personally* elevated by theological virtues, he may operate purely through the mind.[45] Similar assumptions about divine frenzy spilling over into the ability to operate on nature can also be found in Pico and the kabbalistic tradition upon which he clearly depended very heavily.[46] Although there is no medieval Latin antecedent for that specific notion, there is little question that in medieval ritual magic, as in Agrippa, the spiritual and intellectual state of the operator and his relation to the divine are fundamental to the success of magical operations.

Agrippa's suggestion that the performance of high magic is a skill that must be learned also reflects the assumptions of medieval ritual magic:

But it is necessary to come to this purity of soul step by step and as it were through certain grades; for anyone newly initiated in these mysteries does not apprehend straightaway all luminous things, but little by little the mind [*animus*] must become accustomed to them, until the intellect distinguishes itself in us, and applying itself to those things of divine light becomes mingled with them. So the human soul, when it is purged and expiated through religious practices until freed from all diversity, shines forth with a free movement, rises up, seizes divine things, even enlightening itself when it may appear to be enlightened from elsewhere. For then he needs no memorization or demonstration, on account of his own natural aptitude. Then by means of his own mind, which is the chief and driver of the soul, by its own nature imitating the angels, he grasps what he desires, not in succession or in time, but suddenly in a moment. For David learned no letters and yet from being a shepherd was made a seer and most erudite in divine things; Solomon in a single night's dream was filled with the wisdom of all things high and low; and thus also Isaiah, Ezekiel, Daniel, and other prophets and apostles were enlightened. For according to the common opinion of the Pythagoreans and Platonists, the soul is able to acquire adventitiously through the way of purgation, without any other study, perfect knowledge of all knowable things, over and above things held to be intelligible.

It can come through external expiation to the point where each thing may be understood indivisibly through its own substantial form. Moreover the mind [*animus*] is also expiated through cleanness, abstinence, penance, and giving of alms; then they confer certain sacred teachings, as it shall be shown below. For the soul is to be cured by the religious study (a study hidden from the common people), so that, being restored to health, confirmed in truth, and armed with divine weapons, it may not fear any shocks that arise.[47]

There is a good deal in this passage that we must pass over, but let us underscore that it proposes an elaboration upon Platonic-illuminationist epistemology, through which one learns by remembering. Through a variety of methods, including religious activities, ritual performance, and purgative exercises, the operator may attain a state where the divine light brings to actuality forms of the truth lying inchoate in the soul. This passage clearly refers to Neoplatonic theurgy, but it also strongly echoes the promises in the *Ars notoria* and *Liber visionum* of divine enlightenment following religious and contemplative exercises. This association was clear to the editors of Agrippa's *Opera* (1600), for they included the *Ars notoria* in an appendix.

Also of great importance is Agrippa's insistence that the method can be learned only little by little, which, as we have seen, was common in the ritual magic tradition. This is a point of considerable significance, for it strongly distinguishes the magical processes involved from the automatic ones associated with natural magic. Although the contemplative process may eventually yield automatic results, the operator must begin by engaging in religious and purgative exercises in combination with a process of learning and practice. Learning to perform magic was an engaged "magical" confrontation with the divine mysteries. That Agrippa intended this confrontation to be in part textual is suggested not only by the encyclopedic nature of the *De occulta philosophia* but also by his other works. Although these other works have been commonly regarded as indications of Agrippa's ambivalence toward the magical tradition, they may be better understood as autobiographical indications of the process through which he expected his readers to pass.

It is now commonly agreed that Agrippa's *De vanitate* was intended not as a rejection of magic but as a clarification of his position on the subject.[48] The rejections of medieval magic are less than airtight and in fact are very similar to those of his medieval forebears in the ritual magic tradition:

It is true that in my youth I myself wrote three books concerning magic . . . which I entitled *On occult philosophy*, in which whatsoever was erroneous through adolescent curiosity, now more wary, I wish it to be recanted by this palinode: I once wasted much time and substance on those vanities. In the end what I achieved [from this] was that I would know by what reasons it was appropriate to dissuade others from that destruction. For whoever presumes to prophesy and divine, neither in the truth nor in the virtue of God, but in the trickery of demons, according to the operation of evil spirits, and boast themselves to work miracles by the means of magical vanities, exorcisms, incantations, love-potions, agogima, and other demonic works, busied with frauds of idolatry, displaying phantasms and sleights of hand eventually ceasing, they are all with Jamne and Mambre, and Simon Magus destined to the eternal torments of hellfire.[49]

The bad magicians whom Agrippa condemns, Jamne and Mambre, are identi-fied by Paul as the Egyptian magicians in Exodus who competed with Moses and Aaron, matching their miracles with magic. The other, Simon Magus, attempted to purchase the gifts of the spirit from the apostles in Acts because he regarded their miracles as powerful magic. Unlike the other major bibli-cal example of magic, the witch of Endor, these stories oppose bad magic to godly miracles and so implicitly raise the possibility of a godly "magic." These bad magicians ultimately fail because they do not "prophesy" or "divine" in the "truth" or "the virtue of God." This certainly does not exclude, and even strongly suggests, the possibility of a holy and legitimate magic, such as that performed through the virtue of God, as proposed in the *De occulta philos-ophia*. In addition, Agrippa does not reject all the magic of the *De occulta philosophia*: he rejects whatever youthful errors it contains, and he regrets having spent too much time and effort immersed in the magic arts. Agrippa's claim that he realized that it was his responsibility to dissuade others from magical practice may even be taken to mean that the magic was not entirely or inherently bad but merely dangerous and not fit for any but the illuminati. Agrippa had the experience and skills necessary to communicate this infor-mation subtly, dissuading the timorous, ignorant, or ungodly and encourag-ing others in the proper direction. This posture would certainly be consistent with the esoteric spirit of both works. Surely, in a piece that gave no quarter in its attacks on rationalism and human frailty, one might expect a less awkward and equivocal rejection.

Part of what makes Agrippa's rejection of medieval magic so convincing is its comprehensiveness. When Agrippa speaks directly to the question of ritual magic, he evinces a broad knowledge of medieval ritual magic sources. He claims knowledge of the works of Adam, Abel, Enoch, Abraham, Solomon,

Paul, Honorius, Cyprian, Albertus Magnus, Roger Bacon, and Alfonso, king of Castile. Each of these names can be traced to known works of image and ritual magic, or to positive evaluations of magic. Implicitly, the list of texts would include the *Sworn Book of Honorius*, Solomonic ritual magic texts such as the *Vinculum Salomonis* or *Anulus Salomonis*, the *Thesaurus spirituum*, the *Picatrix*, the *Liber Razielis*, and a host of other works. In the next chapter of the *De vanitate*, Agrippa mentions the *Almandal*, the *Pauline Art*, and *Notory Art*. So there is no question about his familiarity with this literature.

At the same time, he rejects the library of medieval magic in a similarly ambiguous way:

> These books, to one examining more carefully the canon of their precepts, the customs of their ceremonies, the nature of their words and characters, the order of instructions, and their insipid diction, openly betray themselves to contain nothing but unadulterated trifles and deceits, and to have been contrived in *later ages by men ignorant of all ancient magic*, the most corrupt contrivers of perdition, from certain profane observations mixed with the ceremonies of our religion grafted with many unknown names and characters, to terrify ignorant and simple people and to strike dumb the irrational and those void of good letters. Yet it does not follow therefore that these arts are fables, for unless they were real, and through them many wonderful and harmful things were accomplished, both divine and human laws would not so firmly have established that they ought to be exterminated from the earth. *Now the reason why these conjurers [Goetici] employ only evil demons is because the good angels appear only with difficulty, being only attendant on the commands of God, and meet [congredior] only with men of a pure heart and holy life. But wicked [angels] easily present themselves for invoking, falsely favoring, imitating divinity, and always ready to deceive with their cunning in order to be venerated or adored.*[50] (Emphasis added.)

Once again, the condemnation is far from comprehensive. First, although this is not explicit, Agrippa clearly assumes the existence of some kind of ancient magic that was implicitly better and that might bear some relationship to the surviving traditions. Second, he makes clear that the surviving traditions may contain some truth, since they were condemned so strongly. Whether he means that shreds of the original magic survive in them, still powerful despite being corrupted, or simply that this magic sometimes actually does work is unclear. Finally, Agrippa notes that the central problem with the existing tradition of ritual magic is that its conjurers make use only of evil spirits, since good angels seldom appear and then only to upright and holy men. The problem with the theurgic arts, which he treats in the next chapter, is the same: angels cannot be compelled by impure men.[51] As we have seen, the same point is made in the *De occulta philosophia:* the high and holy magic of the third book is necessary to avoid demonic deception. In fact, the same argument could have been made by any number of medieval necromancers. Agrippa's rejection of magic in the *De vanitate* is thus vociferous but by no means total. He implies that good magic is possible and does not reject the possibility that good men *could* operate with angels.

The careful and rhetorical shaping of this passage does more than suggest a potentially positive view of magic. Clearly, Agrippa was intimately familiar with the literature of medieval ritual magic. That he simultaneously condemns it and preserves many of its assumptions, structures, and goals may be the strongest indication that he was part of it. After all, unlike most medieval magic texts, the printed versions of Agrippa's works were not anonymous: common sense would suggest that he carefully distinguished his work from those similar, more notorious earlier forms of magic commonly regarded as illicit. But it is not merely that Agrippa protests too much. As we have seen, the authors and scribes of ritual magic perennially reworked the received texts, sometimes copying, sometimes changing, and sometimes rejecting what had gone before. John of Morigny's public and pointed culling of the tradition constituted not the creation of an entirely new one but the reworking of the old. Moreover, John's example demonstrates that the rejection of prior forms of magic by no means prevented an author from using numerous elements of the vociferously rejected antecedents. In fact, such denunciations seem to have been de rigueur for magic's most notorious proponents. More pointedly, like Brother John's, Agrippa's autobiographical accounts have a double effect. Their confessional tone gives the impression of progress toward piety and serves the rhetorical purpose of leading the reader to see his magic as good. They also point to the process through which his readers must themselves inevitably pass.

That Agrippa had undertaken such a positive reformulation is attested in a letter he wrote around the time he was composing the *De vanitate* in the late 1520s, which gives us a closer look at his opinion of magical texts without the *De vanitate*'s dense rhetoric. This letter helps us to understand Agrippa's struggles while also revealing the similarity of his concerns and those of his medieval forebears:

> O how many writings are read concerning the invincible power of the magic art, concerning the prodigious images of the astrologers, the marvelous transformation of the alchemists, and that blessed stone

which Midas-like immediately turns every base metal it touches to gold or silver. All these writings are found vain, fictitious and false as often as they are practiced to the letter. Yet they are propounded and written by great and most grave philosophers and holy men. Who will dare call their teachings false? What is more, it would be impious to believe that they have written falsehoods in those works. Hence the meaning must be other than what the letters yield up.[52]

Here, Agrippa's frustration with occult literature does not take the form of mockery, as it does in the *De vanitate*. Nonetheless, his message is substantially the same: how does one extract truth from this obtuse tradition? Both passages make clear that Agrippa believed that something of value could be extracted from it. The problem was how to interpret the tradition or, perhaps more accurately, how one could discover a good and holy magic. In the end, Agrippa would always insist that truth could be discovered only through divine illumination. But that illumination could take place in two principal ways: through interpretive and prophetic gifts. The latter we have discussed at length; the former deserves a brief examination.

The *De vanitate* argues that scripture contains all knowable things; it is the active intellect, as it were, embodied in a text. Through the divine gift of interpretation, truth may be extracted from it:

But there is another way of knowing, which is in the middle between this and the prophetic vision: this is the fitting of truth to our purged intellect, just as a key to a lock. As the [intellect] is most desirous of all truths, so it is susceptible to all intelligibles. Therefore it is called "passible" since, although we perceive those things without the full illumination which the prophets and those who see divine things draw forth, nevertheless a gate is opened for us, so that by the conformity of the perceived truth to our intellect, and by the light, which illuminates us from the opened inner sanctuary itself, we are rendered much more certain than [we would be] from those apparent demonstrations, definitions, divisions, and compositions of philosophers. And it is granted to us to read and understand not with exterior eyes and ears, but to perceive with better senses, and with the veil lifted and face revealed, to imbibe truth emanating from the marrow of the sacred letters, which those who saw with true perception handed on under wraps, which was hidden from the wise of this world and from philosophical understandings; and we apprehend it with so great a judgment of certitude that all perplexity is removed.[53]

The notion that the Bible is the repository of all knowable things can be traced to Maimonides. A more proximate source is the Abulafian notion that in divine ecstasy the mystic becomes one with the Torah, or simply that interpretation of scripture may be employed in order to achieve mystical illumination.[54] With this lock-and-key analogy, Agrippa's illuminationist epistemology is connected with this intermediary process of interpreting scripture or other texts. Somehow the combination of divine illumination, the "correct" interpretation, and the element of divine truth (to which the interpretation corresponds in form) work together to grant one access to that "truth."

Interestingly, although he has employed abstract and epistemological terms, Agrippa puts great emphasis on the subjective experience of this process and the sense of certainty it gives to the interpreter. This is more than an abstract discussion; as with much of Agrippa's work, it gives the strong impression of autobiography. Agrippa evidently believed, or at least wanted his readers to believe, that he had experienced this himself. If he had, it was undoubtedly a great relief to him. If we take him at his word, he had passed in a hermeneutic spiral through a plethora of opaque magic texts from diverse traditions and a host of references to them in ancient sources. The encyclopedic and vague nature of the *De occulta philosophia* certainly drives the reader into such an interpretive process. Agrippa's revisions to that work and his clarifications in the *De vanitate* plot his own ongoing search for truth and its resolution through his increasing engagement with kabbalist approaches and the use of scripture in his construction of magic.[55] His emphasis on scriptural interpretation no doubt reflects his kabbalist sources and their mystical uses of scripture. It also emphasizes that magic was intimately connected with an extended process of interpretation.

But it cannot be forgotten that Agrippa did not regard magic as an entirely contemplative and mystical affair. A simple concrete example demonstrates how Agrippa understood biblical interpretation, divine illumination, prophesy, and magic to coincide. In his discussions of divine frenzy in the *De occulta philosophia* and of the gift of prophesy in the *De vanitate*, Agrippa uses the example of the ephod. The ephod is a form of vestment described in various places in the Old Testament, a kind of waistcoat with shoulder pieces bound with a belt, under which was worn a tunic. The shoulder pieces were decorated with onyx and bore the names of the twelve tribes of Israel. Over the ephod was worn a breastplate known as "rational judgment," which was also decorated with precious stones and inscribed with the names of the twelve tribes. It was worn by the high priest for ritual purposes and literally as an instrument to bring on prophetic states. Testifying to his increasing turn to scripture, Agrippa added a passage about the ephod to the printed version of the *De occulta philosophia* as an example of holy magic that could bring on divine frenzy. He also described the ephod in the *De vanitate*, using it as an example of how "certain foregoing ceremonies, authority of offices, and communion with sacred things [*communio sacrorum*] are very excellent for this prophetic seizing of the spirit."[56] He later used the term "artifice of prophesy" to describe such exercises, strong evidence that Agrippa regarded the magic of the *De occulta philosophia* as equivalent to the prophetic magic of the Old Testament patriarchs and entirely free from the problems he details in the antimagic chapters of the *De vanitate*. Even if we were to take this to mean something different from the magic of the *De occulta philosophia*, it remains the case that in this example, as elsewhere, Agrippa has returned to scripture to construct a kind of holy magic.

In conclusion, although he focused particularly upon the interpretation of scripture, Agrippa once again returned to divine illumination as the central source for achieving truth and, more specifically, for knowledge relating to the practice of magic. That scripture, rather than the texts of ritual magic, is given primacy is not so divergent from the ritual magic tradition as might first appear. There, too, we have seen the impulse to employ the Bible as an inherently powerful text. The Psalms, the prologue to the Gospel of John, and other significant passages of scripture form a solid base upon which a ritual magic operator might depend. The contemplation of various aspects of the biblical stories is a similar exercise. So, too, whether of biblical origin or not, the standard prayers and liturgical formulae, such as the Pater noster, Ave Maria, Credo, confessional prayers, and exorcisms, were regarded as inherently efficacious and dependably legitimate features of holy magic. The authors of ritual magic were perhaps less self-conscious on this subject than Agrippa, and generally far less subtle. Nevertheless, the impulse to employ more dependable and static textual standards such as the Bible in the construction of holy magic is something that Agrippa shared with the medieval tradition. Certainly, the assumption that magical practices had been revealed to, and passed on by, Old Testament figures such as Solomon and Adam was a constant element in medieval ritual magic.

This discussion of Agrippa raises another point related to the entire history of ritual magic in the West: the influence of Judaic literature. Although the Jewish magic traditions that formed the basis for much of the medieval Latin tradition may not seem as sophisticated as the later kabbalist sources that became so important during the Renaissance, Jewish sources were nonetheless a consistent presence in both Renaissance magic and medieval ritual magic. The Judaic focus upon mysticism, interpretation, vision, and mystical ascent permeated even the more explicitly adjurational texts of Jewish magic that would have been circulating in the later Middle Ages, and—though not so central as in the Arabic material—astrological elements were also present in this tradition.[57] Renaissance thinkers influenced by kabbalism would find familiar features in the ritual magic tradition as a result of its Jewish roots. It should also be no surprise that, as the medieval ritual magic tradition comes to the fore in the Renaissance, we see the beginnings of the *Clavicula Salomonis*'s rise to predominance. This is not to suggest that the use of the term "Solomonic magic" is justified in referring to ritual magic, as there is plenty of medieval ritual magic that is not Solomonic. Nonetheless, the influence of Jewish sources on this tradition is clearly powerful and merits more investigation.

There has long been a tendency to frame our understanding of Agrippa's intellectual journey in terms of crisis. This may well be appropriate. Certainly, everything we know about Agrippa suggests that he suffered from an intemperate existential honesty that made him incapable of withholding his views or expressing them cautiously. Thus we have good reason to take him at his word where he speaks explicitly about his struggles. His own works suggest that the illuminationist skepticism of *De vanitate* and *De occulta philosophia* resulted, at least in part, from the combined difficulties of extracting a coherent form of holy magic from his opaque sources and of squaring it with a Christian perspective. It is certainly reasonable to argue that in this way Agrippa reflects the larger struggle of Renaissance writers with their pagan sources. We may also frame our understanding of Agrippa as a high point in a long line of writers struggling with what I have called Brother John's dilemma. Like John of Morigny and other medieval practitioners of ritual magic, Agrippa had a tense relationship with the written tradition. Its meanings were hidden from plain view and could be discovered only with divine guidance, its inherent imperfections cleansed only through illumination and visionary experience, and its weak footings stabilized only by recourse to conventional religion and scripture. Like his forebears, too, his reworking of the tradition was highly personal and ultimately gave rise to new and varied formulations as others confronted it. When his ghost was conjured, there was no telling what it might say.

As we know, Agrippa's ghost apparently *was* called in the 1560s, along with the ghosts of Adam, Job, Solomon, and Roger Bacon. The operation involved demons and angels and employed standard medieval techniques. The spirits in whose company Agrippa was conjured also suggest these sources. Solomon was the most common pseudonymous author of medieval ritual magic texts, but Adam also appears in texts like the *Liber Razielis* as the original magical practitioner. Although Bacon did have things to say about natural magic, his presence in this company is better explained by his pseudonymous authorship of the standard necromantic work, *Thesaurus spirituum*. Agrippa was not associated with Hermes Trismegistus or Arabic writers, the authors more commonly connected with *naturalia* and astrological image magic, but with the authors of medieval ritual magic works. His magic was understood not as a dramatic break with the medieval past but as a continuation of it.

Conclusion

If we take Ficino and Agrippa as representative of Renaissance interests, we can begin to understand why the broader community of Renaissance occultists had greater enthusiasm for the literature of medieval ritual magic than they did for Scholastic image magic. In the simplest terms, medieval ritual magic and Renaissance magic held similar assumptions, sought similar goals, and often employed nearly identical techniques. Moreover, in both cases, astrological image magic was understood as only one element in a much more expansive system. Significant new currents certainly appeared in the Renaissance. The speculative basis for the magical systems developed by Ficino and Agrippa was in large measure Neoplatonic and kabbalist, but aspiration, myth, and theory are not sufficient for the practice of magic: eventually one must develop a set of techniques. These could not be derived wholly from Neoplatonic or kabbalist sources. Clearly, they did not appear out of thin air. An extensive library and living tradition of high magic already existed, and it provided the base material from which these new systems were formed. More significantly, the notion of what magic might be was historically mediated and was naturally informed by ambient traditions. Surely, we must regard medieval ritual magic, with its religious orientation, its less restrictive methodology, its desire that magic be centered on the operator, its emphasis upon experience of the divine or spiritual, its ambivalent attitude toward texts and writing, and its love-hate relationship with the process of interpretation and discernment as the most significant contemporary living tradition upon and in opposition to which the new approaches were formulated. May we not regard Renaissance magic as the snobby and overeducated brat-child of medieval ritual magic, loudly disavowing the intellectual failings and pretensions of its sometimes less sophisticated parent? And if the inherent commonalities between new and old are not enough, should we not take seriously the assumption of the wider body of sixteenth-century magical practitioners that Renaissance magic did not represent a radical departure from earlier traditions? Were these lesser-known or anonymous scribes and collectors not also represent-atives of Renaissance magic?

Ficino's *De vita coelitus comparanda* has commonly been regarded as representative of the intellectual currents that viewed magic as an exten-sion of natural philosophy. This is true, but only if we simultaneously recognize that this was only one element in a more complex system with considerably higher goals. In his late Neoplatonic sources, theurgic magic was considered an integral part of religious practice. Ficino's use of reli-gious language and the ritual operations in his magic all suggest a similar inclination. The goal of Ficino's system was contemplation and a life in concord with the heavens, which is to say, in accord with the intentions of God. Underlying Ficino's work is an Augustinian morality that insists upon the need to use the gifts at one's disposal for good. More crucially, the stuff of natural philosophy and astrology constituted only one tier in a larger magical hierarchy that included ratiocination and contemplation. Nor were the individual instances of a magical operation or effect ends in themselves but rather elements in a broader set of activities seeking more expansive goals—literally, a way of living. In the same way that Ficino's instructions could not be disengaged from the autobiographical elements of his work, his magic could not be disengaged from the operator upon whose condition it hinged and who not only performed the magic but also personally formed the location, basic mechanisms, and existential reasons for it. Finally, the performance of magic involved more than slavishly fol-lowing a set of instructions; it required a discipline of attentiveness and a process of self-reflection involving direct engagement with the various tra-ditions of astrology. In short, the magic of the *De vita coelitus comparanda* is nonrestrictive, contemplative, operator-centered, and religious. It also hinges upon interpretation.

Much more than Ficino, Agrippa gathered materials from the texts of medieval ritual magic, so it is not surprising that his magical operations *looked* like that form of magic. He harvested a dizzying range of magical and divinatory practices, all of which he subsumed in a single ordered package. He incorporated conventional religious practice, such as the per-forming of religious ritual and religiously motivated acts, and included the use of the Bible as a tool for mystical ascent and the performance of magic. His project was deeply mystical and religious and had as its primary goal the achievement of direct ecstatic experience of the divine. The status of the operator was also fundamental to proper magical practice. If they did not originate with a religiously motivated and ritually purified operator, *all* magical practices were doomed to demonic intrusions. And at the highest level of operation, the magus, immersed in the divine, could act on nature at will by virtue of his elevated and purged status. Agrippa's magic was operator-centered in another significant way: as with Ficino, interpretation was a primary part of the process. Agrippa rejected all independent human systematization and knowledge, including magic, but nonetheless magical knowledge could be founded upon a direct, almost mystical, engagement with magic and religious texts. Agrippan magic had to be learned, not merely performed, and it inherently involved interpretation, discernment, and divine illumination. In part, this involved an engagement with the existing written traditions and, for his readers, with a better organized but similarly vague *De occulta philosophia*. Many of these texts were deceptive and false, and even the best merely pointed toward the truth.

One crucial element distinguishes the magic of Ficino and Agrippa. Unlike their medieval forebears, they explicitly embraced Brother John's dilemma without any attempt to resolve it. In many respects, Ficino and Agrippa took the same approach to texts that medieval ritual magic did. They freely reinterpreted and reconfigured the received traditions of magic. They offered readers wide latitude to determine the nature of the operations they would undertake. They struggled with the problem of what to commit to writing. Their magic could not be performed like a recipe, but only learned. Even so, they worried that their ideas would be misunderstood and corrupted, and this concern found expression in their esoteric approach to writing. Although texts and systems of magic and astrology were essential, both Ficino and Agrippa located truth ultimately in the self-reflective, contemplative, or mystical moment, and explicitly not in the received written traditions. Thus they preserved the essential elements of the dilemma that both problematized and at the same time formed the creative core of ritual magic. In Ficino and Agrippa, however, we see a fuller appreciation and articulation of that dilemma. Ficino explicitly offers a variety of approaches to his readers. Not only does he seem unconcerned by the differences between the various systems of astrology, but he actually appears to revel in them and their poetic power. Their very diversity makes possible the crucial moment in Ficinian magic, textually mediated self-reflection. For his part, Agrippa wrote magical texts that confront the reader with a wide array of traditions. He seems intentionally to drive the reader into precisely the same kind of hermeneutic process through which he himself had passed. Thus Agrippa designed his works to be difficult to read, to be understandable only by the enlightened few; furthermore, he insisted that they provided not the truth itself but simply the means to approach it. In short, both Agrippa and Ficino openly require the reader personally and repeatedly to draw upon the rich hermeneutic of unstable, obscure, multivalent, and even contradictory texts. It could be said that in the magic of Ficino and Agrippa, the processes of interpretation, contemplation, and self-reflection are poised to swallow the magical techniques from which, in some measure, they arose. Thus in Agrippa, and in Renaissance magic in general, we may witness not so much a crisis of Renaissance thought as the greatest creative achievement in a long-standing tradition of ritual magic in which texts, interpretation, doubt, and the numinous stand in constant creative tension.

NOTES

Abbreviations

HMES   Lynn Thorndike, *A History of Magic and Experimental Science*, 8 vols.
                   (New York: Macmillan, 1923–58).
Humphreys Cat.   K. W. Humphreys, ed., *The Friars' Libraries* (London: British Library in
                   Association with the British Academy, 1990).
James Cat.   M. R. James, ed., *The Ancient Libraries of Canterbury and Dover: The
                   Catalogues of the Libraries of Christ Church Priory and St. Augustine's
                   Abbey at Canterbury and of St. Martin's Priory at Dover* (Cambridge:
                   Cambridge University Press, 1903).
SD   Vincent of Beauvais, *Speculum doctrinale*, vol. 2 of *Speculum quad-
                   ruplex: Sive speculum maioris* (Venice: Baltazaris Belieri, 1624); reprint,
                   Graz: Akademische Druck-u. Velagsanstalt, 1964.

Introduction

1. See Yates, *Giordano Bruno and the Hermetic Tradition*, 80–81; HMES, 5:591.

2. See especially Cohn, *Europe's Inner Demons*, 164–205.

3. Brian Copenhaver, Paola Zambelli, and Vittoria Perrone Compagni are notable exceptions.

4. A selective list includes, by Pingree, "Artificial Demons and Miracles"; "Between the *Ghaya* and *Picatrix* I"; "Diffusion of Arabic Magical Texts in Western Europe"; "Learned Magic in the Time of Frederick II"; and (edited by Pingree) *Picatrix*. A selective list of Burnett's works includes "Adelard, Ergaphalau, and the Science of the Stars"; "Arabic, Greek, and Latin Works on Astrological Magic"; *Magic and Divination*; "Scandinavian Runes in a Latin Magical Treatise"; and (translated by Burnett) *Adelard of Bath, Conversations with His Nephew*.

5. By Boudet, see "Les condamnations de la magie"; "L'*Ars notoria* au Moyen Age"; and "Les Who's Who démonologiques." Boudet is also spearheading a new series called Salomon Latinus, to be published in the Micrologus Library.

6. Boudet, "Magie théurgique"; Hedegård, *Liber iuratus Honorii*; Kieckhefer, "Devil's Contemplatives"; Mathiesen, "Thirteenth-Century Ritual"; and Allen, "Summoning Plotinus."

7. On manuscript collection and transmission, see Page, "Image-Magic Texts"; Láng, *Unlocked Books*; and Klaassen, "Medieval Ritual Magic in the Renaissance." On specific texts, see Boudet, *Entre science et nigromance*.

8. See Veenstra, "Venerating and Conjuring Angels"; Veenstra, "Holy Almandal"; and Véronèse, "Contre la divination et la magie à la cour."

9. See John of Morigny, "Prologue to John of Morigny's *Liber visionum*"; the essays in Fanger, *Invoking Angels*; Fanger, "Plundering the Egyptian Treasure"; and Watson, "John the Monk's *Book of the Visions*."

10. On Ficino, see Copenhaver, "Natural Magic, Hermeticism, and Occultism." Copenhaver has written extensively on this topic. See also his "Scholastic Philosophy and Renaissance Magic"; "Astrology and Magic"; and "Renaissance Magic and Neoplatonic Philosophy." See also Celenza, "Late Antiquity and Florentine Platonism." Of Allen's numerous studies of Ficino, see in particular "Summoning Plotinus." A good edition of the *De vita coelitus comparanda* is Kaske and Clark's of 1989. On Pico, see in particular Wirszubski, *Pico della Mirandola's Encounter with Jewish Mysticism*, 132; and Copenhaver, "Magic and the Dignity of Man"; "Secret of Pico's Oration"; and "Number, Shape, and Meaning."

11. See, all by Zambelli, "A propositio del *De vanitate scienciarum*"; "Magic and Radical Reformation"; and "Cornelius Agrippa"; Keefer, "Agrippa's Dilemma"; and Lehrich, *Language of Demons and Angels*. I refer here to Vittoria Perrone Compagni's very useful introduction to Agrippa's *De occulta philosophia* in *De occulta philosophia libri tres*.

12. See Clucas, *John Dee*; Clulee, *John Dee's Natural Philosophy*; and Harkness, *John Dee's Conversations with Angels*.

13. Lucentini and Compagni, *I testi e i codici*. In *L'Ars notoria au Moyen Âge*, Véronèse thoroughly discusses the manuscripts of the *Ars notoria* and a number of related texts. See also Weill-Parot, *Les "images astrologiques" au Moyen Âge*; and Boudet, *Entre science et nigromance*.

14. See Weill-Parot, "Astral Magic and Intellectual Changes."

15. See Véronèse, "La notion d''auteur-magicien.'"

16. See Vickers, review of Zambelli, *L'ambigua natura della magia*. On the "old dirty" magic, see Yates, *Giordano Bruno and the Hermetic Tradition*, 80–81. For my reservations about Vickers's characterization of Renaissance magic, see Klaassen, "Ritual Invocation and Early Modern Science."

17. Eamon, *Science and the Secrets of Nature*, 54.

18. Lehemann, "Collegium Amplonianum," 29 (catalogue reference Math. 54). The 1410 catalogue lists the volume Math. 54 as necromantic. Among the constituent titles it lists can be found *Liber prestigiis*, which is probably Adelard of Bath's translation of Thābit's work on images, and another work on the seven figures of the seven planets, their prayers, and their suffumigations.

19. As Tambiah argues in *Magic, Science, Religion*, applying scientific concerns about causality to the interpretation of nonscientific mentalities is inherently problematic. However, medieval approaches to magic sometimes did concern questions of causality.

20. See Luhrmann's *Persuasions of the Witch's Craft* and "Art of Hearing God." For a discussion comparing medieval and modern techniques, see Mathiesen, "Thirteenth-Century Ritual," 156–57.

21. See Kieckhefer, "Specific Rationality of Medieval Magic."

Part I Introduction

1. *HMES*, 2:835.
2. Howell et al., *Cobbett's Complete Collection of State Trials*, 1:117–18.

Chapter 1

1. Caesarius of Heisterbach, *Dialogus miraculorum*, 5.4.
2. John Gower, *Confessio amantis*, 6.
3. Thomas of Chobham, *Summa confessorum*, 331.
4. Saint Bernardino of Siena, *Sermons*, ed. Nazareno Orlandi, trans. Helen Josephine Robins (Sienna: Tipographia Sociale, 1920), 163–76, cited in Kieckhefer, *Magic in the Middle Ages*, 194.

5. The only explicit discussions of magic occur in the *Speculum doctrinale*. Chapters 119 and 120 contain classifications of magic from Isidore of Seville and Richard of St. Victor. The passages are drawn from the *Etymologies of Isidore of Seville*, 7.8.9, and Richard of St. Victor, *Liber exceptionum*, 1.1.25. The discussion of magic in the *Speculum doctrinale* is otherwise drawn entirely from legal sources. Gratian's *Decretum* provides the bulk of the material for this discussion. Raymond of Penafort is a significant contributor as well. Most of the passages may be found in Raymond of Penafort, *Summa de poenitentia*, fols. 102–105.

6. *HMES*, 2:458.

7. *SD* 16.46. See Richard of St. Victor, *Excerpta*, 1.1.12.8–17.

8. "Idem non condemnatur hic rustici qui seruant tempora ad seminandum, vel arbores incidendas et simila, quae certam et naturalem habent rationem. Idem de physicis circa medicinas dandas, et minutiones faciendas et simila." *SD* 9.121, quoting Raymond of Penafort, *Summa de poenitentia*, fol. 104b.

9. Gratian, *Decretum*, 26.3.1–2. For Augustine's *De divinatione daemonum*, see J.-P. Migne, *Patrologia latina*, 40:581–92; *Corpus scriptorum ecclesiasticorum latinorum*, 41:579–618; for the work in English, see Ruth W. Brown's translation, "On the Divination of Demons."

10. For a survey of Augustine on the subject of magic, see *HMES*, 1:504–27.

11. "Superstitiosum est quicquid institutum est ab hominibus, vel ad colendam sicut Deum creaturam, vel ad consultationes et pacta quaedam significationum, cum daemonibus placita atque faederata, qualia sunt molimina magicarum artium. Ad hoc etiam genus pertinent omnes ligaturae, atque remedia, quae medicorum quoque disciplina condemnat, siue in praecantationibus, siue quibusdam notis, quas characteres vocant." *SD* 9.116. Cf. Gratian, *Decretum*, 26.2.6.

12. *SD* 9.117. Cf. Gratian, *Decretum*, 26.3.2; Augustine, *De divinatione daemonum*, 3.7.

13. Apart from the passage quoted above, the association between paganism and magic is largely implicit in the passages from Augustine included here. Several examples in chapter 116 of the *Speculum doctrinale*, however, suggest this association. Here he speaks of the worship of animals and demons and of the observance of Egyptian days.

14. *SD* 9.115.

15. *SD* 9.121. Cf. Raymond of Penafort, *Summa de poenitentia*, fols. 104–5.

16. *SD* 9.116, 118 121, 122.

17. "Ex hoc potest haberi, quod non sunt reprobanda breuia quae fiunt in ascensione, cum non contineantur nisi verba euangelij. Sed supersitiosum est, si credatur quod minus habeant efficaciae si scribantur post lectum Evangelium, aut post Missam, aut alia die, quam si scribantur cum legantur siue proferantur in ecclesia verba euangelii quae ibi continentur. Illa autem breuia in quibus scribuntur quidam characteres, et quaedam nomina inusitata, quasi nomina Dei ineffabilia, in quibus dicitur: Quicunque portauerit super se instud breue, non periclitabitur sic vel sic, aut istud aut illud sibi euenit, proculdubio reprobanda sunt." *SD* 9.121. *Brevia* in this case must mean "charms." Cf. gloss "f" in Raymond of Penafort, *Summa de poenitentia*, fols. 104–5.

18. "Quapropter sacerdotes per ecclesias sibi commissas, populo Dei omni instantia praedicare debent, vt nouerint haec omnino falsa esse, et non a diuino, sed a maligno spiritu, talia fantasmata mentibus fidelium irrogari, arbitrentur." *SD* 9.118. Cf. Gratian, *Decretum*, 26.5.12.

19. *SD* 9.122. Cf. Gratian, *Decretum*, 26.5.12.

20. Kieckhefer, *Magic in the Middle Ages*, 176. One of the general points of Edward Peters's book on the subject is the transference of antimagic invective from a rhetorical and moral context to a legal one. See Peters, *Magician, the Witch, and the Law*.

21. Peters, *Magician, the Witch, and the Law*, 80.

22. Here I rely heavily on Peters's discussion, ibid., 63–109. For a good discussion of the inclusion of magical arts among the seven liberal arts, see Burnett, *Magic and Divination*, 1–15.

23. Peters, *Magician, the Witch, and the Law*, 93.

24. Kieckhefer, *Magic in the Middle Ages*, 184.

25. Kieckhefer, "Specific Rationality of Medieval Magic," 818.

26. Pingree, "Learned Magic in the Time of Frederick II," 42–43.

27. This position is admirably argued by Nicolas Weill-Parot in his exceptional treatment of astrological image magic, Les "images astrologiques" au Moyen Âge.

28. On theurgy in general, see Shaw, Theurgy and the Soul. For Iamblichus on theurgy and the inadequacies of reason, see Wallis and Gerson, Neoplatonism, 118–23. On theurgy, see Dodds, "Appendix I," in Proclus, Proclus: The Elements of Theology.

29. See Copenhaver, "Astrology and Magic."

30. David Pingree, in "Some of the Sources," has discussed how the confluence of sources ranging from Neoplatonism to rather base forms of magical practice makes for a fundamental tension in this work between otherworldly goals and mundane magical practices. While the tension is not overcome in a particularly satisfying way, the compiler has made efforts to synthesize these divergent traditions, arguing that the profundities and secrets of "science" are only accessed through operibus et experimentis, meaning the mundane magical operations. See Pingree, Picatrix, 3.12.1. There are other modern editions of the Latin Picatrix—for example, Compagni's "Picatrix latinus." For a modern German translation of the Arabic version, see Ritter and Plessner's "Picatrix." An incomplete version of a French translation may be found in Matton, La magie arabe traditionnelle, 243–317. Other works of magic implicitly combine mundane operations with enlightenment. In the case of the Sworn Book of Honorius (see chapter 4), necromantic operations are regarded as a legitimate part of the operations of one seeking the beatific vision. The Ars notoria (also discussed in chapter 4) combines these features as well. Neither of these texts provides theoretical discussions of a broad range of magical operations.

31. For a more complete survey of the philosophical history of astrological image magic, see Weill-Parot, Les "images astrologiques" au Moyen Âge.

32. References to De radiis stellarum give the chapter number followed by the page number(s) in D'Alverny and Hudry's edition of De radiis.

33. For a list of works attributed to al-Kindī approximately 120 years after his death, see Ibn al-Nadim, Fihrist of al-Nadim, 217–18. A useful but outdated version of this list combines the Fihrist titles with titles of extant tracts in Arabic and Latin in Atiyeh, Al-Kindi, 148–210.

34. Al-Kindī, De radiis stellarum, 1 (217–18).

35. Ibid., 3 (224–26).

36. Ibid., 5 (229–33).

37. Ibid., 6 (233–50).

38. Although Albertus Magnus does not mention it, De radiis stellarum was known and commented upon in Scholastic circles after him. See D'Alverny and Hudry's introduction in ibid., 173–79.

39. See Burnett, Magic and Divination, 1–15, 133–45.

40. See Fanger, "Things Done Wisely by a Wise Enchanter."

41. For example, Siger of Brabant cites the text with some approval, while not extending this support to its claims about magical words. See Maurer, "Between Reason and Faith," 18.

42. For a translation and discussion of this text, see Zambelli, Speculum astronomiae and Its Enigma. The authorship of this text is much debated. See Weill-Parot, Les "images astrologiques" au Moyen Âge, 59–60. I have adopted Weill-Parot's approach in identifying the author as the Magister Speculi. For Thorndike's discussion of the subject, see HMES, 2:692–717.

43. "Est enim unus modus abominabilis, qui suffumigationem et invocationem exigit, quales sunt Imagines Toz Graeci et Germath Babylonensis, quae habent stationes ad cultum Veneris, quales sunt Imagines Balenuz et Hermetis, quae exorcizantur per quinquaginta quatuor nomina angelorum, qui subservire dicuntur imaginibus lunae in circulo eius, et forte sunt potius nomina daemonum, et sculpuntur in eis septem nomina recto ordine pro re bona et ordine transverso pro re cuius expectatur repulsio. Suffumigantur etiam pro bona re cum ligno aloes, croco et balsamo, et pro mala re cum galbano, sandalo rubeo et resina, per quae profecto spiritus non congruntur, sed quando Dominus permittit peccatis nostris exigentibus

ut decipiant homines, exhibent se coactos. Haec est idolatria pessima, quae, ut reddat se aliquatenus fide dignam, observat viginti octo mansiones lunae et horas diei et noctis cum quibusdam nominibus dierum, horarum et mansionum ipsarum." *Speculum astronomiae,* 11.4–18 (240–41). I quote from the edition and translation of this work in Zambelli, *Speculum astronomiae and Its Enigma*; page numbers in this edition are provided in parentheses in subsequent citations of this source.

44. "Hic modus etiam a nobis longe sit; suspectus enim est, ne saltem sub ignotae linguae nominibus aliquod lateat, quod sit contra fidei catholicae honestatem." Ibid., 11 (240–41).

45. "The third type is [that] of astrological images, which eliminates the filth, suffumigations and invocations, and does not allow exorcisms or the inscription of characters, but obtains [its] virtue solely from the celestial figure." "Tertius enim modus est imaginum astronomicarum, qui eliminat istas spurcitias, suffumigationes et invocationes non habet, neque exorcizationes aut characterum inscriptiones admittit, sed virtutem nanciscitur solummodo a figura caelesti." Ibid., 11.103–6 (246–47).

46. Ibid., 246–49. Charles Burnett has demonstrated that the Magister Speculi condemned Adelard of Bath's translation of Thābit's *De imaginibus* as necromantic because it retains the ritual aspects of the original text. Burnett, *Magic and Divination*, 1–15. All known British manuscripts are of the other translation, by John of Seville.

47. "Partem vero quae est de imaginibus astronomicis propter vicinitatem quam habent ad necromanticas, non defendo aliter quam secundum quod superius in earum capitulo dictum est, eas nancisci virtutem a figura caelesti iuxta verbum Ptolemaei nonum . . . et nisi quia nihil prohibet eas defendere secundum quod possunt negari vel defendi." *Speculum astronomiae,* 11.1–7 (240–41). I have modified the translation slightly here.

48. Ibid., 121. On the influence of the *Speculum astronomiae*, see chapter 2.

49. Aquinas, *De occultis operibus naturae*; the Latin text is included at 191–97 (parenthetical page numbers in subsequent citations of this source are to the Latin). I quote from McAllister's translation in *Letter of Saint Thomas Aquinas* and give page references in parentheses for the Latin text in the same volume. See also Weill-Parot, *Les "images astrologiques" au Moyen Âge*, 226–27.

50. "Ita omnes virtutes et actiones mediorum corporum transcendentes virtutes elementorum, consequuntur eorum proprias formas, et reducuntur sicut in altiora principia in virtutes corporum coelestium, et adhuc altius in substantias separatas" Aquinas, *De occultis operibus naturae*, 15 (196).

51. "Possibile tamen est quod in uno individuo ejusdem speciei virtus et operatio consequens speciem remissius vel intensius inveniatur secundum diversam dispositionem materiae et diversum situm corporum coelestium in generatione hujus vel illius individui." Ibid., 16 (196).

52. "Tales autem virtutes si quae essent in artificiatis, ex coelestibus corporibus nullam formam consequerentur; cum forma artificis aliud nihil sit quam ordo compositio et figura, ex quibus prodire non possunt tales virtutes et actiones. Unde patet quod si quas tales virtutes artificiata perficiant, puta quod ad aliquam sculpturam moriantur serpentes aut immobilentur animalia vel laedantur, non procedit hoc ab aliqua virtute indita et permanenti, sed ex virtute agentis extrinseci, quod utitur talibus sicut intrumentis ad suum effectum." Ibid., 17 (196).

53. "Sicut autem imagines ex materia naturali fiunt, sed formam sortiuntur ex arte; ita et verba humana materiam quidem habent naturalem, silicet sonos ab hominis ore prolatos, sed significationem quasi formam habent ab intellectu suas conceptiones per tales sonos exprimente. Unde pari ratione nec verba humana habent efficaciam ad aliquam immutationem corporis naturalis ex virtute alicujus causae naturalis, sed solum ex aliqua spirituali substantia." Ibid., 19 (197).

54. See Weill-Parot, *Les "images astrologiques" au Moyen Âge*, 223–302. For a discussion of Ficino's treatment of the text, see Copenhaver, "Scholastic Philosophy and Renaissance Magic."

55. *HMES*, 2:462–63.

56. *SD* 9.115–21, cols. 848–53.

57. "Pictaciola pro quauis infirmitate scripta, super homines aut animalia ponunt praeter symbolum." *SD* 9.122, col. 853.

58. Vincent of Beauvais, *Speculum naturale*, 8.35 and 8.77.

59. Flint, *Rise of Magic*, 128.

Chapter 2

1. "Dixit Balenut: Ymago fit in prima hora diei ad ligandum homines ut non loquantur aliud de eo cum facta fuerit, vel unum verbum malum in sempiternum. Fundatur igitur ymago cuius medietas sit ex argento et alia medietas ex stanguo fuerit ad mensuram 4 palmarum ad ymaginem ipsius pro quo facis, et in prima hora diei. Et sit sculptum in capite ipsius nomen domini imaginis et in pectore nomen domine hore prime cuiusque dierum fuerit: et sit scriptum in ventre eius nomen domini ymaginis et ista sunt nomina subfumigacionis cum aloe et sanatar rubeo; et inuolues in panno albo et mundo, postea sepelias ipsam in porta eius, et est ligatio parata ad omnes linguas ligandas." London, British Library, Harley 80, fol. 79r.

2. "Hic est preciousus liber magnus signorum cethel, atque secretus quem fecerunt filii israel in deserto post exitum ab egipto, secundum motus et cursus syderum . . . . Si inueneris in lapidem sculptum virum sedentem super aratrum longibardum [*sic*] ceria [cervice? London, British Library, Sloane 1784, fol. 5r has *ceruicem curuatum*] curuata, habentem in collo quatuor homines iacentes, et teneat in manibus uulpem et turturem, hoc sigillum, ad collum suspensum, ad omnes plantationes valet, et ad invenciones thesaurorum. Argumentum cuius est: accipiat lanam nigram puram absque tinctura vt eam natura produxit et fac inde culcitam facere, [qua] palea tritici impleatur, et puluinar similiter, quod super culcitam ponatur, et desuper dormiat et sompniabit omnes thesauros regionis in qua fuerit et qualiter eos habere poterit." Oxford, Bodleian Library, Digby 193, fol. 30r.

3. For works of Arabic image magic and their manuscripts, witnesses may be found in Carmody, *Arabic Astronomical and Astrological Sciences*. See also Thorndike, "Traditional Medieval Tracts." Much of this has been superseded by the work of Charles Burnett, David Pingree, Paolo Lucentini, and Vittoria Perrone Compagni. See the numerous articles by Charles Burnett listed in the bibliography. See in particular Pingree, "Diffusion of Arabic Magical Texts" and "Learned Magic in the Time of Frederick II." For image magic works with Hermetic associations, see Lucentini and Compagni, *I testi e i codici*. For a modern edition of the *De imaginibus*, see that of Carmody in *Astronomical Works of Thâbit ibn Qurra*, 167–97. See also *HMES*, 1:663–66. For Thetel's *De imaginibus*, see Jean Baptiste Pitra's edition in *Spicilegium Solesmense*, 3:335–37. For the Hermetic *De quindecim stellis*, see *De quindecim stellis quindecim lapidibus*, in Delatte's *Textes latins et veiux français*, 242–43; for the version attributed to Enoch, see the same work, 276–88. On engraved gems, see Thorndike, "Traditional Medieval Tracts," 235. Other recent editions of texts in this tradition include Compagni's edition of the *Liber orationum planetarum septem* in her "Una fonte ermetica: Il liber orationum planetarum." The *De viginti quattuor horis* and the *Liber lune* may be found in Lucentini, "L'ermetismo magico nel secolo XIII."

4. Pingree notes that Thetel's work on images was probably "composed in Greek in late antiquity since it is stated that Galen carried the sigil found in a dark green jasper. The images described in the text are often reminiscent of those that are found on the amulets of Roman Egypt and Syria." Pingree, "Diffusion of Arabic Magical Texts," 64–65.

5. See Klaassen, "Ritual Invocation and Early Modern Science."

6. I draw here largely upon Pingree, "Diffusion of Arabic Magical Texts." Sophie Page has further supplemented this work by identifying transmission from Paris to St. Augustine's Abbey in Canterbury. See her "Magic at St. Augustine's."

7. Among books owned by Allen, we find Al-Kindī's *De radiis stellarum*, Digby 91, fols. 80–127, and Digby 183, fols. 38–44. As an example of magic-oriented experiments, the *Liber vaccae* may be found in Digby 71, fols. 36–55, among alchemical material. Another collection of experiments makes up MS 67. An *Ars notoria* fragment may be found in Digby 218, fols. 104r–105v.

8. Oxford, Bodleian Library, Ashmole 1471; Oxford, Corpus Christi, 125; and London, British Library, Harley 80 all contain numerous works of image magic. See Dee, *John Dee's Library Catalogue*.

9. The only major exceptions to this rule in England are two codices owned by John Erghome (see chapter 3). Other examples include Lehemann, "Collegium Amplonianum," 29 (catalogue reference Math. 54), in the fifteenth-century collection of Amplonius Ratnick, and Firenze, Biblioteca nazionale centrale di Firenze, II.iii.214. The latter is described in some detail in Pingree, "Learned Magic in the Time of Frederick II."

10. Two codices in Erghome's collection include works from the standard bibliography of image magic together with works of explicitly necromantic magic (discussed at length in chapter 3). London, Society of Antiquaries, 39 is another British example (discussed in chapter 5). Two continental examples are Firenze, Biblioteca Medicea Laurenziana, Plut. 89, sup. 38 (s. xv) and Firenze, Biblioteca nazionale centrale di Firenze, II.iii.214 (s. xv).

11. I cite only British examples. Cambridge, University Library, Gg.vi.3; London, British Library, Royal 12.C.XVIII; London, British Library, Sloane 312 (both constituent collections); London, Society of Antiquaries, 39; London, Wellcome Library, 510; Oxford, Corpus Christi, 221; and—all in Oxford, Bodleian Library—Ashmole 1471, Bodley 463, Digby 57, Digby 193, Digby 194, and Selden Supra 76. Among manuscripts known from medieval catalogues are York (Humphreys Cat.), Austin Friars A8 383 and Canterbury (James Cat.), St. Augustine's Abbey 1275 and 1161. I cite the shelfmarks from K. W. Humphreys's edition of the medieval catalogue of the abbey of the Austin Friars at York and the M. R. James edition of the Library of St. Augustine's Abbey. All subsequent citations of volumes in these catalogues employ this form.

12. A rare exception to this rule is Cambridge, University Library, Ff.vi.53 (1391), which is made up largely of legal and literary texts. It contains no texts on astrology and none involving any physical or practical application except two lapidaries, one of them the text by Thetel.

13. Firenze, Biblioteca Medicea Laurenziana, Plut. 30, Cod. 29.

14. Boston, Countway Library of Medicine 7; Royal 12.C.XVIII; Ashmole 1471; Digby 57; Digby 79; Canterbury (James Cat.), St. Augustine's Abbey 1275 and 1161.

15. Society of Antiquaries 39, fols. 18–24. I include Ashmole 346 in this discussion, although it is an early sixteenth-century collection. For a full discussion of this manuscript and its relation to Society of Antiquaries 39, see chapter 5.

16. Galen's *Liber de spermate* appears at fols. 68r–71v, a *Vocabularium herbarum et medicamentorum* at 134v–136r, and Constantinus Africanus's *Liber de coitu* at fols. 173v–179v, followed at fols. 184v–188r by four treatises ascribed to Hippocrates.

17. See, for example, Vaticano (Città del), Biblioteca Apostolica Vaticana, Pal. lat. 1116; Erfurt, Wissenschaftliche Bibliothek, Amplon., quarto 174; and København, Kongelike Bibliotek, Gl. Kgl. S. 1658.

18. Canterbury (James Cat.), St. Augustine's Abbey 1161.

19. James, *Ancient Libraries of Canterbury*, lxxxii.

20. Venn and Venn, *Alumni Cantabrigienses*, 1:4.27.

21. Singer, *Catalogue of Latin*, 3:763–65.

22. See, for example, London, Wellcome Library, 117.

23. Ibid., 116; Ashmole 1471; Cambridge, University Library, Ff.vi.53; and Sloane 1784. For a continental example, see Oxford, Bodleian Library, Canon. misc., 285.

24. Canterbury (James Cat.), St. Augustine's Abbey 1277; Digby 37, fols. 4–42; York (Humphreys Cat.), Austin Friars A8 362. See Friedman, "Secretum Philosophorum."

25. The *Secretis fratri Alberti* appears in Canterbury (James Cat.), St. Augustine's Abbey 1275, and also in Digby 37, fols. 46–55. The *Secretum secretorum* appears in Bodley 67, fols. 1–59r, and Digby 228, fols. 27v–40v. Extracts appear in London, Society of Antiquaries, 39, fols. 21–23.

26. See, for example, Bodley 463, a Spanish manuscript that contains multiple works on astrology in addition to a work on magical images.

27. Known cases of transmission, such as that between Society of Antiquaries 39 (see chapter 5) and Ashmole 346 (see chapter 3), principally involve works on magic.

28. Weill-Parot, *Les "images astrologiques" au Moyen Âge*, 602–22.

29. Canterbury (James Cat.), St. Augustine's Abbey 1140 (= Oxford, Bodleian Library, Rawlinson C. 117), 1166 (= Harley 13); Selden Supra 76, fols. 47r–60v; York (Humphreys Cat.), Austin Friars A8 159, 275, 362, 364, 385, and 452. For continental examples, see Edinburgh, Royal Observatory, Cr.3.14; London, Institution of Electrical Engineers, Thompson Collection S.C. MSS 3/5; and a no longer extant book of the original Amplonian collection: Lehemann, "Collegium Amplonianum," 21 (catalogue reference Math. 9).

30. See, for example, Erfurt, Wissenschaftliche Bibliothek, Amplon., quarto 189; Firenze, Biblioteca Medicea Laurenziana, Plut. 30, Cod. 29; München, Bayerische Staatsbibliothek, Clm 27; Paris, Bibliothèque nationale de France, lat. 7440; Vaticano (Città del), Biblioteca Apostolica Vaticana, Pal. lat. 1381 and 1445.

31. Canterbury (James Cat.), St. Augustine's Abbey 1275 and 1277. Although 1277 survives as Corpus Christi 125, the tract by Qusta ibn Luca has not survived with it. For more on this treatise, see the discussion of Michael Northgate below. For a continental example, see Firenze, Biblioteca nazionale centrale di Firenze, II.iii.214.

32. The Magister Speculi refers to this work generally at the beginning of the eleventh chapter and gives an incipit for a book of Balenuz called *De horarum opere*. *Speculum astronomiae*, 11.47–48 (Zambelli, 242–44). The entry *Belenus de ymaginibus* appears in Canterbury (James Cat.), St. Augustine's Abbey 1275. Royal 12.C.XVIII also contains a work on images attributed to Belenus at fols. 12r–15r. The incipit given by the Magister Speculi, *Dixit Balenuz qui et Apollo dicitur: Imago prima*, identifies the work with this copy. In the *Speculum* the author notes that this is joined (*adjungitur*) to the *Liber lune*. This text appears to be a condensed version of the latter part of the *Liber lune*, as it appears in Harley 80, fols. 77v–81r.

33. York (Humphreys Cat.), Austin Friars A8 362, 364, and 375. Among the books of Toz Graecus, the *Speculum* condemns *De imaginibus Veneris*. *Speculum astronomiae*, 11.56–59 (242–43); Thorndike, "Traditional Medieval Tracts," 248. The *De lapidibus Veneris*, a part of which appears in Oxford, Bodley 463, fol. 78, is simply a work on precious stones and their powers.

34. Carmody, *Arabic Astronomical and Astrological Sciences*, 63; Thorndike, "Traditional Medieval Tracts," 247; *Speculum astronomiae*, 11.69–71 (244–45); Corpus Christi 125, fols. 70–75 (?) (although this does not appear in the entry for this codex as Canterbury [James Cat.], St. Augustine's Abbey 1277); York (Humphreys Cat.), Austin Friars A8 375. A text on the rings of the seven planets appears in Society of Antiquaries 39, fols. 6v–8v, although the incipit does not correspond to the one given by the Magister Speculi (*Divisio lunae quando impleta fuerit etc.*). A ring is described for each planet, which is to be made in the hour of the moon for that planet.

35. York (Humphreys Cat.), Austin Friars A8 362 lists a text that could be *De quatuor annulis*. Canterbury (James Cat.), St. Augustine's Abbey 1538 and 1603 list *De annulis Salomonis*, as does the *Speculum astronomiae*, 11.76–78 (244–45). See Thorndike, "Traditional Medieval Tracts," 250. A sixteenth-century collection (Sloane 3847, fols. 66v–81) contains a *De quatuor annulis* attributed to Solomon.

36. "In nomine domini hic est preciosis liber magnus signorum cethel atque secretus, quem fecerunt filii israel in deserto post exitum ab egipto, secundum motus et cursus siderum." Digby 193, fol. 30r. The text is substantially the same in Selden Supra 76, fols. 109v–115r; Digby 79, fols. 178v–179v; and Corpus Christi 221, fols. 55–57.

37. Biblioteca Apostolica Vaticana, Pal. lat. 1381. Thābit's *De imaginibus* occurs at fol. 88r, the *Speculum astronomiae* extract at fols. 11v–12v. Naturally, it is conceivable that these two texts did not derive from the same original volume.

38. Burnett, *Magic and Divination*, 7.

39. Throughout this section I rely heavily upon the description of John Argentine in Talbot and Hammond, *Medical Practitioners in Medieval England*, 112–15.

40. Oxford, Corpus Christi, 255, fols. 206v–209v.

41. Oxford, Bodleian Library, Ashmole 1437, sec.1, fols. 11r–30v, sec. 2, fols. 1–20v, and sec. 3, pp. 21–181.

42. Emden, *Biographical Register of the University of Cambridge*, 16.

43. Armstrong, "Italian Astrologer," 449; Rhodes, "Princes in the Tower." Rhodes criticizes earlier work by Armstrong in which Armstrong misidentifies Argentine as a Strasbourg doctor. In "Italian Astrologer," Armstrong correctly identifies the doctor as John Argentine. In an addendum in the July 1962 issue of the *English Historical Review*, the editor and Rhodes apologize to Armstrong and note that they had not yet seen his article.

44. Rhodes, "Provost Argentine of King's." Rhodes makes no mention of Society of Antiquaries 39, the manuscript examined here. See also Emden, *Biographical Register of the University of Cambridge*, 15–16; Talbot and Hammond, *Medical Practitioners in Medieval England*, 112–15.

45. Emden, *Biographical Register of the University of Cambridge*, 509; Venn and Venn, *Alumni Cantabrigienses*, 1:4.27.

46. For a discussion of this manuscript, see chapter 5.

47. Pingree, "Diffusion of Arabic Magical Texts," 102.

48. Emden, *Biographical Register of the University of Cambridge*, 15.

49. No such ownership mark appears in the Society of Antiquaries manuscript.

50. Rhodes, "Provost Argentine of King's," 208.

51. Pingree, "Diffusion of Arabic Magical Texts," 98.

52. In fact, the third part of this study suggests that humanist interests may have been partly responsible for the decline in copying of the standard medieval texts of image magic.

53. See Leland, "Witchcraft and the Woodvilles."

54. On the *Sompnia Danielis*, see Kruger, *Dreaming in the Middle Ages*, 7–16.

55. Pingree, "Diffusion of Arabic Magical Texts," 94.

56. Thorne, *William Thorne's Chronicle of Saint Augustine's*, 422; James, *Ancient Libraries of Canterbury*, lxxxii, 348–49.

57. My discussion of John of London and Michael Northgate draws heavily upon Knorr, "Two Medieval Monks," and Page, "Magic at St. Augustine's," 27–29.

58. James, *Ancient Libraries of Canterbury*, lxxvii.

59. The entry for 1538 appears to have been duplicated in error as 1603. However, it is conceivable that it is an exact copy, which would bring the total to five.

60. Page, "Magic at St. Augustine's," 29.

61. Pingree, "Diffusion of Arabic Magical Texts," 86.

62. See Province of Canterbury, *Registrum Roberti Winchelsey*, 1:914. See also Emden, *Donors of Books to St. Augustine's*, 14.

63. James, *Ancient Libraries of Canterbury*, lxxvii.

64. Northgate, *Dan Michel's Ayenbite of Inwyt*. Available in a partial modern English translation by A. J. Wyatt as *The Ayenbite of Inwyt (Remorse of Conscience)* (London: W. B. Clive, 1889).

65. Northgate, *Dan Michel's Ayenbite of Inwyt*, 19, 40–41, 43. See also Kittredge, *Witchcraft in Old and New England*, 51.

66. Knorr makes this case in "Two Medieval Monks."

67. *HMES*, 2:390–92. See also Friedman, "Prioress's Beads 'of Smal Coral,'" 301–5.

68. *HMES*, 2:389.

69. Thomas of Cantimpré, *Liber de natura rerum*, 91–96.

70. I am indebted to Mildred Budney for her advice on the dating of this binding.

71. Baxter, *Bestiaries and Their Users*, 199.

72. Page, "Magic at St. Augustine's," 30–31.

Chapter 3

1. Canterbury (James Cat.), St. Augustine's Abbey 1275, 1277 (now Oxford, Corpus Christi, 125), 1538 (1603); London, British Library, Harley 80 and Royal 12.C.XVIII; York (Humphreys Cat.), Austin Friars A8 362, 364, and 375; and, all in Oxford, Bodleian Library, Ashmole 346, Bodley 463, and Digby 228. This list represents at least eight different scribes or collectors, given that John Erghome owned all of the magical material from York.

2. London, Society of Antiquaries, 39, fols. 21–23, and Ashmole 346, fols. 116–117v. The source cited is the *Secretum secretorum*, and so this may not be the condemned material.

3. Canterbury (James Cat.), St. Augustine's Abbey 1275.

4. London, British Library, Royal 12.C.XVIII, fols. 12–15.

5. Bodley 463, fols. 77r–78v.

6. For the *Liber lune*, see Harley 80, fols. 77v–78v.

7. For a discussion of this strange little work, see Page, "Magic at St. Augustine's," 126–55, 217–39; Corpus Christi 125, fols. 175 and 62r–63v.

8. Canterbury (James Cat.), St. Augustine's Abbey 1275 and 1277 (= Corpus Christi 125, but apparently the text does not survive) include Qusta ibn Luca's *De physicis ligaturis*. The lone copy of the *Speculum astronomiae* is to be found in Digby 228, fols. 76–79. Al-Kindī's *De radiis stellarum* appears in York (Humphreys Cat.), Austin Friars A8 362 and 375.

9. "Cum fuerit luna in alnath, id est in prima mansionem, que est facies martis et est mansio mala, in ipsa facies ymagines separacionis et discordie." Harley 80, fol. 87r.

10. "Haec est idolatria pessima, quae, ut reddat se aliquatenus fide dignam, observat viginti octo mansiones lunae et horas diei et noctis cum quibusdam nominibus dierum, horarum et mansionum ipsarum. A nobis longe sit iste modus: absit enim ut exhibeamus creaturae honorem debitum creatori." *Speculum astronomiae*, 11.15–20 (240–41). Again, I quote from the edition and translation of this work in Zambelli, *Speculum astronomiae and Its Enigma*; page numbers in this edition are provided in parentheses in subsequent citations of this source.

11. It also appears in York (Humphreys Cat.), Austin Friars A8 159, although this codex contains no magical works.

12. Edinburgh, Royal Observatory Cr.3.14 contains an *Ars notoria* and at least a portion of the *Speculum astronomiae*. Firenze, Biblioteca nazionale centrale di Firenze, II.iii.214 contains a wide variety of magical material, including ritual magic, as well as Qusta ibn Luca's *De physicis ligaturis*.

13. Kieckhefer, *Forbidden Rites*, 10.

14. The listed titles are *Noua cirurgia magri Henr' de amunda villa*, *Experimenta diuersa in physica et Cirurgia*, and *Cirurgia extracta de Gilbertina practica puerorum*. James, *Ancient Libraries of Canterbury*, 348.

15. *Speculum astronomiae*, 11.45–55 (240–45).

16. *HMES*, 1:652–57.

17. *HMES*, 1:611. Thorndike refers to a seventeenth-century copy of this text in Sloane 3848, fols. 36–40.

18. Humphreys, *Friars' Libraries*, xxix–xxx.

19. York (Humphreys Cat.), Austin Friars A8 362, 364, 371, 375, 383, 385, and 452. Numbers 385 and 542 include only the *De radiis stellarum* and no practical text on magic. Codex 371 includes only the *Ars notoria* and thus does not concern us here.

20. *HMES*, 2:53–59.

21. For the *Pronostica Socratis Basilei*, see *HMES*, 2:115.

22. Burnett, "Adelard, Ergaphalau, and the Science of the Stars," 173.

23. For a discussion of this work, see chapter 4.

24. On this example, and for a broader examination of dream interpretation in magical literature, see Klaassen, "Magical Dream Provocation."

Part II Introduction

1. John of Morigny, *Liber visionum*, 49 (166). The epigraph is from Fanger and Watson's translation of the "Prologue to John of Morigny's *Liber visionum*." Citations of the *Liber visionum* include the page numbers from this translation in parentheses. The Latin reads, "Omnibus visionibus leuiter non credas uel acquiescas, set consilio saluatoris proba spiritus si ex Deo sint et discretionem ipsorum precibus impetres a Spiritu Sancto." The synopsis provided below is from the same source; a synopsis of Part I of John's book, based on Graz, Universitätsbibliothek, 680, may also be found in Fanger, "Plundering the Egyptian Treasure," 242–49.

2. John of Morigny, *Liber visionum*, 31 (192–93).

3. The parallels between this story and that of Abraham Abulafia are interesting. Abulafia also claimed to have had a prophetic vision of the divine but said later that some visions were sent by demons to confuse him. In fact, he said, he "groped about like a blind man at midday for fifteen years with Satan to his right." This did not prevent him from being convinced of the truth of his visionary experiences. Scholem, *Major Trends in Jewish Mysticism*, 127.

4. Sensitivity to subtle moral or theological issues may also have motivated John's concern with demonic involvement. Augustine warned against the use of any strange words, and Aquinas rejected the *Ars notoria* in part because it employed incomprehensible orations. These prohibitions may have driven John to remove the *verba ignota* from the Solomonic *Ars notoria* when he produced the *Liber visionum*. The injunctions against unknown words in magic were common and derive ultimately from Augustine. See, for example, Augustine, *De doctrina christiana*, 19–21. As Fanger suggests, John may be referring to the *verba ignota* that Aquinas mentions in *Summa theologiae*, 2.2.96.

5. Watson, "John the Monk's *Book of the Visions*," 168.

6. "Nota quod nichil debes agere minuere vel mutare de omnibus que scripsimus tam in orationibus quam in figuris, ymaginationibus et institutionibus, nisi a Deo vel Virgine gloriosa tibi prius fuerit divinitus inspiritum, id est revelatum." Ibid., 204–5.

7. For a very useful and insightful discussion of the problem of visions and truth, see Christian, *Apparitions in Late Medieval and Renaissance Spain*, 3–9.

8. John of Morigny, *Liber visionum*, 49 (161–62).

9. This observation notwithstanding, the text itself appears to be endogenous to the Christian Latin world, not translated or adapted from a Hebrew original. See Boudet, "L'*Ars notoria* au Moyen Âge."

10. Fanger, "Plundering the Egyptian Treasure," 229. Fanger demonstrates that John evidently regarded this "plundering" as a part of a divine project guided by angels and the Virgin. His "purifying" consisted in part of adding to the beginning of the text the cycle of prayers he had composed, and of stripping out from the Solomonic version the words said to be transliterated from ancient languages. Ibid., 220–22.

11. John notes, for example, that visions and other revelations come "according to the merits of the operator": "Et que in aliis libris longo tempore et maximis et fastidiosis librorum voluminibus graviter et prolixe . . . , in hoc libro prepaucis placidisque orationibus, angelorum reuelacione ac inaudita uerborum eorum subtilitate, necnon et intemerate . . . virginis Marie visione, apparicione, consolacione et procuracione, *secundum operantis merita*, breui tempore." John of Morigny, *Liber visionum*, 1 (166).

12. "Cum igitur hanc scienciam predictam exercerem multas alias visiones mirabiles vidi que non tangunt propositum nostrum, per quas nigromanciam sciui in utraque specie cum ipsius artis librorum adiutorio." Ibid., 20 (181).

13. "Ego, frater Iohannes, postquam dimisi artem notoriam declinaui ad artes nigromancie, et in ipsa preualui tantum quod nouam nigromanciam componerem et quod Annulos Salomonis fabricarem." Ibid., 24 (186).

14. "Et cum esse non posset per doctrinam successiuam propter meam paupertatem, et in predicto libro continebatur qualiter ad propositum meum attingere per doctrinam subitaneam potuissem, idcirco, omnibus alijs studijs dimissis, cepi in ipsa frequencius studere, et in tantum studui quod qualiter operari deberem sciui." Ibid., 15 (178).

15. For an example of a text rearranged by an unknown later redactor, see Watson's analysis of Hamilton, Ontario, McMaster University Library, 107 (formerly unnumbered manuscript), in "John the Monk's *Book of the Visions*," 206–15. Prayers were also extracted from John's text, rearranged, abbreviated, and put to other uses; see, e.g., Fanger and Láng, "John of Morigny's *Liber visionum*."

16. See Klaassen, "Unstable Texts and Modal Approaches."

17. For a useful discussion of this term with reference to medieval ritual magic, see Fanger's introduction to *Invoking Angels*.

Chapter 4

1. Caesarius of Heisterbach, *Dialogus miraculorum*, 10.4. For the English translation, see *Dialogue on Miracles*, 2:174.

2. See Véronèse, "Magic, Theurgy, and Spirituality," 38–39.

3. Ibid., 43–49.

4. See Camille, "Visual Art in Two Manuscripts." For Aquinas's discussion of the *Ars notoria*, see Aquinas, *Summa theologiae*, 2.2.96.1.

5. Véronèse, "Magic, Theurgy, and Spirituality," 49–59.

6. For a necromantic emulation, see Kieckhefer, *Forbidden Rites*, 193–96; München, Bayerische Staatsbibliothek, Clm 849, fols. 3r–5v. The sixteenth-century necromantic collection Sloane 3853 also contains prayers from the Solomonic *Ars notoria* at fols. 159v–174v, making clear that, at least in the sixteenth century, the boundaries between necromancy and the *Ars notoria* were porous.

7. The Old Compilation *Liber figurarum* was designed to work with approximately ninety figures; John cuts this down to eight images in the New Compilation text. See discussion in Fanger, "Covenant and the Divine Name," in Fanger, *Invoking Angels*, 194–99.

8. Prayers extracted from the *Ars notoria* are mentioned in one of the volumes held at St. Augustine's Abbey at Canterbury. The *Ars notoria* in Sloane 3853 (fols. 159v–174v) does not include figures or descriptions of them; and at the end of the copy of John of Morigny's work in Hamilton, Ontario, McMaster University Library, 107 (fols. 80v–83v), we find appended a set of prayers "pro scientia adipiscenda" drawn from the *Ars notoria* but not mentioning it by name.

9. For example, Aquinas's condemnation of the art is based in part upon his demonstration that demons cannot illuminate the intellect, although they may be able to relate some small portions of the sciences in words. *Summa theologiae*, 2.2.96.1.

10. *HMES*, 2:281–83.

11. See Véronèse, *L'Ars notoria au Moyen Âge*, 297–98; London, British Library, Sloane 513, 1712, 3008, and 3846. See also London, British Library, Harley 181; Oxford, Bodleian Library, Bodley 951 and, also from the Bodleian, Ashmole 1515 and Jones 1.

12. Canterbury (James Cat.), St. Augustine's Abbey 1539 (1603); York (Humphreys Cat.), Austin Friars A8 371 and 362 (includes two versions); and Powicke, *Medieval Books of Merton College*, 213 (catalogue no. 999).

13. A printed version of an *Ars notoria*, not the version in Bodley 951, appears in at least four early seventeenth-century editions of Agrippa's *Opera*. Although their exact dates are unknown, three of these may be traced to the Beringi at Lyon, and each of them contains the *Ars notoria*. The first line of the preface differs in each: "Non dubito, quem titulus Libri no" (Lyon [Lugduni] Beringi Fratres [16??] A); "Non dubito quin titulus Libri nostri de Occul-" (Lyon [Lugduni] Beringi Fratres [16??] B); and "Non dubito quin titulus libri nostri de Occulta" (Lyon [Lugduni] Beringi Fratres [16??] C). See Ferguson, *Bibliographical Notes*. Ferguson's search was not exhaustive, and there may well be other editions. One edition, or possibly two, of Agrippa's *Opera* appeared in Strasbourg in the early sixteenth century, published by Zetzner. The *Ars notoria* was not only among the texts included with Agrippa's works but was evidently deemed important enough to advertise its presence on the title page. While these volumes have been attributed to the Beringi (and indeed the title page of the first volume employs the Beringi seal and claims Lyon as the place of publication), the device and motto of Zetzner appear on page 135 of the appendix. I have examined a single codex containing volumes 1 and 2 and the appendix (Strasbourg: Zetzner, 1605A). John Ferguson has examined a similar (perhaps the same) edition in which two of the three volumes appear as separate codices (Strasbourg: Zetzner, n.d., and Strasbourg: Zetzner, 1605B). This fact, and a discrepancy between his description and the volume I have seen, suggests two editions rather than one. See Ferguson, *Bibliographical Notes*, 19–21. For an English translation related to the version contained in Bodley 951, see Robert Turner's 1657 translation, *Ars notoria: The Notory Art of Solomon*.

14. See Peterson, *Lesser Key of Solomon*.

15. An *Ars notaria* may be found in the list of books Warden Richard Fitzjames borrowed from Merton College Library. The first word of the second folio is given as *haybala*, making it unlikely that this text concerns notarial abbreviations. See Powicke, *Medieval Books of Merton College*, 213 (catalogue no. 999).

16. For a discussion of intellectual reactions to the text, see Véronèse, "L'*Ars notoria* au Moyen Âge et à l'époque moderne," 1:637–76.

17. Harley 181 contains three different versions of the genre. Sloane 3853 is a necromantic collection in which I have identified a previously unknown version. Ashmole 1515 contains an attempt at a translation of the Solomonic text. I discuss all of these versions in chapter 6. For the condemnations of the *Ars notoria*, see Bujanda, Davignon, and Stanek, *Index de Venise*, 1549, 412, 434. See also *HMES*, 6:146.

18. John of Morigny's condemnation of heresy probably resulted from the fact that he taught his methods and disseminated copies of his text (which in all forms includes instructions for how it should be taught to others; see his *Prima practica* as it appears in Fanger and Watson's edition, part 2.3, based on London, British Library, Additional 18057, fols. 69v2–70v1). For a discussion of the condemnation, see Watson, "John the Monk's *Book of the Visions*," 163–64; and Fanger, "Plundering the Egyptian Treasure," 222–25. See also Viard, *Les Grandes Chroniques de France*, 9:23–24.

19. See, for example, the collection of Richard Dove, Sloane 513, discussed below.

20. See Kieckhefer, "Devil's Contemplatives"; Véronèse, "L'*Ars notoria* au Moyen Âge et à l'époque moderne," 1:115–58.

21. These are both versions of the *Ars brevis*, a spin-off of the *Ars notoria*. Bell, "Cistercian at Oxford."

22. As noted above, a work of necromancy appears together with a work on the notory art in an indenture to the Merton College Library in 1483. Given the first word of the second folio (*haybala*), this must be the *Ars notoria*. Powicke, *Medieval Books of Merton College*, 213–15 (catalogue nos. 999 and 1053). The work appears in Erghome's compendium of superstitious works (York [Humphreys Cat.], Austin Friars A8 362) but also in another of his volumes (A8 371) with works on natural philosophy and experiments. Sloane 3853, analyzed below, contains a shortened Solomonic *Ars notoria*. See chapter 6.

23. The version at Merton College evidently contained *verba ignota*. In the shorter versions, these were often removed. The shortened versions all tend to describe themselves as such, e.g., *Ars notoria brevis et bonis*. All of these employ the standard title and/or are ascribed to Solomon.

24. Both of these texts may be found in Harley 181, discussed in chapter 6.

25. Kieckhefer, *Forbidden Rites*, 193–96.

26. Oxford, Bodleian Library, Rawlinson liturg. D. 6; Mainz, Stadtbibliothek Mainz, I 138; and München, Universitätsbibliothek, Oct. Cod. 213. See Fanger and Láng, "John of Morigny's *Liber visionum*."

27. Camille, "Visual Art in Two Manuscripts."

28. Viard, *Les Grandes Chroniques de France*, 9:23–24.

29. Fanger, "Plundering the Egyptian Treasure," 222–25.

30. Canterbury (James Cat.), St. Augustine's Abbey 209, 1616, and 1791.

31. Ibid., 1603. This entry appears to be duplicated in entry 1538 of the same library. Additions in paretheses are mine.

32. *Speculum astronomiae*, 11.23 (Zambelli, 240–41); *HMES*, 2:699. Some of the manuscripts of the *Rings of Solomon* include explicitly necromantic practices (e.g., Firenze, Biblioteca nazionale centrale di Firenze, II.iii.214, fols. 26v–29v, and Firenze, Biblioteca Medicea Laurenziana, Plut. 89, sup. 38, fols. 211–24), while others are more like regular astrological image magic (Sloane 3847, fols. 66v–81).

33. See, for example, Graz, Universitätsbibliothek, 680, which contains a wide range of devotional material, including sermons, in addition to a copy of John of Morigny's *Liber visionum*. Oxford, Bodleian Library, Lyell 51, fols. 86–120 contains a section in a fifteenth-century Austrian hand that includes what appears to be the *Ars memorativa* together with sermons, the *Ars predicandi*, a work on the virtues and vices, and a section of the *Ars brevis* of Ramon Llull.

34. A text attributed to Augustinus, "Manuale de salute sive aspiratione animae ad deum," appears in several early modern editions. There is a single limited-edition modern reprint, Heireman's *Alosti in Flandria*.

35. This work by the late thirteenth-century Franciscan James of Milan was previously attributed to Bonaventure. A fourteenth-century reworking of the text was produced by the English mystic Walter Hilton. See Bonaventure, *Opera omnia Sancti Bonaventurae*, 12:631–703; [James of Milan], *Goad of Love*, 42.

36. The suggested exclusions derive from the M. R. James edition of the catalogue. For a modern edition, see Pseudo-Dionysius, *De caelesti hierarchia*.

37. Gams, *Series episcoporum ecclesiae catholicae*, 596.

38. Canterbury (James Cat.), St. Augustine's Abbey 767, 276. Additions in paretheses are mine.

39. See, for example, Erfurt, Wissenschaftliche Bibliothek, Amplon., quarto 28. It contains, among other material, a work on the seven virtues and a treatise on the Lord's Prayer. Interestingly, the codex also includes a treatise on the *ars dictamini*. Graz, Universitätsbibliothek, 1016 contains books 2–4 of Lombard's *Sentences* and, interestingly, an exegetical note on Exodus 20:20 about sacrificing to false gods. See also the examples discussed above, Graz, Universitätsbibliothek, 680, and Oxford, Bodleian Library, Lyell 51, fols. 86–120.

40. "Et tu, qui es deus meus, qui in principio creasti celum et terram et omnia ex nichilo, qui in spiritu tuo omnia reformas, comple, instaura, sana animam meam, vt glorificem te per omnia opera cogitationum mearum et verborum meorum. Deus, pater, orationem meam confirma, et intellectum meum auge, et memoriam meam ad suscipiendam beatam visionem tuam meo viuente corpusculo et ad cognoscendam super excelsam et super eternam tuam essenciam, qui viuis et regnas per infinita secula seculorum." Sloane 3853, fol. 162v.

41. For example, a prayer of confession appears in Rawlinson D. 252, fols. 49r–50r, as part of preparations for necromantic rituals. See chapter 5.

42. Thorndike notes that the name Bartholomeus de Rippa Romea also appears among the authorities cited by Camilo Lunardi in *Speculum lapidum*, although he tentatively connects the name with Bartholomew of England. *HMES*, 6:310. (For editions of the *Speculum lapidum*, see chapter 6, note 40.) London, Wellcome Library, 116, 1–37, contains a work on stones and images for stones attributed to Bartholomeus de Rippa Romea. The material is actually drawn directly from the *De mineralibus*, by Albertus Magnus, and *De lapidibus*, attributed to Albertus. The fourteenth-century date and English origin of the manuscript are not incompatible with Thorndike's suggestion. However, that the work is drawn directly from Albertus and not from Bartholomew of England's encyclopedia, *De proprietatibus rerum*, suggests that de Rippa Romea may well have been a different person.

43. Rorem, *Pseudo-Dionysius*, 47–58.

44. Chapter 2 is titled "That divine and heavenly things are appropriately revealed, even through dissimilar symbols." In an elaboration of his apophatic theology, Pseudo-Dionysius argues that incongruous images are more effective for contemplative efforts, especially for the inexperienced, because they do not lead one astray. Less startling images might lead one to assume that God was literally like them, a false assumption by definition. It should be clear, however, that Pseudo-Dionysius principally discusses scriptural imagery. Rorem, *Pseudo-Dionysius*, 57–58, 73.

45. Watson, "John the Monk's *Book of the Visions*," 174. It should be noted that Watson was not aware of this manuscript record when he made this astute comparison.

46. That Walter Hilton had rewritten the *Stimulus amoris* meant that more English manuscripts circulated under this title. This increases the possibility that this text was the one by Hilton, which makes it more likely that this codex is of English origin. It remains possible, however, that the title refers to the earlier work by James of Milan. It should be observed that Walter Hilton, who rewrote substantial portions of this work in his version by the same title, tended to avoid the more abstract language of Pseudo-Dionysius, as well as such topics as divine union. The work may be seen as part of an overall movement away from abstract spirituality and toward a more Christocentric one. In fact, Hilton regarded the work as a weapon against false mysticism. *Goad of Love*, 24.

47. See Veenstra, "Honorius and the Sigil of God." My descriptions of this work and of the textual traditions of the *Sworn Book of Honorius* draw heavily upon this essay.

48. For an edition of the texts in this tradition, see Hedegård, *Liber iuratus Honorii*.

49. Veenstra, "Honorius and the Sigil of God," 178.

50. Ibid., 155–60.

51. Recent research by Tanya Luhrmann on the affective techniques of contemporary evangelical Christianity reveals the powerful impact of such exercises. See Luhrmann, "Art of Hearing God."

52. See Kieckhefer, "Devil's Contemplatives"; Veenstra, "Honorius and the Sigil of God," 168–73.

53. Veenstra, "Honorius and the Sigil of God," 174–75.

54. Hedegård, *Liber iuratus Honorii*, 298–336.

55. In the original version, the vision of God also brings about a consecration of the sigil. Veenstra, "Honorius and the Sigil of God," 159–60.

56. Ibid., 175–79.

57. "Qui consulente angelo hocroel nomine volumina artis magice deffloravit, nobis florem accipiens et aliis cortices dimitendo." Hedegård, *Liber iuratus Honorii*, 61.

58. For a very insightful discussion of the question of religion and necromancy, see Kieckhefer, "Holy and the Unholy."

Chapter 5

1. See, for example, Coleman, *Communing with the Spirits.*

2. Butler, *Ritual Magic,* 17.

3. For the classic text, see Pingree's edition of the *Picatrix.*

4. Richard Kieckhefer has tentatively identified the idea of exorcism, exorcist manuals, and the clerical underworld as key elements in the development of necromancy. *Magic in the Middle Ages,* 151–56, 165–75.

5. See, for example, Acts 19:12–15. Jewish exorcists invoked the names of Jesus and Paul in an operation but failed because the spirit did not know who the exorcists were (i.e., they were not Christians).

6. Boudet and Véronèse, "Le secret dans la magie rituelle," 105–11. For more on the *Clavicula Salomonis* and its use in necromantic manuals, see below.

7. For sixteenth-century uses of this text by British scribes, see chapter 6.

8. Veenstra, "Holy Almandal."

9. *Speculum astronomiae,* 11 (Zambelli, 240–51). For a discussion of these texts, see Boudet, *Entre science et nigromance,* 145–55. See also Weill-Parot, *Les "images astrologiques" au Moyen Âge,* 52–62.

10. Kieckhefer, *Magic in the Middle Ages,* 151–56.

11. John of Morigny was one such monk-necromancer. Caesarius of Heisterbach presents the monastery as the refuge of the ex-necromancer. Caesarius, *Dialogue on Miracles,* 318–20. One of the more dramatic and entertaining examples is the romance of Eustace the Monk that Kittredge mentions in *Witchcraft in Old and New England,* 45–46. Eustace, trained at Toledo by the devil, ultimately becomes a powerful necromancer and pirate. See Cannon, "Battle of Sandwich"; *Roman d'Eustache Le Moine.*

12. Boudet and Véronèse argue that the prologues of several works of explicit conjuring depict the knowledge they contain as redemptive. It might be more accurate to say that it was "restorative," for it did not restore humanity to a prelapsarian state—only Christ's sacrifice could accomplish that—but rather assisted humanity in its fallen state. "Le secret dans la magie rituelle," 118–25.

13. See Klaassen, "Learning and Masculinity."

14. Kieckhefer, in "Holy and the Unholy," has noted this positive treatment of necromancy.

15. Duvernoy, *Le registre d'inquisition de Jacques Fournier,* 128–43. This formed the basis for a discussion in Le Roy Ladurie, *Montaillou,* 342–56.

16. Salimbene de Parma, *Chronicle of Salimbene de Adam,* 6–7; *Monumenta Germaniae historica,* Scriptores 32.32.

17. Caesarius of Heisterbach, *Dialogus miraculorum,* 5.4 (for the English translation, see *Dialogue on Miracles,* 279–81).

18. See, for example, Oxford, Bodleian Library, Rawlinson D. 252, fols. 66v–67v.

19. See Moore, "New Sects and Secret Meetings."

20. Sophie Page has suggested a tension between the "rationalizing" processes of writing or copying a text and the acceptance of its bizarre or shocking details. "Magic and the Pursuit of Wisdom," 55. Richard Kieckhefer discusses the interplay of holy and unholy in "Holy and the Unholy."

21. For the most recent discussion of the *Clavicula Salomonis,* particularly its presence in the medieval library, see Boudet and Véronèse, "Le secret dans la magie rituelle." For a discussion of the *Almandal,* see Veenstra, "Holy Almandal" and "Venerating and Conjuring Angels." For a discussion of the *Liber Razielis* and *Liber Theysolius,* see Page, "Magic and the Pursuit of Wisdom." The *Thesaurus spirituum* remains unexamined except for the brief treatments cited below. Attributed to Rupertus Lombardus, or sometimes Robertus Longobardus, the text (or portions of it) also travels under the names *Practica nigromantiae, Preceptualis ars magice,* and in one case *Dannet.* If we take surviving manuscripts as a rough indicator (and overlook the considerable variation in contents), it was one of the most common works of conjuring in the

late Middle Ages. It is also listed in Trithemius's bibliography of necromantic works. See the text of this work in Zambelli, *White Magic, Black Magic*, 104. The section of this text known as the *Practica nigromantiae* is attested in a German fragment of the fourteenth century and a British manuscript of the fifteenth. Eight additional manuscripts of the sixteenth and seventeenth centuries also survive. It is not impossible that the shorter *Practica nigromantiae* might have been incorporated into the longer text, but Trithemius's citation of the *Thesaurus spirituum* around 1500 makes clear that this longer work is at least fifteenth-century in origin, as are the prologue and the attribution to Rupertus Lombardus. The longer versions contain four sections concerned entirely with conjuring demons, including conjurations and advice on times of operation. Shorter versions sometimes contain a volume of precepts and sometimes only the initial seven rules. See Berlin, Staatsbibliothek Preussischer Kulturbesitz, Codices Elecorales Recentores 184, fols. 146ff.; London, Society of Antiquaries, 39, fols. 15rff.; London, Wellcome Library, 110, fols. 57r–98, and—all in London, British Library—Additional 36674, fols. 149ff.; Sloane 3850, fols. 117b–129; and Sloane 3885, fols. 26–57.

22. "Et aperuit Rachiel librum et legit in auribus Ade. Audiuit autem adam verba libri sancta ex ore angeli et eiecit se super faciem suam ad teram cum magno timore. Cui dixit Rachiel Surge adam et confortare et non habeas timorem . . . . Recipe librum istum de manu mea et respice in eo quia per ipsum scies et intelliges." München, Bayerische Staatsbibliothek, Clm 51, fol. 6r.

23. Veenstra, "Holy Almandal," 195–96.

24. On the requirement of secrecy in ritual magic, see Boudet and Véronèse, "Le secret dans la magie rituelle," 111–13.

25. Ibid., 117–18.

26. Page, "Magic and the Pursuit of Wisdom," 43–44; Vaticano (Città del), Biblioteca Apostolica Vaticana, Reg. lat. 1300, fol. 11v.

27. Boudet and Véronèse, "Le secret dans la magie rituelle," 116.

28. Ibid., 112–13. On the *Liber Theysolius*, which provides these instructions, see Page, "Magic and the Pursuit of Wisdom," 45.

29. Boudet and Véronèse eloquently argue this point in "Le secret dans la magie rituelle," 125–29.

30. Because it relied on printed sources, E. M. Butler's well-known and otherwise useful survey, *Ritual Magic*, did not treat a substantial portion of the late medieval literature.

31. The foundational work in this area is Kieckhefer's *Forbidden Rites*.

32. Oxford, Bodleian Library, e Mus. 219, fols. 186–188r.

33. London, British Library, Sloane 430, fol. 2v, and Sloane 3556, fol. 1v. Both images are reproduced in Page, *Magic in Medieval Manuscripts*.

34. Powicke, *Medieval Books of Merton College*, 215 (catalogue no. 1053). Warden Richard Fitzjames borrowed this manuscript on 19 May 1483, and the record describes it simply as "a book of necromancy." This need not mean that it literally contained either true necromancy or that it was a collection. However, the record of the volume is from the fifteenth century, which makes it unlikely that it was a work of image magic, because the use of the term "necromantia" to describe image magic appears to have been an earlier habit. Assuming that the contents *were* necromantic, it is likely that it was a collection, as that is the usual form of this genre when it occupies an entire codex. See ibid., 213.

35. See, for example, Oxford, Bodleian Library, Tanner 407, 167ff.; Sloane 314, fol. 106v; and Sloane 3849, fols. 17–19.

36. Sloane 430, fol. 2v, and Sloane 3556, fol. 1v.

37. Sloane 314, fol. 106v.

38. Louis, *Commonplace Book of Robert Reynes*, 169, quoted in Kieckhefer, *Forbidden Rites*, 97.

39. Sloane 121, fols. 90v–93v. See Kieckhefer, *Magic in the Middle Ages*, 171.

40. Philip, *Bodleian Library*, 93–98.

41. See Fanger and Láng, "John of Morigny's *Liber visionum*."

42. When some sixteenth-century manuscripts managed to find their way into the early major book collections, many were collected because they were copies owned by such significant figures as Simon Forman, not necessarily because of their necromantic content.

43. Sloane 121, fols. 90v–93v. Kieckhefer mentions this manuscript and also ponders possible reasons for the presence of the necromantic experiment among these tricks and sleights of hand. *Magic in the Middle Ages*, 171. In his later book, *Forbidden Rites*, he suggests that we regard the creation of illusion as a category of magical performance. This manuscript would suggest that illusion magic was a genre that cut across usually distinct forms of magic, from parlor tricks to demonic conjurations.

44. "Vt milites armati bellantes videatur. In mancione 3a fac fieri anulum auream concauum, in cuius concauitate ponas pergameneum virgineum, in quo fiunt scripta de sanguine hominis hec nomina: denetica alibiat stablacctis virciseri. Anulo sic completo, tene ipsum die sequenti <in> aurora introitu alicuius campi et suffumiga ipsum cum <. . .> hominis mortui et dic, flexis genibus versus campum, hanc oracionem. 'Domine deus omnipotens, qui de ultimo celo vides abbissos, qui homines ad ymaginem et similitidinem tuam formasti, per quem viuunt viuentes et moriuntur morientes largitatem tue benignitatis, exoro quatinus quacumque die uel hora tangam anulum de saliua mea isti Spiritus, quorum nomina sunt intus inclusa, faciant armatos milites bellantes ante occulos illarum, quibus voluero apperere.' In hoc [f]acto, tange terram cum anulo faciendo hac signum [symbol]. Postea involue sindone nigra, et custo eum mundissime, et cum volueris operari, dic, tangendo cum saliua tua anulum, 'O vos spiritus, quorum nomina intus sunt inclusa, coniuro vos per illum, cui debetis principaliter obedire, quatinus quod desidero faciatis.' Hoc dicto videbis mirabilia." Society of Antiquaries 39, fols. 2v–3r. (Punctuation mine. Angle brackets indicate mutilation.)

45. Ibid., fol. 2r. For a discussion of the use of these "historiola," see Frankfurter, "Narrating Power."

46. Swartz, "Scribal Magic and Its Rhetoric."

47. Pingree, "Learned Magic in the Time of Frederick II," 42–43.

48. "Domine deus omnipotens qui olim aquam in vinum transmutasti et qui de ultimo celo vides abbissas." Society of Antiquaries 39, fol. 3r.

49. "Et est unus liber *De septem anulis septem planetarum* qui sic incipit: *Divisio lunae quando impleta fuerit etc.*" *Speculum astronomiae*, 11.69–71 (244).

50. Vaticano (Città del), Biblioteca Apostolica Vaticana, Pal. lat. 1375, fol. 270v. The first images correspond.

51. The text appears after the first chapter, at fol. 6v, but belongs later in the text, where its incipit is given as the first chapter in a section that discusses the use of the sigils of the planets, at fol. 8v.

52. Zambelli, *White Magic, Black Magic*, 104.

53. "Item nota quod quilibet bene potest facere exorsismum in qualibet hora noctis excepta hora matutinali vel qua cantatur matutine nam spiritus multi abhorrent venire dum hore sunt sacre quia diuinitas dei expellit demones et ideo in illa hora non est bona inceptio exorsismorum." Society of Antiquaries 39, fol. 16v.

54. "Nota quod quatuor reges princip[a]les non possunt constringi in aliqua hora diei nisi in crepusculo noctis Item spiritus dic[t]i reges non possunt constringi nisi ante primam Item principes, a tertia usque meridiem, et a sexta usque ad vesperas, uel ad co[m]pletorium. Item miche<. . .>es, a sexta hora usque ad completorium, vel ad completoria usque ad defeccam solis diei." Ibid., fol. 17v. (The angle brackets indicate mutiliation.)

55. A text on the four princes is mentioned in the *Speculum astronomiae*, 11.24 and 79 (240–41 and 244–45), under the title *De tribus figuris spirituum qui dicuntur principes in quatuor plagis mundi*. Necromantic rituals involving or mentioning the four kings may also be found. See, for example, Rawlinson D. 252, fols. 103r–107r, a ritual invocation of four spirits with power in matters of theft—Theltrion, Spireon, Botheon, Mahireon—who are under the four kings. See also Sloane 3853, fols. 138–141, *Speculum quatuor regum*. Trithemius also lists this text in his bibliography of magic texts. Zambelli, *White Magic, Black Magic*, 103.

56. See Burnett, *Magic and Divination*, 1–15.

57. See Kieckhefer, "Holy and the Unholy."

58. Rawlinson D. 252, fol. 35v. Hereafter cited by folio number alone.

59. The initial reference to the *Vinculum Salomonis* appears at fol. 62v. The text itself appears at fol. 87v.

60. The *Liber consecrationum* appears at fols. 81r–87r and the *Coniuracio licentialis* at fol. 36v.

61. Surviving manuscripts titled *Pentaculum Salomonis* include Rawlinson D. 252, fol. 87v; London, Wellcome Library, 110, fols. 36r–38v; Firenze, Biblioteca Medicea Laurenziana, Plut. 89, sup. 38, fol. 116r–v. The work also appears in the catalogue of John Erghome's books (York [Humphreys Cat.], Austin Friars A8 362, t). Surviving texts not titled but identified as *Pentaculum Salomonis* include Cambridge, University Library, Ll.i.12, fol. 9r–v, and Firenze, Biblioteca Medicea Laurenziana, Plut. 89, sup. 36, fol. 234r–v. A *Sigilla Salomonis* appears in Rawlinson D. 252, fol. 23v. In *Les "images astrologiques" au Moyen Âge*, p. 634, Weill-Parot notes that it appears in chapter 6 of Giorgio Anselmi's *Opus de magia disciplina* (Firenze, Biblioteca Medicea Laurenziana, Plut. 44, Cod. 35 [s. xvi]) and also in Vat. lat. 5333, which contains only the fourth part of the treatise. A *Liber pentaculorum Salomoni* and possibly the *Vinculum Salomonis* under the title *Vinculum spirituum* appear in the bibliography of magic books by Trithemius. See Zambelli, *White Magic, Black Magic*, 106. Surviving manuscripts of the *Liber consecrationum* can be found in Berlin, Staatsbibliothek Preussischer Kulturbesitz, Codices Elecorales Recentores 184, fols. 45–145; Sloane 3826 (s. xvi), fols. 58–65; Sloane 3846, fols. 158v–164r; Sloane 3853, fols. 64–69; and Sloane 3854, fols. 68–76. The text also appears in the collection of John Erghome (York [Humphreys Cat.], Austin Friars A8 385, r).

62. "Per potentissimum et corroboratum nomen dei El forte et admirabile ego impero tibi exorzizo et coniuro te spiritum presentis thesauri custodem cuiuscumque fueris ordinis potestatis generis aut virtutis per eum qui dixit fiat et facta sunt. Et per omnia nomina ipsius et per nomen et in nomine Joth Vahu et he quod Adam audiuit et locutus est et per nomen et in nomine Agla vel Ely quod Noe audiuit et liberatus est cum octava sua familia a diluvio." London, Wellcome Library, 110, fol. 38r. "*Per potentissimum et coroboratum nomen dei El, forte et admirabile, vos exorcizamus potenter, coniuramus cogente, et imperamus vobis per illum qui dicit et mandauit et omnia facta fuerunt et per omnia nomina eius et per nomen et in nomine y. et vv et X quod est, per quod adam prothoplaustus audiuit et locutus est, et per nomen et in nomine Meth phennoyphaton, quod adam nominauit in introitu inferni et liberatus est a morte eternal, et per nomen et in nomine Agla Ely quod noe nominauit et liberatus est a diluuio cum vniuersis famulis quod ducebat.*" Rawlinson D. 252, fol. 87v. A third version, in Firenze, Biblioteca Medicea Laurenziana, Plut. 89, sup. 38, fol. 116r, has only the vaguest similarities to these two texts. The title also appears among the books of John Erghome, as noted above.

63. The following segments, which are fairly typical, describe the uses for Psalm 21. "Si incideris inter inimicos tuos et timueris maliciam eorum, dic septies hunc psalmum et salu-aberis." Rawlinson D. 252, fol. 126r. "Si incideris in manus inimicorum, seu iniquorum hominum et timueris malitiam eorum, dic hunc psalmum septies, et saluaberis ab eis et scribe eum in lamina uitrea, et karacteres istas et suffumiga cum mastice et dillue eas cum aqua munda et infunde in porta iminici tui et fugient a te. [characters]." Firenze, Biblioteca Medicea Laurenziana, Plut. 89, sup. 38, fol. 318r.

64. "Exorcizo vos creaturas planetarum dedicatas eorum spiritibus et in earum horis fabricatas et earum potencia factas per Uryel Salatiel Acoel." Rawlinson D. 252, fol. 80v. "Exorciso vos creaturas planetarum spiritibus dedicatas horisque eorum fortitudinis fab-ricatas per uriel salatiel acoel." København, Kongelike Bibliotek, Gl. Kgl. S. 1658, fol. 245.

65. Kieckhefer, *Forbidden Rites*, 256–86; Rawlinson D. 252, fols. 81r–87r. The text starts on fol. 81r, but the text parallel to the Munich handbook does not pick up until fol. 85r, where it follows the version on fols. 135r–139r (Kieckhefer's second column) fairly consistently for a few pages and then ends abruptly at fol. 87v, after the prayer for consecrating the book.

66. Sloane 3854, fols. 68–76. The text corresponds in a rough fashion alternately to both texts in München, Bayerische Staatsbibliothek, Clm 849. About halfway through, at fol. 72, the text breaks off entirely from the other two examples and gives specific instructions on the consecration of a circle.

67. "Quicumque vult saluus esse, ante omnia opus est in isto opere ut teneat catholicam fidem. Quam nisi quisque integram inuiolatamque seruauerit, absque dubio in eternum peribit." Fol. 81r.

68. Kieckhefer, *Forbidden Rites*, 8–10.

69. Fols. 1–23, 92–94, 109–10, 139v–142, and 159–62, for example, are taken up with a number of experiments of this kind.

70. John of Salisbury, *Frivolities of Courtiers*, 146–47; Kieckhefer, *Magic in the Middle Ages*, 151; *HMES*, 2:168.

71. Cellini, *Vita*, 1.64–65. For an English translation, see *Autobiography of Benvenuto Cellini*, 118–22.

72. For treasure hunting, see fol. 156. For the discovery of thieves or finding stolen goods, see fols. 103–107r, 109–118v, 121v–124v, and 126–130. Rings for love occur at fols. 45–46. An experiment to discover who has known a woman may be found at fols. 109–110.

73. Kittredge, *Witchcraft in Old and New England*, 185–213.

74. For example, fols. 38v and 63r. At fol. 114r prayers for divine assistance in a conjuring ritual are interspersed with the psalms. The psalm lines appear in rubric (represented here by underlining), followed by the prayer written out in full. "<u>Domine exaudi oracionem etc.</u> O Adonay sanctissime, el potens . . . . <u>Ostende nobis domine misericordiam tuam et salutare tuum etc.</u> Creator Adonay qui verus est dator scienciarum." See Psalms 101 and 84.

75. Duffy, *Stripping of the Altars*, 124.

76. "Quando sol est in signe calido et sicco, bonum est coniurare spiritus infernales. In signo calido et humido, spiritus aereos. In signo frigido et humido, spiritus aquaticos. In signo frigido et sicco, spiritus terreos." Fols. 29r–30v.

77. "Vide ergo semper quod aura sit serena antequam incipias facere circulum. Si autem, in faciendo circulum, surrexerunt nubes, noli amplius facere. Si autem, post factum circulum et peractum, surrexerunt nubes, tunc operare, quia signum est quod bene expedies." Fol. 31r.

78. The same angel names appear next to each day of the week on fol. 33v, but the order shifts in a circular fashion with each day. The fourth angel of the current day becomes the first angel of the subsequent day. In a circular fashion the first three are moved to the end of the subsequent day. Hence the first three days of the week (from Sunday) run as follows:

Die dominica. Raphael. Anael. Michael. Gabriel. Captiel. Samael. Satquiel.
Die lune. Gabriel. Captiel. Satquiel. Samael. Raphael. Anael. Michael.
Die Martis. Samael. Raphael. Anael. Michael. Gabriel. Captiel. Satquiel.

79. The materials correspond marvelously with the characteristics of the planets that are associated with the days. For example, aloe is used for Monday, pepper for Tuesday (Mars), and red sandalwood and saffron for Sunday. Fol. 34v.

80. "Et vos Angeli gloriosi prenominati mee questiones quam volo querere scitis, auxiliatores et mihi omnibus negociis meis adiutores." Fol. 33v.

81. "Anulus mercurij debet fieri de cupro, sicut est mars [*sic*], ad habendum omnem scienciam et victoriam in omni placito cuiuscunque domini, et quod non condempnaberis ab aliquo iudice. Quando vis operare, sis ieiu[n]us die [sigil for mercury] usque ad noctem. Eadem nocte, cum sanguine vulpis vel mureligi, fac istum caracterem [figure] et nomen angeli, quod est yparon, in pelli hirti, et quando venis coram iudice vel aliquo alio homine, scribe hunc karacterem in pectore tuo vel in fronte cum nomine Angeli, et tene cedulam in manu tua, et ipse non habebit potestatem condempnandi te, et facies anulum in die [sigil for mercury] et eius hora." Fol. 80r–v.

82. "Exorcizo vos creaturas planetarum dedicatas eorum spiritibus et in earum horis fabricatas et earum potencia factas, per Uryel Salatiel Acoel et per potenciam, que vobis condonata est in creacione vestra in principio, quibus dicens 'Relinquo munera que sunt preciosa, ita quod vos ad illa adiuuetis que desiderare volo et petere, et quod tale adiuuamentum prebeatis ad quales particulos, estis fabricate vel scripte estis per virtutem per quam vos constrinxi estis, prestante deo in secula seculorum amen.'" Fol. 80v. (I exorcise you, creatures of the planets, consecrated to their spirits and constructed in their hours and made by their power, through Uryel, Salatiel, Acoel, and through the power which was bestowed upon you in your creation in the beginning, saying to them [i.e., Uryel, etc.]: "I relinquish gifts which are precious so that you may furnish benefit to those things which I wish to desire and seek, and so that you may furnish such benefit to those particulars, you [i.e., the rings] were constructed or you were inscribed through the power by which I have constrained you: you exist with God disposing forever and ever, amen.") The opening line echoes the first line in the standard exorcism for salt in the preparation of holy water. "Exorciso te creatura salis per deum. . . ." *Manuale ad usum percelebris*, 1.

83. See Sutton and Visser-Fuchs, "Cult of Angels"; Keck, *Angels and Angelology*; Veenstra, "Holy Almandal."

84. München, Bayerische Staatsbibliothek, Clm 849, fols. 3r–5v; Kieckhefer, *Forbidden Rites*, 193–96.

85. "De aliquo loco thesaurum Afferat scilicet Aurum Argentum aut gemmas." Fol. 162v.

86. "Pro bonis angelis dic istud. Raphael, Gabriel, Michael, Cherubyn, Ceraphyn, Arriel, Pantaseron, Mucraton, Sandalon, et vos angeli gloriosi mee questiones quam volo etc." Fol. 14v.

87. "Et vos Angeli gloriosi prenominati mee questiones quam volo querere scitis auxiliatores et mihi omnibus negociis meis adiutores." Fol. 34r.

88. "Deinde pone te ad lectum et ad te veniat senex barbatus qui tibi de omnibus respondebit." Fol. 99v.

89. See, for example, London, British Library, Harley 181, fols. 75r–81v. I discuss this portion of this sixteenth-century manuscript in chapter 6. For more on dreams in ritual magic texts, see Klaassen, "Magical Dream Provocation."

90. This is also the case in the Harley manuscript just cited.

91. "Memoria irreprehensibilis, sapiencia incomprehensibilis, efficacia incontradicibilis impleat conscientiam meam. Sapiencia tua, dulcedo et gratie tue mentem meam inn[e]at [muniat in *Ars notoria*]. Omnes sancti angeli tui, cum omnibus virtutibus celi, faciem meam et cor meum sine fine intueri et illuminare desiderent. Sapiencia qua omnia fecisti, intelligencia qua omnia reformasti, beatitudinis perseverancia qua angelos constituisti, dilectio et largitatis caritas, qua adam omnem scienciam docuisti, informet, repleat, instruat, corrigat, instauret, et reficiat me, ut fiam prudens in mandatis intelligendis et suscipiendis angelorum tuorum et spirituum visione et notici[a], in salutem corporis et anime mee et omnium credencium in nomine tuo, quod est benedictum in secula Amen.

"Te igitur omnium pater simplex exoro, et in tua pietate tota confido. Exaudi ergo petitionem meam, [qui] ad te deuote clamantes benigniter exaudis. Da, queso, domine deus meus mihi graciam sapienciam virtutem et potenciam, quatinus angelus vel angeli, scilicet iste vel isti .N., quociens ipsum vel ipsos inuocauero, mihi benigniter appareat, [velut] et peticionem meam veracem sufficiant perimplere, per gloriosam magestatem tuam et nomen sanctum benedictum in eternum, qui viui[s] et regna[s], deus per omnia secula seculorum Amen." Fol. 78r–v.

92. "Memoria irreprehensibilis, sapientia incontradicibilis, efficacia impermutabilis Deus eterni consilii angelis, amplectatur cor meum dextera tua, impleat conscientiam meam memoria tua et odor unguentorum tuorum et dulcedo gratie tue, muniat mentem meam splendor Spiritus Sancti, caritas qua angeli faciem tuam cum omnibus celi uirtutibus intueri sine fine desiderant, sapientia qua omnia fecisti, intelligentia qua omnia reformasti, beatitudinis perseuerentia qua angelos restituisti, dilectio qua hominem lapsum ad celestia erexisti,

doctrina qua Adam omnem scientiam docere dignatus es, informa, reple, muni, corrige et refice me, ut fiam nouus in mandatis tuis intelligendis et in suscipienda scientia in salutem corporis et anime mee et omnium fidelium credentium in nomine tuo, quod est benedictum in secula seculorum, amen." *Ars notoria*, Version A, 36. I quote from Véronèse's edition, *L'Ars notoria au Moyen Âge*, 46-47. I have underlined the parallel passages.

93. See, for example, fols. 22v, 12v, and 14r. On demands that demons not mock the operator, see fol. 37.

94. "When he appears, give him or them kind entertainment & then ask what is just & lawfull & that which is proper & suitable to his office & you shall obtain it." Veenstra, "Holy Almandal," 226. Veenstra's edition is based on an abbreviated version of the text, Sloane 2731, that has been absorbed into the *Lemegeton*. The passage is essentially the same in two other contemporary versions, Sloane 3648 and 3825.

Part III Introduction

1. Weill-Parot discusses this in different terms. He suggests an increasing boldness in pushing the boundaries of Scholastic thought in the texts in the fifteenth century, continuing into the sixteenth. See "Astral Magic and Intellectual Changes."

2. See Klaassen, "Medieval Ritual Magic in the Renaissance."

3. The spurious *Fourth Book of Occult Philosophy* passed through three Latin editions (Marburg, 1559, and Paris, 1565 and 1567). It was also published in English translation in London in 1655 and 1665.

4. A Latin edition of the *Fourth Book of Occult Philosophy* appeared in the 1600 and 1630 editions of Agrippa's *Opera*, published in Lyon. There were three printed editions of the *De occulta philosophia* in the sixteenth century. Agrippa personally oversaw the publication of an edition at Cologne in 1533 by Johannes Soter. Its publication had been delayed by the intervention of the Dominican inquisitor Conrad Köllin of Ulm. A partial edition may have been printed in Antwerp in 1531 and in Paris by Christianus Wechelus. Subsequent editions include three early seventeenth-century editions of his *Opera* published in Lyon, one or two in Strasbourg, and an English edition in London in 1651. See Ferguson, *Bibliographical Notes*. An *Ars notoria* is included in at least one edition of Agrippa's *Opera*. Another was published in English translation in London in 1657. A wide variety of other texts concerning ritual magic were also published in the various Beringi Fratres editions of Agrippa's *Opera*. For example, the copy used for the Georg Olms reprint (1970) includes such texts as "De speciebus magiae ceremonialis," "De illorum daemonum qui sub lunari collimitio versantur," and "Libri arbatel magiae." The *British Library Short Title Catalogue* lists the following thirteen editions of the *De triplica vita*, the third part of which is the *De vita coelitus comparanda*: Florence, 1489, 1490, and 1501; Argen., 1511; Venice (?), 1525 (?); Basel, 1532; Paris, 1547; Lyon, 1560 and 1584; Paris (?), 1616; Strasbourg, 1521; and Venice, 1498 and 1520 (?). For my discussion of this work and its commonalities with the ritual magic tradition, see chapter 7.

5. For example, the 1489 edition of the *De triplica vita* appears in the Syon Monastery library in the early sixteenth century. Bateson, *Catalogue of the Library of Syon Monastery*, B 27. A database of book lists in Renaissance England published by the Folger Shakespeare Library (general editor R. J. Fehrenbach) lists nine occurences of the *De occulta philosophia* (object names 93.70, 94.16, 112.78, 126.21, 127.90, 133.110, 133.140, 146.114, and 146.220) and three of the *De triplica vita*, of which the *De vita coelitus comparanda* is a part (object names 110.230, 112.166, and 133.233). See http://wmpeople.wm.edu/site/page/rjfehr/home (accessed 1 June 2012).

6. See Davies, *Cunning-Folk*, 1-10. This text was used as kind of primer of the "old religion" and *grimoire* within years of its first publication. See Klaassen and Phillips, "Return of Stolen Goods."

Chapter 6

1. The angel names correspond loosely to those in Vaticano (Città del), Biblioteca Apostolica Vaticana, Reg. lat. 1300, fol. 49v; and London, British Library, Sloane 3853, fols. 46r–49v.

2. The practice is mentioned in a list of operations suitable for particular hours of the day or night in London, Society of Antiquaries, 39, fols. 15–17. It also appears in Oxford, Bodleian Library, Rawlinson D. 252, fol. 31v, in a similar list. It appears in Trithemius's bibliography of magic works. See Zambelli, *White Magic, Black Magic*, 103. See also below on Gilbert.

3. London, British Library, Royal 17.A.XLII, fols. 12r–13r, 38v–39v, and 53v–54r correspond, respectively, to passages on fols. 128r–v, 129r–130r, and 130r–v. Another prayer, on fol. 130v, may have been drawn from the *Sworn Book*, as it corresponds to Royal 17.A.XLII, fol. 52v. It also has the same incipit as a prayer for "pleasantness in speaking" found in Sloane 3846, fol. 25r. Fols. 28r–44v of Royal 17.A.XLII also correspond to passages on fols. 160r–177r. I am indebted to the online transcriptions of Joseph Peterson (http://www.esotericarchives.com), in which some of the relationships between these manuscripts are identified.

4. Véronèse, "L'*Ars notoria* au Moyen Âge et à l'époque moderne," 1:1–17. I have included manuscripts of the *Ars Paulina*. I have also included the three manuscripts copied by Simon Forman (1600–1601) among the sixteenth-century manuscripts, because I discuss them here and because they might arguably represent the interests of a sixteenth-century practitioner. Had the dates been strictly applied, the apparent decline would be more dramatic.

5. London, British Library, Harley 181, fol. 2r. The text also appears in Wien, Österreichische Nationalbibliothek, 11321, fols. 131r–146v.

6. Fols. 1–17. See Véronèse, "L'*Ars notoria* au Moyen Âge et à l'époque moderne," 1:276–77.

7. Fols. 75r–81r. See also Sloane 3846, fols. 182rff. For more on this text, see Véronèse, "La notion d'"auteur-magicien.'"

8. "Et si bene in operatione processeris, ipsamque in consuetudinem duxeris, apparebit tibi CRUCIFIXUS interdum etiam non rogatus, loqueturque tecum ore ad os, sicut amicus ad amicum, docens in pluribus veritatem a qua poteris scire omnis questionis dubie veritatem, vel pro te vel pro alio. Nam per hanc artem cognoscuntur preterita, presentia, et futura, consilia et secreta regum, rita spirituum, peccata hominum, status mortuorum. Etiam scire poterimus occultas cogitaciones, et earum actiones, eventum futurorum, thesaurum absconditum, furem, latronem, valetudinem amici et inimici. Complementum artium, Alkimiam, medicinam, theologiam, reliquasque scientias vel artes, mineras, vires, virtutes, lapidium vim, et colligationes verborum, officia et nomina spirituum, atque karacteres bonorum et malorum, proprietatesque creaturarum, ceteraque in mundo scibilia per istud experimentum leniter consequeris." Harley 181, fol. 8ov.

9. London, British Library, Additional 36674, fols. 60r–61r. Emendations and additions indicated in square brackets.

10. For Gilbert's performance of this ritual, see ibid., fols. 51r–53v. The four princes are mentioned in the *Speculum astronomiae*, 11.23 and 79. For other medieval examples of conjurations of the four kings, see Rawlinson D. 252, fols. 15r–24r, 103r–107r; and Society of Antiquaries 39, fol. 17v. The names Gilbert uses correspond to those listed by Agrippa as princes of the four points of the compass; see *De occulta philosophia*, 2.7. Rituals for speaking with the dead through the conjuration of Azazel occur in a variety of sources. See Oxford, Bodleian Library, Ballard 66, fols. 33–39 (s. xvii); Sloane 3884, fols. 47–56 (s. xvi); and Rawlinson D. 252, fols. 66v–68r.

11. On these changes, see Klaassen, "Ritual Invocation and Early Modern Science."

12. "O god of Aungelles, god of Archaungells; god of Patriarches, god of Prophetts, god of vs sinners; O lord be my help, that this my worke may proceed in good tyme, to thy glorie, O god; and to learninge, and noe Art else, glorifie the in all workes. Amen. Let not euyll spyritt enter my mynde o god, nor nothinge else but all to thy glorie o god; for learning is all my desier, lord thou knowest; euen as yt was to thy seruaunt Solomon; O lord sende me somme of this good hiddenn worke, that hath not been reuealed to noe mann. Then for that cause

I desier the O god to sende yt mee, that in these our laste daies yt may be knowenn. Amen. Amen, lord, Amen with your Pater noster." Additional 36674, fol. 47r.

13. For the new form of show stone, see ibid., fol. 56r. For the prayer dictated by Solomon, see fol. 47r.

14. Deborah Harkness's *John Dee's Conversations with Angels*, for example, makes great strides in confronting the intellectual challenge of the angel conversations.

15. See ibid., 9–59.

16. Of the various works on Dee, the most sensitive treatment of his magical operations and his eschatological project is unquestionably Harkness's. For a partial early edition of the conversations, see Dee, *True and Faithful Relation*.

17. Veenstra, "Honorius and the Sigil of God," 180–81.

18. Harkness, *John Dee's Conversations with Angels*, 11.

19. Ibid., 96.

20. The classic example, al-Kindī's *De radiis stellarum*, 6 (D'Alverny and Hudry's edition, 233–50), also associates magical qualities with words from primordial languages, which maintain an ontological connection with divine forms due to their proximity to creation.

21. See, for example, Sloane 3850, fols. 143–166, which frequently renders *fiat* as *fiate* and *aliter* as *alitere*. The scribe of Ashmole 1378 slavishly copied a Latin text, including the empty space for an initial left in the original text. He was evidently not aware of this common medieval practice and seems to have considered the empty square area somehow important. This, combined with his poor knowledge of Latin, resulted in the following first line: "Equantur orations cum predidentia experimenta cenaris probare" (68)!

22. For a useful discussion of the use of the vernacular that goes beyond the association between literacy and heresy, see Hudson, *Premature Reformation*, 390–445.

23. For a valuable discussion of the nature of the fairy in literature, see Woodcock, *Fairy in "The Faerie Queene,"* and Briggs, *Anatomy of Puck*.

24. For a discussion of the connection between necromancy and Shakespeare's *Tempest*, see Mowat, "Prospero's Book." For a curious example of fairy conjuring in Oxford, Bodleian Library, e Mus. 173, fol. 37r–v, see Klaassen and Bens, "Six Rituals to Attain Invisibility." For other examples of ritual magic works involving fairies, see Sloane 1727; Ashmole 1406; Washington, D.C., Folger Shakespeare Library, X. d. 234 and V. b. 26.

25. Conjurations for Oberion appear in Rawlinson D. 252, fols. 139r and 144r.

26. Kassell, "'All this land full fill'd of faerie.'"

27. It appeared appended to the seventeenth-century editions of Agrippa's *Opera* and John French's 1655 English translation of the *Fourth Book of Occult Philosophy*, but also independently in a German edition in Paris in 1567.

28. Scot, *Discouerie of Witchcraft* (1665), 376–430.

29. For a mid-seventeenth-century copy of the *Fourth Book*, see London, Wellcome Library, 10. Another late sixteenth- or early seventeenth-century example is Sloane 3851, which contains, in addition to the *Fourth Book*, also the work titled *Arbatel*.

30. On the Royal manuscript, see Mathiesen, "Thirteenth-Century Ritual," 145. For the passage on angels, see Sloane 3846, fol. 21r. He quotes from *De occulta philosophia*, 3.21.

31. Sloane 3849, fol. 38v, and Oxford, Bodleian Library, e. Mus 238, fols. 4r, 3v, and 2r.

32. See, for example, Sloane 3884. Fols. 40v–44 refer to Cornelius Agrippa and Peter Abano, whose spurious works occur together in editions of the *Fourth Book of Occult Philosophy*. Fols. 75–91 of Sloane 3851 contain the entire text of this work, and Additional 36674, fol. 23, contains extracts.

33. See Estes, "Reginald Scot and His 'Discoverie of Witchcraft.'"

34. The *Clavicula Salomonis* appears at fols. 1–66r, the *Liber quatuor annulis* at fols. 66v–81v, the *De quindecim stellis* at fols. 84r–97v, and the *Liber imaginum* at fols. 101r–112r.

35. See, for example, Sloane 3826, Sloane 3850, Sloane 3883, Wellcome 426, and Ashmole 1442.

36. Late sixteenth-century versions are Ashmole 244 and Sloane 3822. Pingree, *Picatrix*, xv–lxix. See also Pingree, "Diffusion of Arabic Magical Texts," 102.

37. For more detail, see Klaassen, "Medieval Ritual Magic in the Renaissance."

38. It is also worth keeping in mind that the figures presented here make the conservative assumption that manuscripts mentioned in medieval library catalogues were produced at roughly the time of the catalogue's production (i.e., the latest possible date). Many, no doubt, predated the catalogue by a century or two.

39. Weill-Parot, *Les "images astrologiques" au Moyen Âge*, 592. This suggestion is also problematic, because most astrological image magic texts are contained in larger codices whose contents are nonmagical. Thus, while the copying of such texts may be a significant moment for the study of image magic, their survival or destruction was probably unrelated to their magical content. Exceptions could include the destruction of an entire codex for the sake of a few folios or the cutting out of folios containing magic.

40. I have employed Leonardus's 1717 edition of the *Speculum lapidum*. It was published in Latin editions in 1502 (Venice), 1516 (Venice), and 1610 (Paris). Italian editions date from 1565 and 1617. An English edition was printed in 1750 in London; see *HMES*, 6:298–302.

41. Among those with this standard medieval pattern are Cambridge, University Library, Kk.i.1; Conte de Sarzana, Private Library, unnumbered (a large collection of image magic works); Oxford, Bodleian Library, Canon. lat. 500 (*Picatrix* extract); and Oxford, Bodleian Library, Ashmole 346 (the collection of an early sixteenth-century British doctor).

42. See, for example, Cambridge, University Library, Additional 3544; Sloane 3846; Sloane 3847; Oxford, Bodleian Library, e Mus. 173; and Rawlinson D. 253. The substantial presence of the *Liber Razielis* in Lübeck, Bibliothek der Hansestadt, Math. 4° 9 suggests that this is a similar case. In the case of Gent, Centrale Bibliotheek der Rijksuniversiteit, 1021, which I have not seen, it appears to be a copy of one of the printed editions of Pseudo-Agrippa and so would also follow a similar pattern. It is interesting to note that some of the earliest known large collections of magical works, Pingree's proposed thirteenth-century exemplar for Firenze, Biblioteca nazionale centrale di Firenze, II.iii.214, and the large volumes owned by John Erghome in the library of the York Austin Friars follow this same pattern. See Klaassen, "English Manuscripts of Magic," 9–11.

43. See, for example, Forman's and Ashmole's notes on magic in Sloane 3822. The volume includes notes on the creation of sigils (fols. 7r–24v) and letters from Thomas Hyde offering information on talismans extracted from manuscripts at Oxford (fols. 91r–93v), but it is also peppered with ritual magic operations (fols. 27r, 84r–v, and 172r) and ritual additions to the making of sigils (fols. 34r–35v). This manuscript gives the impression that Ashmole was mining astrological image magic texts for magic that worked, and that practical application and experiment, more than the preservation of prior intellectual traditions, drove his activities. For a discussion of Forman's exercises, see Kassell, "Economy of Magic in Early Modern England."

44. On the growing popular appetite for the secrets of the learned, see Eamon, *Science and the Secrets of Nature*.

45. Tester, *History of Western Astrology*, 218–19.

46. Copenhaver, "Tale of Two Fishes."

47. *HMES*, 5:1–4.

48. In Zambelli's recent edition of the work, only four of the fifty-two manuscripts of the *Speculum astronomiae* listed derive from the sixteenth century. See *Speculum astronomiae and Its Enigma*, 204–5.

Chapter 7

1. Nauert, *Agrippa and the Crisis of Renaissance Thought*, 231–36.

2. For an extensive scholarly discussion of this issue, see Kieckhefer, "Specific Rationality of Medieval Magic." Kieckhefer's main point is that medieval thinkers conceived of magic as

rational, which is to say that they thought it could work and that its workings were governed by principles (of theology or physics) that could be articulated coherently. On demons and the intellectual world of the sixteenth century, see Clark, *Thinking with Demons*. Also useful are Brian Copenhaver's various articles on the subject, in particular "Scholastic Philosophy and Renaissance Magic." The naturalistic explanation of demons extends back at least as far as Augustine, who discusses their abilities in relation to their physical makeup. The problem with employing them in divination was their mendaciousness and the lack of trust in God that such divination would involve. See Augustine, *De divinatione daemonum*. Aquinas's treatment similarly deals with the physical abilities and nature of demons (*Quodlibet* 4.16). Examples could be multiplied endlessly.

3. Wirszubski, *Pico della Mirandola's Encounter with Jewish Mysticism*, 133–60. See also Pico, *Syncretism in the West*, 128–32. The usual assumption has been that Ficino, being the teacher and elder, had a formative influence on Pico's thinking about magic. Stephen Farmer, the editor of the latter work, has suggested that it may well have been the reverse (118–20).

4. Agrippa took his discussion on finding one's genius substantially from Ficino. This in turn appears in British manuscripts (see below).

5. See Copenhaver, "Renaissance Magic and Neoplatonic Philosophy"; "Scholastic Philosophy and Renaissance Magic"; and "Iamblichus, Synesius, and the Chaldean Oracles." This subject has more recently been revisited by Nicolas Weill-Parot and Christopher Celenza. See Weill-Parot, *Les "images astrologiques" au Moyen Âge*, 639–755; Celenza, "Late Antiquity and Florentine Platonism."

6. See Kaske and Clark, "Introduction," in Ficino's *De vita coelitus comparanda*, 61.

7. Yates, *Giordano Bruno and the Hermetic Tradition*, 68–76.

8. Ficino's version of the magical room contains astrological images. *De vita coelitus comparanda*, xix. For an example from a ritual magic collection, see the *Thesaurus spirituum* in Sloane 3853, fol. 6.

9. Kaske and Clark, "Introduction," 62.

10. Ibid., 61.

11. *HMES*, 4:562.

12. Allen, *Platonism of Marsilio Ficino*, 115; Voss, "Orpheus redivivus," 236.

13. Kaske and Clark, "Introduction," 55–70.

14. "Quoniam vero coelum est harmonica ratione compositum moueturque harmonice, et harmonicis motibus atque sonis efficit omnia, merito per harmoniam solam non solum homines, sed inferiora haec omnia pro viribus ad capienda coelestia praeparantur. Harmoniam vero capacem superiorum per septem rerum gradus in superioribus distribuimus: per imagines videlicet (ut putat) harmonice constitutas, per medicinas sua quadam consonantia temperatas, per vapores odoresque simili concinnitate confectos, per cantus musicos atque sonos, ad quorum ordinem vimque referri gestus corporis saltusque et tripudia volumus; per imaginationis conceptus motusque concinnos, per congruas rationis discursiones, per tranquillas mentis contemplationes." *De vita coelitus comparanda*, 22 (362–63). Quotations are from Kaske and Clark's edition, with page numbers of their translation in parentheses.

15. As Weill-Parot has demonstrated, Ficino's new approach to astrological image magic solved many of the philosophical difficulties presented by texts of heavily ritualistic astrological image magic. For a lengthy discussion of this issue, see Weill-Parot, *Les "images astrologiques" au Moyen Âge*, 639–755.

16. Imagination was a physical power, and the psychosomatic powers of this feature of human psychology had long been the subject of Scholastic discourse. On the physical nature of the imagination in medieval and Renaissance psychology, see Harvey, *Inward Wits*.

17. Copenhaver's analysis of the *De vita* in "Iamblichus, Synesius, and the Chaldean Oracles" suggests that Ficino struggled with his sources in the desire to draw something legitimate from the theurgic practices of later Neoplatonism. Because he was greatly enamored of magical practices that might have efficacy beyond purely physical and medical effects, but duly wary of the implications for Christian orthodoxy, his position remained ambiguous. On

theurgy, see Shaw, *Theurgy and the Soul*. Chris Celenza has emphasized the post-Plotinian nature of Ficino's ideas in "Late Antiquity and Florentine Platonism."

18. *De vita coelitus comparanda*, 15 (316–17).

19. On star souls, see Ficino, *Commentary on Plato's Symposium on Love*, 6.4. See also Walker, *Spiritual and Demonic Magic*, 45, quoted in Kaske and Clark, "Introduction," 59. On demons and mirrors, see Kodera, "Narcissus, Divine Gazes," 302.

20. Kaske and Clark, "Introduction," 23–29.

21. Walker, *Spiritual and Demonic Magic*, 20.

22. Allen, "Summoning Plotinus."

23. Allen, *Star-Crossed Renaissance*, 12–18.

24. In "Inward Zodiac," Melissa Meriam Bullard discusses the arguments put forward by Charles Trinkhaus in an unpublished paper (688–89). For a summary of the debates over Ficino's position on astrology, see Allen, *Platonism of Marsilio Ficino*, 183n27.

25. "Ut prospere vivas agasque, imprimis cognosce ingenium, sidus, genium tuum et locum eisdem convenientem. Hic habita. Professionem sequere naturalem." *De vita coelitus comparanda*, 23 (370–71).

26. "Quicunque sanae mentis suique compos nascitur, est a coelo ad honestum aliquod opus et vitae genus naturaliter institutus. Quisquis igitur coelum optat habere propitium, hoc opus, hoc genus imprimis aggrediatur, hoc sedulo prosequatur, coelum enim suis favet inceptis. Ad hoc impsum vero prae caeteris es natura factus, quod primum a teneris annis agis, loqueris, fingis, optas, somnias, imitaris; quod tentas frequentius, quod facilius peragis, quo summopere proficis, quo prae ceteris delectaris, quod relinquis invitus. Hoc est sane ad quod te coelum rectorque coeli genuit . . . . Quicunque igitur per argumenta quae modo diximus suum ingenium perscrutatus ita naturale suum opus inveniet, invenerit simul suum sidus et daemonem. Quorum exordia sequens aget prospere, vivetque feliciter, alioquin et fortunam experietur adversam et coelum sentiet inimicum." Ibid., 23 (370–71).

27. "Sive igitur ab illa quam in superioribus narrabam experientia dilligentiaque, sive ab hac arte quam modo recensui, primum investigemus naturae daemonisque instinctum, infortunatum esse censebimus, qui officium nullum profitetur honestum. Nam et ducem professionis re vera non habet, qui opus honestum non aggreditur; et ducem naturalem vix ullum habet, quoniam stellarum daemonumque sive angelorum ducum divinitus ad custodiam dispositorum officium est agere semper et excellenter atque latissime. Infortunatum insuper eum, ut supra diximus, qui professione naturae contraria diversum a genio subit daemonem." Ibid., 23 (374–75).

28. Ibid., 24 (378–81), 15 (316–17).

29. Wirszubski, *Pico Della Mirandola's Encounter with Jewish Mysticism*, 133–60.

30. Kaske and Clark, "Introduction," 18–23.

31. Allen, "Summoning Plotinus," 83–85.

32. Ficino, *Letters of Marsilio Ficino*, 1:44.

33. *HMES*, 6:146–50.

34. Bacon was probably included because of his mythic connection with necromancy and his pseudonymous authorship of the *Thesaurus spirituum*. He appears very rarely in medieval collections of image magic, where some of his works could, at least in theory, be mentioned.

35. Compagni, "Introduction," in Agrippa, *De occulta philosophia libri tres*, 17.

36. A good summary of the first two books may be found in Yates, *Giordano Bruno and the Hermetic Tradition*, 131–37.

37. At first glance, this work appears to be radically opposed to the *De occulta philosophia* in almost every way. On the one hand, we have an encyclopedic, esoteric, and perhaps credulous occult handbook in which, although he does not tell us everything, Agrippa gives the impression of having worked everything out. In the *De vanitate*, on the other hand, he makes a rhetorical attack—sometimes elegant and witty, sometimes vituperative and clumsy—on all human claims to truth, including those of the magical traditions. He proposes instead that our access to truth may come only through inspired interpretation of scripture and

prophetic revelation. That Agrippa published a revised and expanded version of the *De occulta philosophia* shortly after the *De vanitate* appeared has given the impression of intellectual instability at best, and, at worst, the sense that he was simply attempting to cover his tracks. Whatever truth there may be in these impressions, there can be little question that Agrippa did intend that his enlightened students would read the two works in tandem, with the *De vanitate* as a clarification of his position in the *De occulta philosophia*. Rather than rehearse what is now an extensive literature, I take this position for granted. For more information, see Compagni's introduction to *De occulta philosophia libri tres*, 1–53; Zambelli, "Cornelius Agrippa"; Zambelli, "A propositio del *De vanitate scienciarum*"; and Nauert, *Agrippa and the Crisis of Renaissance Thought*, 157–221. In particular, Nauert points to Agrippa's early concerns about the use of rationality as an approach to God (200). See also Keefer, "Agrippa's Dilemma." For a discussion of the debate prior to 1965, see pp. 157–59 of Nauert's book.

38. Lehrich's recent book, *The Language of Demons and Angels*, has discussed very convincingly what I call the hermeneutic spiral produced by Agrippa's approach.

39. "Tempus est nunc ad altiora nos convertere et ad eam magiae portionem, quae nos docet callere et scire leges religionum et quomodo veritatem religione divina debeamus adipisci et quomodo animum et mentem, qua sola possumus veritatem coprehendere, rite debeamus excolere . . . . Quicunque vero religione relicta naturalibus tantum confidunt, solent a malis daemonibus saepissime falli; ex intellectu autem religionis contemptus medelaque nascitur vitiorum et contra malos daemones tutamentum: denique nil Deo gratius et acceptius quam homo perfecte pius ac vere religiosus, qui tam homines caeteros praecellit, quam ipse a diis immortalibus distat. Debemus nos igitur prius quidem purgatos offerre et commendare divinae pietati et religioni et tunc divinum illud ambrosianum nectar ... soptis sensibus, tranquilla mente expectare, laudantes, et adorantes supercoelestem illum Bacchum, summum deorum et sacerdotum, antistitem, regenerationis autorem, quem bis natum veteres cecinere poëtae, a quo tam divinissimi rivi in corda nostra emanant." *De occulta philosophia*, 3.1. I quote the Latin text from Compagni's edition of Agrippa's *De occulta philosophia libri tres*, 402–3. Subsequent parenthetical page references are to this edition. I have also found John French's translation (London, 1651) useful, and his elegant translation significantly informed mine.

40. "Sciendum ergo quod, sicut per primi agentis influxum saepe producitur aliquid sine cooperatione mediarum causarum, sic etiam per solum opus religionis fit aliquod sine applicatione naturalium coelestiumque virtutum; sed nemo potest operari per puram et solam religionem, nisi qui totus factus est intellectualis. Quicunque autem sine admixtione aliarum virtutum per solam religionem operatur, si diu perseveraverit in opere, absorbetur a numine nec diu poterit vivere." Ibid., 3.6 (414–15).

41. Ibid., 3.6–35 (414–506), 3.36–44 (506–42), 3.45–54 (542–66).

42. Yates, *Giordano Bruno and the Hermetic Tradition*, 138–40. This contrasts sharply with her comprehensive treatment of the second book. Her summary gives the impression of a heavily "Hermetic" document.

43. Lehrich, *Language of Demons and Angels*, 202–3.

44. "Mens itaque nostra pura atque divina, religioso amore flagrans, spe decora, fide directa, posita in culmine et fastigio humani animi, veritatem attrahit omnesque rerum tam mortalium quam immortalium status, rationes, causas et scientias in ipsa veritate divina, tanquam in quodam aeternitatis speculo, intuetur, subito comprehendens. Hinc provenit quod nos in natura constituti ea quae supra naturam sunt cognoscimus ac inferiora quaeque intelligimus atque non modo ea quae sunt et quae fuerunt, verumetiam eorum quae mox fient et quae longe post futura sunt assidue recipimus oracula. Praeterea non solum in scientiis et artibus et oraculis mens eiusmodi virtutem sibi divinam vendicat, verumetiam in rebus quibusque per imperium transmutandis miraculosam suscipit potentiam. Hinc provenit nos in natura constitutos aliquando supra naturam dominari operationesque tam mirificas, tam subitas, tam arduas efficere, quibus obediant manes, turbentur sidera, cogantur numina, serviant elementa; sic homines Deo devoti ac theologicis istis virtutibus elevati imperant

elementis, pellunt nebulas, citant ventos, cogunt nubes in pluvias, curant morbos, suscitant mortuos." *De occulta philosophia* 3.6 (414).

45. Technically, Agrippan magic proposes (in at least one of its forms) that the individual is purged and that the image of God is analogous in function to a magical talisman. Ibid., 3.49 (553).

46. In his chapter on magic in *Pico della Mirandola's Encounter with Jewish Mysticism*, Wirszubski suggests that the division Pico draws between practical and speculative Kabbalah is by no means clear (152).

47. "Oportet autem pedetentim et velut per gradus quosdam ad hanc animi puritatem pervenire; neque enim unusquisque de novo iis mysteriis initiatus statim lucida omnia comprehendit, sed assuefaciendus paulatim est animus, quousque in nobis emineat intellectus ac divinae lucis applicans illis permisceatur. Anima itaque humana quando rite fuerit purgata et expiata, tum ab omni varietate soluta, libero motu foras emicat, sursum ascendit, divina capit, etiam seipsam erudit, quando forte aliunde erudiri videtur; neque enim commemoratione neque demonstratione tunc indiget ob naturalem sui solertiam, tum per mentem suam, quae animae caput et auriga est, suapte natura angelos imitata, non successione, non tempore, sed subitaneo momento quod cupit assequitur. David enim literas non didicit et ex pastore effectus est vates et divinarum rerum scientissimus; Solomon in unius nocts somnio omnium superum et inferum sapientia repletus fuit; sic Esaias, Ezechiel, Daniel, caeterique prophetae et apostoli eruditi sunt. Potest enim anima, quae communis Pythagoreorum et Platonicorum sententia est, per viam purgatoriam absque alio studio adventitiam, super iam desuper habita intelligibilia perfectam omnium scibilium scientiam acquirere; potest etiam per extrinsecam expiationem ad hoc devenire ut omnia per substantialem suam formam indivisibiliter intelligat. Purgatur autem animus et expiatur per munditiam, per abstinentiam, per poenitentiam, per eleemoysna; tum etiam conferunt ad idem sacra quaedam instituta, ut hic inferius patebit. Curanda enim est anima per religionum studia, vulgo quidem occulta, ut sanitati retituta, veritate firmata et divinis praesidiis munita non timeat suorientes concussiones." *De occulta philosophia*, 3.53 (563–64).

48. Some of what follows has already been discussed in Zambelli, "Cornelius Agrippa."

49. "Verum de magicis scripsi ego juvenis adhuc libros tres ... quos de Occulta philosophia nuncupaui, in quibus quidquid tunc per curiosam adolescentiam erratum est, nunc cautior, hac palinodia recantatum volo: per multum enim temporis et rerum in his vanitatibus olim contrivi. Tandem hoc profeci, quod sciam, quibus [edition has: quem iis] rationibus oporteat alios ab hac pernicie dehortari. Quicunque enim non in veritate, nec in virtute Dei, sed in elusione daemonum, secundum operationem malorum spirituum, divinare et prophetare praesumunt, et per vanitates magicas, exorcismos, incantationes, amatoria, agogima, et caetera opera daemoniaca, et idololatriae fraudes exercentes, praestigia et phantasmata ostentantes mox cessantia, miracula sese operari jactant, omnes hi cum Iamne et Mambre, et Simone mago aeternis ignibus cruciandi destinabuntur." Agrippa, *De vanitate*, 48 (82). Page citations are to the edition of this work in Agrippa's *Opera* (Lyon, 1600). In Timothy 3:8, Iamnes and Mambres (or Jannes and Jambres) are the names given to Pharaoh's magicians (Exodus 7). *The Pennitence of Iamne et Mambre* is an apocryphal work. See Dobschütz, *Decretum Gelasianum*, 12, 84, 122, 306.

50. "Qui libri tamen acutius inspicienti, suorum praecetorum canonem, rituum consuetudinem, verborum et characterum genus, extructionis ordinem, insulsam phrasin, aperte sese produnt non nisi meras nugas ac imposturas continere, ac posterioribus temporibus ab omnis antiquae magiae ignaris perditissimis perditionum artificibus esse conflatos, ex prophanis quibusdam observationibus nostrae religionis caeremoniis permixtis insitisque ignotis multis nominibus et signaculis, ut perterreant rudes et simplices, et stupori sint insensatis, et his, qui nesciunt bonas literas. Neque tamen propterea patet has artes fabulas esse, nam nisi revera essent, atque per illas multa mira ac noxia fierent, non tam arcte de illis statuissent divinae ac humanae leges, eas exterminandas esse de terra. Cur autem Goetici illi solis malis utantur daemonibus, ea ratio est, qui boni angeli difficile comparent, quia Dei jussum

expectant, nec nisi mundis corde et vita sanctis hominibus congrediuntur: mali autem faciles se exhibent ad invocandum, falso faventes et divinitatem mentientes, semper praesto, vt astu suo decipiant, ut venerentur, ut adorentur." Agrippa, *De vanitate*, 45 (75).

51. Ibid., 46 (76–77).

52. "O quanta leguntur scripta de inexpugnabili magicae artis potentia, de prodigiosis astrologorum imaginibus, de monstrifica alchimistarum metamorphosi, deque lapide illo benedicto, quo, Midae instar, contacta aera mox omnia in aurum argentumve permutentur: quae omnia comperiuntur vana, ficta et falsa, quoties ad literam practicantur. Atque tamen traduntur ista scribunturque a magnis grauissimisque philosophis et sanctis viris, quorum traditiones quis audebit dicere falsis? Quinimo credere impium esset, illos data opera scripsisse mendacia. Alius est ergo sensus, quam literis traditur." Agrippa, *Epistola* 5.14, in *Opera*, 2:873–74, translated and quoted in *HMES*, 5:132. The letter is dated 1527.

53. "Sed alia constat cognoscendi via, quae inter hanc et propheticam visionem media est, quae est adaequatio veritatis cum intellectu nostro purgato, veluti clauis cum sera, qui ut est veritatum omnium cupidissimus ita intelligibilium omnium susceptiuus est. atque idcirco intellectus passibilis vocatur, quo etsi non pleno lumine percipimus ea, quae depromunt prophetae, et hi qui ipsa divina conspexerunt, aperitur tamen nobis porta, ut ex conformitate veritatis perceptae, ad intellectum nostrum, et ex lumine, quod ex ipsis penetralibus apertis nos illustrat, multo certiores reddamur, quam ex philosophorum apparentibus, demonstrationibus, definitionibus, diuisionibus et compositionibus, daturque nobis ut legamus et intelligamus, non oculis et auribus exterioribus, sed percipiamus melioribus sensibus, et ablato velamine et revelata facie hauriamus veritatem, a medulla sacrarum literarum emanantem, quam sub velaminibus tradiderunt hi, qui vero intuitu conspexerunt, quae a sapientibus huius mundi et philosophis cognitionibus abscondita est, eamque nos tanto certitudinis judicio apprehendimus, ut omnis amoveatur perplexitas." Agrippa, *De vanitate*, 98 (225).

54. On the Bible in Maimonides and kabbalism, see Idel, *Absorbing Perfections*, 272–313, 482–92. The latter section discusses the impact of these notions in the Renaissance. On Abulafia and kabbalism, see Scholem, *Major Trends in Jewish Mysticism*, 137–41.

55. Compagni's edition of this work identifies the passages from the original version, written in 1510.

56. "Ad quam quìdem Propheticam spiritus correptionem nonnunquam praeviae quaedam caeremoniae, et officij authoritas, sacrorumque communio plurimum praestant: sicvti de Balaam exemplificat Scriptura. Et alibi de applicatione Ephod, et Evangelista testatur de Caipha, quia prophetauit, cum esset Pontifex anni illius." Agrippa, *De vanitate*, 99 (292–93).

57. See, for example, Schäfer, "Merkavah, Mysticism, and Magic." See also Kanarfogel, *"Peering Through the Lattices."* For a discussion of this literature and also of the connections with Renaissance thought, see Idel, *Absorbing Perfections*, 482–92.

BIBLIOGRAPHY

Primary Sources in Manuscript

Manuscripts that do not survive but are known through medieval catalogues are identified in the notes in the form of a conventional manuscript descriptor that also includes a reference to the modern catalogue. Thus York (Humphreys Cat.), Austin Friars A8 383 refers to a manuscript once held in the library of the Austin Friars at York and described in K. W. Humphreys's edition, where it is numbered A8 383. Full references to the editions of medieval catalogues may be found in the Selected Printed Primary Sources section below.

Berlin, Staatsbibliothek Preussischer Kulturbesitz
    Codices Elecorales Recentores 184

Boston, Countway Library of Medicine
    7

Cambridge, University Library
    Additional 3544
    Ff.vi.53, Gg.vi.3, Kk.i.1, and Ll.i.12

Edinburgh, Royal Observatory
    Cr.3.14

Erfurt, Wissenschaftliche Bibliothek
    Amplonian Collection, quartos 28, 174, and 189

Firenze, Biblioteca Medicea Laurenziana
    Plut. 30, Cod. 29
    Plut. 44, Cod. 35
    Plut. 89, sup. 36 and 38

Firenze, Biblioteca nazionale centrale di Firenze
    II.iii.214

Gent, Centrale Bibliotheek der Rijksuniversiteit
    1021

Graz, Universitätsbibliothek
    680 and 1016

Hamilton, Ontario, McMaster University Library
    MS 107

København, Kongelike Bibliotek
    Gl. Kgl. S. 1658

London, British Library
    Additional 18057 and 36674
    Harley 13, 80, and 181
    Royal 12.C.XVIII and 17.A.XLII
    Sloane 121, 312, 313, 314, 430, 513, 1712, 1727, 1784, 2731, 3008, 3556, 3648, 3822,
    3825, 3826, 3846, 3847, 3848, 3849, 3850, 3851, 3853, 3854, 3883, 3884, and 3885

London, Institution of Electrical Engineers
    Thompson Collection S.C. MSS 3/5

London, Society of Antiquaries of London
    39

London, Wellcome Library
    10, 110, 116, 117, 426, and 510

Lübeck, Bibliothek der Hansestadt
    Math. 4° 9

Mainz, Stadtbibliothek Mainz
    I 138

München, Bayerische Staatsbibliothek
    Clm 27, 51, and 849

München, Universitätsbibliothek
    Oct. Cod. 213

Oxford University, Bodleian Library
    Ashmole 244, 340, 346, 391, 393, 1378, 1406, 1416, 1437, 1442, 1471, 1473, and 1515
    Ballard 66
    Bodley 67, 463, 464, 951, and Additional B. 1
    Canon. lat. 500
    Canon. misc., 285
    Digby 37, 57, 71, 79, 91, 183, 193, 194, 218, and 228
    e Mus. 173, 219, and 238
    Lyell 51
    Rawlinson C. 117, D. 252, and D. 253
    Rawlinson liturg. D. 6
    Selden Supra 76
    Tanner 407

Oxford University, Corpus Christi College
    125, 221, and 255

Paris, Bibliothèque nationale de France
    Lat. 7440 and 9336

Turin, Biblioteca nazionale
    E. V. 13

Vaticano (Città del), Biblioteca Apostolica Vaticana
    Pal. lat. 1116, 1375, 1381, and 1445
    Reg. lat. 1300
    Vat. lat. 5333

Washington, D.C., Folger Shakespeare Library
    V. b. 26 and X. d. 234

Wien, Österreichische Nationalbibliothek
    11321

Selected Printed Primary Sources

Adelard of Bath. *Adelard of Bath, Conversations with His Nephew: On the Same and the Different, Questions on Natural Science, and on Birds.* Translated by Charles Burnett. Cambridge Medieval Classics 9. Cambridge: Cambridge University Press, 1998.

Agrippa, Heinrich Cornelius von Nettesheim. *De occulta philosophia libri tres.* Edited and translated by Vittoria Perrone Compagni. Leiden: Brill, 1992.

_____. *Henry Cornelius Agrippa, His Fourth Book of Occult Philosophy: Of Geomancy, Magical Elements of 'Peter De Abano,' Astronomical Geomancy, the Nature of Spirits, 'Arbatel' of Magick.* Translated by Robert Turner. London: John Harrison, 1655.

_____. *Of the Vanitie and vncertaintie of Artes and Sciences....* Translated by James Sandford. London: H. Bynneman, 1575.

_____. *Opera.* 2 vols. Lyon: Beringi Fratres, 1600.

_____. *Three Books of Occult Philosophy.* Translated by John French. London: Printed by R.W. for Gregory Moule, 1651.

Albertus Magnus. *The Secrets of Albertus Magnus. Of the Vertues of Hearbes, Stones, and certaine Beasts. Wherevnto is newly added, a short discourse of the seauen Planets gouerning the Natiuities of Children. Also a Booke of the same Author, of the maruellous things of the worlde, and of certaine effects caused by certaine Beasts.* London: V. V. Iaggard, 1599.

Al-Kindī, Yaʿqūb ibn Ishāq. *De radiis stellarum.* In *De radiis*, ed. M. T. d'Alverny and F. Hudry. *Archives d'Histoire Doctrinale et Littéraire du Moyen Âge* 41 (1974): 139–260.

Aquinas, Thomas. *De occultis operibus naturae ad quemdam militem ultramontanum.* In *The Letter of Saint Thomas Aquinas*, ed. and trans. Joseph Bernard McAllister, 191–97. Washington, D.C.: Catholic University of America Press, 1939.

Ars notoria: The Notory Art of Solomon, Shewing the Cabalistical Key of Magical Operations.... Translated by Robert Turner. London: J. Cottrel, 1657.

Augustine. *De divinatione daemonum.* In *Patrologia latina*, ed. J.-P. Migne, 40:581–92.

_____. "On the Divination of Demons." Translated by Ruth W. Brown. In Augustine, *Treatises on Marriage and Other Subjects*, trans. Charles T. Wilcox et al. and ed. Roy J. Deferrari, 417–40. Fathers of the Church 27. Washington, D.C.: Catholic University of America Press, 1955.

Bayerische Akademie der Wissenschaften. *Mittelalterliche Bibliothekskataloge Deutschlands und der Schweiz.* 9 vols. Munich: C. H. Beck, 1918–2009.

Bonaventure. *Opera omnia Sancti Bonaventurae.* Edited by Adolphe C. Peltier. 15 vols. Paris: L. Vivès, 1864–71.

Bujanda, J. M. de, R. Davignon, and E. Stanek. *Index de Venise, 1549, Venise et Milan, 1554, Index des livres interdits.* Vol. 3 of *Index des livres interdits*, ed. J. M. de Bujanda, 10 vols. Sherbrooke: Le Centre d'Études de la Renaissance, Éditions de l'Universite de Sherbrooke, 1987.

Caesarius of Heisterbach. *The Dialogue on Miracles*. Translated by Henry von Essen Scott
and C. C. Swinton Bland. Edited by George Gordon Coulton. 2 vols. London:
Routledge, 1929.

———. *Dialogus miraculorum: Textum ad quatuor codicum manuscriptorum editionisque
principis fidem accurate*. Edited by Joseph Strange. 2 vols. Cologne: J. M. Heberle,
1851.

Canterbury, Province of. *Registrum Roberti Winchelsey Cantuariensis Archiepiscopi A.D.
1294–1313*. Transcribed and edited by Rose Graham. 2 vols. Oxford: Oxford University Press, 1952, 1956.

Cellini, Benvenuto. *The Autobiography of Benvenuto Cellini*. Translated by George Anthony
Bull. Harmondsworth, Middlesex: Penguin, 1986.

Dee, John. *The Hieroglyphic Monad*. York Beach, Me.: Samuel Weiser, 2000.

———. *John Dee's Library Catalogue*. Edited by R. J. Roberts and Andrew G. Watson. London: Bibliographical Society, 1990.

———. *The Private Diary of Dr. John Dee: And the Catalogue of His Library of Manuscripts,
from the Original Manuscripts in the Ashmolean Museum at Oxford, and Trinity
College Library, Cambridge*. Edited by James O. Halliwell-Phillipps. New York: AMS
Press, 1968.

———. *A True and Faithful Relation Of What passed for many Yeers Between Dr. John Dee . . .
And Some Spirits. . . .* Edited by Meric Casaubon. London: Printed by D. Maxwell
for T. Garthwait, 1659.

Enoch. *De quindecim stellis quindecim lapidibus quindecim herbis et quindecim imaginibus*.
In *Textes latins et vieux français relatifs aux Cyranides*, ed. Louis Delatte, 276–88.
Paris: E. Droz, 1942.

Ficino, Marsilio. *Commentary on Plato's Symposium on Love*. Edited and translated by Sears
Reynolds Jayne. Dallas: Spring Publications, 1985.

———. *De vita coelitus comparanda*. In *Three Books on Life*, trans. and ed. Carol V. Kaske
and John R. Clark, 236–393. Binghamton, N.Y.: Medieval and Renaissance Texts and
Studies, in conjunction with the Renaissance Society of America, 1989.

———. *The Letters of Marsilio Ficino*. Translated by members of the Language Department of the School of Economic Science, London. 8 vols. New York: Gingko Press,
1985–2009.

———. *Marsilio Ficino and the Phaedran Charioteer: Introduction, Texts, Translations*. Edited
and translated by Michael J. B. Allen. Berkeley and Los Angeles: University of California Press, 1981.

Fournier, Jacques. *Le registre d'inquisition de Jacques Fournier*. Edited by Jean Duvernoy.
Toulouse: Bibliothèque Meridionale, 1965.

Heireman, K., ed. *Alosti in Flandria anno M°CCCC°LXXIII: Facsimile van de drie oudste
Zuidnederlandse drukken Aalst 1473*. Brussels: Gemeentekrediet, 1973.

Hermes. *De quindecim stellis quindecim lapidibus quindecim herbis et quindecim imaginibus*.
In *Textes latins et vieux français relatifs aux Cyranides*, ed. Louis Delatte, 235–75.
Paris: E. Droz, 1942.

———. "Una fonte ermetica: Il liber orationum planetarum." Edited by Vittoria Perrone
Compagni. *Bruniana e Campanelliana: Ricerche Filosofiche e Materiali Storico-Testu-
ali* 7 (2001): 189–97.

Hermes [Belenus]. *Liber lune*. Edited by Paolo Lucentini. In *Sic itur ad astra: Studien zur
Geschichte der Mathematik und Naturwissenschaften; Festschrift für den Arabisten
Paul Kunitzsch zum 70. Geburtstag*, ed. Menso Folkerts and Richard Lorch, 444–50.
Wiesbaden: Harrassowitz, 2000.

Honorius. *Le grimoire du Pape Honorius*. Rome [Paris?], 1800.

———. *Liber iuratus Honorii: A Critical Edition of the Latin Version of the Sworn Book of
Honorius*. Edited by Gösta Hedegård. Stockholm: Almquist & Wiksell, 2002.

Howell, Thomas Bayly, Thomas Jones Howell, William Cobbett, and David Jardine, eds. *Cobbett's Complete Collection of State Trials and Proceedings for High Treason and Other Crimes and Misdemeanors from the Earliest Period to the Present Time.* 33 vols. London: R. Bagshaw, 1809–26.

Humphreys, K. W., ed. *The Friars' Libraries.* London: British Library in association with the British Academy, 1990.

Ibn al-Nadim, Muḥammad ibn Isḥāq. *The Fihrist of al-Nadim: A Tenth-Century Survey of Muslim Culture.* Edited by Bayard Dodge. New York: Columbia University Press, 1970.

Isidore of Seville. *The Etymologies of Isidore of Seville.* Edited and translated by Stephen A. Barney with the collaboration of Muriel Hall. Cambridge: Cambridge University Press, 2006.

James, M. R., ed. *The Ancient Libraries of Canterbury and Dover: The Catalogues of the Libraries of Christ Church Priory and St. Augustine's Abbey at Canterbury and of St. Martin's Priory at Dover.* Cambridge: Cambridge University Press, 1903.

[James of Milan.] *The Goad of Love: An Unpublished Translation of the Stimulus amoris, Formerly Attributed to St. Bonaventure.* Translated by Walter Hilton. Edited by Clare Kirchberger. London: Faber and Faber, 1952.

John of Morigny. "The Prologue to John of Morigny's *Liber visionum*: Text and Translation." Translated and edited by Claire Fanger and Nicholas Watson. *Esoterica: The Journal of Esoteric Studies* 3 (2001): 108–217. Available online at http://www.esoteric.msu .edu/VolumeIII/Morigny.html.

John of Salisbury. *Frivolities of Courtiers and Footprints of Philosophers: Being a Translation of the First, Second, and Third Books and Selections from the Seventh and Eighth Books of the Policraticus of John of Salisbury.* Edited by Joseph B. Pike. Minneapolis: University of Minnesota Press, 1938.

Lehemann, Paul, ed. "Collegium Amplonianum." In Bayerische Akademie der Wissenschaften, *Mittelalterliche Bibliothekskataloge Deutschlands und der Schweiz,* 2:1–41. Munich: C. H. Beck, 1928.

Leonardus, Camillus. *Speculum lapidum.* Hamburg: Christianum Liebezeit, 1717.

Manuale ad usum percelebris ecclesie sarisburensis. Edited by A. Jeffries Collins. London: Henry Bradshaw Society, 1960.

Northgate, Michael. *Dan Michel's Ayenbite of Inwyt: Introduction, Notes, and Glossary.* Edited by Pamela Gradon and Richard Morris. Oxford: Oxford University Press, 1979.

Peterson, Joseph H., ed. *The Lesser Key of Solomon: Lemegeton Clavicula Salomonis.* York Beach, Me.: Weiser Books, 2001.

"Picatrix": Das Ziel des Weisen von Pseudo-Maǧriṭi. Translated by Helmut Ritter and Martin Plessner. London: Warburg Institute, 1962.

Picatrix: The Latin Version of the Ghayat al-Hakim. Edited by David Pingree. London: Warburg Institute, 1986.

"Picatrix latinus: Concezioni filosofico-religiose e prassi magica." Edited by Vittoria Perrone Compagni. *Medioevo* 1 (1975): 237–345.

Pico della Mirandola, Giovanni. *Syncretism in the West: Pico's 900 Theses (1486); The Evolution of Traditional Religious and Philosophical Systems, with Text, Translation, and Commentary by Stephen Alan Farmer.* Edited by Stephen Alan Farmer. Tempe: Medieval and Renaissance Texts and Studies, 1998.

Proclus. *Proclus: The Elements of Theology.* Edited by E. R. Dodds. Oxford: Clarendon Press, 1933.

Pseudo-Agrippa, Heinrich Cornelius von Nettesheim. *Henrici Cornelii Agrippae liber quartus de occulta philosophia, seu De cerimoniis magicis. Cui accesserunt, Elementa magica Petri de Abano, philosophi.* Marburg, [1559?].

Pseudo-Dionysius the Areopagite. *De caelesti hierarchia, in usum studiosae iuventutis.* Edited by Peter Hendrix. Leiden: Brill, 1959.

Raymond of Penafort. *Summa de poenitentia et matrimonio cum glossis.* Rome, 1605.

Reynes, Robert. *The Commonplace Book of Robert Reynes of Acle: An Edition of Tanner Ms 407.* Edited by Louis Cameron. New York: Garland, 1980.

Richard of St. Victor. *Liber exceptionum: Texte critique avec introd., notes et tables.* Edited by Jean Chatillon. Paris: J. Vrin, 1958.

Roman d'Eustache Le Moine. Edited by Francisque Michel. Paris: Silvestre, 1834.

Salimbene de Parma. *The Chronicle of Salimbene de Adam.* Edited by Joseph L. Baird, Giuseppe Baglivi, and John Robert Kane. Medieval and Renaissance Texts and Studies 40. Binghamton, N.Y.: Medieval and Renaissance Texts and Studies, 1986.

Scot, Reginald. *The Discouerie of Witchcraft.* London, 1584.

Solomon. *The Key of Solomon the King (Clavicula Salomonis): Now First Translated [from Latin, French, and Italian] and Edited from Ancient Mss. in the British Museum.* Edited and translated by S. L. MacGregor Mathers. London: Kegan Paul, Trench, Trübner, 1909. Reprint, London: Routledge and Kegan Paul, 1972.

Thābit ibn Qurra. *De imaginibus.* In *The Astronomical Works of Thâbit ibn Qurra,* ed. Francis J. Carmody, 167–97. Berkeley and Los Angeles: University of California Press, 1960.

Thetel. *De imaginibus.* In "Cethel aut veterum Judaeorum Phisilogorum de Lapidibus Sententie," in *Spicilegium Solesmense,* vol. 3, ed. Jean Baptiste Pitra, 335–37. Paris: Institutus Franciae, 1852.

Thomas of Cantimpré. *Liber de natura rerum.* Berlin: Walter de Gruyter, 1973.

Thomas of Chobham. *Summa confessorum.* Edited by F. Broomfield. Louvain: Editions Nauwelaerts, 1968.

Thorne, William. *William Thorne's Chronicle of Saint Augustine's Abbey, Canterbury.* Enlarged and expanded by Thomas Sprott and Roger Twysden. Translated by A. H. Davis. Oxford: Basil Blackwell, 1934.

Véronèse, Julien, ed. *L'Ars notoria au Moyen Âge: Introduction et édition critique.* Florence: Edizioni SISMEL, 2007.

Vincent of Beauvais. *Speculum naturale.* Venice: Hermannus Liechtenstein, 1494.

———. *Speculum quadruplex: Sive speculum maioris.* 4 vols. Venice: Baltazaris Belieri, 1624. Reprint, Graz: Akademische Druck-u. Verlagsanstalt, 1964–65.

Zambelli, Paola, ed. *The Speculum astronomiae and Its Enigma: Astrology, Theology, and Science in Albertus Magnus and His Contemporaries.* A critical edition of the *Speculum astronomiae,* edited and translated by Paola Zambelli, with the assistance of Stefano Caroti, Michela Pereira, Stefano Zamponi, Charles F. S. Burnett, K. Lippincott, and David Pingree, and with extensive critical commentary by Paola Zambelli. Dordrecht: Kluwer, 1992.

Zohar: The Book of Enlightenment. Translated by Daniel Chanan Matt. London: Paulist Press, 1983.

Secondary Sources

Allen, Don Cameron. *The Star-Crossed Renaissance: The Quarrel About Astrology and Its Influence in England.* New York: Octagon Books, 1966.

Allen, Michael J. B. *The Platonism of Marsilio Ficino: A Study of His Phaedrus Commentary, Its Sources and Genesis.* Berkeley and Los Angeles: University of California Press, 1984.

———. "Summoning Plotinus: Ficino, Smoke, and the Strangled Chickens." In *Reconsidering the Renaissance,* ed. M. di Cesare, 63–88. Binghamton, N.Y.: Medieval and Renaissance Texts and Studies, 1992.

Allen, Michael J. B., Valery Rees, and Martin Davies, eds. *Marsilio Ficino: His Theology, His Philosophy, His Legacy*. Leiden: Brill, 2002.

Armstrong, C. A. J. "An Italian Astrologer at the Court of Henry VII." In *Italian Renaissance Studies: A Tribute to the Late Cecilia M. Ady*, ed. Ernest Fraser Jacob, 157–78. New York: Barnes and Noble, 1960.

Ash, Eric H. *Power, Knowledge, and Expertise in Elizabethan England*. Baltimore: Johns Hopkins University Press, 2004.

Atiyeh, George Nicholas. *Al-Kindi, the Philosopher of the Arabs*. Rawalpindi: Islamic Research Institute, 1966.

Bailey, Michael D. *Battling Demons: Witchcraft, Heresy, and Reform in the Late Middle Ages*. University Park: Pennsylvania State University Press, 2003.

———. "The Disenchantment of Magic: Spells, Charms, and Superstition in Early European Witchcraft Literature." *American Historical Review* 111, no. 2 (2006): 383–404.

Baldwin, R. "John Dee's Interest in the Application of Nautical Science, Mathematics, and Law to English Naval Affairs." In *John Dee: Interdisciplinary Studies in English Renaissance Thought*, ed. Stephen Clucas, 97–130. Dordrecht: Springer, 2006.

Barb, A. A. "Three Elusive Amulets." *Journal of the Warburg and Courtauld Institutes* 27 (1964): 1–22.

Bateson, Mary, ed. *Catalogue of the Library of Syon Monastery, Isleworth*. Cambridge: Cambridge University Press, 1898.

Bautier, Anne-Marie. "*Spiritus* dans les textes antérieurs à 1200: Itinéraire lexicographique médolatin; Du souffle vital à l'au delà maléfique." In *Spiritus: IV° Colloquio internazionale, Roma, 7–9 gennaio 1983*, ed. Marta Fattori and M. Bianchi, 113–32. Rome: Edizioni dell'Ateneo, 1984.

Baxter, Ron. *Bestiaries and Their Users in the Middle Ages*. Stroud, Gloucestershire: Sutton, 1998.

Beitchman, Philip. *Alchemy of the Word: Cabala of the Renaissance*. Albany: State University of New York Press, 1998.

Bell, David. "A Cistercian at Oxford: Richard Dove of Buckfast and London." *Studia Monastica* 31 (1989): 67–87.

Besterman, Theodore. *Crystal-Gazing: A Study in the History, Distribution, Theory, and Practice of Scrying*. New York: University Books, 1965.

Blair, Ann. "Mosaic Physics and the Search for a Pious Natural Philosophy in the Late Renaissance." *Isis* 91, no. 1 (2000): 32–58.

Blair, Ann, and Anthony Grafton. "Reassessing Humanism and Science." *Journal of the History of Ideas* 53, no. 4 (1992): 535–40.

Boudet, Jean-Patrice. "L'*Ars notoria* au Moyen Âge: Une résurgence de la théurgie antique?" In *La magie: Actes du colloque international de Montpellier (25–27 mars 1999)*, vol. 3, *Du monde latin au monde contemporain*, ed. Alain Moreau and Jean-Claude Turpin, 173–91. Montpellier: Publications de la Recherche Université Paul-Valéry, 2000.

———. "Les condamnations de la magie à Paris en 1398." *Revue Mabillon*, n.s., 12 (2001): 121–57.

———. *Entre science et nigromance: Astrologie, divination et magie dans l'Occident médiévale (XIIe–XVe siècle)*. Paris: Publications de la Sorbonne, 2006.

———. "Magie théurgique, angélologie et vision béatifique dans le *Liber sacratus sive juratus* attribué à Honorius de Thèbes." In *Mélanges de l'École Française de Rome: Moyen-Âge* 114, no. 2 (2002): 851–90.

———. "Les Who's Who démonologiques de la Renaissance et leurs ancêtres médiévaux." *Médiévales* 44 (2003): 117–40.

Boudet, Jean-Patrice, and Julien Véronèse. "Le secret dans la magie rituelle médiévale." *Micrologus* 14 (2006): 101–50.

Brann, Noël L. *The Abbot Trithemius (1462–1516): The Renaissance of Monastic Humanism*. Leiden: Brill, 1981.

———. *Trithemius and Magical Theology: A Chapter in the Controversy over Occult Studies in Early Modern Europe*. Albany: State University of New York Press, 1999.

Bremmer, Jan N., and Jan R. Veenstra, eds. *The Metamorphosis of Magic from Late Antiquity to the Early Modern Period*. Louvain: Peeters, 2002.

Briggs, Katherine M. *The Anatomy of Puck: An Examination of Fairy Beliefs Among Shakespeare's Contemporaries and Successors*. London: Routledge and Kegan Paul, 1959.

Buck, August, ed. *Die okkulten Wissenschaften in der Renaissance*. Wiesbaden: Harrassowitz, 1992.

Bullard, Melissa Meriam. "The Inward Zodiac: A Development in Ficino's Thought on Astrology." *Renaissance Quarterly* 43 (Winter 1990): 687–708.

Burnett, Charles. "Adelard, Ergaphalau, and the Science of the Stars." In *Adelard of Bath: An English Scientist and Arabist of the Early Twelfth Century*, ed. Charles Burnett, 133–208. London: Warburg Institute, 1987.

———. "Arabic, Greek, and Latin Works on Astrological Magic Attributed to Aristotle." In *Pseudo-Aristotle in the Middle Ages*, ed. J. Kraye, W. F. Ryan, and C. B. Schmitt, 84–96. London: Warburg Institute, 1986.

———. *Magic and Divination in the Middle Ages: Texts and Techniques in the Islamic and Christian Worlds*. Aldershot: Variorum, 1996.

———. "Scandinavian Runes in a Latin Magical Treatise." *Speculum* 58, no. 2 (1983): 419–29.

Burnett, Charles, and W. F. Ryan, eds. *Magic and the Classical Tradition*. London: Warburg Institute, 2006.

Butler, E. M. *The Myth of the Magus*. Cambridge: Cambridge University Press, 1948.

———. *Ritual Magic*. Cambridge: Cambridge University Press, 1949.

Camille, Michael. "Visual Art in Two Manuscripts of the Ars Notoria." In *Conjuring Spirits: Texts and Traditions of Medieval Ritual Magic*, ed. Claire Fanger, 110–39. University Park: Pennsylvania University Press, 1998.

Cannon, Henry Lewis. "The Battle of Sandwich and Eustace the Monk." *English Historical Review* 27 (1912): 649–70.

Carmody, Francis J. *Arabic Astronomical and Astrological Sciences in Latin Translation: A Critical Bibliography*. Berkeley and Los Angeles: University of California Press, 1956.

Celenza, Cristopher. "Late Antiquity and Florentine Platonism: The 'Post-Plotinian' Ficino." In *Marsilio Ficino: His Theology, His Philosophy, His Legacy*, ed. Michael J. B. Allen, Valery Rees, and Martin Davies, 71–97. Leiden: Brill, 2002.

Christian, William A. *Apparitions in Late Medieval and Renaissance Spain*. Princeton: Princeton University Press, 1981.

Clark, Stuart. *Thinking with Demons: The Idea of Witchcraft in Early Modern Europe*. Oxford: Oxford University Press, 1997.

Clucas, Stephen, ed. *John Dee: Interdisciplinary Studies in English Renaissance Thought*. Dordrecht: Springer, 2006.

———. "'Non est legendum sed inspicendum solum': Inspectival Knowledge and the Visual Logic of John Dee's *Liber mysteriorum*." In *Emblems and Alchemy*, ed. Alison Adams and Stanton J. Linden, 109–32. Glasgow: Glasgow Emblem Studies, 1998.

———. "*Regimen Animarum et Corporum*: The Body and Spatial Practice in Medieval and Renaissance Magic." In *The Body in Late Medieval and Early Modern Culture*, ed. Darryll Grandley and Nina Taunton, 113–29. Aldershot: Ashgate, 2000.

Clulee, Nicholas H. *John Dee's Natural Philosophy: Between Science and Religion*. London: Routledge, 1988.

Cohn, Norman. *Europe's Inner Demons: An Enquiry Inspired by the Great Witch-Hunt*. New York: Basic Books, 1975.

Coleman, Martin. *Communing with the Spirits: The Magical Practice of Necromancy*. York Beach, Me.: S. Weiser, 1998.

Connolly, Margaret. "A Prayer to the Guardian Angel and Wynkyn de Worde's 1506 Edition of *Contemplations of the Dread and Love of God*." *Manuscripta* 45–46, no. 1 (2001–2): 1–17.

Copenhaver, Brian P. "Astrology and Magic." In *The Cambridge History of Renaissance Philosophy*, ed. Eckhard Kessler, Jill Kraye, Quentin Skinner, and Charles B. Schmitt, 264–300. Cambridge: Cambridge University Press, 1988.

————. "Iamblichus, Synesius, and the Chaldaean Oracles in Marsilio Ficino's *De vita libri tres:* Hermetic Magic or Neoplatonic Magic?" In *Supplementum festivum: Studies in Honor of Paul Oskar Kristeller*, ed. James Hankins, John Monfasani, and Frederick Purnell Jr., 441–55. Binghamton, N.Y.: Medieval and Renaissance Texts and Studies, 1987.

————. "Magic and the Dignity of Man: De-Kanting Pico's Oration." In *The Italian Renaissance in the Twentieth Century*, ed. Allen J. Grieco, Michael Rocke, and Fiorella Gioffredi Superbi, 295–320. Florence: Leo S. Olschki, 2002.

————. "Natural Magic, Hermeticism, and Occultism in Early Modern Science." In *Reappraisals of the Scientific Revolution*, ed. David C. Lindberg and Robert S. Westman, 261–301. Cambridge: Cambridge University Press, 1990.

————. "Number, Shape, and Meaning in Pico's Christian Cabala: The Upright Tsade, the Closed Mem, and the Gaping Jaws of Azazel." In *Natural Particulars: Nature and Disciplines in Renaissance Europe*, ed. Anthony Grafton and Nancy Siraisi, 25–76. Cambridge: MIT Press, 1999.

————. "Renaissance Magic and Neoplatonic Philosophy: *Ennead* 4.3–5 in Ficino's *De vita coelitus comparanda.*" In *Marsilio Ficino e il ritorno di platone: Studi e documenti*, ed. Gian Carlo Garfagnini, 351–69. Florence: L. S. Olschki, 1986.

————. "Scholastic Philosophy and Renaissance Magic in the *De vita* of Marsilio Ficino." *Renaissance Quarterly* 37, no. 4 (1984): 523–54.

————. "The Secret of Pico's Oration: Cabala and Renaissance Philosophy." In *Renaissance and Early Modern Philosophy*, ed. Peter A. French, Howard K. Wettstein, and Bruce Silver, 56–81. Oxford: Blackwell, 2002.

————. "A Tale of Two Fishes: Magical Objects in Natural History from Antiquity Through the Scientific Revolution." *Journal of the History of Ideas* 52, no. 3 (1991): 373–98.

Couliano, Ioan P. *Eros and Magic in the Renaissance*. Translated by Margaret Cook. Chicago: University of Chicago Press, 1987.

Davies, Owen. *Cunning-Folk: Popular Magic in English History*. London: Hambledon and London, 2003.

————. *Grimoires: A History of Magic Books*. Oxford: Oxford University Press, 2009.

Dobschütz, Ernst von. *Das decretum Gelasianum de libris recipiendis et non recipiendis: In kritischem Text hrsg. und untersucht von Ernst von Dobschütz*. Leipzig: J. C. Hinrichs, 1912.

Duffy, Eamon. *The Stripping of the Altars: Traditional Religion in England, c. 1400–c. 1580*. New Haven: Yale University Press, 1992.

Dupèbe, Jean. "L'*Ars notoria* et la polémique sur la divination et la magie." In *Divination et controverse religieuse en France au XVIe siècle*, 122–34. Paris: École Normale Supérieure de Jeunes Filles, 1987.

Eamon, William. *Science and the Secrets of Nature: Books of Secrets in Medieval and Early Modern Culture*. Princeton: Princeton University Press, 1994.

————. "Technology as Magic in the Late Middle Ages and the Renaissance." *Janus* 70 (1983): 171–212.

Easlea, Brian. *Witch Hunting, Magic and the New Philosophy: An Introduction to Debates of the Scientific Revolution, 1450–1750*. Atlantic Highlands, N.J.: Humanities Press, 1980.

Elliott, Dyan. *Fallen Bodies: Pollution, Sexuality, and Demonology in the Middle Ages*. Philadelphia: University of Pennsylvania Press, 1999.

Emden, Alfred Brotherston. *A Biographical Register of the University of Cambridge to 1500*. Cambridge: Cambridge University Press, 1963.

————. *A Biographical Register of the University of Oxford to 1500*. 3 vols. Oxford: Clarendon Press, 1957–59.

_____. *A Biographical Register of the University of Oxford, A.D. 1501 to 1540*. Oxford: Clarendon Press, 1974.

_____. *Donors of Books to St. Augustine's Abbey, Canterbury*. Oxford: Oxford Bibliographical Society, 1968.

Estes, Leland L. "Reginald Scot and His 'Discoverie of Witchcraft': Religion and Science in the Opposition to the European Witch Craze." *Church History* 52, no. 4 (1983): 444–56.

Evans, Robert John Weston, and Alexander Marr, eds. *Curiosity and Wonder from the Renaissance to the Enlightenment*. Aldershot: Ashgate, 2006.

Fanger, Claire, ed. *Invoking Angels: Theurgic Ideas and Practices, Thirteenth to Sixteenth Centuries*. University Park: Pennsylvania State University Press, 2012.

_____. "Plundering the Egyptian Treasure: John the Monk's Book of Visions, and Its Relation to the Notory Art of Solomon." In *Conjuring Spirits: Texts and Traditions of Medieval Ritual Magic*, ed. Claire Fanger, 216–49. University Park: Pennsylvania State University Press, 1998.

_____. "Signs of Power and the Power of Signs: Medieval Modes of Address to the Problem of Magical and Miraculous Signifiers." PhD diss., University of Toronto, 1993.

_____. "Things Done Wisely by a Wise Enchanter: Negotiating the Power of Words in the Thirteenth Century." *Esoterica* 1 (1999): 97–132.

_____. "Virgin Territory: Purity and Divine Knowledge in Late Medieval Catoptromantic Texts." *Aries* 5, no. 2 (2005): 200–224.

Fanger, Claire, and Benedek Láng. "John of Morigny's *Liber visionum* and a Royal Prayer Book from Poland." *Societas Magica Newsletter* 9 (2002): 1–4.

Faraone, Christopher A., and Dirk Obbink. *Magika Hiera: Ancient Greek Magic and Religion*. New York: Oxford University Press, 1991.

Fehrenbach, Robert J., and E. S. Leedham-Green, eds. *Private Libraries in Renaissance England: A Collection and Catalogue of Tudor and Early Stuart Book-Lists*. 7 vols. Binghamton, N.Y.: Medieval and Renaissance Texts and Studies, 1992–2009.

Ferguson, John. *Bibliographical Notes on the Treatises De occulta philosophia and De incertitudine et vanitate scientiarum of Cornelius Agrippa*. Edinburgh: For private circulation, 1924.

Finamore, John F. *Iamblichus and the Theory of the Vehicle of the Soul*. Chico, Calif.: Scholars Press, 1985.

Flint, Valerie I. J. *The Rise of Magic in Early Medieval Europe*. Princeton: Princeton University Press, 1991.

Forman, Simon. *The Autobiography and Personal Diary of Dr. Simon Forman: . . . from A.D. 1552 to A.D. 1602, from the unpublished manuscripts in the Ashmolean Museum, Oxford . . . .* Edited by James Orchard Halliwell. London: For private circulation, 1849.

Frankfurter, David. "Narrating Power: The Theory and Practice of Magical *Historiola* in Ritual Spells." In *Ancient Magic and Ritual Power*, ed. Marvin W. Meyer and Paul Allan Mirecki, 457–76. Leiden: Brill, 1995.

Frazer, James George. *The Golden Bough: A Study in Magic and Religion*. 3rd ed. 13 vols. London: Macmillan, 1911–15.

Friedman, John B. "The Prioress's Beads 'of Smal Coral.' " *Medium Aevum* 39 (1970): 301–5.

_____. "Secretum Philosophorum." In *Conjuring Spirits: Texts and Traditions of Medieval Ritual Magic*, ed. Claire Fanger, 77–86. University Park: Pennsylvania State University Press, 1998.

Gams, Pius Bonifatius. *Series episcoporum ecclesiae catholicae*. 2nd ed. Leipzig: Hiersemann, 1931.

Gibbons, B. J. *Spirituality and the Occult from the Renaissance to the Modern Age*. London: Routledge, 2001.

Graf, Fritz. *Magic in the Ancient World*. Translated by Franklin Philip. Cambridge: Harvard
    University Press, 1997.
Grafton, Anthony. "Geniture Collections, Origins and Uses of a Genre." In *Books and the
    Sciences in History*, ed. Marina Frasca-Spada and Nick Jardine, 49–68. Cambridge:
    Cambridge University Press, 2000.
———. *Magic and Technology in Early Modern Europe*. Washington: Smithsonian Institution
    Libraries, 2005.
Grafton, Anthony, and Moshe Idel, eds. *Der Magus: Seine Ursprünge und seine Geschichte in
    verschiedenen Kulturen*. Berlin: Akademie Verlag, 2001.
Grafton, Anthony, and Nancy G. Siraisi, eds. *Natural Particulars: Nature and the Disciplines
    in Renaissance Europe*. Cambridge: MIT Press, 1999.
Grendon, Felix. *Anglo-Saxon Charms*. [Folcroft, Pa.]: Folcroft Library Editions, 1974.
Haines, John. "Did John of Tilbury Write an *Ars notaria?*" *Scriptorium* 62, no. 1 (2008):
    48–73.
Hall, A. Rupert. "Magic, Metaphysics, and Mysticism in the Scientific Revolution."
    In *Reason, Experiment, and Mysticism in the Scientific Revolution*, ed. Maria
    Luisa Righini Bonelli and William R. Shea, 275–82. New York: Science History
    Publications, 1975.
Hamesse, Jaqueline. "*Spiritus* chez les auteurs philosophiques des 12e et 13e Siècles." In
    Spiritus: IVº Colloquio internazionale, Roma, 7–9 gennaio, 1983, ed. Marta Fattori
    and M. Bianchi, 157–90. Rome: Edizioni dell'Ateneo, 1984.
Hankins, James, John Monfasani, and Frederick Purnell Jr., eds. *Supplementum festivum:
    Studies in Honor of Paul Oskar Kristeller*. Binghamton, N.Y.: Medieval and Renais-
    sance Texts and Studies, 1987.
Hansen, Bert. "Science and Magic." In *Science in the Middle Ages*, ed. David C. Lindberg,
    483–506. Chicago: University of Chicago Press, 1978.
Harkness, Deborah E. *John Dee's Conversations with Angels: Cabala, Alchemy, and the
    End of Nature*. Cambridge: Cambridge University Press, 1999.
Harvey, E. Ruth. *The Inward Wits: Psychological Theory in the Middle Ages and the Renais-
    sance*. London: Warburg Institute, 1975.
Henry, John. "Magic and Science in the Sixteenth and Seventeenth Centuries." In *Compan-
    ion to the History of Modern Science*, ed. Robert C. Olby, Geoffrey N. Cantor, John R.
    R. Christie, and Michael J. S. Hodge, 583–96. London: Routledge, 1990.
Hillgarth, J. N. *Who Read Thomas Aquinas?* Toronto: Pontifical Institute of Mediaeval Stud-
    ies, 1992.
Hirsch, Rudolf. *The Printed Word: Its Impact and Diffusion (Primarily in the Fifteenth–Six-
    teenth Centuries)*. London: Variorum Reprints, 1978.
Holmes, Oliver Wendell. *The Guardian Angel*. Boston: Ticknor and Fields, 1867.
Hudson, Anne. *The Premature Reformation: Wycliffite Texts and Lollard History*. Oxford:
    Clarendon Press, 1988.
Huffman, William H. *Robert Fludd and the End of the Renaissance*. London: Routledge,
    1988.
Idel, Moshe. *Absorbing Perfections: Kabbalah and Interpretation*. New Haven: Yale University
    Press, 2002.
———. *Kabbalah: New Perspectives*. New Haven: Yale University Press, 1988.
———. "Saturn, Schabbat, Zauberei und die Juden." In *Der Magus: Seine Ursprünge und
    seine Geschichte in verschiedenen Kulturen*, ed. Anthony Grafton and Moshe Idel,
    209–50. Berlin: Academie Verlag, 2001.
Isaacs, Ronald H. *Ascending Jacob's Ladder: Jewish Views of Angels, Demons, and Evil Spirits*.
    Northvale, N.J.: Jason Aronson, 1998.
Kanarfogel, Ephraim. "*Peering Through the Lattices*": Mystical, Magical, and Pietistic Dimen-
    sions in the Tosafist Period*. Detroit: Wayne State University Press, 2000.

Kassell, Lauren. "'All this land full fill'd of faerie,' or Magic and the Past in Early Modern England." *Journal of the History of Ideas* 67, no. 1 (2006): 107–22.

———. "The Economy of Magic in Early Modern England." In *The Practice of Reform in Health, Medicine, and Science, 1500–2000: Essays for Charles Webster*, ed. Margaret Pelling and Scott Mandelbrote, 43–57. Aldershot: Ashgate, 2005.

———. *Medicine and Magic in Elizabethan London: Simon Forman, Astrologer, Alchemist, and Physician*. Oxford: Clarendon Press, 2005.

———. "Reading for the Philosophers' Stone." In *Books and the Sciences in History*, ed. Marina Frasca-Spada and Nick Jardine, 132–51. Cambridge: Cambridge University Press, 2000.

Keck, David. *Angels and Angelology in the Middle Ages*. New York: Oxford University Press, 1998.

Keefer, Michael H. "Agrippa's Dilemma: Hermetic 'Rebirth' and the Ambivalences of *De vanitate* and *De occulta philosophia*." *Renaissance Quarterly* (Winter 1988): 614–53.

Kieckhefer, Richard. "The Devil's Contemplatives: The *Liber iuratus*, the *Liber visionum*, and Christian Appropriation of Jewish Occultism." In *Conjuring Spirits: Texts and Traditions of Medieval Ritual Magic*, ed. Claire Fanger, 250–65. University Park: Pennsylvania State University Press, 1998.

———. "Erotic Magic in Medieval Europe." In *Sex in the Middle Ages: A Book of Essays*, ed. Joyce E. Salisbury, 30–55. New York: Garland, 1991.

———. *Forbidden Rites: A Necromancer's Manual of the Fifteenth Century*. Stroud, Gloucestershire: Sutton, 1997.

———. "The Holy and the Unholy: Sainthood, Witchcraft, and Magic in Late Medieval Europe." *Journal of Medieval and Renaissance Studies* 24 (1994): 355–85.

———. *Magic in the Middle Ages*. Cambridge: Cambridge University Press, 1989.

———. "The Specific Rationality of Medieval Magic." *American Historical Review* 99, no. 3 (1994): 813–36.

Kittredge, George Lyman. *Witchcraft in Old and New England*. New York: Russell and Russell, 1956.

Klaassen, Frank. "English Manuscripts of Magic, 1300–1500: A Preliminary Survey." In *Conjuring Spirits: Texts and Traditions of Medieval Ritual Magic*, ed. Claire Fanger, 3–31. University Park: Pennsylvania State University Press, 1998.

———. "Learning and Masculinity in Manuscripts of Ritual Magic of the Later Middle Ages and Renaissance." *Sixteenth Century Journal* 38, no. 1 (2007): 49–76.

———. "Magical Dream Provocation in the Later Middle Ages." *Esoterica: The Journal of Esoteric Studies* 8 (2006): 120–47.

———. "Medieval Ritual Magic in the Renaissance." *Aries* 3, no. 2 (2003): 166–99.

———. "The Middleness of Ritual Magic." In *The Unorthodox Imagination in Medieval Britain*, ed. Sophie Page, 131–65. Manchester: Manchester University Press, 2011.

———. "Religion, Science, and the Transformations of Magic: Manuscripts of Magic, 1300–1600." PhD diss., University of Toronto, 1999.

———. "Ritual Invocation and Early Modern Science: The Skrying Experiments of Humphrey Gilbert." In *Invoking Angels: Theurgic Ideas and Practices, Thirteenth to Sixteenth Centuries*, ed. Claire Fanger, 341–66. University Park: Pennsylvania State University Press, 2012.

———. "Three Early Modern Magic Rituals to Spoil Witches." *Opuscula: Short Texts of the Middle Ages and Renaissance* 1, no. 1 (2011): 1–10.

———. "Unstable Texts and Modal Approaches to the Written Word in Medieval European Ritual Magic." In *Orality and Literacy: Reflections Across Disciplines and Cultures*, ed. Keith Thor Carlson, Kristina Fagan, and Natalia Khanenko-Friesen, 217–43. Toronto: University of Toronto Press, 2011.

Klaassen, Frank, and Katrina Bens. "Six Rituals to Attain Invisibility." In *Opuscula: Short Texts of the Middle Ages and Renaissance*. Forthcoming.

Klaassen, Frank, and Christopher Phillips. "The Return of Stolen Goods: Reginald Scot, Religious Controversy, and Magic in Bodleian Library, Additional B. 1." *Magic, Ritual, and Witchcraft* 1, no. 2 (2006): 135–76.

Klaniczay, Gábor. *The Uses of Supernatural Power: The Transformation of Popular Religion in Medieval and Early-Modern Europe.* Edited by Karen Margolis. Translated by Susan Singerman. Princeton: Princeton University Press, 1990.

Knorr, Wilbur. "Two Medieval Monks and Their Astronomy Books: MSS. Bodley 464 and Rawlinson C. 117." *Bodleian Library Record* 14 (1993): 269–84.

Kodera, Sergius. "Narcissus, Divine Gazes, and Bloody Mirrors: The Concept of Matter in Ficino." In *Marsilio Ficino: His Theology, His Philosophy, His Legacy*, ed. Michael J. B. Allen, Valery Rees, and Martin Davies, 285–306. Leiden: Brill, 2002.

Kristeller, Paul Oskar. *The Philosophy of Marsilio Ficino.* Translated by Virginia Conant. New York: Columbia University Press, 1943.

Kruger, Steven F. *Dreaming in the Middle Ages.* Cambridge: Cambridge University Press, 1992.

Láng, Benedek. *Unlocked Books: Manuscripts of Learned Magic in the Medieval Libraries of Central Europe.* University Park: Pennsylvania State University Press, 2008.

Lehrich, Christopher I. *The Language of Demons and Angels: Cornelius Agrippa's Occult Philosophy.* Leiden: Brill, 2003.

Leland, John. "Witchcraft and the Woodvilles: A Standard Medieval Smear?" In *Reputation and Representation in Fifteenth-Century Europe*, ed. Douglas Biggs, Sharon D. Michalove and Albert Compton Reeves, 267–88. Leiden: Brill, 2004.

Le Roy Ladurie, Emmanuel. *Montaillou: the Promised Land of Error.* Translated by Barbara Bray. New York: G. Braziller, 1978.

Levi-Strauss, Claude. "The Sorcerer and His Magic." In *Magic, Witchcraft, and Curing*, ed. John Middleton, 23–41. Austin: University of Texas Press, 1977.

Lucentini, Paolo. "L'ermetismo magico nel secolo XIII." In *Sic itur ad astra: Studien zur Geschichte der Mathematik und Naturwissenschaften; Festschrift für den Arabisten Paul Kunitzsch zum 70. Geburtstag*, ed. M. Folkerts and R. Lorch, 409–50. Wiesbaden: Harrassowitz, 2000.

Lucentini, Paolo, and Vittoria Perrone Compagni. *I testi e i codici di Ermete nel Medioevo.* Florence: Polistampa, 2001.

Luhrmann, Tanya M. "The Art of Hearing God: Absorption, Dissociation, and Contemporary American Spirituality." *Spiritus: A Journal of Christian Spirituality* 5, no. 2 (2005): 133–57.

———. *Persuasions of the Witch's Craft: Ritual Magic in Contemporary England.* Cambridge: Harvard University Press, 1989.

Maclean, Ian. "Foucault's Renaissance Episteme Reassessed: An Aristotelian Counterblast." *Journal of the History of Ideas* 59, no. 1 (1998): 149–66.

Malinowski, Bronislaw. *Magic, Science, and Religion, and Other Essays.* Garden City, N.Y.: Doubleday, 1954.

Marquès-Rivière, Jean. *Amulettes, talismans et pantacles dans les traditions orientales et occidentales.* Paris: Payot, 1972.

Mathiesen, Robert. "A Thirteenth-Century Ritual to Attain the Beatific Vision from the *Sworn Book of Honorius of Thebes*." In *Conjuring Spirits: Texts and Traditions of Medieval Ritual Magic*, ed. Claire Fanger, 143–62. University Park: Pennsylvania State University Press, 1998.

Matton, Sylvain, ed. *La magie arabe traditionnelle.* Paris: Retz, 1976.

Maurer, Armand. "Between Reason and Faith: Siger of Brabant and Pomponazzi on the Magic Arts." *Medieval Studies* 18 (1956): 1–18.

Maxwell-Stuart, P. G., ed. and trans. *The Occult in Early Modern Europe: A Documentary History.* New York: St. Martin's Press, 1999.

———. *Wizards: A History.* Stroud, Gloucestershire: Tempus, 2004.

McKnight, Stephen A., ed. *Science, Pseudo-Science, and Utopianism in Early Modern Thought*. Columbia: University of Missouri Press, 1992.

Mebane, John S. *Renaissance Magic and the Return of the Golden Age: The Occult Tradition and Marlowe, Jonson, and Shakespeare*. Lincoln: University of Nebraska Press, 1989.

Moore, R. I. "New Sects and Secret Meetings: Association and Authority in the Eleventh and Twelfth Centuries." In *Voluntary Religion*, ed. W. J. Sheils and Diana Wood, 47–68. Oxford: Blackwell, 1986.

Mowat, Barbara A. "Prospero's Book." *Shakespeare Quarterly* 52, no. 1 (2001): 1–33.

Nauert, Charles Garfield. *Agrippa and the Crisis of Renaissance Thought*. Urbana: University of Illinois Press, 1965.

Newman, William R. *Promethean Ambitions: Alchemy and the Quest to Perfect Nature*. Chicago: University of Chicago Press, 2004.

Newman, William R., and Anthony Grafton, eds. *Secrets of Nature: Astrology and Alchemy in Early Modern Europe*. Cambridge: MIT Press, 2001.

Nitzsche, Jane Chance. *The Genius Figure in Antiquity and the Middle Ages*. New York: Columbia University Press, 1975.

Olsan, Lea. "Charms and Prayers in Medieval Medical Theory and Practice." *Social History of Medicine* 16 (2003): 343–66.

———. "Charms in Medieval Memory." In *Charms and Charming in Europe*, ed. Jonathan Roper, 59–87. New York: Palgrave Macmillan, 2004.

———. "The Language of Charms in a Middle English Recipe Collection." *ANQ* 18, no. 1 (2005): 31–37.

———. "Latin Charms of Medieval England: Verbal Healing in a Christian Oral Tradition." *Oral Tradition* 7 (1992): 116–42.

Osler, Margaret J., ed. *Rethinking the Scientific Revolution*. Cambridge: Cambridge University Press, 2000.

Page, Sophie. "Image-Magic Texts and a Platonic Cosmology at St Augustine's, Canterbury in the Late Middle Ages." In *Magic and the Classical Tradition*, ed. Charles Burnett and W. F. Ryan, 69–98. London: Warburg Institute, 2006.

———. "Magic and the Pursuit of Wisdom: The 'Familiar' Spirit in the *Liber Theysolius*." *Corónica* 36, no. 1 (2007): 41–70.

———. "Magic at St. Augustine's, Canterbury in the Late Middle Ages." PhD diss., Warburg Institute, 2000.

———. *Magic in Medieval Manuscripts*. London: British Library, 2004.

Perrone Compagni, Vittoria. "Riforma della magia e riforma della cultura in Agrippa." *I Castelli di Yale: Quaderni di Filosofia* 2 (1997): 115–40.

Peters, Edward. *The Magician, the Witch, and the Law*. Philadelphia: University of Pennsylvania Press, 1978.

Peterson, Eric. *The Angels and the Liturgy*. Translated by Ronald Walls. New York: Herder and Herder, 1964.

Philip, Ian Gilbert. *The Bodleian Library in the Seventeenth and Eighteenth Centuries*. Oxford: Clarendon Press, 1983.

Pingree, David. "Artificial Demons and Miracles." *Res Orientales* 13 (2001): 109–22.

———. "Between the *Ghaya* and *Picatrix* I: The Spanish Version." *Journal of the Warburg and Courtauld Institutes* 44 (1981): 27–56.

———. "The Diffusion of Arabic Magical Texts in Western Europe." In *La diffusione delle scienze islamiche nel Medio Evo europeo*, 57–102. Rome: Accademia Nazionale dei Lincei, 1987.

———. "From Hermes to Jabir and the *Book of the Cow*." In *Magic and the Classical Tradition*, ed. Charles Burnett and W. F. Ryan, 19–28. London: Warburg Institute, 2006.

———. "Learned Magic in the Time of Frederick II." *Micrologus* II (1994): 39–56.

———. "Plato's Hermetic *Book of the Cow*." In *Il Neoplatonismo nel Rinascimento*, ed. P. Prini, 133–45. Rome: Istituto della Enciclopedia Italiana, 1993.

———. "Some of the Sources of the Ghâyat al-Hakim." *Journal of the Warburg and Courtauld Institutes* 43 (1980): 1–15.

Platt, Peter G., ed. *Wonders, Marvels, and Monsters in Early Modern Culture*. Newark: University of Delaware Press, 1999.

Powicke, Frederick Maurice. *The Medieval Books of Merton College*. Oxford: Clarendon Press, 1931.

Rhodes, Dennis E. "The Princes in the Tower and Their Doctor." *English Historical Review* 77 (1962): 304–6.

———. "Provost Argentine of King's and His Books." *Transactions of the Cambridge Bibliographical Society* 2, part 3 (1956): 205–12.

Roper, Jonathan, ed. *Charms and Charming in Europe*. New York: Palgrave Macmillan, 2004.

Roper, Lyndal. *Religion and Culture in Germany (1400–1800)*. Leiden: Brill, 2001.

Rorem, Paul. *Pseudo-Dionysius: A Commentary on the Texts and an Introduction to Their Influence*. New York: Oxford University Press, 1993.

Rosenwein, Barbara H., and Lester K. Little. *Debating the Middle Ages: Issues and Readings*. Malden, Mass.: Blackwell, 1998.

Scarre, Geoffrey. *Witchcraft and Magic in Sixteenth- and Seventeenth-Century Europe*. Atlantic Highlands, N.J.: Humanities Press International, 1987.

Schäfer, Peter. "Merkavah, Mysticism, and Magic." In *Gershom Scholem's "Major Trends in Jewish Mysticism" Fifty Years After: Proceedings of the Sixth International Conference on the History of Jewish Mysticism*, ed. Peter Schäfer and Joseph Dan, 59–78. Tübingen: J. C. B. Mohr, 1993.

Schaffer, Simon. "Occultism and Reason." In *Philosophy, Its History and Historiography*, ed. A. J. Holland, 117–43. Dordrecht: D. Reidel, 1985.

Scholem, Gershom. *Major Trends in Jewish Mysticism*. New York: Schocken Books, 1941.

Scribner, Robert W. "The Reformation, Popular Magic, and the 'Disenchantment of the World.'" *Journal of Interdisciplinary History* 23, no. 3 (1993): 475–94.

Shaked, Shaul, ed. *Officina magica: Essays on the Practice of Magic in Antiquity*. Leiden: Brill, 2005.

Shapin, Steven. *The Scientific Revolution*. Chicago: University of Chicago Press, 1996.

———. *A Social History of Truth: Civility and Science in Seventeenth-Century England*. Chicago: University of Chicago Press, 1994.

Shaw, Gregory. *Theurgy and the Soul: The Neoplatonism of Iamblichus*. University Park: Pennsylvania State University Press, 1995.

Shumaker, Wayne. *The Occult Sciences in the Renaissance: A Study in Intellectual Patterns*. Berkeley and Los Angeles: University of California Press, 1972.

Singer, Dorothea Waley. *Catalogue of Latin and Vernacular Alchemical Manuscripts in Great Britain and Ireland, Dating from Before the Sixteenth Century*. 3 vols. Brussels: Lamertin, 1928–31.

Skemer, Don C. *Binding Words: Textual Amulets in the Middle Ages*. University Park: Pennsylvania State University Press, 2006.

Stephens, Walter. *Demon Lovers: Witchcraft, Sex, and the Crisis of Belief*. Chicago: University of Chicago Press, 2002.

Styers, Randall. *Making Magic: Religion, Magic, and Science in the Modern World*. Oxford: Oxford University Press, 2004.

Sutton, Anne F., and Livia Visser-Fuchs. "The Cult of Angels in Late Fifteenth-Century England: An Hours of the Guardian Angel Presented to Queen Elizabeth Woodville." In *Women and the Book: Assessing the Visual Evidence*, ed. Lesley Smith and Jane H. M. Taylor, 230–65. Toronto: University of Toronto Press, 1997.

Swartz, Michael D. *Scholastic Magic: Ritual and Revelation in Early Jewish Mysticism*. Princeton: Princeton University Press, 1996.

———. "Scribal Magic and Its Rhetoric: Formal Patterns in Medieval Hebrew and Aramaic Incantation Texts from the Cairo Genizah." *Harvard Theological Review* 83, no. 2 (1990): 163–80.

Talbot, Charles H., and Eugene Ashby Hammond. *The Medical Practitioners in Medieval England: A Biographical Register*. London: Wellcome Historical Medical Library, 1965.

Tambiah, Stanley Jeyaraja. *Magic, Science, Religion, and the Scope of Rationality*. Cambridge: Cambridge University Press, 1989.

Tester, S. J. *A History of Western Astrology*. Woodbridge, Suffolk: Boydell Press, 1987.

Thomas, Keith Vivian. *Religion and the Decline of Magic*. New York: Scribner, 1971.

Thorndike, Lynn. *A History of Magic and Experimental Science*. 8 vols. New York: Macmillan, 1923–58.

———. "Traditional Medieval Tracts Concerning Engraved Astrological Images." In *Mélanges Auguste Pelzer*, 217–74. Louvain: Bibliothèque de l'Université, 1947.

Traister, Barbara Howard. *Heavenly Necromancers: The Magician in English Renaissance Drama*. Columbia: University of Missouri Press, 1984.

Travaglia, Pinella. *Magic, Causality, and Intentionality: The Doctrine of Rays in al-Kindi*. Florence: SISMEL/Edizioni del Galluzzo, 1999.

Veenstra, Jan R. "Cataloguing Superstition: A Paradigmatic Shift in the Art of Knowing the Future." In *Pre-Modern Encyclopaedic Texts: Proceedings of the Second COMERS Congress, Groningen, 1–4 July 1996*, ed. Peter Binkley, 169–80. Leiden: Brill, 1997.

———. "The Holy Almandal: Angels and the Intellectual Aims of Magic." In *The Metamorphosis of Magic from Late Antiquity to the Early Modern Period*, ed. Jan N. Bremmer and Jan R. Veenstra, 189–229. Louvain: Peeters, 2002.

———. "Honorius and the Sigil of God: The *Liber iuratus* in Berengario Ganell's *Summa sacre magice*." In *Invoking Angels: Theurgic Ideas and Practices, Thirteenth to Sixteenth Centuries*, ed. Claire Fanger, 151–91. University Park: Pennsylvania State University Press, 2012.

———. *Magic and Divination at the Courts of Burgundy and France: Text and Context of Laurens Pignon's Contre les devineurs (1411)*. Leiden: Brill, 1998.

———. "Venerating and Conjuring Angels: Eiximenis's *Book of the Holy Angels* and the Holy Almandal, Two Case Studies." In *Magic and the Classical Tradition*, ed. Charles Burnett and W. F. Ryan, 119–34. London: Warburg Institute, 2006.

Venn, John, and J. A. Venn, comps. *Alumni Cantabrigienses: A Biographical List of All Known Students, Graduates and Holders of Office at the University of Cambridge, from the Earliest Times to 1900*. 4 vols. Cambridge: Cambridge University Press, 1922–54.

Véronèse, Julien. "L'*Ars notoria* au Moyen Âge et à l'époque moderne: Étude d'une tradition de magie théurgique (XIIe–XVIIe siècle)." 2 vols. PhD diss., Université Paris X–Nanterre, 2004.

———. "Contre la divination et la magie à la cour: Trois traités adressés à des grands aux XIVe et XVe siècles." *Micrologus* 16 (2006): 405–31.

———. "God's Names and Their Uses in the Books of Magic Attributed to King Solomon." *Magic, Ritual, and Witchcraft* 5, no. 1 (2010): 30–50.

———. "Magic, Theurgy, and Spirituality in the Medieval Ritual of the *Ars Notoria*." In *Invoking Angels: Theurgic Ideas and Practices, Thirteenth to Sixteenth Centuries*, ed. Claire Fanger, 37–78. University Park: Pennsylvania State University Press, 2012.

———. "La notion d''auteur-magicien' à la fin du Moyen Âge: Le cas de l'ermite Pelagius de Majorque († v.1480)." *Médiévales* 51 (2006): 119–38.

Viard, Jules, ed. *Les grandes chroniques de France*. 10 vols. Paris: Honoré Champion, 1920–53.

Vickers, Brian, ed. *Occult and Scientific Mentalities in the Renaissance*. Cambridge: Cambridge University Press, 1984.

———. Review of Paola Zambelli, *L'ambigua natura della magia*. *Isis* 85 (1994): 318–20.

Voss, Angela. "Orpheus redivivus: The Musical Magic of Marsilio Ficino." In *Marsilio Ficino: His Theology, His Philosophy, His Legacy*, ed. Michael J. B. Allen, Valery Rees, and Martin Davies, 227–41. Leiden: Brill, 2002.

Waite, Gary K. *Heresy, Magic, and Witchcraft in Early Modern Europe*. Houndmills, Basingstoke: Palgrave Macmillan, 2003.

Walker, Daniel P. *Spiritual and Demonic Magic from Ficino to Campanella*. London: Warburg Institute, 1958.

Wallis, R. T. *Neoplatonism*. With a foreword and bibliography by Lloyd P. Gerson. 2nd ed. London: Hackett, 1995.

Watson, Nicholas. "John the Monk's *Book of the Visions of the Blessed and Undefiled Virgin Mary, Mother of God*: Two Versions of a Newly Discovered Ritual Magic Text." In *Conjuring Spirits: Texts and Traditions of Medieval Ritual Magic*, ed. Claire Fanger, 163–215. University Park: Pennsylvania State University Press, 1998.

Webster, Charles. *From Paracelsus to Newton: Magic and the Making of Modern Science*. Cambridge: Cambridge University Press, 1982.

Weill-Parot, Nicolas. "Astral Magic and Intellectual Changes (Twelfth–Fifteenth Centuries): 'Astrological Images' and the Concept of 'Addressative' Magic." In *The Metamorphosis of Magic from Late Antiquity to the Early Modern Period*, ed. Jan N. Bremmer and Jan R. Veenstra, 167–87. Louvain: Peeters, 2002.

——— . *Les "images astrologiques" au Moyen Âge et à la Renaissance: Spéculations intellectuelles et pratiques magiques (XIIe–XVe siècle)*. Paris: Honoré Champion, 2002.

Wirszubski, Chaim. "Francesco Giorgio's Commentary on Giovanni Pico's Kabbalistic Theses." *Journal of the Warburg and Courtauld Institutes* 37 (1974): 145–56.

——— . *Pico della Mirandola's Encounter with Jewish Mysticism*. Cambridge: Harvard University Press, 1989.

Wolfson, Elliot R. *Abraham Abulafia—Kabbalist and Prophet: Hermeneutics, Theosophy, and Theurgy*. Los Angeles: Cherub Press, 2000.

——— . "Mystical Rationalization of the Commandments in the Prophetic Kabbalah of Abraham Abulafia." In *Perspectives on Jewish Thought and Mysticism*, ed. Alfred Ivry, Elliot R. Wolfson, and Allan Arkush, 331–80. Amsterdam: Harwood Academic Publishers, 1998.

——— . *Through a Speculum That Shines: Vision and Imagination in Medieval Jewish Mysticism*. Princeton: Princeton University Press, 1994.

Woodcock, Matthew. *Fairy in "The Faerie Queene": Renaissance Elf-Fashioning and Elizabethan Myth-Making*. Aldershot: Ashgate, 2004.

Yates, Frances. *Giordano Bruno and the Hermetic Tradition*. Chicago: University of Chicago Press, 1964.

——— . *The Occult Philosophy in the Elizabethan Age*. London: Routledge and Kegan Paul, 1979.

Zambelli, Paola. "A propositio del *De vanitate scienciarum et artium* di Cornelio Agrippa." *Rivista Critica di Storia della Filosofia* 15 (1960): 166–80.

——— . *L'ambigua natura della magia: Filosofi, streghe, riti nel Rinascimento*. Milan: Il Saggiatore, 1991.

——— . *L'apprendista stregone: Astrologia, cabala e arte lulliana in Pico della Mirandola e seguaci*. Venice: Marsilio, 1995.

——— . "Cornelius Agrippa, ein kritischer Magus." In *Die okkulten Wissenschaften in der Renaissance*, ed. August Buck, 65–90. Wiesbaden: Harrassowitz, 1992.

——— . "Magic and Radical Reformation in Agrippa of Nettesheim." *Journal of the Warburg and Courtauld Institutes* 39 (1976): 69–103.

——— . *White Magic, Black Magic in the European Renaissance: From Ficino, Pico, Della Porta to Trithemius, Agrippa, Bruno*. Leiden: Brill, 2007.

Zambelli, Paola, and Tiberio Russiliano. *Una reincarnazione di Pico ai tempi di Pomponazzi*. Milan: Il Polifilo, 1994.

Zika, Charles. "Reuchlin's *De verbo mirifico* and the Magic Debate of the Late Fifteenth Century." *Journal of the Warburg and Courtauld Institutes* 39 (1976): 104–38.

INDEX

Abulafia, Abraham, 229 n. 3
Adam, 214
Adelard of Bath
    Liber prestigiorum, number of copies, 44
    on necromancy, 26
    translations by: *De imaginibus*, 46–47; in
        migration of texts, 36
Agrippa, Cornelius
    approach, 217–18
    De occulta philosophia, 199–217; Agrippa's
        rejection of, 207–10, 214; astrological
        image magic in, 181; centrality of
        operator in, 205–6; demons in, 202–3,
        209–10; influence of, 199; kabbalism
        in, 200; magic as skill in, 206–7;
        necromancy in, 204–5; organization of,
        200–201; printed, popularity of, 177;
        recent scholarship on, 7–8; religious
        magic in, 203–4; ritual magic in, 203–4;
        techniques and approaches in, 201–2
    De vanitate, 201, 207–8, 245 n. 34
    existential crisis of, 214
    influence of, 199–201
    magic of, reformulation of, 200
    scribal references to, 162
Albertus Magnus, influence on moralists, 19
alchemical codices
    astrological image magic in, 41
    Harley 181 as, 166–67
alchemy. *See also specific texts*
    in *Ars notoria*, 167
    engraved stones in, 41
Alfonso, court of, in migration of image magic
    texts, 36
Al-Kindī, Ya'qūb ibn Ishāq
    cosmology of, 24–25
    in debate on images, 2–3
    De radiis stellarum: in Allen collection, 37;
        codex classification of, 77; decline in
        interest in, 184; in Erghome collection,
        65–66, 69; on natural explanation for
        magic, 24–26; popularity of, 43, 222
        n. 38
Allen, Michael J. B., 7, 193–94

Allen, Thomas, collection of, 37
Almandal, 117, 120–22
amulets, in Rawlinson collections, 144–45
angel(s)
    in *Ars notoria*, 81, 91, 93
    belief in, 11
    compelled appearance of, 209–10
    conflation with other beings, 147
    Dee's conversations with, 171–73
    in development of necromancy, 116–17
    devotion to, 147–48
    guidance by, 108–9, 112, 121
    knowledge acquired through, 147–51, 152
    in *Liber lune*, 63
    names of. *See* names
    in necromancy, 129–30
    in Northgate collection, 101–2
    questioning, 144
    in Society of Antiquaries 39, 128–30
    summoning of. *See* necromancy
    summoning *vs.* binding, 133–34
    in *Sworn Book of Honorius*, 67, 108–9
    in visions of Brother John, 81–82, 85
angel magic, 146–55. *See also* necromancy
annotations
    in Dee collection, 37
    in Rawlinson D. 252, 136
antiquity, Renaissance enthusiasm for, 187–88
apothecary, image magic used by, source of,
    13–14
Aquinas, Thomas
    influence on moralists, 19
    influence on Pico della Mirandola, 190
    on power of artificial forms, 29–30
Arabic tradition, in necromantic texts, 116
Arbatel, editions of, 177
Argentine, John
    background of, 47–48, 227 n. 43
    collection of: attribution of, 48, 49, 227
        n. 49; collections included in, 127;
        content of, 128–34, 236 n. 51; medical
        texts in, 41; necromantic texts in,
        127–34; preservation of, 125; *Speculum
        astronomiae* and, 44–45, 226 n. 34